A Walk About Guide to Alaska

Vol. Two: The Chugach Mountains

By Shawn Lyons

Copyright 1999 by Shawn R. Lyons

Published by Shawn R. Lyons
3407 Turnagain Street. # 9
Anchorage, Alaska 99517

Produced and printed in Alaska

Printed by Professional Color Graphics
5611 Silverado Way, Suite D
Anchorage, Alaska 99518

First printing, Summer of 1999

Edited by Mary E. Lyons, Marthy W. Johnson and Richard Larson
Design and layout by Larson Graphics
Maps by Richard Larson of Larson Graphics
Photos by Shawn R. Lyons

Cover: On the ridge south of Rendezvous Peak looking down upon the headwaters of the South Fork of Eagle River with (left to right) Cantata Peak and Calliope Peak on the skyline.

Designed and layed out on a Macintosh computer running OS 8.5. Software used includes: Adobe Photoshop, Adobe PageMaker, Macromedia Freehand, and Microsoft Word.

Library of Congress Catalog Card Number: 99-62672

ISBN: 1-888125-47-0

Dedication

This book is dedicated to the memory of Dorothy Eaton,
My "Alaskan Mother" (1925-1997)

She never asked me where I'd been or if I had fun
Instead she only asked, "Did you go alone?"
By that question alone she showed how much she cared
Both for me and the country I wandered through.

Acknowledgement

Every book—no matter who the author is or when they wrote—is the result of a plethora of influences. This book is no different. A lifetime of reading, hiking, camping, talking and listening is contained in the pages of this book. So where does one begin doing the thanking? Perhaps with those whose influence on these pages are most direct. These are the people who told me about any one or more of the trails in this book, or kept me informed about new trails being built and old trails being repaired or re-routed. In this regard, I'd like to thank, first and foremost, Al Meiners, Superintendent for Chugach State Park; Asta Spurgis, director of the Eagle River Visitor's Center; and my friends Tucker Spohr, Alan Julliard, and Paul Berryhill, who took me on my first trips into the Chugach Mountains during my first few years of living in Anchorage. I'd also like to thank all the people—both friends and strangers—with whom I ever swapped ideas and information about trails and routes. Whether that information was exchanged while standing on some trail or leaning over some beer makes little difference: it was all helpful.

Next, I'd like to thank all the people who helped in any way specifically with this book. These people include my mother who proofread the entire book (she has always been one of the best editors I know); Richard Larson, whose patience and artistic insight was responsible for the maps, the page layout and the overall design; and Scott Nissenson of Professional Colorgraphics who oversaw the final editing and printing. Then, of course, many thanks are due to Mike Campbell, my patient editor at "The Anchorage Daily News," through whose hands many of these articles first passed.

In addition, I'd like to acknowledge the influence of all the authors of all the books that ever put an image or an idea into my head—from Sappho to Dylan Thomas and Lao Tsu to Martin Buber. Along with these authors, I am also indebted to the specific group of other writers who have narrated all the fact and fictional tales about hiking or climbing that line my shelves. Whether it is Dante Alighieri toiling with reverent heart up Mount Purgatory or W.E. Bowman stumbling with a good humored grin up Rum Doodle, they have all been a source of both entertainment and inspiration. Finally, last—but certainly not least—I'd like to thank all the people who've ever gone on hikes with me to anywhere at any time and somehow still found it in their hearts to remain friends when it was over and done.

Warning

The trails in this book are, with only one or two exceptions, officially recognized and maintained trails, but this does not mean they are always tame or easy. Many streams and creeks, for instance, have no bridges over them, nor are there many—if any—signs that indicate the direction to go or the distance gone once one leaves a trailhead. Neither, with the except for along one or two trails, are there any cabins or shelters in the Chugach.

Once you leave the trailhead, you are, for all intents and purposes, on your own. This is even more true once you get off-trail. There you are entirely on your own, wholly reliant on your own skills and judgment. This means having the ability to set up a safe campsite at night in regard to both the animal life and the elements is essential. It also means having the ability to find a feasible route during the day up mountains, over passes, across creeks, and through brush. For this reason alone, good map-reading skills are essential in negotiating most of the off-trail options in this book. For that matter, good map reading skills are helpful even if you don't plan to get off trail—just so you always know where you are and what options are available to you in case of emergency. But even more than maps, you should bring a thorough understanding of your own abilities and limitations as well as all the common sense you can muster. Most accidents can be prevented with a little caution and a little insight—and a lot of common sense. The only thing you should not bring with you is exclusive knowledge as to where you are going and how long they plan to be gone. You should make sure that someone—a friend, co-worker or

family member—knows where you are going no matter how short or long the trip. Even afternoon trips up Flattop can be dangerous; so leave an itinerary.

In short, if you wish to do any of the on- or off-trail trips in this book, you should 1) bring adequate equipment and maps of the area 2) be certain of your capabilities to survive in very rugged, wild country on your own and 3) leave a detailed itinerary and schedule with someone—anyone—in case something happens to you out there.

Yet regardless of how untamed these areas are, many of them are, nevertheless, under private ownership. Most of the Chugach Mountains are indeed within the bounds of the Chugach State Park. Most of the trailheads, however, border private land. On rare occasions, as was the case with the Rabbit Creek Trail, lands on which the trailhead is located are bought by individuals. Overnight, what once provided public access has become private land. So be sure to check with local authorities as to availability of certain trails— especially the beginning of trails along roads and highway. This book will note—whenever possible— whether or not a trail is at all under any type of private ownership. Ownership situations change, however, and what may be public access one day can be private property the next—and, fortunately, vice versa. Ultimately it is the hiker's individual responsibility to know where they can and cannot go. Addresses of various organizations and officials that can be questioned as to the accessibility of certain trails can be found in the appendix at the back of the book.

Table of Contents

A wonderful day for a stroll in a valley.

Introduction

Every time I become lost in the clouds, I think of the first hike my father ever took me on in the White Mountains of New Hampshire. It was a hike which should have deterred me from ever going to the mountains again.

Growing up in the Boston area, the White Mountains in New Hampshire were the constant against which I measured my growing up. Before I ever saw those mountains, they were established in my mind as a place of distant mystery where only older people were allowed to go. Every year I'd stand in the driveway on an early morning in June or July and watch as my two older brothers, Terry and Tim loaded their packs into the trunk of the family car and headed north to those mountains with my father. Sometimes they went with Fred Fiola and his two sons, Jimmy and Freddy; they never took me, however, or, for that matter, my younger brother Robert who was two years younger than I. Neither of us was considered old enough yet.

My father had been hiking and climbing in the White Mountains for decades, long before I was even a gleam in his eye. Nor had the famous hut system that is there now even been conceived by any of the hierarchy of the Appalachian Mountain Club. He could remember when Mitzpah Springs and Tuckerman's Ravine had only one lean-to while along Franconia Ridge and farther south beyond Cannon Mountain it was difficult to find any shelter at all. I think he can even remember when the Kangemangus Highway was nothing but a dirt road. Back then, in the 1930s and 40s (minus the years he spent as a paratrooper in the war), long before hiking became fashionable and certainly long before the advent of freeze-dried and other specialty foods for hikers, my father would carry two weeks' supply of heavy canned foods into those mountains and just hike and hike along those then little used trails.

By the time I was born, however, all this was starting to change. The Appalachian Mountain Club which had jurisdiction over the White Mountains was starting to build its famous full-service hut system, and hikers by the thousands were migrating from all over New England—and especially from the metropolitan Boston area—to those mountains only two or three hours north of us. Every year my father and older brothers were part of this summer exodus. I pleaded with my parents to let me go as well. But like all children in similar situations we were simply told, "You're not old enough yet." So every year, on a very early Saturday morning in July, I stood with my mother, my sister Kathleen, and brother Robert in the driveway and watch them go.

When I was seven, though, Robert and I were finally deemed *old enough*. Our introduction and initiation to the White Mountains were finally at hand. It wouldn't be a full-fledged hiking and camping trip, though. Nor would we be going with just Dad, Terry and Timmy and hike with a pack on our backs into some lean-to where we'd spend the night and climb some peak the next day. (We still weren't *old enough* for really roughing it.) We weren't even going into the high mountains, such as those in the Presidential Range or along Franconia Ridge. Instead, the entire family—Mom and Dad, Terry, Timmy, Kathy, and even Robert and myself—along with the Gavins who were visiting from New Jersey (Mrs. Gavin was an old college friend of my mother's) would drive to a campground in the southern White Mountains. After spending the night there, we would climb Mount Chocorua the next day.

Compared to most summits in the White Mountains, Mount Chocorua wasn't much of a mountain. It wasn't even 4,000 feet high. It was a mere runt of a mountain compared to the big 5,000-, and 6,000-foot peaks that rose farther north. But its entire summit, Terry and Timmy kept on telling me as the trip got closer and closer, was one big rock that you sometimes even had to use your hands to climb—it was that steep! This big bubble top of granite that made up the summit cone was where the mountain got its sobriquet the "Matterhorn of New England." With the top so bare, the view, I was also told, was spectacular. All this was well and good—frosting on the cake, as it were, but that's not what was most important to me. I didn't even mind that we were not going farther north to the higher mountains in the range. All that really mattered to me was that it was a peak in the White Mountains. I was finally going to the White Mountains!

It wasn't at all what I expected. In fact, it's a wonder I ever returned to the mountains after that first trip because all I remembered was rain and clouds. I remember the rain pattering on the tarp my father had strung between the two cars in the campground. (Most of us slept under this, though a couple of the more fastidious adults slept in the back of the station wagon.) All night it rained. In time, water began to ooze along the ground under the tarp. If it hadn't been for the plastic ground cover my father had also placed on the ground underneath us, both our sleeping bags and we would've been very wet—and very miserable—by morning.

By morning the rain had stopped. The clouds, however, didn't break. All day long as we climbed the muddy trail up through the hardwoods and into the sweet-smelling softwoods and evergreens, the clouds remained overhead. By the time we were winding through the krummholz at tree line with their rainy day smell (a smell that I have never since forgotten and which, surprisingly, brings back nothing but fond memories), we were actually in the clouds.

I'd never been in the clouds before. I'd spent my whole life up to that day below them. The novelty didn't last long, though. Damp and cold, I would've preferred a sunny and warm view—as I thought it was supposed to be in the mountains. After all, all the slides my father showed every year of other trips always showed my two brothers standing high on exposed sunny ridges beneath a blue sky and before wide, hazy expanses. At seven years old, I figured that was what it was always like in the mountains: sunny and blue. Obviously, however, that was not the truth of the matter.

"Don't we get it to be sunny and warm after climbing so long?" I asked Terry at one point. He only laughed at me. He might've also called me stupid—it wouldn't have been the first time.

Fortunately for my short attention span, as the novelty of being in the clouds began to end another novelty began: the summit cone rock. It was, of course, impossible to see how big the rock was. But I could at least sense how big it was just by how long it took us to scramble up—at least it seemed a long time to my young perception. Up cracks, across slabs and even along a couple of wet ledges, we continued to climb, a thin line of ghostly people barely visible in the swirling mist. In the muffled quiet, our voices carried only a little farther than our eyesight.

Then, finally, after one last pull up one last slab of cold granite, we were holding onto the steel rod imbedded on the summit. Hemmed in on all sides by close clouds, we could barely see beyond our outstretched hands. For all our effort, though, my father gave us Chunkies—the standard snack food on all our hikes. That was some consolation—but not much. Maybe, I thought, the kids at school will be impressed. But it would be literally months until school started again.

Considering the cold rain, the wet clouds and the lack of view, one would think that I would've sworn off hiking and climbing for the rest of my life. If I wanted to stand in the cold rain, there were plenty of places to do that—with a lot less effort. I didn't have to drive to New Hampshire and climb a mountain. I could've just stood outside our home on a blustery March day. But somehow, *where* I got wet and cold mattered. The mountain myth that I had so long nurtured didn't get washed away in the rain or get lost in those clouds.

Maybe it was just because that rain and those clouds weren't in my own back yard; maybe it was because there was still the promise of a long, green view on a golden day; or maybe it was simply because I had actually climbed a mountain (or had been told I'd climbed a mountain, because I experienced no actual proof of it other than the fact that we'd climbed a long time before reaching the top of a single rounded rock somewhere in the clouds)—I'm not sure why, but I was eager to go back to the mountains the next year.

So my climb up Mount Chocorua was not the end of my hiking and climbing career. It was only my beginning. Every year after that Robert and I were able to go with my father to the more northern and higher mountains of the Presidential Range. Such fabled places—fabled at least to me—as Pinkham Notch, Tuckerman's Ravine, the Boot Spur Trail and Lakes of the Clouds Hut—all of which are found on Mount Washington—as well as Garfield Hut to the north and Mitzpah Springs to the south and seemingly countless other places, all became more than just names in one of my older brothers' stories or a place on a map; they became physically real and familiar places to me. I could actually make them part of my own stories now.

All in all, though, it didn't matter to me where my father took us. Everywhere we went was Shangri-La. It didn't even matter that the rain and mist I had first encountered on Mount Chocorua were discovered to be in no way unique to the White Mountains. As in the Chugach, one simply learned to live with rain while out hiking. Most days of the year on Mount Washington are, in fact, cloudy (365 out of 365 days according to one tongue-in-cheek statistic), but it made the few glimpses of sunshine and the fewer panoramas of the earth below all the more rewarding.

I was defintely hooked on hiking.

In time, like my father before me, I hiked all over the White Mountains. By the time I graduated from high school I knew those mountains intimately, and had also hiked the Appalachian Trail from Georgia to Maine and the Long Trail from Massachusetts to Canada, along the crest of the Green Mountains in Vermont. In time, I also hiked and climbed in the Rockies, Mexico, Nepal, Pakistan, and the Yukon. It was the hiking and climbing possibilities that first drew me to Alaska twelve years ago. Yet if it weren't for that first climb up Mount Chocorua with my father so many, many years ago, I might've gone to any of these places. I might never have hiked at all.

After my first climb, thoiugh, it's still a wonder that I ever wanted to go hiking again. By the same token, considering the difficulty I had in publishing my first book, it's a wonder why I should ever have wanted to publish again. Right then and there, when I finally had my first book in hand, I should have sworn off ever wanting to produce another.

First, there had been the problem of writing and rewriting and rewriting again and again in the ongoing—and futile—search for what Ezra Pound calls "the perfect word." Second, there was the seemingly constant problems and delays that go along with publishing and distributing one's own book. The long process, from hiring a copy editor, getting someone to do the maps and page layouts, and then finding someone yet again to do the printing and binding, right up to finally getting the finished product on the shelves of stores is fraught with delays and problems. No matter how diligent my co-workers were, every step in the process seemed to epitomize Murphy's Law: "Whatever can go wrong, will."

Why submit myself to that ordeal again? After all, I have a whole library. Why add another to one of the shelves? I am no Frost, or Dickinson, or Dickens or Swift—and I'm certainly no Homer or Shakespeare! It seemed a worthless endeavor to toil over word after word, sentence after sentence, and paragraph after paragraph just to add another book to a world already overloaded with mediocrity. Like Huck Finn, after finishing one book I should've sworn off ever doing another. I didn't, though, and I have no logical explanation for it other than that I like to write and like almost all writers, I like to see my work in print. Like a mountaineer standing on the summit of a peak, it signifies a moment of completion (as well as, I'll admit, vain gratification).

That, plus the favorable reception of my first book, has compelled me to gladly undergo the trials and tribulations of producing another book. (Ah, what would Huck Finn say?) Like the first guide, this second volume is devoted to the trails in a specific area of South-Central Alaska—in this instance the trails in Chugach State Park.

And like the first volume, the bulk of this book is a collection of first-person narratives about my experiences on various trails and mountains. However, realizing that many readers use my columns as guides for where to go and what to do, this book also includes specific guidebook information about the trails. In this way, by providing both first-person articles as well as trail guide information, I have satisfied both the *armchair traveler* and the *active reader*.

Some regular readers of my column have told me they spend as little time outdoors as possible. It's flattering that people who aren't outdoor enthusiasts still find pleasure in my scribblings. For these *armchair travelers* I wanted to put together a book through which they could continue to enjoy the mountains vicariously. With that in mind, I decided to make the bulk of the book a collection of first-person narratives.

For those readers, on the other hand, who want to know where a hike is—as well as how far away, how long, how difficult or easy, how scenic and how safe it is—I've added at the end of each article a *Walk-About Guide* for each trail. This will answer the most common questions people may have about where a trail is as well as what a trail is like. The guide, then, is for any one who wants to know not only where to go, but what it is like when they get there.

In some instances, after the Walk-About Guide to a specific trail, I've also included optional excursions that are essentially *off-trail hikes*. Continuing beyond the end of a specific trail, these options will outline climbs up nearby mountains, or traverses along nearby ridges, or even, at times, ways to connect one trail with another. These additional hikes are titled *Option A*, *Option B*, and *Option C* etc. depending on how many off trail hikes are possible from the access of one particular trail.

Many of the trails in the Front Range, as well as all over Alaska, for that matter, climb no farther than up to a lake or a pass where they come to an abrupt stop. The crumbling magnificence of high summits may tower all around against the blue sky; the trail, however, more often than not, doesn't seek to climb them. Only occasional trails, like those up Point Hope, Flattop, Wolverine Peak and O'Malley Peak climb to a point where the earth and sky merge. Most other trails—Hidden Lake, Middle Fork, and McHugh Lake as well as Rabbit Lake, Falls Creek, Symphony Lake and Peters Creek and even the Pioneer Ridge among many others— go only so far before dead-ending in the valleys below. But that doesn't mean the hike has to end. The Options following some Walk-About Guides will allow the more experienced and adventurous reader to climb out of the valleys below into the heights above.

Off trail options, however, are not always feasible. Wandering off trail along any section of Ship Creek, Thunderbird Falls or Eklutna Lake to the north, or Gull Rock, Ptarmigan Lake or even Johnson Pass trails on Kenai Peninsula to the south (which are contained in Volume I of this series of books) will immerse the hiker in a jungle of brush; whereas wandering off the end of Golden Fin Lake or Rainbow Lake trails also on the Kenai Peninsula will result in a dunking. Wandering off other trails, however, can be far more dangerous than having to tangle with some brush or having to practice one's dog paddle. Exploring beyond the end of Byron Glacier Trail, for instance, will expose the hiker to the high risks inherent in any traverse across a glacier or any climb up a near-vertical slope. Lacking the skills and equipment to negotiate such terrain can easily result in serious injury or worse. For these reasons, optional hikes will only be listed where they can be done by anyone with stamina, experience and map-reading skills.

This overall concept of a *First Person Guide Book*, combining as it does, first person narratives with guidebook information will, I hope, accommodate armchair travelers as well as active readers who can create their own outdoor experiences. Of course I realize that in trying to accommodate everyone, I may end up pleasing no one. I'll take that chance. I'd like to think, however, that there is at least one armchair traveler and one active reader who will find this book satisfying and/or useful. If so, I will be satisfied that the work that went into this second *First Person Guidebook* will have been worth it.

View from Eagle River Nature Center.

Grading Trails

A SYSTEM TO RATE THE HIKES

If you are ready to leave father and mother, brother and sister, and wife and child and friends, and never see them again, —if you have paid your debts, and made your will, and settled all your affairs, and are a free man, then you are ready for a walk.
(from "Walking" by H.D. Thoreau)

Very few people are as serious as Thoreau was about his hiking. Most people consider it only a diversion from the every day working world, through which they can clean the spirit, reduce stress or get some exercise. And so not every one has the inclination, or time or energy to spend the long hours that Thoreau spent wandering in the countryside around Concord or climbing Mount Katahdin. Different strokes for different folks, as the saying goes.

Like Thoreau, I take my hiking seriously too. Like him, I leave everything behind me when I go out on a hike—especially a long hike. Except for his climb up Katahdin, Thoreau did little climbing or scrambling, but it's difficult to go anywhere in the Chugach without at least some of this. The hikes I take usually include a substantial amount of both. H.D. and I simply have different ideas of what's fun when we step into the great outdoors—as do most of us.

Though hiking is fun, there are limits—both physical and mental—to everything, which is why most people want to know how easy or difficult any outing will be. Nobody wants to overstep their abilities. Nobody wants to bite off more than they can chew, no matter how good it tastes. So it seems appropriate to provide a grading system for this book indicating the level of difficulty of each trail or climb.

In devising such a system there are some questions that had to be asked. Should a climb's difficulty be classified according to its overall elevation gain or how steep it is? Some elevation gains, like the climb up Bird Ridge, are continuous and steep whereas others, like the climb to Powerline Pass, are long and shallow. Should the long, shallow climb be rated the same as the short, steep one? Should the Turnagain Arm Trail which gains over 1,000 feet in elevation over nine miles of short ups and downs be rated the same as the climb up the new McHugh Creek Trail which gains over 1,000 feet in one long steady climb? And what about the difference between climbing on trails and climbing over trackless tundra? Should O'Malley which has a well-beaten track to its summit be rated the same as Tikishla which doesn't? And should a narrow and rocky trail be rated the same as a wide and smooth trail?

In the end, I decided it best to grade climb difficulty according to three factors: 1) whether it's on trail or not, 2) how steep and high elevation gains are, and 3) how long it is. All three are important in determining both how difficult and how long any hike or climb will take.

Then there's the question of children. Many children between, say, the ages of eight and twelve are perfectly capable of making the eight-mile round trip to the summit of Wolverine and back, or even the twelve more level miles to the Williwaw lakes and back. But what they're physically capable of doing, they're not always psychologically capable of doing.

I don't have any children. But growing up as one of six, I do have some memories of what it was like to be surrounded by children. (And if it was trying for me at times, I can only imagine what it must have been like for my parents!) One of my most vivid memories is the long pilgrimage we'd take at least once a summer from Boston to the White Mountains in New Hampshire. Before even leaving Massachusetts, the car would begin to echo with six voices asking in cacophonous counterpoint, "Are we there yet?"

Even when my father took me and my younger brother Robert on our first hike up Mount Washington, the climb to Tuckerman's Ravine, which is only a third of the way up the mountain, seemed to take forever—especially carrying a twenty pound load. We were certainly physically capable of doing it; but it seemed so long!

So whether the child is young enough to be carried, or old enough to carry him/her self, the distance on some of these climbs may prove a more mental than physical strain. So it would be hard to establish a grading system that works for all ages. In the end, all I can suggest is to use your instinct and make. Remember, however, that it is always better to err by going on too short a hike than to over extend them on too long a hike.

In establishing this, I've adopted a system numbered 1 through 7 that is in part like that used in rock-climbing circles. The major difference is that level 5 in my system is still non-technical scrambling and 6 is technical. (In the rock-climbing system levels 5 and 6 are classified as indirect and direct aid technical climbs which are further differentiated by the use of decimals.) So here they are:

Grade 1: Flat, wide trail with a minimum of elevation gain (less than 250 feet per mile). Examples of Grade 1 would be the Johnson Pass Trail, the Eklutna Lake Trail and the Coastal Trail.

Grade 2: Rougher trail with longer and slightly steeper climbs (250 to 750 feet per mile). Examples of Grade 2 would be the Middle Fork Trail, Resurrection Pass Trail and the upper section of Powerline Pass Trail.

Grade 3: Steep trail with long, continuous climbs (750 or more feet per mile). Examples of Grade 3 would be Bird Ridge, portions of Wolverine Peak and Pioneer Peak.

Grade 4: No trail. Tundra walking with little or no bushwhacking on flat terrain or with only moderate gains in elevation (250 to 750 feet per mile). Examples of Grade 4 would be the last mile or so to Ship Pass or the hike from Williwaw Lakes to Long Lake.

Grade 5: No trail. Tundra walking and/or bushwhacking with substantial elevation gains climbs (500 to1,500 feet per mile). Examples of this would be climbs up the Ramp and Temptation as well as hikes up to Sheep Valley above Eagle River or to the summit of McHugh Peak from off the McHugh Creek Trail.

Grade 6: No trail. Requires use of hands. Very rough and steep terrain of mostly boulders, rocks and scree in which the climbs are long and steep (1,500 feet or more per mile). Climb or scramble often includes some exposure. Examples would include the summit ridge of Tikishla Peak, the climb up Hidden Peak from Hidden Lake and Ptarmigan Peak from either Flattop or Powerline Pass Trail.

Grade 7: Get out your ropes. Steep and exposed enough to require at least some belayed climbing and even the placement of some protection.

To augment this grading system, I have provided other (sometimes redundant) information at the end of every first person narrative to further help readers decide which trail or hike best suits them. This includes the location and distance from Anchorage, the trail's mileage, condition, and total elevation gain, expected hiking time for the average hiker, as well as campsites and cabins that can be utilized for more extended hikes. In addition, I have listed the USGS maps of the area of the trail or trails mentioned in every article. This is for those wanting more detailed topography than provided by the maps accompanying each article.

This grading system is just the second of ten informational categories found in the ***Walk-About Guides*** after each article. Preceding the **Trail Grade** will be **Trail Location**, which will tell how to drive to the trailhead and, if necessary, how to get to the trail from the parking area. It also provides directions through any confusing sections of the trail that may be caused by the crisscrossing of this trail with other trails or roads, or where the trail may all but disappear in tundra or open country. (Because I don't have an odometer in my car that registers tenths of miles, I've given the approximate distance of the trailhead to the nearest milepost on the highway mentioned.)

Following the Trail Grade will be **Trail Condition**. This section will briefly provide information regarding the state of each trail—whether it is rocky, muddy, narrow and/or overgrown path or, conversely, whether it is a flat, dry, wide and/or open road bed. I felt this was necessary because the amount of climbing done on a trail is not the only criteria involved in determining how easy or hard a trail is. Oftentimes footing can slow a person down as much—or more—than a climb.

The **Trail Mileage** is next. This includes, wherever applicable, both the one-way and round-trip mileage for any trail or hike. Traverses, on the other hand, have only the one way mileage.

Next on the list is **Total Elevation Gain** of a trail. This is, as close as I can calculate, the total gain and loss over every little knoll, spur and hill from the beginning to the end of a trail. In some cases, this amounts to little more than the difference in height from the beginning of the trail to the top of a pass or the highest point along any trail; in other cases, where the hike may go over two or more very substantial ridges (or climb two or more summits), it is the total elevation gain of all the major climbs along a trail or hike—and therefore substantially higher a total than simply subtracting the elevation of the highest point from the lowest point along any trail or hike.

Following Total Elevation Gain will be **Highest Point**. The figure given in this section is simply the highest point above sea level reached along the trail.

Then comes **Normal Hiking Time**, which is the number of hours or days it takes most people to hike the specific trail or trip. There are of course some people, like skiers and runners in training, who will go faster than the time mentioned; there are others, with small children or in a large party, who may go slower than given times. But I believe the guidelines will accommodate the pace of most people. The person who can judge that the best, though, is the hiker.

Campsites will include both cabins and designated places to pitch a tent along any trail as well as other unofficial possibilities. Please remember, though, that it is against the law to build a fire inside Chugach State Park, so bring a stove. It's a good idea to bring a stove anyway because rain—which is certainly not an uncommon climatic occurrence in South-central Alaska—could make building a fire very frustrating. Bringing a stove also saves the nearby forest from being stripped beyond all recognition by the need for firewood.

Best Time refers to nothing more than the most favorable time of year in which to see the trail in question. Experienced hikers and outdoor travelers could cover any trail mentioned any time of year, but they should be aware of avalanche conditions, which can turn even the easiest of trails into a very dangerous—and even deadly—hike. Devil's Pass, for instance, on the Kenai Peninsula is a very easy and safe trail in the summer: it has a low grade climb and good footing. But in winter, this gentle trail becomes a death trap amid the avalanches that rumble down the steep-sided gorge the trail slabs through for four miles. So just because a trail is easy in the summer does not mean it's safe in winter.

Then finally, there is the category of **USGS Maps**. This lists nothing more than the United States Geological Survey Maps showing the trail area. Sometimes, but not very often, they even show the trail.

Besides the USGS maps, there are also a series of maps called Alaska Road and Recreation Maps, which have as much detail as the USGS maps but also list all the current trails and trailheads for which they provide small trail descriptions, points of interest, facilities available in nearby towns or villages, points of interest, fishing spots and other visitor information. These two-sided maps are also bigger and show far more territory for a much lower cost than the USGS maps.

The advantage of the USGS maps, however, is that they are all-inclusive. Get enough of them and they will show every square foot of Alaska in an easily understood grid system that allows sections to be placed next to each other—as contiguously well as above and below each other—to create a larger and larger map. There is, furthermore, a USGS map for any area you may plan to hike.

Finally, a note about the maps that accompany each Walk-About Guide. Though they are largely self-explanatory, the reader should note that the shading on the maps indicate changes in elevation. The darkest gray is water and the white is permanent snow. In between these two extremes is a lighter gray shading which indicates below tree line while the darker gray areas denote above tree line.

All the maps in this book also label all the other trails found in the vicinity of the highlighted trail that corresponds to each Walk-About Guide. Walk-About Guides and specific maps to many of these secondary labeled trails—if they are officially recognized trails—can be found in other chapters in this book. However, there are other trails labeled on the maps—some of which I never knew existed until poring over these finished maps—for which Walk-About Guides will not be found in this book. These trails are not only very difficult to find and follow, but neither are they recognized or maintained by either the National Forest Service or the Chugach State Park (which is probably why many of them are so difficult to find and follow!). Many of them are also on private property or are simply winter trails which become non-existent in the warmer seasons when most people do their hiking, which are two good reasons not to include them in any guidebook. (In order to prevent the book from becoming too long, I had to establish strict criteria as to what to include and what not to include.) This book contains Walk-About Guides to trails only officially recognized and maintained by the state within the bounds of Chugach State Park.

Though I am including one chapter on what I carry in my pack at all times, I do not, overall, consider this a *how-to* book. Many of the narratives do make mention of what I did when confronted with certain conditions and animals, but this is not a book about how to respond to bears, how to analyze snow conditions, how to react to the continuous weather changes of south-central Alaska, or how to perform a plethora of crafts and exercise a myriad of skills—all of which at any given moment could mean the difference between life and death. There are other books for that—such as 55 Ways to the Wilderness in South-central Alaska by Helen D. Nienhueser and John Wolfe Jr., A Naturalist's Guide to Chugach State Park by Jenny Zimmerman and Hiking Alaska by Dean Littlepage. All three books have excellent—and mandatory—reading on equipment and snow conditions for anyone who intends to venture out into the Alaska wilds.

Neither is this a guide to flora and fauna—knowledge about which I am sorely lacking. For those interested in identifying wild life and plant life, there are many good publications including Guide to the Birds of Alaska by Robert H. Armstrong (who also has written some reference books about fish and fishing in Alaska), Field Guide to Alaskan Wildflowers by Verna E. Pratt (which is one of a number of books on wildflowers in Alaska by the same author), Alaska Trees and Shrubs by Leslie A. Vierick and Elbert A. Little, Jr., and Mammals of Alaska published by Alaska Geographic Society. This is not even a book that will be very helpful to mountain bikers. For those wishing to bicycle the trails in Alaska, the best guide is Richard Larson's Mountain Bike Alaska: 49 Trails in the 49th State. Instead, this is a book for those who just want to read, or to read and hike.

In conclusion I will say, that in addition to what I put in my pack, I always carry an ice ax in the spring, fall and winter and I always use a walking stick—which I've discovered has far more uses than for just walking in the summer and early fall. I highly recommend to anyone venturing into the mountains that they carry one of these tools. That, along with the following chapter is the best advice I can give to any and all who are inspired to go and explore some of the trails mentioned in this book. These few tips might not seem like much but they have, along with my pack, saved my life more than once.

Looking up Rabbit Creek from McHugh Peak.

My Pack

For over twenty years, I have carried the same pack. Limp with age, it hangs off my shoulders like a bag of potatoes. In addition, the padding on the back side is so thin, that I can feel every awkward bulge and point of the load inside rubbing against the small of my back. At the beginning of every hike I'm constantly punching here and pushing there to readjust the load before it hangs comfortably. It's also scuffed and faded. Dirt streaks, water stains, and frayed stitches are all evident of its old age and long use. The tan cordura of its main compartment is, however, still water repellent and sturdy to the touch; and the leather that protects its base, though scored and streaked, has yet to be punctured by stone or branch.

Neither is the pack I carry the epitome of modern outdoor technology. There is no internal frame and no padded waist strap to ease some of the stress of the load. In addition, there is no hi-tech strap system to finely balance the weight and size of the load to the body. Nor do any detachable pockets, ski slots or accessory buckles grace its exterior. All it is a bucket of cloth with a few accessory patches on the outside. And this bucket is not even waterproof! Instead, I've lined it with a garbage bag to be certain that everything inside will stay dry—even if I tumble into a stream. Over the bucket fits a top which contains one decently sized zip pocket just big enough to carry a map and a few other items I want within easy reach.

Yet despite its being old and ugly, I carry this worn, sagging sack of a pack on every trip I make—whether that trip is an hour stroll up Flattop or a twenty-four hour hike through the Talkeetnas. I never go hiking without it. For despite being old and ugly, this faded, sagging pack is often the last buffer between me and death. That may sound melodramatic, but it's not. It's the truth. Being able to put on a extra jacket when the temperature drops or a raincoat when it starts to precipitate has staved off hypothermia more times than I can count. Being able to don a head lamp when day deepens into night has, more than a few times, allowed me to still find my way. Having that extra candy bar or Pop-Tart when the energy wains, has more than once given me the strength to go the last miles when I've gone out too far or too deep for my own good. Even having that extra pair of socks or mittens for the phalanges has saved more than one toe or finger when the stars have come out and the frost gets thick. There's no doubt that my pack has had to be my home on my back, containing all the comforts and necessary means of survival for the thin-skinned and weak-stomached human creature who carries it.

Knowing that it is my means of survival in the wilds, I've been very careful about what I put in this pack. This is for two reasons: I want to keep the load light, and I want to keep the load simple. If weight was no consideration, then I could obviously carry everything for every occasion. Too a heavy a load, however, can be just as dangerous as too light a load because it tires the body and slows the pace, which can lead to exhaustion and hypothermia. So I want to carry what I need to insure that I survive, but not necessarily carry what I may want to make me comfortable. I also want to keep the load simple, so that my choices will be simple. I don't carry three different weight sweaters or two hats or even a wide choice in menu. These things merely add weight and confusion to the pack.

I start with the bucket, which I fill with items necessary to the body's survival. First I think of long term survival. What is the worst weather I can encounter? coldest temperature? Harshest precipitation? Highest winds? And how much could all these changes slow me down? I assume the worst. So first I pack a thick fiber pile jacket that I stuff into the bottom of the pack. Alongside this I push a knee-length rain parka, that even if it makes me sweat, still keeps me warm. Finally, I shove down alongside the parka a pair of neoprene gloves, that will keep the fingers warm while climbing in wet snow or hiking in the rain. Then I think about food to sustain me if I'm out longer than I expect to be— which is far too often. So inside the jacket and park I nestle a quart-size Tupperware container filled with candy bars, pop tarts, energy bars and vitamins. These items take care of most extreme condition changes.

Next, I start thinking of the smaller changes in air and body temperatures. To be comfortable from hour to hour I carry a green stuff sack containing smaller items that can easily be lost in the corners and folds of the pack if they are put in separately. The stuff sack is always easily found, even late in the darkest night. It contains extra mittens with waterproof shells, wool socks, waterproof socks, a wool cap, a long underwear top and a headlamp. If it's early spring or fall I might also put in some long underwear bottoms and a pair of instep crampons. In this stuff sack I also carry a small zippered nylon wallet in which I put the car keys and some cash—because I sometimes come out of the wilds far from where I went in and the money comes in handy for a bus, a taxi or even just a drink at any convenience store or bar that happens to be nearby. (The Turnagain House, for instance, is a wonderful place to sip a hot drink on a cold winter night while waiting for a ride after having done the Arctic Valley—Indian Pass traverse.) Then I squeeze in another red stuff sack of food—high energy food such as hard candies and a few more candy bars.

At the top of the bucket I fold a wind suit—that is if it's not cold enough to be wearing it at the start of the hike. The reason I make the wind suit so readily accessible is because to me it's an all-purpose piece of clothing that not only protects the body from the wind, but can also keep the body warm on a cold day as well as keep out a spitting rain or dry snow on a gray day. It's also very light, the parka and pants weighing only a few ounces total, that it's value far outweighs the effort of carrying it. I never leave home without it. It is, in short, the clothing that I always have with me even on the shortest hikes on the warmest days. Alongside it I slip a plastic, quart-size water bottle, which I usually don't fill unless it's a winter hike/climb or my intended route is over a long, high ridge or any other place where water may be scarce. Finally, I pack one last item: a zip-lock bag containing a roll of toilet paper—which I also never leave home without.

Now, having taken care of the body's overall protection and sustenance, I pack the flap pocket with items specifically needed for each individual trip. First, I pack the appropriate maps for the area. I slide them into zip-lock bags for protection and lay them as flat as possible along the bottom of the pocket. In another zip-lock plastic bag I carry a small note pad, pen and pencil for taking notes and jotting down ideas while on the hike itself. Into this second plastic bag I also put a wrist watch. Then I slip in a sierra cup for drinking out of springs and streams. If I think I might need them in the first few hours of the hike, I also insert sunglasses and/or an extra pair of light gloves. Finally, I slip in a brand new multi-tooled, all-purpose, top-of-the-line Swiss Army Knife which was recently given to me as a gift. It's a bit heavy, but it does have just about every tool for every emergency. All it lacks is the Saint Bernard with the flask of brandy under its chin.

Depending on the weather, I start every hike wearing a pair of shorts, a turtle neck shirt and a visored cap and, depending on where I'm going, carrying either an ice ax or walking stick. All these things I can either put into or somehow attach to the pack if necessary, so the pack can, in essence, carry everything I have with me.

My pack epitomizes my deepest fears of the worst weather in the pile jacket and rain parka I have stuffed in its base, but it also embodies my greatest hopes for the perfect day in the sunglasses and shorts I either carry in the flap or wear. It also carries the food I need for energy and, by extension, survival. But my pack also keeps me on route—or opens up other options—through the maps in the top flap. It allows me to travel after dark: with the headlamp in the bucket, and even allows me to keep records of my deepest thoughts with the pen and paper that are always close at hand.

My pack is, in short, my closest and most constant companion. It has been the means to my survival many times though I never gave it a thought simply because it was always there, close at hand, with everything I needed for almost every situation.

Trail crew near Eagle River Nature Center.

CHAPTER 1

New Snow, Old Memories

Snow lay like a like a long, wide sheet over the surface of the still frozen lake below us. Snow lay like a discarded, crocheted shawl over the rocky facades and cloud-piercing summits of the peaks above us. Snow— new snow, in fact—lay like a vast, white dust cover over the tundra all around us. The stagnating snows of spring had fallen once again in the high country, transforming the landscape into a vast, silent room—a museum hall of impersonal, static marmoreal repose.

But to one who had spent time in this room when the rippling waters lapped against the lichen-covered rocks and soft breezes bent the tundra grasses and flowers with their breath, this room will never be truly idle or frozen. It will always contain a seed that can be sparked to life by the simple act of being remembered. And some of us did remember.

I, for one, remembered being on this trail, the Rabbit Lake Trail, about five years ago, before one lower section of it with the surrounding acreage was bought by a land speculator. He barred all travel across his property in the hope that the state would buy the land back from him. The state never did.

After spending a number of thankless years guarding his land, the owner had moved his trailer home off the land some time the year before. Since then hikers have once again started to use this old trail as the easiest way of accessing Rabbit Lake and McHugh Lake valleys. Anyone who does use the trail is still technically trespassing, but I prefer to think of it as hikers simply taking back a right that was originally theirs.

As I stood with Sheenagh, Frank, Susan, Clifford and Tom on a low ridge above Rabbit Lake, I remembered hurrying up valley in the golden light of a late August morning to begin a marathon climb of all twelve 5,000-plus-foot peaks in the Front Range. My friend Alan Julliard was with me. He would accompany me as far as the base of South

1

Suicide before he would turn back down valley to other responsibilities in the city below. I remembered the blue sky overhead, and the last, warm mists lifting from the twin summits of South and North Suicide Peaks above. I also remembered the gurgling stream running down beside us and the light breeze brushing against the backs of our necks. I also remembered how the ground squirrels chattered out warnings as we passed—just as they had on the early part of this day's hike.

For even though this upper concave of the valley was draped in a quieting quilt of new snow, it hadn't been like that on the first few miles of the hike. Just three miles back, the world had not been covered in snow. It had been alive with green. Already, early-season flowers polka-dotted the open hillside below us while new shoots of grass blushed the hillside above as we meandered slowly up the first miles of the trail. Nor were these the only signs of spring. There were also rivulets gurgling down from the slopes of Flattop, birds whistling from nearby copses of greening willow and alder, and a hazy combination of bugs and pollen floating in the warm air around us. Meanwhile, through the vortex of the valley far below moved the distant rumbling waters of Rabbit Creek rushing their way downward to the sea.

Back there, on the first miles of the trail, was the land of moving time, where the new season was overlapping the old, where memory and desire were melding into one, the former reborn in change and the latter born in change. At snowline, however, we came upon the great gate between the towering mass of Ptarmigan Peak on our left and the broad back of McHugh Peak on our right, and the world quieted. The sun disappeared—gone for what turned out to be almost the entire remainder of the hike. The landscape was suddenly bleak and lifeless—a wash of undefining gray. The air became damp and cold. The sky became dark and oppressive. It were as if we had suddenly moved back in time, back into the realm of forgetful sleep, a sleep without memory or desire—a winter sleep where time stood still.

Soon after, though we had done little or no climbing, the path began to cross wide swaths of old snow. Debris of avalanches lay across the trail fanning out at the bottom of wide chutes and meadows still buried under deep, hard drifts of snow. Soon we found ourselves stepping through small blotches of fresh snow that had fallen just the night before. Winter was obviously not in retreat up here. On the contrary, it still held

2

sovereignty.

Finally coming up over one final rise, we were looking down on the snow-entombed waters of Rabbit Lake. To our left was the deep, snow-filled trough of Rabbit Creek. No moving water was visible or audible on this day. There was only a ditch of heavy, wet snow. To our right, the landscape rose steeply up to the crest of a high ridge, the east ridge of Ptarmigan, close to 1,500 feet overhead. From there, the ridge swung in a great jagged arc to the northeast before swinging around again to the south where, in one mighty, rock- and snow-laden thrust upward, it rose into the high, sky-dominating summit of North Suicide Peak. From this great summit, the ridge descended into the horseshoe-shaped pass of Windy Gap, along the vortex of which stretched a heavy cornice that hung out over Rabbit Lake like a frozen whitecap in the sea. From here the ridge ascended steadily once more in a long, smooth line to the coned summit of South Suicide Peak, after which, in rocky undulations, it finally began its long sporadic descent toward Turnagain Arm.

Sporadic flashes of sunlight darted across the valley floor. Some never touched us while others just brushed our faces for a moment before rushing on again. Meanwhile, above us, like ghosts, the high summits appeared and disappeared behind scudding clouds that drifted like smoke rising from the immense caldron in the gap between the two Suicides. The steamy clouds never hid the mountains for long, though. After drifting slowly upward to veil the summits in momentary shrouds, they hung on the wary heights for but a moment and then moved gloomily on.

Despite the grand—and gloomy—mix of mountains and clouds before us, the landscape was remarkably quiet. Not a sound could be heard anywhere. Even the wind, which we could see moving the clouds far above us, was unheard. We indeed seemed frozen in time.

At the lake we wandered off in different directions to follow our own pursuits. Frank sat down before a lone rock to fill his notebook with another one of his fine miniature paintings. The Suicides were too close for proper perspective, so he chose as his subject Homicide Peak which glared menacingly over the north ridge of North Suicide. Sheenagh sat down beside him to keep him company. Tom then wandered off alone to explore the north shore of the lake while Susan, Clifford, and I crossed the snow-choked stream bed of Rabbit Creek to make the short climb to the top of the low ridge that separated the McHugh Creek and Rabbit

Creek drainages. Standing at the crest of the rounded ridge we faced a hard wind and lightly blowing snowflakes down the long, winding McHugh Creek valley to the shimmering waters of Turnagain Arm, where the sun was shining. It all looked so remote and foreign.

It shouldn't have been, though. I'd been up and down that valley numerous times just as I'd been up the Rabbit Creek Valley we'd just traversed. As I stood there with the wind in my face and the snow ricocheting off my parka, I thought of other days, some in sun and some in clouds, some in snow and some in rain, days I had spent trudging up these valleys to climb the various peaks that rose around us. Sometimes with friends, sometimes alone, I had climbed to all the summits of the mountains above almost more times than I could count. In every season, in every conceivable type of weather, I had stood on those summits.

But there would be no climbing today. Instead, on this day I would only look up and remember those other days and other climbs, like the time Alan and I became stranded for a night in the clouds on North Suicide, or the hot Labor Day we spent climbing along the summit ridge of McHugh Peak, and another, hotter, Labor Day spent on the ridge between Ptarmigan Peak and Rabbit Lake with Georgia Gustafson and Donna Schwirtz. Then there was the cool July morning Paul Berryhill and I traversed the entire ridge from South Suicide Peak over to Powerline Pass, and the wintry September day the year before when I had had to kick steps through some already hardened new snow up to the summit of South Suicide. Each one of these trips remained far from forgotten. Each one was as vivid in my memory as an owl's hoot on a crisp, quiet winter night.

My father's memories of the war were probably just as clear and hard. On the other side of the continent he was probably—at that very same moment—sitting in the evening light of the living room in our home outside Boston and, like me, thinking back to other days spent among other people. My memories, though, were not nearly as long or deep as his—or as consequential as his on this day of all days: Memorial Day. But they did have their similarities. For his memories of World War II were not just of names and faces that were gone, never to come again, but also of people who were still a part of his every waking day.

I remembered how during my years of growing up in that house right up until the day I left—his comrades from the 101st Airborne, men

4

with whom he'd labored through North Africa, Sicily, Italy, and later France, Belgium and finally Germany, would call him up at all hours of the day and night. No matter what the time or what his mood at the moment, he was always happy to hear from them. It was as though he had just been with them yesterday, crawling through the trenches of Bastogne or sharing a bottle of wine and the company of a woman while on leave in Rome. I remembered how they'd come to the house while I was growing up—Al "the Pal" Mury, Jay Karp, "Doc" Moore, Vin Tofany, and even a general or two—and how they'd stay up late into the night. Long after dinner was over they'd still be sitting at the dining room table with half-finished carafes of wine and the last of the desserts and dishes before them glasses of brandy in hand, talking of old and new times. I knew, even as young as I was then, that there was an inseparable bond between them, that the horror and glory of their shared experience had tied them together in friendship from that time to this, and from this time till the end of their days.

And that, to me, is also a part of Memorial Day.

That inseparable bond is not just among the living. The distinct experience of those years at war also bound my father and his veteran comrades to the memory of all their other comrades in the 463rd Parachute Field Artillery Battalion—the first airborne unit in the U.S. Army. It also bound them to all the other thousands in the 101st Airborne Division to which they were attached as well as to the hundreds of thousands of other men and women who served in the Allied cause and did not come back from that great war. Their young faces are still remembered by the now old men who once stood and fought beside them.

And that, too, is a part of Memorial Day.

Yet though my memories of this Memorial Day—and all the days that had gone before it—would never have the meaning and suffering (thankfully) of my father's memories of World War II, they would, both now and in the future, be important to me for the deeds done and the sights seen as well as for those friends with whom they were shared.

Rabbit Creek Trail

Note: As of this writing, some of the first miles of Rabbit Creek Trail are under private ownership, so technically, any who uses this trail is trespassing. However, since the owner failed to compel the state to buy back his land, he has removed his trailer home from the area. Since then hiker's have begun once again to use this trail to access the Rabbit Lake and McHugh Creek drainages.

Trail Location: The Rabbit Creek trailhead is located at the very end of Canyon Road in the upper Rabbit Creek valley. To get there, drive south on the Seward Highway from downtown Anchorage to the DeArmoun Road exit. At the end of the ramp, turn left and follow DeArmoun Road toward the mountains. About 3.5 miles from the highway, cross Hillside Road and continue uphill on what is now Upper DeArmoun Road. Just over 1 mile up this road turn right and downhill onto Canyon Road. This road snakes around, passing many side streets for almost 2 miles, becoming rougher and rougher the higher it winds, and dead ends at a gate. The road from this point on *is* the trail. (Due to the roughness of the road, some vehicles may not be capable of reaching as far the gate. If so, you can simply park on either side of the road and walk the rest of the distance. However, most cars should be able to reach the wide turn-around area in the road just around the corner from the gate.)

Trail Grade: This trail, being almost entirely an old dirt road, is predominantly a grade 1 hike, with only very short sections of grade 2 (such as where the land owner tore up the trail with a backhoe to discourage people from trespassing).

Trail Condition: Because it is a road, the trail condition is excellent, except, as stated before, where the owner tore up almost 1 mile of trail with a backhoe. In this section, there are roots to avoid, ditches to climb in and out of and, on rainy days, many deep puddles.

Trail Mileage: The one way distance from the gate to the shore of Rabbit Lake is just over 5 miles, for a round-trip total of 10 miles.

Total Elevation Gain: Approximately 1,300 feet.

High Point: The highest point reached is just over 3,100 feet above sea level at the point where the trail passes over top of the bluff just before reaching Rabbit Lake.

Normal Hiking Time: Many runners do this round trip to the lake and back in 2 to 2.5 hours. Hikers, however, should expect to take anywhere from 3 to 8 hours, depending on their ambition and condition.

Campsites: There are plenty of campsites along the west and south shore of Rabbit Lake and the north shore of McHugh Lake. There are also numerous places to camp along the upper ends of both McHugh Creek and Rabbit Creek. Be sure to bring a gas stove, though, as there is no wood available.

Best Time: This trail is best hiked from mid-June to mid-September when the valley is usually free of snow. It also makes a fine snowshoe hike or ski outing in the winter with only minimal avalanche risk in the valley.

USGS Maps: Anchorage A-7 and A-8 SE.

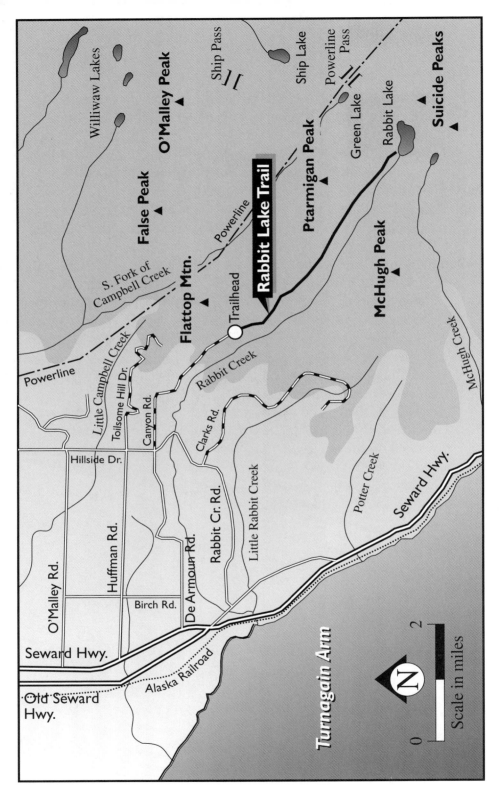

Williwaw Lakes

O'Malley Peak ▲

Ship Pass

Ship Lake

Powerline Pass

Suicide Peaks ▲ ▲

False Peak ▲

Green Lake

Rabbit Lake

Rabbit Lake Trail

Ptarmigan Peak ▲

S. Fork of Campbell Creek

Powerline

Flattop Mtn. ▲

Trailhead

McHugh Peak ▲

Little Campbell Creek

Powerline

Toilsome Hill Dr.

Canyon Rd.

Rabbit Creek

McHugh Creek

Clarks Rd.

Hillside Dr.

Little Rabbit Creek

Rabbit Cr. Rd.

Potter Creek

Seward Hwy.

Huffman Rd.

De Armour Rd.

O'Malley Rd.

Birch Rd.

Turnagain Arm

Seward Hwy.

Alaska Railroad

Old Seward Hwy.

N

Scale in miles

0   2

8

Spring in the high country of the Chugach Mountains.

RABBIT CREEK TRAIL TO THE
SUMMIT OF SOUTH SUICIDE PEAK

Note: The difficulty of this trip—both due to the total elevation gain as well as the rocky traverse along Suicide Peak's southwest ridge—should make most people think twice about doing it with children or if they themselves do not have at least some rock scrambling experience and are not in at least decent physical condition. For those who are capable and willing, this climb is one of the grandest in the Front Range of the Chugach.

Trail Location: From the shore of Rabbit Lake turn right (south), cross Rabbit Creek and cross over the low ridge to McHugh Lake. (To get to the shore of Rabbit Lake see WALK-ABOUT GUIDE TO RABBIT CREEK TRAIL.) Cross McHugh Creek just below the lake and begin to climb the broad, yet steep tundra slope on the other side of the ridge. At the top of the ridge (the southwest ridge of the mountain), turn left (northeast) up the ridge. Stay on the ridge, going over or around the gendarmes and rock pillars and scree slopes that block the way, until the broad tundra slope below the final summit cone is reached. From here, follow the crest of the ridge—with the precipitous west face of the mountain on your left. For those who want to avoid the west face, it is possible to corkscrew up and around to the right. (It is also possible to reach the summit of South Suicide, as well as North Suicide, by climbing directly up the gully between them to the upper right hand side of Windy Gap. The loose scree that fills this entire gully from top to bottom, however, makes this anything but an easy climb. It should not require any roped climbing if one stays in the

10

gully; however, it should only be attempted by experienced rock scramblers.) Truly ambitious hikers may even want to continue down into the very appropriately named Windy Gap, so named because of the ferocious south winds that funnel up and through it. (I had to literally drag myself across on one occasion the winds were so strong.) From there continue up to the summit of North Suicide (5,065 feet) and possibly even continue the traverse down the knife-edged ridge over to the long east ridge of Ptarmigan Peak where, if one feels like they've climbed enough for one day, a gentle descent can be made back to Rabbit Lakes. For those who still want to climb more, they have the option of continuing west along the very steep and jagged ridge to Ptarmigan Peak and back down to the Rabbit Creek Trail or north along the back of the ridge, up over the next ridge and all the way down to Powerline Pass. There they can pick up the Powerline Pass Trail and follow it out to Glenn Alps. Any one of these extensions of the climb up South Suicide makes for an incredibly long, but spectacular day.

NOTE: Though most of the climbing beyond North Suicide is grade 5 and 6, there is one narrow notch on the saddle between North Suicide Peak and the east ridge of Ptarmigan Peak that may require some grade 7 climbing. So you might want to bring a rope. Some may also find a rope useful at times while coming down the rocky north ridge of North Suicide Peak or along the jagged east ridge of Ptarmigan Peak.

Trail Grade: Rabbit Creek Trail to Rabbit Lake is predominantly grade 1 (with small sections of grade 2), whereas crossing the trail-less tundra over to McHugh Lake is predominantly grade 3. Beginning with the climb up the slope on the opposite side of the lake, however, the grade rises quickly to levels 5 and 6, where it stays for almost the entire climb to the summit.

Trail Condition: This trip has almost every possible trail condition, from easy, flat trail to open, wide tundra, to very steep, scree streaked tundra, to rocky, hand over hand scrambling along the ridge and in the last two or three hundred yards to the summit.

Trail Mileage: From the shore of Rabbit Lake to the summit of South Suicide Peak is a total distance of just over 3 miles for a round trip total of 6 miles. From the trailhead of Rabbit Creek Trail to the summit and back is a total round trip distance of 16 miles.

Total Elevation Gain: The total elevation gain from the trailhead of Rabbit Creek Trail to the summit of South Suicide Peak is 3,105 feet.

High Point: The highest point reached, the summit of South Suicide Peak, is 5,005 feet above sea level.

Normal Hiking Time: The length and difficulty of this trip requires either one very long day of hiking and climbing or two shorter days.

Campsites: Though there are a plethora of fine places to pitch a tent along McHugh Creek or by McHugh Lake, there are no campsites on the climb itself. Be sure to bring a gas stove, as there is no wood available.

Best Time: The best time to do this climb is mid-June to August, just after the last snow melts and before the first snow falls.

USGS Maps: Anchorage A-7 and A-8 SE.

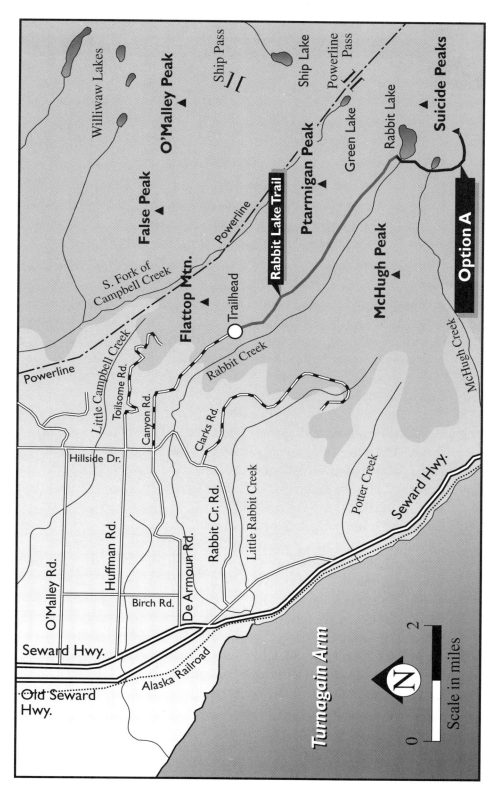

Williwaw Lakes

O'Malley Peak ▲

Ship Pass

Ship Lake

Powerline Pass

Suicide Peaks ▲

False Peak ▲

S. Fork of Campbell Creek

Ptarmigan Peak ▲

Green Lake

Rabbit Lake

Rabbit Lake Trail

Powerline

Flattop Mtn. ▲

Trailhead

McHugh Peak ▲

McHugh Creek

Option A

Powerline

Little Campbell Creek

Toilsome Rd.

Canyon Rd.

Rabbit Creek

Clarks Rd.

Hillside Dr.

Rabbit Cr. Rd.

Little Rabbit Creek

Potter Creek

Seward Hwy.

Huffman Rd.

De Armoun Rd.

O'Malley Rd.

Birch Rd.

Seward Hwy.

Old Seward Hwy.

Alaska Railroad

Turnagain Arm

N

Scale in miles

0   2

13

RABBIT CREEK TRAIL TO THE
SUMMIT OF McHUGH PEAK

Note: This hike/climb is a very scenic, but harder, alternative round trip return to the McHugh Creek Picnic Area. Instead of going back down the trail, this route traverses the summit ridge of McHugh Peak, crossing over four different peaks—the highest being the summit of McHugh Peak itself (4,301 feet)—before descending once again to the McHugh Creek Trail for the descent back to the highway.

Trail Location: From the end of the Rabbit Creek Trail at the shore of Rabbit Lake, turn right, cross Rabbit Creek and climb to the low ridge that separates the Rabbit Creek from the McHugh Creek drainage. (To get to the end of Rabbit Creek Trail see WALK-ABOUT GUIDE TO RABBIT CREEK TRAIL.) From this low ridge, the route bears left, or southwest, up the shallow ridge. Stay on the crest, climbing and scrambling in a few spots—none of which are dangerously exposed—for as long as desired. After the summit is reached, continue down the ridge for as long as desired, keeping a close eye on McHugh Creek Trail which should be visible far down the left, or east, slope. Before that trail enters the woods, descend to it down any preferred slope. Then follow the McHugh Creek Trail left, and back up the valley. Pass McHugh Lake and re-cross the low ridge back to the shore of Rabbit Lake and the Rabbit Creek Trail. An alternative to descending to the McHugh Creek Trail is to either back track the way you came or, if not too far down the ridge, descend off the right hand side of the ridge to the Rabbit Creek Trail. This second option should not be attempted unless the Rabbit Creek Trail is clearly visible, otherwise the hikers may find themselves going down the wrong drainage and, after some difficult bushwhacking, coming out of the woods in Bear Valley.

Trail Grade: The route along the crest of the ridge is a grade 4 climb from end to end.

Trail Condition: The crest of the ridge alternates between being rocky with short sections of scree—which may require some use of hands—and gentle stretches of easy tundra walking. The sometimes steep descent back to the trail will alternate between scree and tundra and meadow.

Trail Mileage: The entire ridge crest is almost 4 miles long, for a round trip total via a return trip up McHugh Creek Trail of 18 to 20 miles or, if backtracking along the ridge, anywhere from 16 to 18 miles to and from the trailhead of Rabbit Creek Trail.

Total Elevation Gain: Hiking from the low ridge between McHugh Lake and Rabbit Lake entails a climb of just under 1,100 feet. From the trailhead to the summit of McHugh Peak is just over 2,500 feet.

High Point: The highest point attained on this hike is 4,301 feet above sea level at the summit of McHugh Peak.

Normal Hiking Time: The round trip to and from the Rabbit creek trailhead via the McHugh Peak ridge will take 6 to10 hours depending upon the condition and ambition of the hiker(s).

Campsites: Though there are numerous places to pitch a tent on the tundra near the lakes, there is only one possible campsite on the ridge itself. It is just to the right of the summit of the first peak south of McHugh Peak itself and about 3 miles from Rabbit Lake. Be sure to bring a gas stove, though, as there is no wood available.

Best Time: June to September is the best time of year in which to do this hike.

USGS Maps: Anchorage A-7 and A-8 SE.

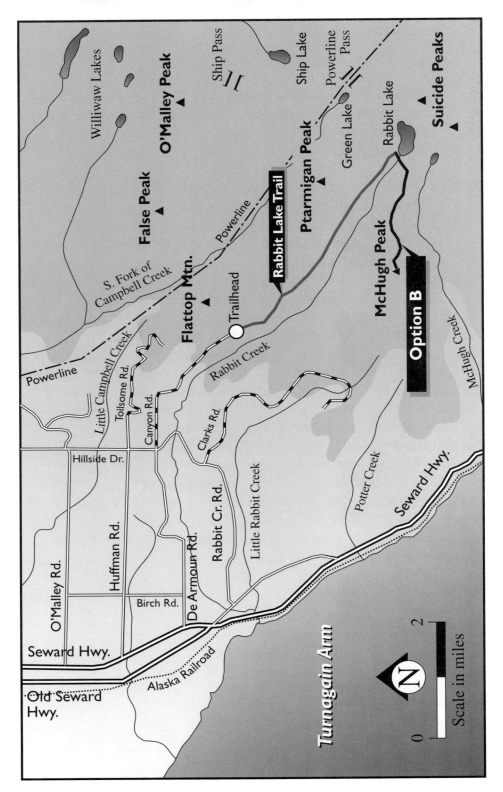

16

Descending the north ridge of North Suicide Peak.

RABBIT CREEK TRAIL TO THE
SUMMIT OF PTARMIGAN PEAK

Note: This is not a particularly dangerous climb—*if* one stays on the south west side of the mountain. However, it should not be attempted by novice hikers in that it requires quite a bit of rock scrambling up some relatively steep gullies as well as along the rocky summit ridge.

Trail Location: About 2.5 miles from the beginning of the Rabbit Creek Trail, a mile or so after leaving the torn up section of the trail, bear left off the trail anywhere and begin to climb toward the obvious spired summit that can be seen above and to the left. This is Ptarmigan Peak. (To get to Rabbit Creek Trail, see WALK-ABOUT GUIDE TO RABBIT CREEK TRAIL.) Some hikers may prefer to simply climb up to Ptarmigan Pass where a small tarn on the opposite side of the Pass is a delightful spot. Anyone wanting to climb Ptarmigan Peak, though, should continue climbing toward the summit, always staying on the right, or southwest side of the ridge (as the west and north faces are mostly sheer cliffs and *very* dangerous). If one feels one's self getting too close to the cliffs on the left, simply keep shifting to the right and continue climbing. The upper portions of the mountain will require some decisions about route making—such as what gully to climb or when to continue right— but if one persists upward, the summit (marked by a register and plaque located along the ridge just to the west) will be reached. Experienced rock scramblers may even want to continue east from here to the junction with the ridge that extends from North Suicide Peak to Powerline Pass. From there it is an easy descent down a wide tundra slope to the northeast corner of Rabbit Lake. Then follow the shoreline back to the Rabbit Creek Trail.

Trail Grade: The climb to the summit of Ptarmigan as well as along the entire length of the ridge fluctuates between grades 5 and 6—with a lot more 6 than 5.

Trail Condition: The higher one climbs, the rougher and more difficult the route becomes. It is, however, a pretty straightforward climb to the summit. Beyond the summit, though, the ridge is a series of rocky spires and gendarmes that will probably require considerable backtracking and route finding skills as many ledges and gullies dead end—which results in considerable up and down and back and forth climbing and scrambling. The ridge, though, is passable. It's just a matter of being patient with all the twists and turns along its crest.

Trail Mileage: From the trailhead of Rabbit Creek Road to the summit of Ptarmigan Peak is roughly 4.5 miles, for round trip total of 9 miles. To continue down the ridge to Rabbit Lake is at least another 3 miles—especially with all the twists and turns that traverse entails—for a round trip total of at least 16 very slow miles.

Total Elevation Gain: From the trailhead to the summit of Ptarmigan Peak requires a climb of almost 3,100 feet.

High Point: The highest point reached—whether the traverse of the entire ridge is done or not—is the summit of Ptarmigan Peak which is 4,880 feet above sea level.

Normal Hiking Time: The round trip to the summit and back should taken anywhere from 6 to 10 hours, whereas the traverse of the entire ridge should be about 9 to 13 hours.

Campsites: There are no campsites anywhere along the ridge.

Best Time: The best time to make this climb and/or traverse is anywhere from mid-June to September.

USGS Maps: Anchorage A-7 and A-8 SE.

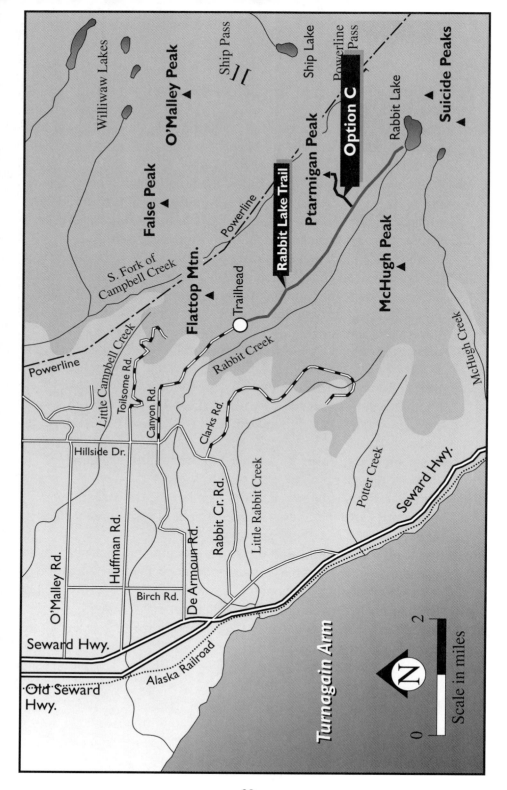

Williwaw Lakes

O'Malley Peak ▲

O'Malley Peak

Ship Pass

Ship Lake

Powerline Pass

Suicide Peaks ▲

Rabbit Lake

Suicide Peaks ▲

False Peak ▲

Ptarmigan Peak

Option C

Powerline

Rabbit Lake Trail

S. Fork of Campbell Creek

McHugh Peak ▲

McHugh Creek

Flattop Mtn. ▲

Trailhead

Powerline

Little Campbell Creek

Rabbit Creek

Toilsome Rd.

Canyon Rd.

Clarks Rd.

Hillside Dr.

Rabbit Cr. Rd.

Little Rabbit Creek

Potter Creek

Seward Hwy.

Huffman Rd.

De Armour Rd.

O'Malley Rd.

Birch Rd.

Seward Hwy.

Alaska Railroad

Turnagain Arm

Old Seward Hwy.

N

0

2

Scale in miles

Above Turnagain Arm near McHugh Peak looking south toward Kenai Peninsula and Mount Augustine on the horizon.

CHAPTER 2

The Rarest Dream That E'er Dull'd Sleep

The faint shadow of footprints in the gray snow at my feet were the only clue as to which way to go. They were my lifeline. The clouds had closed in so tight—to within a few feet—that they blocked all visiblity in every direction. All I could see were those footprints appearing out of the mists before me and disappearing into the mists behind me as I moved. It was like climbing in a long, narrow tunnel.

Rocks appeared and disappeared at the shadowy borders of sight. Brush dripping with cold beads of mist came and went at the shifting edges of vision. But nothing else moved. No creature stirred. No bird sang. I was isolated and alone.

Then the tundra underfoot disappeared. I crossed two steep-angled fields of mushy snow and clambered up a muddy rock rib, my feet slipping with every step on the mushy talus. My fingers were white with cold, my breath was a heavy, condensed cloud from exertion. I wondered if I was getting anywhere—if I was even going the right way. For one fleeting moment, I even wondered if I'd be able to get back to where I started.

I could've been anywhere: days deep in the Wrangell-St. Elias Range, seasons deep in the Brooks Range, or even miles deep in the Talkeetna Mountains. But I wasn't in any place so exotic and wild as these. This was on Flattop Mountain—old familiar Flattop which can be seen from all over Anchorage and reached by car in minutes. Less than two miles up a gently graded trail from the parking lot to the summit, it's considered a choice family destination, or a fine place for an evening's meditation, or even for a concentrated training run.

But on this Saturday morning it was none of these. It seemed as wild and remote as anywhere in Alaska. I certainly didn't know it would be like this when, with a few free hours before me, I decided to drive to Glen Alps and go for a run. After all, it was close, familiar and also, especially out along the trail leading to Powerline Pass, scenic. That's what it was usually like, but not today. On this day, the usual was not at all the norm. Instead it was like Alice's trip through the looking glass where everything familiar was turned topsy-turvy and nothing was as it should be and often not even what it seemed.

Of course I should've realized that the unusual was a distinct possibility as I drove out of the city. For even though the city was bathed in sunlight, the mountains were shrouded in clouds—and clouds always bring out the worst in the mountains. Still, I was going to Flattop, old familiar Flattop. It had a trail and it was close to the parking lot. So why worry?

When I arrived at the parking lot it was quiet—eerily quiet and deserted compared to usual—with only two other cars sitting empty in the gray mist and not a person in sight. Nor was the mountain in sight. Donning gloves and a hat, I stepped into the dank, chilly air and started jogging down the trail toward Powerline Pass to warm up before my climb. Dodging puddles, jumping mud holes and skipping over ice patches, I was soon out under the powerlines. Normally from this spot the view is magnificent with O'Malley Peak, Hidden Peak, the Ramp, the Wedge, Ptarmigan and Flattop forming a vast amphitheater around the fall line of the valley down which flow the turbulent waters of Campbell Creek. From this vantage, over the two saddles of Ship Pass to the northeast and Powerline Pass due east, one can usually see other, more distant summits. Behind, to the west, the view over the city and Cook Inlet and Mount Susitna beyond is usually no less spectacular. On a truly blue day even Denali, Foraker and Hunter are visible to the north.

But on this Saturday morning there was nothing to be seen. Even the powerlines, which should have been only fifty feet or so overhead, were hidden. Nor was nearby Campbell Creek, which flowed just sixty feet below on the left, at all visible. Instead, from out of the mists circling over that hidden ravine off to the left there drifted up the muffled roar of volumes of tumbling water. On a sunny day, the creek's waters sparkled like diamonds, but on this day the distant rumble sounded ominous—like the River Styx in the ancient underworld—as it rushed down toward the sea, whose cold waves foamed and frothed somewhere at the far edge of the Anchorage Bowl.

This was not the Powerline Pass I knew. This was another land, a wilder, forgotten land. A land of lifeless gray and confounding mists. A landscape removed from memory, and even time. I felt an inexplicable sense of loneliness and desolation.

But as I jogged slowly back down the trail, following my own footprints across the snow and through the mud, the oppressive clouds around me started to lift. Tantalizing glimpses of the exposed flanks of nearby mountains came and went in the mists. It was, I thought, time to climb Flattop.

The summit of Flattop is only 1.6 miles from the parking lot. Yet in that short distance, the view of the city—and of all the wilderness surrounding it—expands dramatically. If the clouds did clear, I would get a wonderful view to take home with me. Little did I know that I would never get the view. What I got instead was a glimpse of a side of Flattop very few people ever see.

Back at the parking lot, I got my camera and started to climb toward the summit. The trail was almost entirely clear of snow, which I took as an auspicious omen. It was also surprisingly dry, which was another good sign. Stunted spruce and willow swayed in the cool breeze now blowing over the surrounding gentle meadows. Then the clouds began to break apart overhead. In turn, I started to feel more ambitious—even more adventuresome.

When I reached the gap where the Blueberry Hill Trail led off to the right and climbed the round hill above the parking lot and the Flattop Trail climbed left toward the summit, I went straight ahead, splitting the two trails, and, striking off on my own, headed toward the south side of the mountain.

What's the danger? It's only Flattop—and Flattop's not even a mountain. It's just the end of a ridge. Or so I thought.

Little did I know that I'd just walked through the looking glass into another world. Soon the clouds closed in again, the snow appeared in abundance, and the gentle meadows tilted into steep slopes. I climbed on.

I didn't climb with my previous abandon, though. Suddenly Flattop had become like all other mountains both near and far. No longer was it a tame, easy hike, but a tiring—and even dangerous—climb.

24

Every year the newspaper seemed to list at least one fatality due to an accident on this one mountain. I was just now beginning to realized why. It can happen with one unguarded step on one steep trail, or one one careless move on one unnoticed ledge. The smallest mistake can get someone to be hurt, or even killed.

Soon the visibility was all but nil. It became virtually impossible to tell where I was. All I knew for sure was that the summit was still above me, so up I went. I passed over the prints of other hikers, kicked across snowfields troughed by the marks of body sledding. I even found fifteen cents in the gravel as I pulled myself over a wet, rocky outcrop. But these were all signs of human life from another day and another time.

On this day I was alone. I didn't feel in danger, though, as much as I felt misplaced. I didn't feel fear, as much as I felt disoriented. After all, this was just Flattop. It was, however, a Flattop I'd never experienced. This was a Flattop with no human presence nearby and with no sign of civilization with in sight. It was no longer the tame, easy mountain I'd always know.

I didn't know how far I'd come, how far I had to go. Nor did I have any idea how much time had passed. But then who does in a dream?

Years ago, on a long bus ride from Nepal to India, I had stopped in Agra to see the Taj Mahal. I was appalled to find it defaced by graffiti both painted and carved into its once white, pristine walls. Now it was old, scarred and dirty, and no different from Grand Central Station in New York City or the Golden Gate Bridge in San Francisco. It had become common and familiar. Consequently, it has become a victim of the same contempt with which we have come to treat so much that is rare and wonderful—which, in turn, results in the willful desecration of the once radiant and revered.

Later that night, however, a transformation had occurred. Anders, a Swede I was traveling with at the time, and I sneaked back onto the grounds and unrolled our sleeping bags alongside the marble fountains in front of the tomb. There, beneath the magic of the stars, and accompanied by the musical tinkling of the fountains, the blue wash of the moon's light took back the passing years, rolled up the centuries of neglect and abuse, until that magnificent building became once again sparkling and clean, and wonderful to behold. There were no graffiti disfiguring the walls, no cracks marring the foundation and columns, and no piles of dirt swept in the corners. Nor were there any crowds jostling back and forth. There was nothing to dispel the magic. The Taj Mahal was once again what it was meant to be: a majestic and glittering tribute to a lost loved one

So was I once again, at least for a few moments, transported from the actual to the ideal. I was no longer hiking up Flattop. Instead, I was climbing through an unaffected wilderness on a faraway, magic mountain. I followed bear tracks across a high snowfield and listened to the silence of a land void of human presence. It was as magical as that night in India.

> This is the rarest dream that e'er dull'd sleep
> Did mock sad fools withal.
> (from Pericles by Shakespeare)

Such deceiving magic is fleeting, though. On that night in India, when the light of the common day was spreading across the lawns before the Taj Mahal and the toe of a guardsman was nudging us awake, the magic was gone with the rising sun's hard light of reason. So did the magic on Flattop end when I climbed out of the brush and rocks onto the trail just a hundred yards below the summit. In that moment, the trackless world of Alaskan wilderness had once again become just a well-trodden hill overlooking Anchorage.

After the last short climb up the last rocks to the summit, I walked once around the wide top in the still, close clouds. There was, of course, nothing to see except nearby wet stones and cold snow. No wind stirred. No sound was heard except the scraping of my running shoes over the gravel and my own steady breathing. A posted sign suggested that I be cautious while descending.

I sighed. I had passed back through the looking glass.

I came down the normal, familiar route on the dirty, and snow-covered, rutted trail. On my way I passed ten people going up. Some I stopped to chat with, others I gave just a quick greeting or a nod of acknowledgment. But if the truth be told, I felt disoriented and a little bit disappointed by this sudden contact with all these people. I wondered if Alice had felt the same way after coming back through the looking glass.

I wondered if she, like me, was half inclined to go back through the looking glass and never return. Of course, that would have been impossible. No dream is that obedient or abiding.

We can escape the common world, but never for long—and only rarely.

As I stood in the parking lot gazing back up toward the clearing summit, I knew I had been given a rare glimpse of Flattop's dark, magical side. What had started off as an innocent outing had become an unalterable act of initiation. This mountain, once so familiar and common, would never be the same to me again.

Flattop Mountain

Note: This little mountain—which is actually only a bump at the end of a 6 mile long ridge that extends due west off the backbone of the Front Range just south of Powerline Pass—is probably the most popular climb in all of Alaska. It is the preferred choice of people looking for an evening hike after work in the summer, for mountain runners looking for a good workout, for school outings, for families and friends to get some fresh air together on a weekend afternoon, and even for climbers to lug heavy loads up and down in training to climb Mt. McKinley. It is, in short, an all-purpose, mountain. One reason for its popularity is that it is right next door to the highest concentration of people in Alaska—the city of Anchorage. In addition to that, it is neither too short, or too long for most people looking for a little outdoor exercise. On a clear day it also affords wide-angle views of Turnagain Arm and Knik Arm and the hovering mountains that rise above them on the distant, hazy horizons. One can see from Mt. Redoubt to Mt. McKinley.

The ambitious hiker need not stop at the summit of Flattop, though. With some determination it's possible to continue along the ridge for approximately three miles, climbing Peak Two and Peak Three in the process (Option A). The truly determined can even cross the next valley and climb with great caution—which means keeping always to the right (south) side of the ridge in order to avoid the rock cliffs on the west and north sides of the ridge—Ptarmigan Peak (4,880 feet) and from there continue all the way down the ridge before descending into Powerline Pass (Option B). (A first person account of this ridge climb is the subject of the narrative in the next chapter.)

However, despite its popularity, Flattop should not be taken lightly. The same blasting high winds, smothering clouds and blistering blizzards that torment the mountains nearby—as well as the city below— do not ignore this mountain either. Always bring warm clothes and a few extra candy bars or food to stave off any sudden change in the weather or loss of visibility. Also, the rock cliffs just off the trail near the summit and the bordering edges of the broad, flat summit itself, have claimed the lives of many people who forgot that mountains are always dangerous— no matter how many people climb any particular one like Flattop.

Trail Location: The trail to the summit of Flattop begins at the Glen Alps Park Entrance located just below tree line in the foothills of the Front Range that dominates the eastern horizon above Anchorage. To get to Glen Alps go east up O'Malley Road from its intersection with the Seward Highway. Follow O'Malley approximately 4 miles to Hillside Road. Turn right onto Hillside Drive and drive for another mile or so to Upper Huffman Road, which is on the left just after a sign for Chugach State Park. Follow Upper Huffman Road for 3/4's of a mile and take a right onto the appropriately named Toilsome Hill Drive. This road, upon which chains, studs and/or four-wheel drive are recommended in winter, switchbacks and winds its way for two more miles before the entrance to Glen Alps parking lot appears on the left hand side at the top of one last short, steep hill. The trail begins by climbing the elegant wooden staircase at the far end of the parking lot on the right.

Trail Grade: The grading on this mountain varies from a 1 to 2 on the lower part of the mountain where a newly constructed trail winds around Blueberry Hill (the low, round hill directly above the parking lot) to the south side of the mountain. From here, the trail gets steeper, though the rocks and logs that have been put in to prevent erosion and provide steps make for excellent footing even on the wettest of days. Farther up, on the summit cone itself, the trail gets a little rocky but the new switchbacks still make the climbing relatively easy. Only the last few feet to the summit may require any use of hands. But because it is still a trail, even this short steep section can be given a rating no higher than 3, which is also true of the last bit of trail that crawls up a short gully to the summit plateau.

Trail Condition: With the completion of the new trail in 1996, the trail conditions have improved dramatically. The climb up the northern side of the mountain to the notch just below the summit as well as the climb down from the same point used to be a hard and treacherous climb up a very steep, short scree slope. But now with the trail going around and up the opposite side of the mountain that climb has been eliminated. The trail has been laid out to prevent having to do any scrambling up and down scree. Even many of the big boulders that made the summit cone itself a climb of uncertain and unsteady footing have been removed from the walled in tread of the new trail. All one has to do is stay on the trail and the footing should be good to excellent all the way up the mountain.

Trail Mileage: The climb to the summit is 1.6 miles for a round trip total to and from the parking lot of just about 3.2 miles.

Total Elevation Gain: The climb from the parking area to the summit entails a climb of 1,252 feet.

High Point: The summit of Flattop is 3,510 feet above sea level.

Normal Hiking Time: The round-trip to the summit and back should take anywhere from 45 minutes to 5 hours depending on whether you're running, hiking, carrying or leading a child, or examining the numerous flowers at your feet.

Campsites: There are no campsites to speak of, though the Powerline valley below does have ample places to pitch a tent. Wherever you camp, though, please bring a stove because campfires are prohibited inside park limits.

Best Time: Winter mountaineers may love the training they can get in the couloirs and gullies on the upper slopes of this mountain. Winter is, however, a dangerous time to be on the mountain: avalanches, cornices, and steep snow fields are all a threat in the season. Most people, therefore, should consider climbing Flattop from June to October.

USGS Maps: Maps Anchorage A-8 SE.

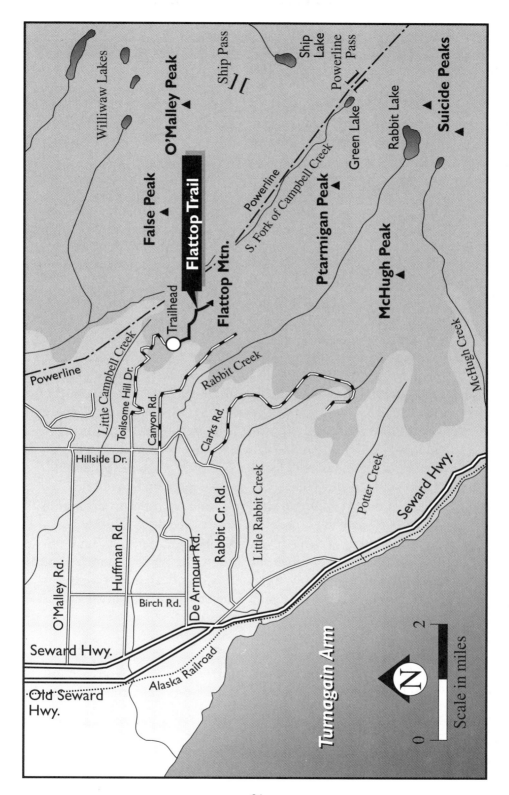

Williwaw Lakes

O'Malley Peak ▲

Ship Pass

Ship Lake

Powerline Pass

Suicide Peaks ▲
▲

False Peak ▲

Flattop Trail

Flattop Mtn. ▲

Trailhead

Powerline

S. Fork of Campbell Creek

Green Lake ▲

Rabbit Lake

Ptarmigan Peak ▲

McHugh Peak ▲

McHugh Creek

Little Campbell Creek

Toilsome Hill Dr.

Canyon Rd.

Powerline

Rabbit Creek

Clarks Rd.

Hillside Dr.

Potter Creek

Seward Hwy.

De Armour Rd.

Rabbit Cr. Rd.

Little Rabbit Creek

O'Malley Rd.

Huffman Rd.

Birch Rd.

Seward Hwy.

Old Seward Hwy.

Alaska Railroad

Turnagain Arm

N

0 ———— 2
Scale in miles

Blueberry Loop Trail

Trail Location: The Blueberry Loop Trail, which circumnavigates Blueberry Hill, the lower knoll located just west of Flattop on the same ridge, is actually a shorter, easier version of the Flattop Trail. So, in that most of this trail is one and the same as the lower portion of the trail up Flattop, follow the same directions to Glen Alps parking area and the beginning of that trail as found in WALK-ABOUT GUIDE TO FLATTOP. Continue following the directions for the Flattop Trail as it leaves the parking lot and starts up to the first trail junction at the northern base of Blueberry Hill. The trail sign here will point right (west) away from Flattop as it begins its circumnavigation by going around the front of Blueberry Hill. Follow this wide and easy trail around to the south side of the mountain and back to the notch where a second trail junction is located. This is where Blueberry Loop Trail and Flattop Trail part company. At this point, the trail up Flattop takes a right hand turn and crosses the base of the notch before continuing on up the ridge, The Blueberry Loop Trail, on the other hand, goes straight ahead, continuing back around the north side of Blueberry Hill. Within a quarter mile, the first trail junction will be reached again. The parking lot is only a short way down to the right from this point.

Trail Grade: This wide, easy, and mostly flat trail never rises in difficulty to more than a Grade 1.

Trail Condition: Considering that this trail was cut by a bulldozer, after which it was covered with loose gravel, it is (with the exception of the bike trails and any other paved trails) one of the smoothest, widest trails in the Chugach—and perhaps even all of Alaska.

Trail Mileage: The entire loop is only 1 mile in distance.

Total Elevation Gain: 400 feet.

High Point: The highest point reached on this trail is 2,500 feet above sea level at the saddle between Blueberry Hill and Flattop Mountain.

Normal Hiking Time: This hike can take anywhere from less than 10 minutes for a runner in a hurry to over an hour for a family in no hurry.

Campsites: There are no places to camp in this area. (The nearest places to camp are either farther up the Powerline Pass Valley to the northeast and Rabbit Creek Valley to the southeast.) There are, however, many places for a picnic, including the top of Blueberry Hill itself which can be reached after a short climb up the tundra from any point along the trail.

Best Time: The best time to do this hike is from June to September. It can also be done as a winter hike, if one doesn't mind tramping through snow and fighting the usually strong winds that roar down off of Powerline Pass and Windy Notch between North and South Suicide peaks.

USGS Maps: Anchorage A-8 SE.

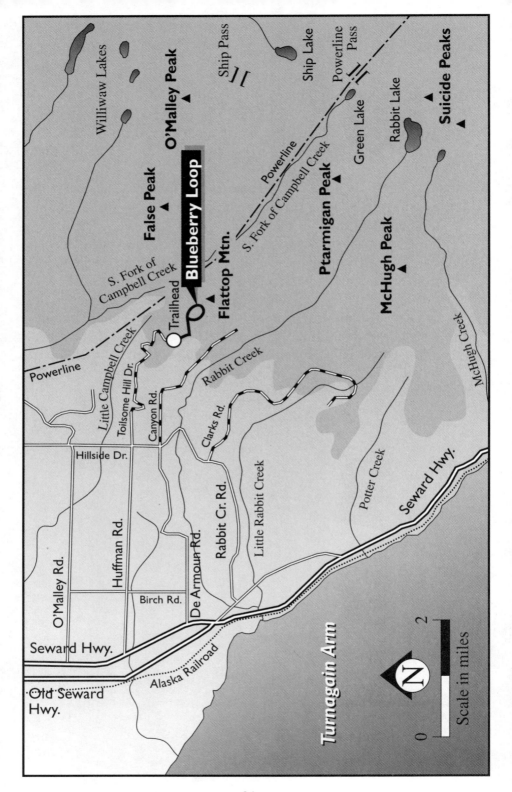

Williwaw Lakes

O'Malley Peak ◄

Ship Pass

Ship Lake

Powerline Pass

Suicide Peaks ◄
◄

Rabbit Lake

False Peak ◄

Blueberry Loop

Powerline

S. Fork of Campbell Creek

Green Lake

Ptarmigan Peak ◄

McHugh Peak ◄

Flattop Mtn. ◄

S. Fork of
Campbell Creek

Trailhead ●

Little Campbell Creek

Powerline

Toilsome Hill Dr.

Canyon Rd.

Rabbit Creek

Clarks Rd.

McHugh Creek

Hillside Dr.

O'Malley Rd.

Huffman Rd.

Birch Rd.

De Armoun Rd.

Rabbit Cr. Rd.

Little Rabbit Creek

Potter Creek

Seward Hwy.

Seward Hwy.

Alaska Railroad

Old Seward
Hwy.

Turnagain Arm

N

0   2

Scale in miles

34

On the Flattop Trail with the city of Anchorage below.

Anchorage Overlook

Trail Location: This short, entirely paved trail is ideal for the handicapped and other people physically unable to walk any distance, and yet still wants to enjoy a wide, spacious view of Anchorage. It begins in the Glen Alps parking area. (To get there, see WALK-ABOUT GUIDE TO FLATTOP TRAIL.) The Overlook Trail begins on the left (northeast) side of the parking lot near the outhouse. Just follow the paved walkway up around the small knoll to where there are benches and even a wind-screened viewing platform.

Trail Grade: This is perhaps the only trail in this book that it isn't difficult enough to deserve a rating of Grade 1. Instead, it is Grade 1/2.

Trail Condition: Considering that this is an asphalt paved trail from end to end, the condition is excellent. In fact, the trail is easier to walk on than the parking area surface!

Trail Mileage: From the parking area to the overlook is 0.1 miles for a round trip total of less than a quarter mile.

Total Elevation Gain: From the parking area to the overlook, the elevation gain is just under 50 feet.

High Point: The highest point reached is 2,258 feet at the overlook itself.

Normal Hiking Time: The round trip to and from the parking area can be done in a matter of minutes. But for those who want to enjoy the view or the warm afternoon sun (if either or both are out—which is *iffy* at best), they might want to allow a lot more time.

Campsites: There are no available places to camp at or near the overlook. However, the overlook itself is a fine place to enjoy a picnic lunch or an evening snack.

Best Time: The best time to do this hike is from early June to late September.

USGS Maps: Anchorage A-8 SE.

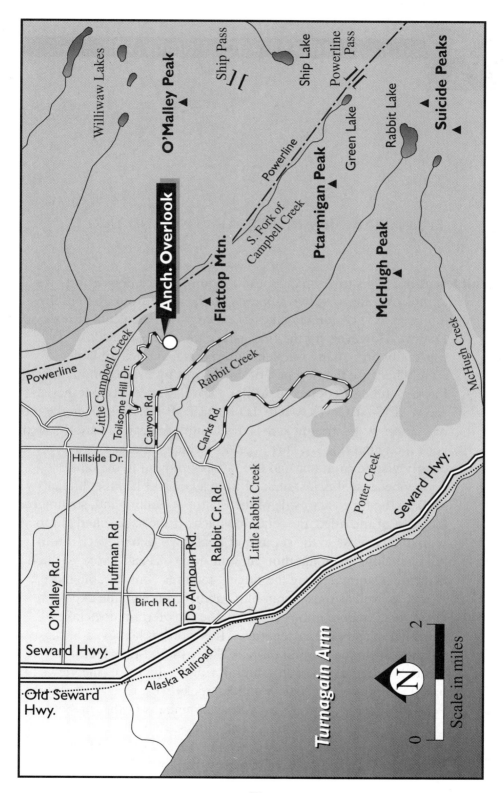

Williwaw Lakes

O'Malley Peak

Ship Pass

Ship Lake

Powerline Pass

Suicide Peaks

Rabbit Lake

Green Lake

Ptarmigan Peak

Powerline

S. Fork of Campbell Creek

Anch. Overlook

McHugh Peak

McHugh Creek

Flattop Mtn.

Little Campbell Creek

Powerline

Rabbit Creek

Toilsome Hill Dr.

Canyon Rd.

Clarks Rd.

Hillside Dr.

Potter Creek

Seward Hwy.

O'Malley Rd.

Huffman Rd.

De Armour Rd.

Rabbit Cr. Rd.

Little Rabbit Creek

Birch Rd.

Seward Hwy.

Turnagain Arm

Alaska Railroad

Old Seward Hwy.

N

Scale in miles

0   2

OPTION "A"

FLATTOP MOUNTAIN TO PEAKS TWO AND THREE

Trail Location: This trip, which doesn't require tremendous effort,
climbs over the next two summits up the ridge from Flattop. In
doing so, it very quickly takes one away from the usual crowds on
Flattop. However, for the first part of the climb, crowds—
especially on a sunny weekend afternoon—are unavoidable
simply because the first part of this hike is up to the summit of
Flattop. It begins at the Glen Alps Park Entrance. (To get there,
see WALK-ABOUT GUIDE TO FLATTOP TRAIL). From the top
of Flattop, walk straight across the summit plateau toward the next
peak along the ridge. (This   peak—which is Peak Two—is
clearly visible from one end of Flattop's summit to the other
simply because it is just under 1 mile away and 100 feet higher.)
Walk to the far eastern side of the Flattop's summit and, staying on
the crest of the ridge, descend down across the saddle and climb
with relative ease to the summit of Peak Two (3,658 feet). From
here, reaching the long, thin summit ridge of Peak Three—which
is the next summit along the ridge—requires considerable more
energy as well as rock scrambling ability. Though the exposure
along this 2 mile climb is minimal, the rock terrain does take
some nerve and skill to negotiate. It is worth it,however, because
the view from the summit of Peak Three (4,500-plus feet)—
located at the far end of the summit ridge—there are fine views of
broad Ptarmigan Pass below and the rocky west face of Ptarmigan
Peak itself across the pass as well as mountains farther up both the
Campbell Creek and Rabbit Creek valleys. From here it is possible
to 1) retrace your steps back down the ridge, 2) descend into
Ptarmigan Pass and follow the narrow trail out of the mouth of the

tarn up in the left hand (northeast) corner of the pass and down to Powerline Trail or 3) descend into Ptarmigan Pass and turn down the gentler slope to the right (south) that drops down to Rabbit Lake Trail. (If you do follow option 3, be sure to spot a car at the trailhead of Rabbit Lake Trail, otherwise you will have to make the long climb back up over Flattop in order to get back to Glen Alps parking area.)

Trail Grade: As stated in the Walk-About Guide to Flattop, the trail up to the summit of Flattop is predominantly grades 1 and 2 with short sections of grade 3 in the last climb up the summit cone to the top. From the summit of Flattop to the summit of Peak Two is mostly grade 4 climbing with some boulder hopping at the top of Peak Two which are almost grade 5. From the summit of Peak Two to Peak Three is also mostly grade 4, but along this climb there are definite long sections of grade 5 climbing as well.

Trail Condition: From the summit of Flattop to Peak Two it is mostly open tundra with some sections of scree and boulders, whereas from the summit of Peak Two to Peak Three it's mostly rocky with long sections of scree and boulders.

Trail Mileage: From the parking lot at Glen Alps to the summit of Peak Two is just over 2.5 miles for a round trip total of at least 5 miles. It is just about 2 miles farther down the ridge to the summit of Peak Three for a round trip total to and from Glen Alps parking area of almost 9 miles.

Total Elevation Gain: From Glen Alps parking lot and over the summit of Flattop to the Summit of Peak Two entails climbing 1,700 vertical feet. Whereas from the Glen Alps parking lot to the summit of Peak Three entails climbing just over 2,600 vertical feet.

High Point: The highest points reached are either the summit of Peak Two at 3,658 feet above sea level or, farther along the ridge, the summit of Peak Three at just over 4,500 feet above sea level.

Normal Hiking Time: The climb to and from the parking lot at Glen Alps to Peak Two should take anywhere from 1.5 hours to 6 hours depending on the ambition and condition of the party involved. The climb from Glen Alps to Peak Three should take much longer—anywhere from 3 hours to 8 hours, again depending on the condition and ambition of the hiker(s).

Campsites: There are occasional campsites along the entire ridge—including the summit of Flattop itself—but none of these have any water. In fact, there are no water sources at all along the ridge until the descent into Ptarmigan Pass—which is a fine campsite. Wherever you camp, though, please bring a stove because campfires are prohibited inside park limits.

Best Time: The best time to do either of these hikes is from mid-June to late August. It can be done in winter, but there are very real avalanche dangers along the whole ridge, so exercise caution at all times.

USGS Maps: Both trips are just barely contained on Anchorage A-8. (Those wishing to descend into Ptarmigan Pass or to have a better idea of what lays beyond the end of this route—including *Option C* in this Walk-About Guide—should also consider getting Anchorage A-7 as well.)

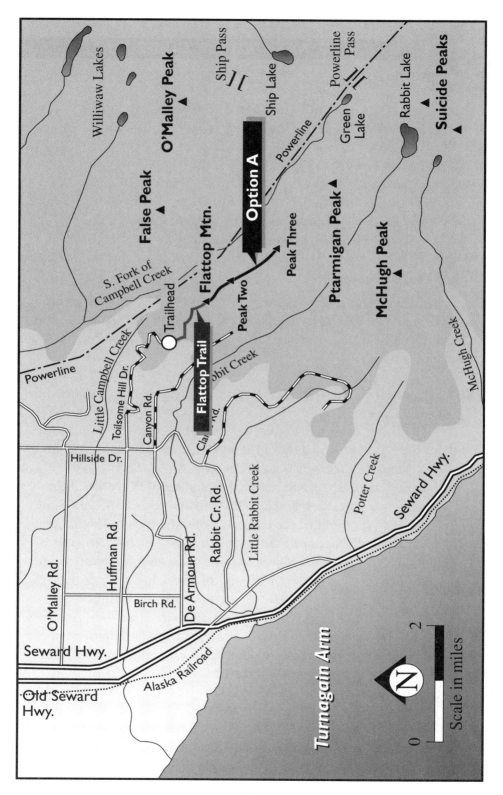

Williwaw Lakes

O'Malley Peak ▲

Ship Pass

Ship Lake

Powerline Pass

Rabbit Lake

Suicide Peaks ▲
▲

False Peak ▲

Powerline

Green Lake

Flattop Mtn. ▲

Option A

S. Fork of Campbell Creek

Peak Three

Ptarmigan Peak ▲

McHugh Peak ▲

Trailhead

Peak Two

Little Campbell Creek

Powerline

Flattop Trail

Toilsome Hill Dr.

Canyon Rd.

Rabbit Creek

McHugh Creek

Hillside Dr.

Clark Rd.

Little Rabbit Creek

Potter Creek

Seward Hwy.

Rabbit Cr. Rd.

O'Malley Rd.

Huffman Rd.

De Armour Rd.

Birch Rd.

Seward Hwy.

Turnagain Arm

Old Seward Hwy.

Alaska Railroad

N

Scale in miles

0   2

RIDGE TRAVERSE FROM FLATTOP MOUNTAIN
TO POWERLINE PASS

Note: This is a trip which should only be considered by those who are both well-practiced rock scramblers and well-conditioned athletes. It is not for any one who gets nervous in high places or has questionable route finding abilities.

Trail Location: This trip is a continuation of the two hikes described in OPTION A - FLATTOP MOUNTAIN TO PEAKS TWO AND THREE. It continues those trips all the way up the ridge, over Ptarmigan Peak down the ridge and over another unnamed 4,630 foot summit, after which it climbs over two more knolls to almost the very end of the ridge before descending to Powerline Pass. From Peak Three descend into Ptarmigan Pass (3,585 feet) and, keeping to the right of the ridge to avoid the rock faces on the north and west faces of Ptarmigan Peak, begin corkscrewing around to the summit. There is some rock scrambling up steep gullies before the summit is finally reached, but it is not overly exposed or dangerous. (However, if any one is at all nervous doing these rock scrambles, it is not advisable that they continue the trip any farther than this summit, for from here to the end of the ridge the rock scrambling and scree climbing get a lot worse before they get any better.) From the summit of Ptarmigan, continue down the ridge, staying as close to the crest as possible. There will be places where 100 to 200 feet down-climbing onto the right (south) face of the ridge will have to done in order to avoid cliffs. Occasionally, as the climb proceeds, there will also be places on the left (north) side of the ridge that can be skirted along or down climbed to avoid rock ledges on the ridge top. But generally, one can stay within shouting distance of the top. When the grass slopes not far beyond the next unnamed 4,630 foot peak and about 1.2 air miles from the summit of Ptarmigan are reached, one has the option of descending to the north shore of Rabbit Lake and following that around to pick up the Rabbit Creek Trail. For those wishing to go on to Powerline Pass, continue bearing left up the crest of the ridge, pass over a small rib of rocks and, once certain of being beyond the last cliffs on the left hand side of the ridge, descend to the left down the long scree and grass slope into Powerline Pass itself. From here, one can walk the Powerline Trail back to Glen Alps.

Trail Grade: Up to the summit of Flattop Mountain, this trip is mostly grade 2, with only one small section of grade 3. From Flattop to Ptarmigan Pass it is almost entirely grade 4 climbing with some sections of grade 5. Then from Ptarmigan Pass to Powerline Pass or Rabbit Lake is almost entirely grade 6 with what for some people might even be grade 7 climbing in some sections of. The only place where it reverts to a lower grade is once on the grass slopes over 1.2 air miles from the summit of Ptarmigan Peak where it is a comfortable, and welcome, grade 4. Going out either Powerline Trail or Rabbit Creek Trail is grade 1 to 2.

Trail Condition: This route has, in fact, very little trail, except for some sporadic goat trails on the grass slopes at the far end of the ridge. For the most part it is all scree, ledges, cliffs and boulders. These conditions under foot—and under hand—makes for very slow going. However, for those who like this type of rock scrambling and boulder hopping, there are not many finer, more interesting ridges close to Anchorage on which to indulge these whims.

Trail Mileage: From Glen Alps parking lot to Powerline Pass is roughly 9 to 10 miles—and possibly even a mile or so longer, considering all the ups and downs and back and forth climbing along the ridge. To this add the 5.5 miles of the Powerline Trail for the walk out for a total of 15 to 17 miles.

Total Elevation Gain: The cumulative gain from Glenn Alps all the way to Powerline Pass is—allowing for the up and down climbing along the ridge—approximately vertical 5,800 feet.

High Point: The highest point reached along the entire ridge is 4,880 feet above sea level at the summit of Ptarmigan Peak.

Normal Hiking Time: This hike can be done by well conditioned and experienced scramblers in one long day. Others may wish to take two days to do it, though that brings up the problem of having to carry relatively heavy packs on a very difficult route.

Campsites: Ptarmigan Pass and Powerline Pass are the only truly decent places to camp along the entire ridge. It is possible to camp on the grass slopes located way down the ridge beyond Ptarmigan Peak, but there is no water sources here, which means having to having to carry the additional weight of enough water to last the night as well as part of the next day. Wherever you camp, though, please bring a stove because campfires are prohibited inside park limits.

Best Time: The best time to do this hike is from mid-June to late August. Extreme avalanche dangers along the entire length of the ridge make it a very dangerous place to be in the winter.

USGS Maps: Anchorage A-7 and A-8.

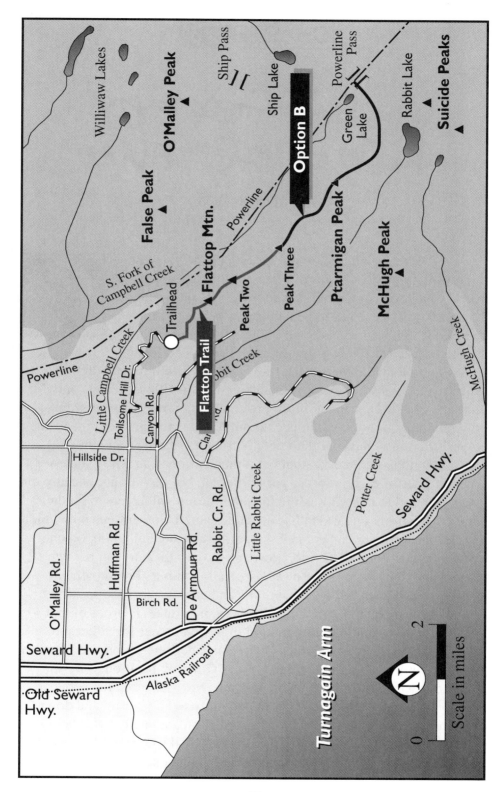

Williwaw Lakes

O'Malley Peak ▲

Ship Pass

Ship Lake

Powerline Pass

Suicide Peaks

Rabbit Lake ▲

False Peak ▲

Option B

Green Lake

O'Malley Peak

Flattop Mtn. ▲

Powerline

Ptarmigan Peak

▲

S. Fork of Campbell Creek

Peak Three

McHugh Peak ▲

Peak Two

Flattop Trail

○ Trailhead

Little Campbell Creek

Rabbit Creek

Powerline

Toilsome Hill Dr.

Canyon Rd.

McHugh Creek

Hillside Dr.

Clark Rd.

Little Rabbit Creek

Potter Creek

Rabbit Cr. Rd.

De Armour Rd.

Seward Hwy.

O'Malley Rd.

Huffman Rd.

Birch Rd.

Turnagain Arm

Seward Hwy.

Alaska Railroad

Old Seward Hwy.

N

Scale in miles

0   2

CHAPTER 3

A Different Kind of Fun

INTRODUCTION

It is expected that by the autumn of 1999, the new safer trail up to the summit of Flattop will, after much work, finally be completed. Of course, if there's going to be a new trail, there has to be a group of people willing to build it. The Kenai National Forest, maintained as it is by the U.S. Department of the Interior, has professional crews to build and maintain the trails located within its jurisdiction. Chugach State Park, however, maintained, as its title indicates, only by the state of Alaska, cannot afford professional crews. Instead, it must rely predominantly on volunteers to build and maintain the trails inside its jurisdiction. I have worked with both types of crews and have enjoyed both experiences—that is, as much as one can enjoy such work! The attitudes of each crew are very different, but this is only because one group is hired to the work while the other group volunteers to do the work. Therefore, one group has deadlines and the other does not, which, in turn, means there is there is less goofing around and joking on one crew than the other. They do, however, in their fashion, get the work done—and done well. (The new *safer* trail—with its broad pathway, gentle switchbacks and even handrails and cables—up Flattop, which should be completed by the time this book is printed, is proof of that.)

I have to admit, though, that I didn't volunteer for either job. Instead, I was asked to volunteer. There is a definite difference between the two, but the work is the same for all. Only my position as a columnist writing for the Anchorage Daily News allowed me some leeway to wander more freely from one place to another up and down the mountain in order to cull more information about what was being done where and by whom. But the privilege had its price: I was made the brunt of some jokes about laxness and given a dirty job whenever possible. It was all meant in good fun—at least I think it was! There are just some things one never knows for certain—and perhaps its better that way.

This narrative is my small tribute to those who work—without loosing their sense of play—at building such trails as this new one on Flattop.

A DIFFERENT KIND OF FUN

That was the last time I will volunteer to carry Dick Griffith's coffee.

"Sure," I told Al Meiners in the parking lot, "just leave it in the back of the ATV when you park, and I'll be glad to carry it up to the work site from there."

"Okay," was all Al said with a smirk.

Debra Brown, the coordinator from REI, who was standing nearby only smiled and shrugged her shoulders at Al.

I wondered what was so funny.

Only when I had hiked up to where Al left the ATV in the small gap leading around the back side of the mountain did I finally get the joke—and the joke was definitely on me. For instead of finding the small thermos I expected, there was a four-gallon jug. And it was full of coffee. All the way up the half-finished trail it leaked out the top and splashed over my shorts and down my legs as I trudged awkwardly onward, continually passing that heavy, swaying load from one tired hand to other. Before long I smelled as though I had taken a plunge into the Jolly Green Giant's morning cup of Maxwell House.

There's no doubt that the entire western civilization would come to a grinding halt if for some reason there was suddenly no more coffee. The world as we know it is fueled by coffee. The same is true for trail crews, including the one for whom I was lugging that—I soon came to realize—infamous jug up the mountain.

It was a still, cloudy day on Flattop Mountain that Sunday. A gray chill saturated the air and visibility through the clouds was no more than fifty feet in any direction. But that didn't deter the dozen or so volunteers who had gathered from all over Anchorage for the second day that weekend to build a new, safer trail to the summit of this ever popular peak.

"The clouds are actually a blessing," one worker told me. "There are no distracting views and after yesterday's heat it's much more comfortable for working."

And work they did. This was no Sunday outing. That was obvious when I finally reached the first volunteers working in a long thin line and cutting into the steep slope of the mountain with picks and shovels to widen and level the bed of the trail. One person was also building stone steps around one switchback turn. It was apparent that these weren't just weekend warriors out on a lark; they were crusaders on a mission. But it was a mission with a definite sense of humor.

It was a sense of humor born from being content with both where they were and what they were doing. Recreation, from the French word *recreation*, comes in many shapes and forms. For some it is a form of diversion, a break from their usual schedule or activity; but that also entails another meaning of the word: to make anew. These people were enjoying a diversion from their usual routines or from Monday-through-Friday desk jobs as well as making something anew—and I don't mean just the trail. It was something much more fundamental. For they were making themselves anew. Picking up stones, swinging picks and digging with shovels were a means of harking back to younger, simpler days.

"It's like playing in the sandbox when we were little, only this sandbox is much bigger," Al remarked.

And there was no mother looking out from a kitchen window telling these volunteers to stay out of the mud, either. Not only were they thus escaping the bondage of their desk jobs, but they were also escaping the bondage of their ages. They were kids once again and relishing this opportunity to muck around in the mud, play with trucks and get a little sweaty. Some may call it regression; but I prefer to think of it as re-creation.

"So you're the one who volunteered to carry Dick's coffee," the first crew member laughed at me as I stumbled up onto the newly smoothed trail bed. As if on cue, the other workers all stopped to lean on their picks and shovels to join in the merriment. "Dick's coffee" was obviously infamous to everyone involved—everyone except me, it seemed.

"You'll probably want to bring it up there," one of the other workers told me as he pointed up the trail into the clouds. On I trudged.

Not five minutes later, though, I was dropping my load by the large tool cache that a helicopter had carried to this high saddle a few days before. There I found Al enjoying some lunch along with a few other people taking a short break from their labors.

"Dick's coffee's here," someone called to no one particular, but everyone in general. A few people snickered. But though Dick's coffee may have been an inside joke, it was also a welcome commodity as cups were soon being pushed beneath its spout and filling rapidly with the steaming brown liquid.

Off to the left, where the old trail emerged onto this saddle from the north, red flags and markers warned wayward hikers to be cautious in the work area—and for good reason. Rocks had been moved everywhere: small ones by hand and large ones by a small gas-powered rock tractor. Above me, on the last steep, rocky slope to the summit, more people could be dimly seen swinging picks and carrying stones back and forth to build retainer walls.

"Come on," Al said, "I'll give you a tour of what we're doing up above."

On my laborious hike up with Dick's coffee, I'd already seen how the trail was now to go right through the low gap between Blueberry Hill and Flattop and slab around the sunnier south side of the mountain, which would not only be free of snow earlier in the year, but also provide wonderful views of the Rabbit Creek valley below and Turnagain Arm far beyond. With a wide foot tread and low grade it promised to be a safer trail than that which already existed on the darker, steeper north side of the mountain.

But though the last section of trail up the final summit cone was over the same ground as the old trail, it had required just as much work as the new trail I'd just climbed. Instead of climbing directly to the summit over a loose rock field, it now switchbacked upward on a predominantly smooth and firm rock-stepped tread that was fenced in on both sides by low rock walls that would prevent people from getting lost or tramping on whatever delicate plant life was eking out a meager living among the rocks. It was a trail that anyone could easily follow, though the crew was not finished yet. They were intent on making it as obvious and easy to follow as possible.

As Al and I climbed into the mists, the dull clang of metal on stone echoed around us. Soon afterwards outlines of workers lifting and setting stones, shoveling a smoother path, or prying boulders loose emerged out of the mist. Then there was Dick Griffith himself swinging a pick into the hard embankment.

"Well, it's about time you got here, Lyons," he said looking up from his labors. (You can tell if you're on Dick's good side when he gives you a hard time—at least I like to think so.)

"I brought your coffee," I answered.

"Good going," he said, "so when are you going to get to work?"

"After I get the Grand Tour from Al," I answered.

"Boy, you newspaper people are all alike!" he said straight-faced. I think he was joking, but I couldn't say for certain as I laughed guiltily in response.

But what was going on here was only the first step in the overall plan for the upper reaches of the mountain. The trail would still need a lot more work before Al Meiner's design took its final form. And as we continued to climb past the last workers that final form became more evident.

"See these orange dots painted in the rocks," Al narrated to me as we clambered over the first rock ledges just below the summit. "These mark where we're going to drill holes to put in posts for a hand rail. See, it's going to come up over these ledges providing an obvious and easy climb to the summit. It would be really hard for someone to get lost or fall off."

Even on the best of summer days, I've seen people struggle up these ledges, looking around for a route, searching for something to hold onto. On the other hand, some people can be too nonchalant on these rocks. They think that because it's *only* Flattop no one gets hurt and no one falls off. But people have fallen off the ledges in these last hundred yards or so to the summit—some to their deaths.

On the flat and featureless summit which sits like a high castle keep walled in by steep rock ramparts on all sides, Al also had a plan. "From this last post on the trail up," he said pointing to a single warning sign that's reached just as you level off on the summit, "we're going to extend a number of rails branching off in all directions so if people get lost up here in a fog or in the clouds they should, as long as they can keep moving, eventually run into one of these handrails that will lead them back to this point and to the trail down."

So like great tentacles of an octopus or the web of a spider, these handrails would extend across the summit flats, gathering in the lost and misplaced to a place where they can get down a safe and well-marked trail. It seemed idiot-proof. It also seemed ingenious. All it has to do is save one life to prove that it's both.

To some environmental purists and hard-core climbers all this may seem either unethical or unnecessary, or both. But there should be at least one mountain that's accessible to everyone. In the northeast where I grew up, Mount Washington in the White Mountains, Mount Mansfield in the Green Mountains and Mount Greylock in the Berkshire Mountains all have roads to their summits. Farther south, Clingman's Dome in the Smokey Mountains, Roan Mountain in the Blue Ridge Mountains and, as I recall, the high point in the Shenandoah Mountains all have auto roads up to their summits. Mount Washington even has a cog railroad to the summit as well! Farther west is Pike's Peak with its road and rail; and there may be others in Wyoming, California, Washington and Oregon that I just don't know about (simply because I've done far less hiking and climbing in the west than in the east). The point is that all these mountains are made accessible to one and all regardless of physical conditioning.

To the hardy purist such highly developed mountains may be an eyesore whereas to the weekend tourist they may be a Godsend. But whereas purists can find plenty of other mountains to satiate their yearning, tourists have nothing unless a mountain is made accessible for them. So let there be at least one democratic mountain that is not biased toward age or ability. Let one mountain be as close as possible to equal for all. And let Flattop be that mountain in the Chugach State Park.

I'm not suggesting that we build a road to the top of Flattop (though the trail built around the south side of Blueberry by a small bulldozer looked almost passable by car!) but simply that one mountain should have a route to its top that the young and old, in shape and out of shape, and the novice and experienced hiker can all climb safely and confidently. For the purist and the hard-core there are other mountains— many more mountains, more than could be counted, in fact—that are out there. Some are even within sight of Flattop. From the summit, they can be seen rising in quiet solitude far away from the *madding crowd*.

Later, after doing my work moving rocks on the trail, lifting and grunting along with the rest of the crew, the sun started to feel its way through the clouds just as quitting time approached. One of the last people off the mountain, I (fortunately without Dick's coffee now) reached the parking lot to find it bustling with activity beneath the now blazing blue sky of the late July evening. Everywhere I looked there were cars moving slowly back and forth, jockeying for parking spaces. Scattered among the cars were single hikers and groups of hikers, as well as mountain bikers and hikers with dogs, parents and children, young couples and old couples, athletes preparing to train and families preparing for picnics. Most of them would climb the trail I'd just come down.

Yes, I thought, as I stood with some of the trail crew drinking juice and eating bagels and cookies around Debra's table burdened with drinks and snacks, this is good. Flattop, after all—if for no other reason than its popularity—is everybody's mountain. By the time the improvement's are finished it will be even more so. That's the way it should be. There should always be one mountain for everybody. And there probably will be as long as volunteers like Dick and the rest of the crew get their coffee.

State Park trail crew tool chest near the summit of Flattop.

CHAPTER 4

Two Sides of Summer

It was not a conscious thought. I just suddenly felt the urgent need to hurry. I don't know if it was the darkening sky or the hour of the day, but I felt I should hurry to reach Powerline Pass, which was still a mile up the ridge and more than 1,000 feet below me. Reaching it was going to be far easier said than done, though. The saw-toothed ridge I was toiling to traverse was as much a mind game as it was physical work. It was also very slow—and very dangerous—going. Picking my way around ledges and beneath spires, kicking steps across precipitous snowfields and pulling myself up declivitous gullies, I was lucky if I was to climb only two miles for every one air mile of distance. Not only was it difficult to hurry; it also would have been foolish. There are far too many places all along that sharp-toothed ridge's humongous maze of towering, toppling, shattered and shifting rocks and hard, steep snowfields and scree gullies where any fall could prove fatal—as the signs on the ridge behind me sadly indicated.

Finally, after one long slide down a scree chute, I was dumped onto a broad, grassy slope which went down, and then up over two more cones to where I could at last descend to the pass. The 4,660-foot summit of Homicide Peak leered over the crest of the ridge directly in front of me as I trundled across the open slopes. When I reached the crest of the next rise, however, it was gone, smothered in clouds. But I still didn't feel threatened. After all, the higher peaks on my immediate right as well as other peaks on the north side of Powerline Pass and Campbell Creek valley on my left were still entirely visible.

In retrospect, though, this was just wishful thinking. I was reluctant to look objectively at the world around me after already working so hard to come so far. I had already come all the way down the ridge from Flattop, and regardless of how far I still had to go, I was not ready just yet to go home.

After all, it was the Summer Solstice and I literally had all day and, if necessary, all night—all twenty-four hours—to finish the hike I had planned. And I might need every hour of that day and night. On this, the longest day of the year, as a commemoration, I wanted to hike around the headwaters of the South Fork of Campbell Creek. This meant climbing up Flattop, following the ridge all the way down and across Powerline Pass, then climbing Avalanche Peak, The Wedge, and The Ramp, from which point I'd then follow the ridge back to the top of O'Malley. Perhaps in my own way, I was undertaking an act of sympathetic magic. This ancient form of magic is based on the simple premise that an act performed by man will produce similar results in nature. By hiking and climbing around the headwaters of Campbell Creek, I hoped to imitate the sun's journey not through the day, but also through the year. The result, I hoped, would insure sunny days and warm nights for all the remaining days of the far too short Alaskan summer. Considering how this piece of attempted magical inducement ended, however, maybe I should have never undertaken it. It certainly seemed to prove that the business of magic is not the business for me.

Even the beginning of the hike was not very auspicious, for I didn't reach the parking lot at Glen Alps below Flattop till almost 12:30 p.m. I wasn't going to worry about time, though. After all, it was the Solstice. What did concern me, however, was seeing the summit of Flattop silhouetted boldly against a bank of clouds. The ride up had been a pleasant drive beneath sparkling sunlight. Even the clouds that hovered over the mountains I was driving toward were all lined with silver, promising, I thought, more fair weather than foul. But all that seemed to change the moment I stepped out of the car.

Amazingly, though, as I climbed over the summit less than a half hour later and began working my way down the ridge, the clouds receded before me like an outgoing tide. Only Powerline Pass, somber beneath a black blanket of clouds, gave me reason to have second thoughts. But any reason for any lingering pessimism was short-lived. By the time I had toiled over my third or fourth lump in the ridge, the low, thick clouds had seemingly all evaporated, leaving nothing but a spattering of high, tan-bellied clouds through which hazy shafts of sunlight gleamed triumphantly.

Sunlight and shadow also alternated as far as the eye could see across the Kenai to the south and the high, glacier-girdled mountains to the east. The broad strokes of the gleaming sun had even shredded the darkness over Powerline Pass, leaving wide swaths of bright light crisscrossing its basin. There didn't seem to be a trace of rain in sight.

On the dappled, rocky slopes and meadows over which I climbed life proceeded in its usual patterns without any hindrance or any sign of threat. Flies and bees buzzed lazily over the sparse grasses or hovered over the small clumps of wildflowers that grew under the sheltered shadows of boulders and along the inside corners of gullies. Other, sturdier flowers braved the sporadic open slopes dropping away from the ridge's crest. Bird calls rang from the rocks below while an eagle lumbered nonchalantly over the next ridge above. A light wind blew the sweat from my brow.

But don't get the impression that this was an effortless outing. For every sloping meadow I crossed on my way along the ridge, there were two rock peaks on either end of it to haul myself over with a lot of hand-over-hand scrambling. After one particularly long climb and traverse down a narrow ridge, I imagined I was nearing the summit of Ptarmigan Peak. But when I crested the far end of the ridge, there was no summit nearby; instead, about 700 feet below me extended a broad pass about a half mile across which then rose steeply and suddenly for over 1,300 feet to where the true summit of 4,880-foot high Ptarmigan played hide and seek in some last, lingering mists. It certainly wasn't going to be an easy climb.

Nor were its looks deceptive: it wasn't an easy climb. But then there isn't any easy—or safe—way up Ptarmigan Peak. Even staying on the right (south) side of the ridge and well away from the cliffs and sheer rock faces on the north and west side of the mountain, I found the going in no way easy. Only after lunging up sliding scree, pulling myself over rock outcrops and even dangling over one snow-choked gully, did I finally crest the summit ridge. Ahead of me, peering over the nearer outcrops, was the spire of Ptarmigan's true summit. But before continuing toward it, my attention was drawn to a nearby cairn where I thought there might be a register of some sort. Instead what I found riveted to a rock among the other rocks was a metal plaque etched with these words:

IN MEMORY OF DEPARTED FRIENDS
NICK PRATT
DAN DAUGHERTY
BEN BENSON

It was a lonely place for such a memorial, with only the wind and snow for companions. I wondered if they had met their ends up here in a tragic accident or pathetic fluke of nature, or whether this was simply a place they had loved to climb to while alive and therefore an appropriate place for their memorials after their deaths. Both seemed to be fitting reasons for such a memorial but being alone on that high, precipitous ridge, I found the former reason much more sobering than the latter. It reminded me that these mountains do take lives.

All year round, no matter what the season, no matter what the weather these mountains take lives. We hear about it on the evening news, we read about it in the paper and we shake our heads in sadness; but then we forget. On the next clear, warm day we're out hiking up Flattop or Wolverine, or over Crow Pass, mountain biking around Eklutna Lake, or kayaking along Twenty Mile River. Time passes. Then we read or hear about someone else, and it gives us pause for a few more thoughtful moments. Then we forget again. But we shouldn't feel guilty. It's the human response; and, after all, we are only human. Perhaps W.H. Auden's poem "Musee des Beaux Arts" describes it best. Auden describes how "The Old Masters" were "never wrong" about suffering and when it occurs.

> *About suffering they were never wrong,*
> *The Old Masters: how well they understood*
> *Its human position; how it takes place*
> *While someone else is eating or opening a window or just walking*
> *dully along;*

And how, using Breughel's painting "Icarus" as an example, we usually react to suffering and death.

> *In Breughel's 'Icarus', for instance: how everything turns away*
> *Quite leisurely from the disaster; the ploughman may*

57

Have heard the splash, the forsaken cry,
But for him it was not an important failure; the sun shone
As it had to on the white legs disappearing into the green
Water; and the expensive delicate ship that must have seen
Something amazing, a boy falling out of the sky,
Had somewhere to get to and sailed calmly on.

Most of us don't react so coldheartedly as the ploughman does in the poem, but regardless of tragedy we do still have to carry on and eventually we turn again to our own affairs.

Only I couldn't turn away so easily. I was too close to the suffering, in too similar an adventure to turn away. Just below was what a local avalanche expert had deemed "the valley of death." In one accident in 1997 two people died and ten more were seriously injured when they slipped and fell down a steep, snow-choked couloir just below where I now stood. In 1995 a Fort Richardson soldier was killed in 300-foot fall on the northwest corner of the mountain.

The memorial, the question of how and why it came to be where it was, and the inherent dangers of the high, lonely ridge all combined to have a profound effect upon me. But for how long? A few moments? A minute? Maybe five? After all, I'm only human too, and I had my own affairs to attend to and miles to go. Still, as I turned up the ridge again, some light had gone out of the day, though I couldn't say whether it was the sky darkening overhead or just my sober thoughts.

A few moments later, at 3:30, I finally reached the summit of Ptarmigan only to see a still distant view of Powerline Pass and a long, stone-spired ridge still between us. To the southeast rose the dark twin summits of North and South Suicide while to the northeast, towering far above the pass was Avalanche Peak. Due south were the gray waters of Turnagain Arm, and due north was the O'Malley-Ramp ridge beyond which hovered over the distant summits of Williwaw, Koktoya and the Tanainas. They were almost all in shadows. Where I stood, though, high on a thin, jagged summit between Rabbit Creek and Campbell Creek, sunlight still glared off the hard rocks and dirty patches of snow.

But though surrounded by sunlight, I suddenly felt the urge to hurry. Maybe it was the encroaching dark clouds, or maybe it was the late hour, or the sense of loss and loneliness on this high, barren ridge. I don't know. But I had to get to Powerline Pass. Between me and that goal were two miles of very slow and dangerous ridge scrambling. Not only were there ledges and spires to skirt by going in between and around, as well as over and under, but there were also cliffs to pass and scree chutes to span. In addition to all this, there were still the lingering patches of last winter's snow to traverse—and it was hard and steep, hardly the kind of snow to be crossed in the track shoes I was wearing. Somehow, though, I managed to cross them all, either by methodically gouging out the widest steps my soft shoes could kick or digging with any nearby flat stone.

Ever so slowly I progressed down the ridge. Though I wanted to hurry, I couldn't. The going was just too slow, too uncertain—and never in a straight line. I had to crisscross back and forth over the ridge, as well as move forward down the ridge, in order to find a route. I hugged my way around ledges and crawled beneath spires, and thrashed my way across snowfields. Once or twice I found myself dead-ended at the top of a 50 or 100 foot cliff. Then I'd have to backtrack and, after sliding down some dusty scree slope, have to climb the next muddy scree slope back up to the ridge. At least I was moving, though, and by moving I would eventually get to where I wanted to go—*eventually.*

And eventually I did. For finally, after one last, long slide down a scree gully, I was dumped onto a broad, grassy slope which went down, and then up over two more cones to where I at last, after crossing the last of the cliffs that dropped precipitously off the north side of the ridge, I could descend, at last, into the pass. The clouds were thickening before me, rising slowly up and over the peaks just beyond the last ridge I was now climbing up and over. The higher Suicide Peaks on my right and Avalanche Peak on my left, though, were still entirely visible from bottom to top. That was reason enough to believe the weather still might hold.

Most everyone has heard the old saying, "If you don't like the weather, wait five minutes." Well, the converse also holds true: "If you DO like the weather, wait five minutes." And my five minutes were up. After only a few sliding steps down to the pass, the one small, dark cloud, under which only a few moments before could be seen brilliant sunshine splashing across the Ship Creek valley and beyond, had suddenly become a great big black cloud that filled the whole bowl. Ship Creek Valley was gone and Powerline Pass Peak had disappeared. Even the Ramp off in the distance was succumbing to the onslaught. A few raindrops spotted my shirt as the wind began to rise. For the first time all day, I began to actually think I might not complete the hike.

If the weather got much worse, I would have to make a hasty retreat. All I had in my waist pack was a wind suit, some hard candies, a Snickers Bar, Pop-Tarts and a pocket notebook—barely enough to survive during decent weather. I was not at all prepared to either sit out or walk through a storm. It was my own fault. There was no one, no thing, to blame but me. I had put too much trust in the weather. It had not betrayed me, though. The weather had done only what it always does: change.

The human creature, composed of the contradictory elements of transient flesh and transcendent mind, harbors the perpetual desire for at least some aspect of permanence, even if it has to be imagined. Sometimes this desire for permanence manifests itself in a tendency to believe that what one sees one moment will last forever. Change, though constant and universal, is offensive to our basically conservative nature. Change—especially big changes—disrupt the regular flow of our own seemingly secure and unchanging lives. We are amazed when children we haven't seen for a few years are suddenly a foot taller; we are dismayed when the playground we used to frequent when we were children is now covered—along with three quarters of the rest of the old neighborhood—by a mall; and we are shocked when we first notice the gray in our parents' hairs or the crow's feet around our eyes. We are even dumbfounded when looking back on faded family pictures and black and white snapshots from years ago we notice how much even those closest to us have changed since those pictures were taken. Change always seems to come as a surprise to the human creature. In regard to weather, such a belief can result in being caught in some precarious situations— sometimes even in life-threatening situations. It's happened to me: I've been caught in an electric storm on one of the volcanoes in Mexico, cornered by a whiteout high on Bird Ridge without an ice ax, and forced to bivouac on North Suicide because of a fog that hid my hand in front of my face as well as any route down off the mountain. There have been other instances as well, some occurring more recently than I care to admit.

Still, with only a few raindrops falling and the western side of the pass leading down toward Flattop still in sunshine, I wasn't overly concerned yet. I thought this storm might remain localized, not having enough momentum to push itself over the pass, and so allow me to push on with my hike. But as I began climbing the steep slope toward the summit of Avalanche Peak on the opposite side of Powerline Pass, the clouds pushing up the eastern side of the pass got darker and moodier. They began swirling and boiling. Soon they were spilling up and over the pass like an uncontrollable witch's brew. The rain began to fall more heavily in big, plopping drops.

I stopped to put on my wind-breaker in the gusting wind and rain, and turned to see if there was any hope that the clouds in the pass would break apart. But all I saw were two tiny bicyclists, apparently coming up from Indian, pushing their mountain bikes up out of the boiling clouds. I began to climb again; but for only a moment. For in that moment a loud clap of thunder echoed overhead. Then the rain changed to hail. It was time to get out. So with drops of rain already clinging to my brow, I took one last blinking look at the sky and turned in retreat. There was no way I was going to go up on a ridge with hail bouncing underfoot and a thunderstorm overhead. Then another loud crash of thunder shook the valley. Now it was *really* time to get out.

In a few minutes I was back down at the pass and running along the dirt road to Glen Alps with the rain and hail bouncing at my feet. Up and across two snowfields I quickly shuffled, helping the two cyclists, a man and a woman, lift their bikes across the second, before continuing down the road with the rain and hail still coming down in blinding sheets. I pulled my head into my shoulders like a turtle and pulled my hands up into my sleeves; but there was no escaping the wet and cold. Even running I couldn't generate enough heat to keep warm. It's difficult to stay warm when you're drenched to the very marrow of your bones. I shivered once or twice, but had to keep on running toward the light at the end of the valley.

Soon, the two mountain bikers passed me and I was alone with the storm. Another peal of thunder exploded overhead. I ducked involuntarily. The cold rain was dripping down my back and my fingers were numb. I wasn't frightened, though, as much as just nervous—and terribly uncomfortable. I just wanted to get out—and fast. So I pulled my head low and kept on jogging.

Then, some five or ten minutes later, I noticed the sound of birds in the brush nearby, and felt the rain slackening. I lifted my head just as another mountain biker pedaled furiously by me—but going the other way! I saw that here the trail was only spotted sporadically with raindrops. Little puffs of dust rose around the last heavy drops falling on the roadbed. The storm had obviously not unleashed all its power down this end of the valley.

I passed some hikers. They were completely dry. A streak of sunlight arched over Flattop's lower ridge above me while the leaves of the alder nearby clattered in a dusty breeze. It was as if the storm had never happened. Except for the wet hair falling in my eyes and the squishing of my socks in my soaked shoes, I would've thought it had all been a dream. But it wasn't. The black clouds still hanging over the upper end of the valley behind me were all the evidence I needed of that.

Life was proceeding in its usual nonchalant fashion when I reached the parking lot a little after 7 p.m: two girls were flirting with a boy in a pickup, a father was racing his two youngsters up the nearby paved trail to the overlook of the city below, and another hiker was taking off his boots and wiggling his feet with a satisfied sigh. Meanwhile, almost 3,000 feet above us all, O'Malley Peak was just emerging out of the clouds.

Forty-five minutes later, as I was coming out of Carr's with some groceries for dinner, the mountains above were entirely free of clouds. I could even see sunlight dropping into the trough of Powerline Pass.

The weather had changed again—only this time for the better. But I couldn't help wondering what would've happened if I had not been in a spot from which it was easy to retreat. What if I'd been a half hour farther along my route, near or on the summit of Powerline Pass Peak or over behind the Wedge, or, even worse, struggling along the 5,000-foot ridge between Hidden Peak and O'Malley? What then? Would the thunder and lightning have been more dangerous? Or would I have just been wetter and number for longer as I tried to get out? But these are just questions, nothing but idle speculations, dry thoughts from a warm study and not of much use unless they can be applied to the next time when just as bad—or worse—conditions suddenly rise over the next hill or ridge.

On the ridge between Peak Two and Peak Three and looking toward (l-r) O'Malley Peak, Hidden Peak and The Ramp.

Powerline Trail

Note: For me this trail has very rarely been an end in itself. I often use it to get in or our of the mountains, descending to it from both the south and north in all kinds of weather, or ascending from it to climb one of the mountains or ridgelines that loom above. It has been a lifeline to me in blizzards, thunderstorms, and fogs as thick as custard—a postscript at the long end of a failed day. It has also been a pleasant preamble at the beginning of a bright and promising day. It is a boring trail sometimes, and mysterious at other times, yet it is always momentous to finally step off or step back on to its wide tread, coming and going on any trip. I know that when I am on Powerline Trail, the parking lot is not far away— which can be a great relief sometimes. This is especially true after scrambling through rain or snow, high winds or deep fogs, somewhere in the isolated heights above. On such days, to reach Powerline Trail is to feel like I'm already home. This is because Powerline Trail is the main artery in the valley of the South Fork of Campbell Creek. Off it trails lead to O'Malley Peak, Hidden Lake, and Ship Pass. There are also numerous trail-less hikes and climbs that can be done from the Powerline Pass Trail—everything from a long slog up The Ramp or The Wedge (which can be done by almost everyone) to a technical ice or rock climb up the dramatic north face of Ptarmigan (which should be done by only the experienced few).

Trail Location: The west terminus of Powerline Trail begins at the Glen Alps Park Entrance located just below tree line in the foothills of the Front Range that dominates the eastern horizon above Anchorage. To get to Glen Alps go east up O'Malley Road from its intersection with the Seward Highway. Follow O'Malley approximately 4 miles to Hillside Road. Turn right onto Hillside Drive and drive for another mile or so to Upper Huffman Road, which is on the left just after a sign for Chugach State Park.

Follow Upper Huffman Drive for 3/4's of a mile and take a right onto the appropriately named Toilsome Hill Drive. This road, upon which chains, studs and/or four-wheel drive is recommended in winter, switchbacks and winds its way for two more miles before the entrance to Glen Alps parking lot appears on the left hand side at the top of one last short, steep hill. The trail begins at the trailhead located just to the left of the elegant wooden staircase at the far right hand (southeast) end of the parking lot. Follow this wide, alder-lined trail a trail out to an intersection with a wider trail/dirt road on an open hill crest underneath the powerlines and far above the South Fork of Campbell Creek. From here, the Powerline Trail bears right, staying on the wide dirt road that follows the powerlines down a short hill. At the bottom of the hill , the road levels off to begin its long, very gradual climb to the pass.

The east terminus of the trail is located a short distance from the Seward Highway near the restaurant, Turnagain House. To get there, take a right hand turn onto a gravel road just north of milepost 103 on the Seward Highway, 25 miles south of Anchorage, and directly to the left of the Turnagain House Restaurant. Continue on this road for a half mile to the fork in the road. Go right and continue for a another half mile to the trailhead. At the time of this writing, a massive clean up of a 35,000 gallon gas spill from the nearby pipeline was still underway. When the clean up is finally completed (which might not be for a few years) the trailhead may be moved.

The trail begins on the left hand side of the road and follows Indian Creek upstream to the old trailheads for both Indian Pass Trail and Powerline Trail. The bridge on the left is the Powerline Trail and the way to get to Powerline Pass—as opposed to the opening into the woods on the right which leads to Indian Pass.

Trail Grade: The grading for the first part of this trail to the pass varies between 1 and 2, with almost all of it being safely within 1. From the parking lot to the pass is one long, shallow climb, except for the last mile and a half which steepens considerably as it begins the final rise to the crest of the pass. On the other hand, coming up from the east end of the trail in Indian to the top of the pass is almost all grade 3 and 4 climbing up a very steep road.

Trail Condition: Considering that the trail is actually a wide dirt road, the conditions are almost always excellent. It is good for biking and running as well as hiking. Even in winter the snowmobiles that are allowed to run up and down the valley pack the trail out and make it ideal for snowshoeing and skiing as well as hiking. But beware of avalanche conditions as you approach the pass itself. People on snow-machines and foot have disappeared in a rumbling mass of loosened snow in that upper part of the valley. The first five miles or so of the trail, however, are perfectly safe for winter travel. No matter what the season, though, be prepared for any sudden change in the weather, which can quickly turn any pleasant outing into a trying ordeal.

Trail Mileage: It is 5.5 miles from Glen Alps parking area to the pass, for a round trip total of 11 miles whereas the traverse all the way to the trailhead in Indian is 13 miles one way.

Total Elevation Gain: It is a 1,300 foot climb from Glen Alps to, and a 3,300 foot climb from Indian to Powerline Pass.

High Point: The highest point reached on this trail is 3,550 feet above sea level at the top of the pass.

Normal Hiking Time: Though many runners do the round trip to and from the pass in under 2 hours, a steady, but not labored, stride can hike the same round trip to and from the pass inside of 4 hours. Others with children or with time on their hands may find it takes closer to 5 to 7 hours to go to the pass and back. The one way traverse all the way to Indian will take from 6 to 8 hours.

Campsites: Though there are not many decent campsites in the first 2 or 3 miles of the trail, there are many farther up with no dearth of water. A small lake just off the trail to the right at the base of Ptarmigan Peak is a particularly picturesque spot. There are, however, no adequate campsites on the east side of the pass. Wherever you camp, though, please bring a stove because campfires are prohibited inside park limits.

Best Time: Most of the trail is navigable all year round. As I cautioned before, though, try to avoid the last mile to the pass from the Glen Alps (west) side in winter because of the extreme avalanche danger. The possibility of avalanches is also very high along some of the higher sections of the trail on the east side of the pass.

USGS Maps: Anchorage A-7 and A-8 SE.

66

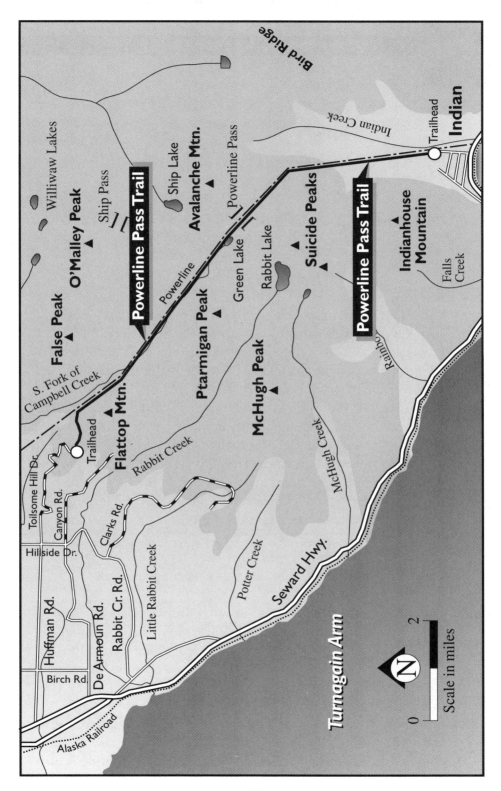

67

POWERLINE TRAIL TO THE SUMMIT OF AVALANCHE PEAK
(also known as POWERLINE PASS PEAK)

Trail Location: Avalanche Peak (which is how the sometimes locally known Powerline Pass Peak is listed on maps) is located at the far east end of the ridge that towers above the north side of Powerline Pass. To get there, follow Powerline Trail from the Glen Alps parking area all the way to the top of the pass. (To get to Powerline Pass Trail, see WALK-ABOUT GUIDE TO POWERLINE PASS TRAIL.) At the crest of the pass, turn left (north) and begin climbing up the broad scree slope to the top of the ridge. Once at the top of the ridge (4,600 feet) turn right and follow the ridge east and away from Powerline Pass. On the left, at the bottom of the precipitous north side of the ridge (which should be approached with extreme caution) are the turquoise waters of Ship Lake while far below on the right can be seen Indian Pass and Turnagain Arm far beyond that. Just under a mile down the ridge, and just over a few smaller knolls and false summits, is the spired, true summit of Avalanche Peak (5,050 feet).

Trail Grade: Powerline Pass Trail is almost entirely grade 1 with only some very short sections of grade 2 on the final climb into the pass. However, from the moment one leaves the trail to the top of the ridge the grade rises quickly—like the elevation—to grade 5 climbing. Then the mile or so ridge walk to the summit levels off to a grade 4 climb.

Trail Condition: Powerline Pass Trail is a wide road with good, solid and level footing almost the entire distance to the pass. Despite there being no trail up to the top of the ridge, the footing is also generally good—especially on the lower slopes which are covered by a fair amount of tundra growth. The higher up one goes, though, the more scree that is encountered, which makes the footing more and more uncertain and tiring—though by no means dangerous. The top of the ridge is almost all scree and boulders, but because the ridge top is more level and less obviously influenced by gravity), it is easier to negotiate than on the climb up to the ridge.

Trail Mileage: From the Glen Alps parking area to the top of the pass is 5.5 miles, while from the pass to the top of Avalanche Peak is at least another 1.5 miles. This gives a one way total of 7 miles or more for a round trip total at least 14 miles.

Total Elevation Gain: The cumulative elevation gain from Glen Alps parking lot to the summit if Avalanche Peak is just under 3,200 feet.

High Point: The highest point reached on this hike is 5,050 feet above sea level at the summit of Avalanche Peak.

Normal Hiking Time: The round trip from Glen Alps to the summit of Avalanche Peak and back should take anywhere from 6 to 10 hours depending on the ambition and condition of the hiker(s).

Campsites: There are some wonderful campsites all along Powerline Trail—particularly around some of the lakes and tarns farther up the valley. It is even possible to camp in the pass itself, though the water sources there are less certain, in that they are more dependent on the amount of recent rain and/or last winter's snowfall. Wherever you camp, though, please bring a stove because campfires are prohibited inside park limits.

Best Time: The best time to do this climb is anywhere from mid-June to late August. Because of the extreme avalanche danger on the open slopes above Powerline Pass it is not recommended as a winter trip.

USGS Maps: Anchorage A-7 and A-8.

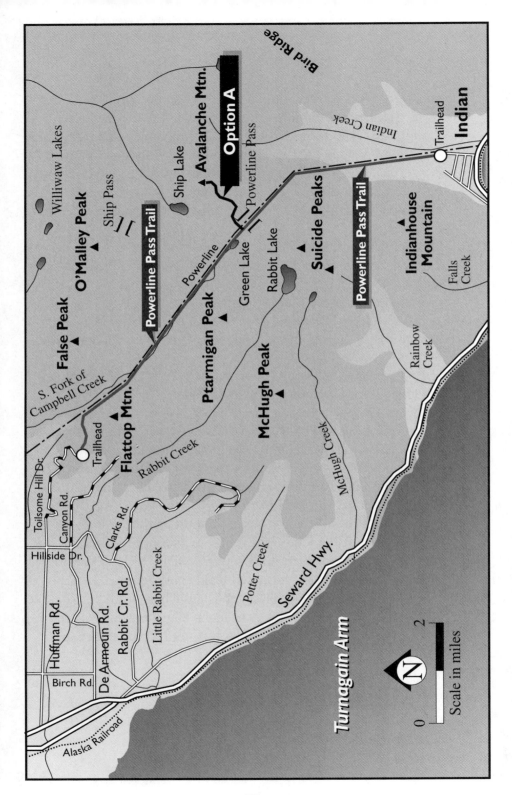

Williwaw Lakes

O'Malley Peak ▲

Ship Pass

False Peak ▲

S. Fork of
Campbell Creek

Flattop Mtn. ▲

Trailhead ○

Tolsome Hill Dr.
Canyon Rd.
Hillside Dr.

Huffman Rd.

De Armoun Rd.

Rabbit Cr. Rd.

Little Rabbit Creek

Birch Rd.

Rabbit Creek

Clarks Rd.

Potter Creek

Ptarmigan Peak ▲

Powerline Pass Trail

Green Lake

Rabbit Lake

McHugh Peak ▲

McHugh Creek

Seward Hwy.

Alaska Railroad

Turnagain Arm

N

Scale in miles

0   2

Ship Lake

Avalanche Mtn. ▲

Option A

Powerline Pass

Powerline

Bird Ridge

Suicide Peaks ▲

Powerline Pass Trail

Indianhouse
Mountain ▲

Falls Creek

Rainbow Creek

Indian Creek

Trailhead ○

Indian

Late fall on Powerline Pass Trail below Blueberry Hill and Flattop.

CHAPTER 5

Some Endings are Beginnings; Some Beginings are Endings

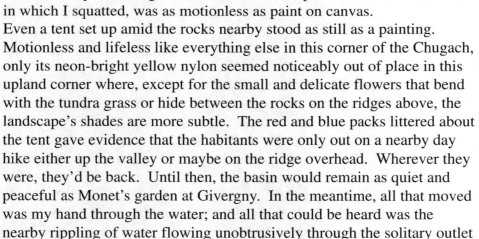

Bending down by the still waters, I swished my hand gently back and forth in the cool, rock-scattered shallows of the high, lonely tarn. No breeze blew, no bird sang. The scalloped sky, which stretched like a canopy across the top of the high, sheer-rock-faced amphitheater in which I squatted, was as motionless as paint on canvas. Even a tent set up amid the rocks nearby stood as still as a painting. Motionless and lifeless like everything else in this corner of the Chugach, only its neon-bright yellow nylon seemed noticeably out of place in this upland corner where, except for the small and delicate flowers that bend with the tundra grass or hide between the rocks on the ridges above, the landscape's shades are more subtle. The red and blue packs littered about the tent gave evidence that the habitants were only out on a nearby day hike either up the valley or maybe on the ridge overhead. Wherever they were, they'd be back. Until then, the basin would remain as quiet and peaceful as Monet's garden at Givergny. In the meantime, all that moved was my hand through the water; and all that could be heard was the nearby rippling of water flowing unobtrusively through the solitary outlet of the lake.

In a matter of yards, though, those gently rippling waters were rushing in leaping cascades down the steep, grassy vale below, only to continue down still farther through the stunted spruce and alder that grew along the upper fringes of tree line and into the wider, deeper Powerline Pass valley. There the waters from this lone lake would converge with the larger, swifter waters of Campbell Creek. Together they'd foam and froth, joined constantly along the way by numerous other streamlets and rivulets draining from the heights above, down the length of that long, open valley. Then, as all this gathering water reached the end of the valley, its velocity and power would increase dramatically as it poured itself over the upper rim of the Anchorage Bowl and, soon after, fall in a white frenzy through the gorge that cut a deep scar in the woodlands far below. From there these same white waters would slow to a calmer clarity as they began their circuitous journey of a last few miles through busy neighborhoods and rustling patches of woodlands, and under roads and highways, and along bike paths and wetlands until just beyond Campbell they would finally drain across the deserted mud flats and merge at last with the far more extensive waters of Cook Inlet, and the vast and soundless depths of the great seas that lay far beyond.

It is a journey little different from the journey that most waters the world over make. The only difference was that these waters I bent beside began their journey here. It was the beginning of my journey as well.

No journey, however, begins in a void. There must be an ending before there can be a new beginning; it is the cyclical nature of life on this planet. And both the water and I had already traveled far—far enough at least to have ended one cycle before being able to make this new beginning.

The waters I touched had already either fallen from the sky as rain, snow, sleet or hail or had formed in the night as frost or dew. From these origins as precipitation and condensation, they had melted and dripped, flowed and fallen into the lake before me. This ended one cycle. There, having reached the end of one journey from the sky to the earth, they began the next journey from the earth back to the sky. First, they had gathered, rising slowly until the whole basin was full. Then, when they at last brimmed the crest of this high, tiny cirque, they began flowing down the channel beside me toward the sea.

I, on the other hand, moved in different, perhaps more self-willed cycles. For one, having the ability to defy gravity, I had consciously hiked the more than five miles up from Glen Alps parking lot. Up the shallow ascent of the broad foot-tread of the Powerline Trail I had come to where, after two and a half miles, Hidden Lake Trail diverged at a ninety-degree angle to the left. From there, I quickly rock-hopped Campbell Creek and immediately began climbing toward the hanging valley below Ship Pass. Up through willow and spruce, over rocks and roots the trail climbed until it leveled out on a shelf above Campbell Creek.

Directly ahead of me now, almost two miles up valley, the long, low saddle of Ship Pass swung against the backdrop of a dull blue sky. I was heading toward that pass; but not to the pass. Upon reaching the first stream that tumbles out of that valley, I didn't cross it to the worn footpath that followed the right hand fork straight up the valley. Instead my way led up the narrow, overgrown path that followed the left hand fork upstream through brambles and bushes toward the low, round bluff that extended like an eroded jetty from the high jagged ridgeline behind it. In the secluded vale behind that bluff lay the waters of Hidden Lake.

The trail steepened noticeably as it began to climb the flank of the valley. Soon I was out of the brambles and bushes below and on the rock-scattered Alpine world above. Though steep, this corner of the Ship Pass valley was particularly lush. Protected from the harsh winds by the ridge and bluff above and watered by the stream flowing nearby, the grass in the hollows here seemed a little taller and greener than it was on the broad flats below Ship Pass, a mile and more off to my right; and the flowers seemed fuller and brighter. If the lake hadn't been so close, I might've laid myself down beside a grassy knoll and slept like Dorothy in the poppy field outside of Oz.

Hidden Lake was close, though—so close that within ten minutes I was bending down beside it. In this, the calm, quiet hour of noon, not a ripple disturbed its clean, clear surface. I leaned over and swished my outstretched hand in its glowing waters. I lifted a cupped handful to my mouth and drank. It was sweet.

Yet even here I didn't rest long. Yes, I'd reached the end of the trail at the lake's shore. But I'd reached this end only to make a new beginning. The journey from the parking lot to the shore of this lake was only the first leg of a longer journey. As in Cartesian geometry it was only a line inside a larger circle, one part of larger whole. As in Buddhist philosophy, it was one turning in a vaster cycle.

For the end of the trail at Hidden Lake did not mean the end of the hike. Instead, it meant the beginning of a better climb. All around me towered the crumbling magnificence of high summits moving against the blue sky. The trail, however, as so often happens in the Chugach—and all over Alaska, for that matter—didn't seek to climb them. But that didn't mean the hike had to end.

As I stood by the lake's glassy waters and gazed upward toward the broken-toothed ridge far above, I knew I was just beginning my day, not ending it. The end of Hidden Lake Trail was just another beginning.

For like the waters in the lake, this place, for me, marked the start of another journey. The difference was that while the waters' way led down, my way led up—up to the jagged ridge line that loomed far overhead in a tight semi-circle around the lake, obliterating any hope of seeing even a glimpse of the northern and eastern horizons. One of those high, jagged spires silhouetted against the sky at the top of the ridge was the summit of Hidden Peak, the highest point on this section of the ridge. When—and if—I reached that point, I intended to follow the ridge back toward Anchorage, passing over the summit of O'Malley Peak and following the trail from there back down to the Glen Alps parking lot.

The steep-sided and rock-scaled bowl, however, would not tolerate rash acts. I had to choose my route with care. On the one hand, if there was too much scree, I would slide backwards a step with almost every exhausting step up. On the other hand, too steep a rock face could mean a long fall backwards if I slipped or a rock came loose. In the end, I chose an obvious gully that didn't look too steep, but still appeared rocky enough to afford solid hand and foot holds. It also more or less followed the fall line straight up the center of the ridge. It would take me right where I wanted to go in the most direct way possible.

With the decision now firmly made, I hopped over the lake's output and after walking less than halfway down the left (north) side of the lake, began climbing the lower scree, picking my way from grass tuft to tuft and boulder to boulder, the short way up to the gully's opening.

Once in the gully, I had to use my hands as well as feet to climb— it was just that steep. The gully itself, one of many ditches gouged by time out of the flank of the ridge, was three to eight feet across and roughly five to ten feet deep. Sometimes I could straddle it in narrow stretches; at other times, I had to cling to the crumbling rocks in its center basin. At other times, I had to use the rocks along one side wall or the other while my feet scrambled for solid footing in the occasional patches of unavoidable scree. I had to clamber around boulders, avoid dripping springs and slippery, lichen-painted shale, and choke down dust from rock falls of my own making. Echoing across the silence of the basin, the rocks would slide, roll and ricochet like pinballs in a clattering cacophony toward the lake below.

Near the top of the gully, I turned just in time to see a hawk winging gently up and over the nearby buttress of the ridge off to my right. With effortless grace, its arched wings stretched motionless in the quiet air, it floated across the rocky escarpment of the mountain before disappearing over its crest and passing into the next valley. Then the stillness fell over the ridge again—but not for long.

From far below there suddenly rose more shattering echoes of falling rocks. It wasn't a rock fall of my doing, though. I hadn't moved. The calls of distant voices, however, told me I was no longer alone. Looking down, far down, I could see that the voices that now sped up to me were those of boys hallooing to each other while they pushed rocks in cracking echoes off the low, rounded ridge on the opposite shore of the lake into the splashing waters below. They looked like ants scurrying to and fro over the puny dust mounds outside their nest.

After examining them for a minute or two, I turned back to my climbing. They must be the ones that belong to that tent down there, I told myself as I grabbed hold of the next rock.

Not long after emerging from the upper end of the gully, I was straddling the ridgetop. From here it was a short but far from straight traverse west to the summit of Hidden Peak. Crisscrossing over the ridgetop to avoid cliffs and traversing across its face, where I was continually clambering in and out of gullies to get around ledges and looming gendarmes, I made my slow, winding way. Finally, after one last exhilarating hand-over-hand climb up a narrow chimney of the final tower I was on the 5,105-foot summit of Hidden Peak.

The crack of stone and the loud voices of the boys below still drifted up through the otherwise silent noon hour. I hardly noticed them. As I dislodged the register from the rocks of the summit's cairn, my thoughts were drifting back to five years before. On that day in mid-August this summit marked the fifth 5,000-plus-foot peak I had climbed; I would climb seven more before I was finished. Nobody before and nobody since (as far as I know) has climbed all twelve five thousand-foot peaks in the Front Range in one day—maybe nobody ever will.

No matter. All I know is that for me, since then, whenever I climb any one of those twelve peaks, a little bit of that day comes back. Sometimes, as on Hidden Peak, I could even read my entry—August 12, 1990—announcing in pencil that the sky was blue and clear and that though I'd reached five summits already, there were still more summits to reach before I could go home.

But sitting here was not the only similarity between that day five years before and this day. The route I took today from the waters of Hidden Lake to O'Malley Peak, the next summit along the ridge, would be the same route I had followed then. Joined by memory and place, the past and present were coming together, merging this day with that day in the past.

Then, as now, I left Hidden Peak after a short stay and followed the high, spired ridge west toward the summit of O'Malley Peak. Now, as then, it took a lot of time to go a short way. Time to crawl around or clamber over high shoulders of rock. Time to lunge across deep gullies of scree. And time to skirt along knife-edged cliffs. All in all, it took almost an hour to traverse the two thirds of a mile to the 5,150-foot summit of O'Malley.

But who can travel in a direct line on a rocky ridge? I had to descend and ascend the ridgetop again and again—sometimes as much as a hundred yards—to get around vertical ledges, across scree-glutted gullies, and climb through lines of looming towers. In the end, the two thirds of a mile distance took probably a mile of climbing to cross.

Five years before in a race against time, I didn't appreciate the time I spent traversing this ridge. But today I did. The mental stimulation of route finding and careful climbing—and the time to revel in it—made this day's traverse almost more memorable than when I made this same traverse five years before. Far below me to the left was the Campbell Creek valley, while far below to the right was the Williwaw Lakes valley. Above them, stretching off to the far ends of the horizons to the north, south and east were countless waves of distant ridges and summits. To the west, directly before me, lay the city of Anchorage and Cook Inlet above which, hovering at the far edge of the world in the farthest west, were the white ramparts of the Alaska Range. I actually wished it would've taken me longer than the hour it did to traverse that ridge. Five years before, though, with so much more to do, I had only wanted to get to the next summit as fast as possible.

Five years before the 5,150-foot summit of O'Malley marked the halfway point of my long day—and night. It was a milestone. Today, however, when I reached the summit of O'Malley, there were no more peaks to climb, no anxious anticipation of what was to come. It was anticlimactic. All the excitement of the climb was now behind me. I was done climbing on this day. I had no more commitments elsewhere among those mountains to fulfill. There was no place to go now but down.

The trail's end at Hidden Lake was the end of my beginning. Now, upon returning, the trail's end at the summit of O'Malley Peak was the beginning of my end.

Oh, I still had five miles or more of hiking to do before I got back to Glen Alps, but it was almost all downhill, and all on trail. I would enjoy the long sliding descent down the scree slope not far below the summit of O'Malley as well as the trek out to the *football field*—the broad and wide tundra plateau below the scree slope which makes O'Malley so conspicuous from the city below. I would even enjoy descending into the Campbell Creek valley. But it would not be the same as the last mile or so I'd just scrambled along the ridge from Hidden Peak.

Back there, between the ends of the two trails, there was some freedom in being so self-guided as well as some excitement in being so self-reliant. The end of the Hidden Lake Trail was the beginning of that self-willed excitement which ended at the start of the O'Malley Peak Trail. From the very first step I took onto that trail, I was once again restricted not only to where it went, but how it got there.

I could've chosen another way back, gotten off the trail and forged my own way down. But why? That would've been only an act of obstinate foolishness. After all, most trails do take the safest and most efficient—while still trying to be the most scenic—route from point to point. So there was no reason to deviate, at least not today. It would've only resulted in more, and perhaps very frustrating, work for myself. That was work I couldn't waste time on today. So I stayed on the *best* route for now.

Behind me, though, back on the open, trackless and trail-less ridge, there was no obviously *best* route. There was only the search for *any* route—and it was entirely up to me and me alone. Five years ago I chose one route. It was a long, arduous, and dangerous route. Yet it was also a wholly fulfilling route—because it was *my* route.

That's the nature of freedom: it is self-determining, self-responsible and wholly self-reliable. And one is only truly free when one is alone. But in our society one is not often alone. Freedom, then, is rare.

It is that single, slim moment when the individual's need and desire are not only one and the same, but entirely one's own. It is that precious moment between having responsibilities to fulfill and laws to obey—both of which are done in relation to other people. To be alone at the outer end of a trail is to have such freedom. In that moment, the trail-less and trackless heights extend outward from the trail's end with indeterminate possibilities. The ridge tops glisten with the morning's dew as the sun's first rays burn away the night's last stars, and the whole day laps at your feet like the waves of a vast, unexplored sea. That is freedom, and that alone is reason enough to seek out such solitude.

Hidden Lake Trail

Note: The Hidden Lake Trail is one of two trails that branch off of Powerline Pass Trail—the other being the O'Malley Peak Trail (mentioned in this article). Hidden Lake Trail leads up into the Ship Pass Valley, a broad Alpine expanse that stretches between The Wedge and The Ramp. The trip to Hidden Lake from where the trail leaves Powerline Pass is only 2.5 miles or so, but it is not the only worthwhile destination in this upper valley. The crest of Ship Pass itself (4,050 feet) (Option A) as well as the summits of The Ramp (5,240 feet) and The Wedge (4,660 feet) (Options B and C) are also popular destinations. A favorite trip of mine is, from Powerline Pass Trail, to climb up to the corner of the south ridge of The Wedge and then follow the goat trail that slabs far above the waters of Ship Lake across the back side of the Wedge over to Ship Pass and then descend down the valley to the Hidden Lake Trail on the return to Glen Alps (Option D). There are, however, more ambitious trips that can begin in this upper valley—such as this one which resulted in a traverse from the summit of Hidden Peak to O'Malley.

Trail Location: The way to Hidden Lake Trail begins at the Glen Alps Park Entrance located just below tree line in the foothills of the Front Range. To get to Glen Alps go east up O'Malley Road from its intersection with the Seward Highway. Follow O'Malley approximately 4 miles to Hillside Road. Turn right onto Hillside Drive and drive for another mile or so to Upper Huffman Road, which is on the left just after a sign for Chugach State Park. Follow Upper Huffman Drive for 3/4's of a mile and take a right onto the appropriately named Toilsome Hill Drive. This road, upon which chains, studs and/or four-wheel drive is recommended in winter, switchbacks and winds its way for two more miles before the entrance to Glen Alps parking lot appears on the left hand side at the top of one last short, steep hill.

From here it is another 2.5 mile hike up Powerline Trail to where Hidden Lake Trail leaves it to begin its steady ascent up into the Ship Pass Valley.

Powerline Trail begins on either of the two trailheads located just to the left of the elegant wooden staircase at the far end of the parking lot. One's the high road, so to speak, and the other's the low road, and they emerge at virtually the same spot: a trail intersection on an open hill crests far above the South Fork of Campbell Creek. From here, the trail bears right, staying on the wide dirt road that leads down a long hill before beginning a long steady climb. The beginning of Hidden Lake Trail, which is about two miles from this point on the Powerline Trail, is clearly marked by a signpost on the left hand side of the trail. From here there is only one questionable spot where hikers may become confused as to which direction to go. This occurs when, after climbing out of the Campbell Creek basin and crossing the bench above, the hiker reaches the bank of the stream flowing down out of the Ship Pass valley. Here the trail forks. One trail crosses the stream and continues up valley, while the other trail—the proper trail to Hidden Lake, which is located high on the north side of the valley—stays on the left hand (west) side of the stream which it follows up through brush to the higher tundra beyond.

Trail Grade: Hidden Creek Trail is almost entirely a grade 2 hike.

Trail Condition: The trail begins almost immediately after a very short descent and a difficult crossing of the South Fork of Campbell Creek. There are rocks on the left hand side of the pool that can be boulder-hopped; however, during flood season or after a heavy rain, when many of these boulders become submerged, even the most acrobatic of hikers will probably end up with wet feet. Nor is this the only water one encounters on this trail: The trail is, in fact, often muddy and wet all the way across the creek's basin as well as up across the first plateau where the trail levels out above. Along the plateau and little farther up there is also some low brush that has to be pushed through and one more easier stream crossing to make before open tundra is reached. From there, it is just a trudge up the tundra to the lake's basin.

Trail Mileage: The one way distance to Hidden Lake is about 4.75 miles for a round-trip total to and from the Glen Alps parking area of just under 9.5 miles.

Total Elevation Gain: The hike from Glen Alps parking area to Hidden Lake entails a climb of roughly 1,500 feet.

High Point: Hidden Lake, the highest point on this trail, is approximately 3,650 feet above sea level.

Normal Hiking Time: Though well conditioned and ambitious hikers and runners often do this trip in 2 to 3 hours, the round trip to Hidden Lake and back *usually* takes 4 to 5 hours for the persistent hiker and 6 to 8 hours for those who like to stop and smell the flowers.

Campsites: Anywhere along the western shore of Hidden Lake is a fine place to camp. There are also plenty of places to pitch a tent all over the upper valley. Wherever you camp, though, please bring a stove because campfires are prohibited inside park limits.

Best Time: May to September are the best times to go to Hidden Lake if you want to hear the water rippling on the shore. The winter months, however, should present no difficulties or dangers for the well-prepared, and always alert hiker. This is not to say, however, that there is no possibility of avalanches along the Hidden Lake Trail. The possibility of an avalanche occurring is always there—especially on the extreme avalanche-prone slopes around the back side of the lake.

USGS Maps: Anchorage A-7, A-8 SE.

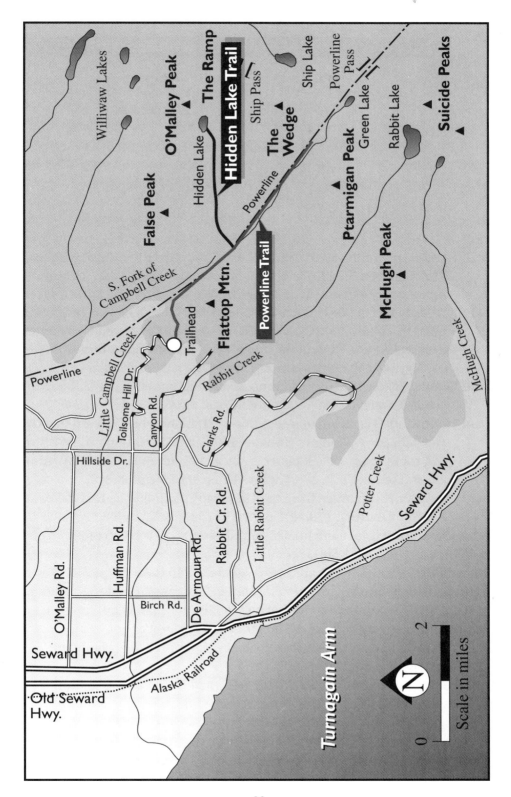

Williwaw Lakes

O'Malley Peak ▲

The Ramp

Hidden Lake Trail

Ship Pass

Ship Lake

Powerline Pass

Suicide Peaks ▲

Hidden Lake

The Wedge ▲

Green Lake

Rabbit Lake

False Peak ▲

Powerline

Ptarmigan Peak ▲

S. Fork of Campbell Creek

Powerline Trail

McHugh Peak ▲

Flattop Mtn. ▲

McHugh Creek

Little Campbell Creek

Powerline

Trailhead

Rabbit Creek

Hillside Dr.

Toilsome Hill Dr.

Canyon Rd.

Clarks Rd.

Rabbit Cr. Rd.

Little Rabbit Creek

Potter Creek

Seward Hwy.

O'Malley Rd.

Huffman Rd.

De Armour Rd.

Birch Rd.

Seward Hwy.

Alaska Railroad

Old Seward Hwy.

Turnagain Arm

N

Scale in miles

0   2

A WALK-ABOUT GUIDE TO

OPTION "A"

HIDDEN LAKE TRAIL TO SHIP PASS

Trail Location: At the base of Ship Pass valley, where the Hidden Lake Trail stays on the left hand side of a small stream, take the first right hand fork across the stream and follow this trail as far as it will go. (To get to Hidden Lake Trail, see WALK-ABOUT GUIDE TO HIDDEN LAKE TRAIL.) At this trail's end, where it eventually peters out in the upper valley, simply continue cross-country over the tundra toward the pass.

Trail Grade: The grade for the climb up to Ship Pass is level 2, rising to levels 3 and 4 on the final climb to the pass.

Trail Condition: Though many sections of Hidden Lake Trail are muddy and wet, the walking is, after an initial section through some brush and rocky trail, almost entirely across soft tundra all the way from the end of Hidden Lake Trail to the crest of Ship Pass.

Trail Mileage: It is 6 miles from the Glen Alps parking area to the crest of Ship Pass for a round-trip total of roughly 12 miles.

Total Elevation Gain: The hike to Ship Pass entails a climb of approximately 1,800 feet.

High Point: It is 4,050 feet above sea level at Ship Pass.

Normal Hiking Time: The climb to Ship Pass varies from 4 to 8 hours also depending on condition and ambition of the hikers involved.

Campsites: Plenty all across the upper valley. Wherever you camp, though, please bring a stove because campfires are prohibited inside park limits.

Best Time: June to September are the best months to hike up to Ship Pass. In the winter this climb can be done, but be watchful of snow conditions on the last few hundred yard climb to the crest. It may not look it, but avalanches can occur here.

USGS Maps: Anchorage A-7, A-8 SE.

84

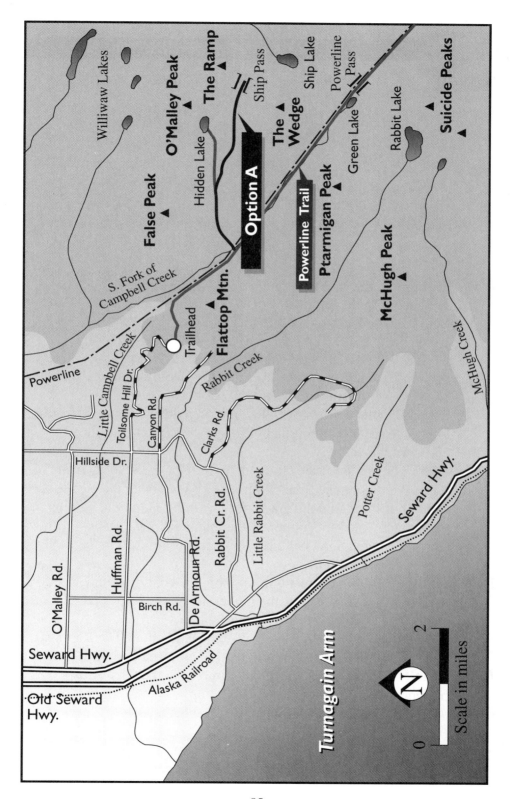

HIDDEN LAKE TRAIL TO THE SUMMIT OF THE RAMP

Trail Location: At the base of Ship Pass valley, where the Hidden Lake Trail stays on the left hand side of a small stream, take the first right hand fork across the stream and follow this trail as far as it will go. (To get to Hidden Lake Trail, see WALK-ABOUT GUIDE TO HIDDEN LAKE TRAIL.) At this trail's end, where it eventually peters out in the upper valley, simply continue cross-country over the tundra toward the pass. Once at the crest of the Pass, turn left (north) and follow the ridgeline all the way to the top of the spired summit that clearly dominates the northeast corner of the valley.

Trail Grade: The grade for the climb up to Ship Pass is level 2, rising to levels 3 and 4 on the final climb to the pass. From the pass to the summit of the Ramp the grade rises with the elevation, passing from grade 4 to 5 the higher up the mountain one climbs—with (for some, what may be) a few moments of grade 6 in the final few feet to the summit.

Trail Condition: From the crest of Ship Pass, the condition underfoot varies from soft tundra to, the higher one gets, steep scree with even some bouldering close to the summit.

Trail Mileage: One way from Glen Alps to the summit of The Ramp is about 6.5 miles for a round trip total of almost a 13 miles.

Total Elevation Gain: It is a 3,100 foot climb from the Glen Alps parking area to the summit of The Ramp.

High Point: The highest point reached is 5,240 feet above sea level at the summit of The Ramp.

Normal Hiking Time: The round trip to and from the parking lot to the summit of The Ramp requires 5 to 9 hours depending on the condition and ambition of the hiker(s).

Campsites: Plenty all across the upper valley. Wherever you camp, though, please bring a stove because campfires are prohibited inside park limits.

Best Time: June to September are the best months to climb The Ramp. In the winter this climbs can be done, but varying snow conditions often transform it from a steady trudge up steep snow to a technical snow or ice climb in which protection may be needed. This is especially true of the last few hundred feet to the summit. No matter how technical it is on a particular day, if done in winter, this climb should always be done with extreme caution and awareness of avalanche conditions.

USGS Maps: Anchorage A-7, A-8 SE.

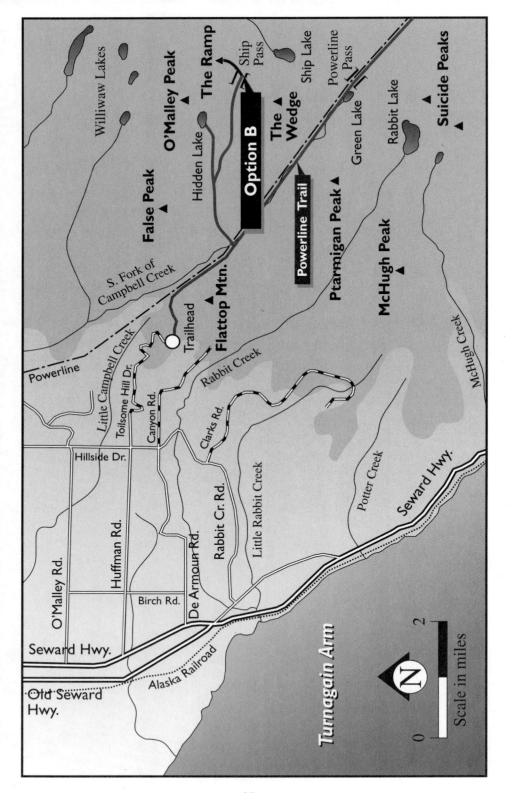

On the sheep trail behind the Wedge.

HIDDEN LAKE TRAIL TO THE SUMMIT OF THE WEDGE

Trail Location: At the base of Ship Pass valley, where the Hidden Lake Trail stays on the left hand side of a small stream, take the first right hand fork across the stream and follow this trail as far as it will go. (To get to Hidden Lake Trail, see WALK-ABOUT GUIDE TO HIDDEN LAKE TRAIL.) At this trail's end, where it eventually peters out in the upper valley, simply continue cross-country over the tundra toward the pass. Once at the crest of the Pass, turn right (south), staying on the top of the pass. At the edge of the pass, simply continue climbing right up the crest of the ridge. Follow the ridge line all the way up to the rounded summit of The Wedge which is the highest point on the south side of the pass.

Trail Grade: From the crest of the pass, the grade increases steadily with the elevation gain. Beginning at grade 3, it soon edges up to grade 4 for the last few yards of climbing up the ridge to the summit

Trail Condition: From the top of Ship Pass to the summit of the Wedge, the climbing is almost entirely on wide, open tundra with only sporadic patches of scree.

Trail Mileage: The climb up to the summit is a little over 6.5 miles for a round trip total to and from Glen Alps parking area of about 12.5 miles.

Total Elevation Gain: It is a 2,550 climb from Glen Alps to the summit of the Wedge.

High Point: It is 4,460 above sea level at the summit of the Wedge.

Normal Hiking Time: The round trip from Glen Alps to the summit of The Wedge and back will take anywhere from 4 to 9 depending on the condition and ambition of the hiker(s).

90

Campsites: Plenty all across the upper valley. Wherever you camp, though, please bring a stove because campfires are prohibited inside park limits.

Best Time: June to September are the best months to climb The Wedge. This climb can also be done in winter, but because of changing snow conditions, this easy trudge up a wide snowfield can be quickly transformed into a technical snow or ice climb. And no matter what the snow conditions, this winter climb should always be done with extreme caution and awareness of avalanche conditions.

USGS Maps: Anchorage A-7, A-8 SE.

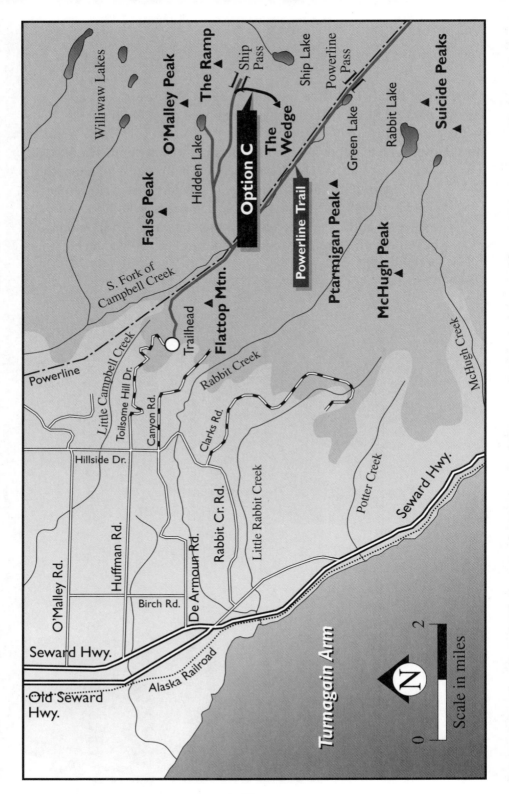

Williwaw Lakes

O'Malley Peak ▲

The Ramp ▲

Ship Pass

Ship Lake

Powerline Pass

Suicide Peaks ▲
▲

Rabbit Lake

Green Lake

Option C

The Wedge ▲

Hidden Lake

False Peak ▲

Powerline Trail

Ptarmigan Peak ▲

McHugh Peak ▲

S. Fork of Campbell Creek

Flattop Mtn. ▲

Trailhead ○

McHugh Creek

Powerline

Little Campbell Creek

Toilsome Hill Dr.

Canyon Rd.

Rabbit Creek

Clarks Rd.

Hillside Dr.

Rabbit Cr. Rd.

Little Rabbit Creek

Potter Creek

Seward Hwy.

O'Malley Rd.

Huffman Rd.

De Armour Rd.

Birch Rd.

Seward Hwy.

Alaska Railroad

Old Seward Hwy.

Turnagain Arm

N

Scale in miles

0   2

92

Approaching the summit of O'Malley Peak from the east with Anchorage Bowl in the background.

CIRCUMNAVIGATION OF THE WEDGE

Trail Location: At the base of Ship Pass valley, where the Hidden Lake Trail stays on the left hand side of a small stream, take the first right hand fork across the stream and follow this trail as far as it will go. (To get to Hidden Lake Trail, see WALK-ABOUT GUIDE TO HIDDEN LAKE TRAIL.) At this trail's end, where it eventually peters out in the upper valley, simply continue cross-country over the tundra toward the pass. Once at the crest of the Pass, turn right (south), staying on the top of the pass. At the edge of the pass, just about where the pass begins to climb more steeply toward the summit of the Wedge, look for an obvious goat trail that slabs around the back of The Wedge. Follow this goat trail all the way across the back of the Wedge to where it joins the ridge crest again. From here descend the relatively steep tundra slope directly down to the Powerline Pass Trail which can be seen far below. Those not wishing to come down just yet may continue—with great care—following the goat trail down the remaining quarter mile of this jagged rock and tundra ridge crest to the base of the rock face of the next ridge (which is the northwest buttress of Powerline Pass Peak) and descend to Powerline Pass Trail from there.

Trail Grade: The climb up to the Ship Pass from the Hidden Lake Trail is mostly grade 2 with an increase to level 3 in the final uphill to up to the top of the pass. The grade, because so much of it is on a trail (albeit unofficial) for the climb around the Wedge is levels 2 to 4. Continuing down the jagged ridge on the other side of the Wedge, even though there is a trail of sorts, is grade 5 simply because one has to use the hands often for certain maneuvers and balance.

Trail Condition: It is all open tundra up to the pass from the end of Hidden lake Trail. Small rocks and dirt, with narrow slides of occasional scree, make up most of the tread along the goat trail. But these are only minor hinderances along this trail which is as solid and sturdy underfoot as many human built trails. The descent to Powerline Trail on the far side of the Wedge reverts once again to open tundra. Though it is a steep descent with some boulder slides, the footing is generally good.

Trail Mileage: The circumnavigation of The Wedge to and from the Glen Alps parking area is between 11 and 12 miles one way.

Total Elevation Gain: The hike around the back of the Wedge entails an overall climb of 1,900 feet.

High Point: The highest point reached on this hike is almost 4,150 feet along the trail behind The Wedge.

Normal Hiking Time: The circumnavigation of The Wedge should take 4 to 8 hours depending on the condition and ambition of the hiker(s).

Campsites: There are plenty of campsites all across the upper valley below Ship Pass as well as on the tundra at the base of the descent on the Powerline Pass side of the traverse. Wherever you camp, though, please bring a stove because campfires are prohibited inside park limits.

Best Time: June to September are the best months to hike around The Wedge. This climb can be done in the winter, but under certain snow conditions it can be a technical snow or ice climb and should be done with extreme caution and awareness of avalanche conditions—which are *always* present whenever any traverse across an open slope is attempted.

USGS Maps: Anchorage A-7, A-8 SE.

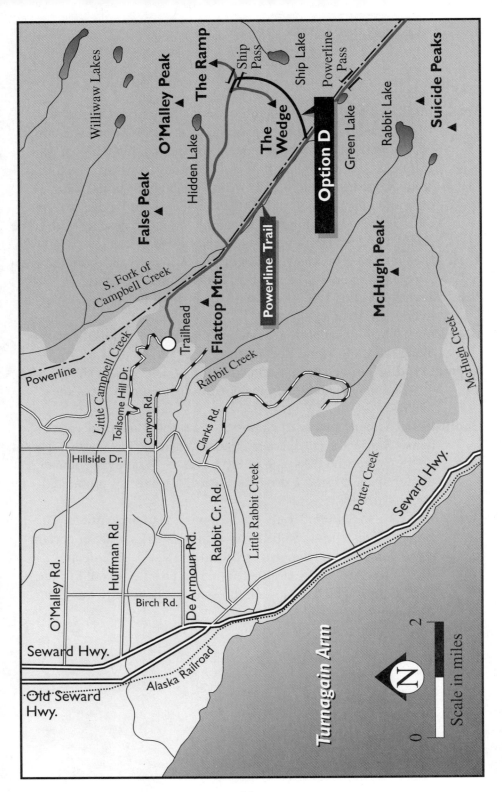

Hidden Lake below Hidden Peak.

Trail Location: The trail to the summit of O'Malley begins, like the
Hidden Lake mentioned above, at Glen Alps parking area.
(To get there, see WALK-ABOUT GUIDE TO HIDDEN LAKE
TRAIL). The trail, which is posted, begins just a little over a half
mile from the start of the Powerline Trail soon after that trail
emerges out of the woods and turns down the wide road under the
powerlines themselves. The sign that marks the beginning of the
climb up O'Malley Peak is less than a hundred yards down
the road on the left hand side. NOTE: This sign does not mention
O'Malley Peak; instead it has the label "Middle Fork Loop Trail."
The first part of this trail is all downhill to a bridge across the
South Fork of Campbell Creek. From here it is all uphill. Soon
after crossing the creek the Middle Fork Loop Trail will bear off
to the left around the front of O'Malley not far beyond the bridge
over the South Fork of Campbell Creek. Do not follow this trail.
Instead, continue climbing toward the of the mountain. The crest
of this first shoulder has a shelf of snow in it well into June and is
a favorite destination for most people. But to stop here is to miss
the so-called "football field," the broad plateau into which the trail
traverses just on the other side of the shoulder. It is this highly
visible *football field* (also referred to at times as *the ballpark*),
located in front of the summit spire itself which makes O'Malley
so easily recognizable from town. A steep, laborious climb up a
wide chute of loose scree at the end of the this plateau then leads
up to a higher ridge crest which is then followed in an easterly
direction as it winds up among boulders and more scree to the
summit.

Trail Grade: From Glen Alps to the summit of O'Malley, this climb
goes through the entire range of levels from 1 to 4, with the level

increasing as the summit gets closer and closer and the trail gets rougher and rougher. The steepest portions, which are the broad swath that leads straight up to the top of the first shoulder and the scree chute that climbs from the "football field" up to the summit ridge, may not be the most technically difficult portions of the climb, but they are physically the hardest.

Trail Condition: The trail condition varies as much as the grade, entailing anything from broad clean trail to loose scree with even some use of hands necessary for balance among the boulders and loose rocks on the high ridge just below the summit.

Trail Mileage: The one way climb to the summit of O'Malley from Glen Alps is about 4.7 miles for a round trip total of approximately 9.5 miles.

Total Elevation Gain: From the parking lot to the summit of O'Malley entails a climb of over 3,150 feet.

High Point: The highest point reached is 5,105 feet above sea level at, not surprisingly, the summit of O'Malley Peak itself.

Normal Hiking Time: This is a full day climb up and over some very rough terrain. Expect to take anywhere from 5 to 7 or 8 to 10 hours depending on conditioning and sure-footedness of the hiker(s)—and the time any one may want to spend at the top enjoying the view.

Campsites: The *football field*, which does have some water sources, including one tarn called Deep Lake located in its northeast corner, is a favorite camping location for a lot of people.

Best Time: The best time to do this climb is from June to September. Only experienced snow and ice climbers should try to climb this peak during the rest of the year.

USGS Maps: Anchorage A-7, A-8 SE.

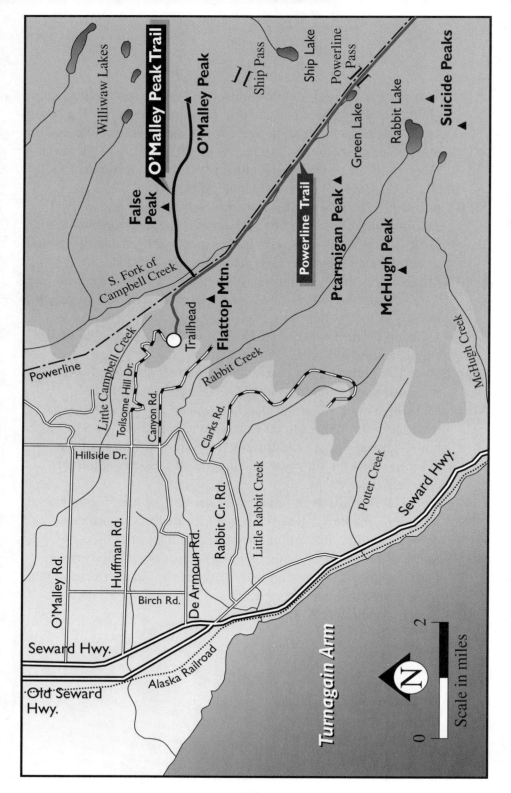

100

The parking lot at Glen Alps on a rare, near empty day.

CHAPTER 6

Ambulation Through a Circle's Evolution

I felt as helpless as a fish left flopping on the sun-sparkled mud by the outgoing tide. Only instead of longing for any watery depths behind me, I was struggling to reach the rocky heights ahead of me. Wallowing in the wet, waist-deep, snow in the center of the mountain's south face, all I longed for was the feel of that solid earth under my feet. I tried wading through the soft drifts, but I only slipped in deeper—up to my waist. I tried crawling over the soft top, but only sank in deeper—up to my chin. I was getting no where fast and no where easy.

Finally, all I could do was half swim and half roll across the seemingly bottomless snow. Only then, pulling myself along with my arms and kicking from behind with my legs, did I finally feel like I was making some progress. Though moving faster, it wasn't any easier. Huffing and puffing, I struggled onward toward the nearest solid ground—a rocky rib that rose out of the snow seventy *very* long feet ahead of me. Behind me spread a half mile of steep, glistening snow and I had no desire to back-track. The wake of my swimming, struggling ascent cut a wide, deep blue swath across its otherwise bright, smooth surface. Winding almost two miles back behind the snowfield, looping down behind a lower buttress, circling through the cirque below and rising back up over the 3,750-foot pass on the far side of the valley could be seen some of the more distant tracks of my passing.

Beyond that I could only imagine seeing the tracks I'd left behind me since morning. In my mind's eye I saw then rising up out of the forests below where I'd begun my hike at Prospect Heights parking area, then pressing across higher alpine meadows where the Middle Fork Trail turned up valley, following the snow-bordered waters of the Middle Fork of Campbell Creek between the long back ridge of Wolverine and the massif of O'Malley Peak. From there they climbed still higher, kicking across the open tundra still carpeted by snow around the Williwaw lakes. Farther up still, I imagined seeing those tracks duck beneath the bases of corniced ridges and pass alongside frozen lakes nestled quietly in the low laps of more massive, towering summits. Then, tracing a blue line across the snow from lake to ever higher lake, those tracks finally climbed up and over the snow-plugged pass. From the crest of that pass I could now actually see them zigzag down across the still ice-hidden headwaters of the North Fork of Campbell Creek into the bowl below only to climb once again up to where I was now floundering—and cursing—in the sun-softened snow on the west face of Koktoya Peak. From here, if I ever got myself out of this morass of snow and up to the summit above, I hoped to follow the North Fork of Campbell Creek down valley to where I could climb over Wolverine Peak and down its western face back to Prospect Heights.

A circle, as defined by Euclidean Geometry, is "a set of all points in a plane that are the same distance from the center. It contains 360 degrees. A radius is a segment of a line connecting the center to any of those point. The radius is always the same length from the center to any one of those points. The circumference of the circle, which is comprised of those equi-distant points, is the distance around the circle."

Of course, this later form of abstract geometry, which this definition is drawn from, is a type of "pure mathematics" dealing as it does with idealized lines and points that are entirely two-dimensional and have no obvious practical application. However, this was not always true of the science of Geometry.

The hike that I was struggling through was actually a form of Geometry that harked back to its origin as a science.

For Geometry in its original form was not an abstract science. The word Geometry itself is actually composed of two Greek words, *geo* which means *earth* and *metrein* which means *measure*. Thus the term originally meant *earth measure*. This is exactly what geometry originally was: a science developed to measure the earth. In a certain sense this is what I was doing while out hiking on this day. The only difference being that I was, in a sense, measuring myself against the earth, not just measuring the earth in and of itself. Herodotus, who is arguably the first great historian (and maybe even the first historian!), credits the Egyptians with having originated the subject of geometry sometime just after 2,000 B.C. Geometry in its original form was also practiced in Babylonia, India and China during the same period. It was also sanctioned by the

103

ancient Jews. It is even made reference to—albeit indirectly—in <u>The Bible</u>.

> *Then he made the molten sea; it was round; it was round,*
> *ten cubits from brim to brim, and five cubits high, and a*
> *line of thirty cubits measured its circumference.*
> (I Kings. 7:23)

Alas, however, not enough information is given as to whether or not there is a radius in this *round* ocean, for whether or not it is a circle in the strict definition of the word is left for the reader to only guess. The term circumference is also given, but there is also reference to diameter (the *brim to brim* measurement). This lack of complete, definitive evidence is one of the major differences between Geometry in this early period of its development and its later forms. Geometry in these early stages was almost wholly an empirical subject. Conclusions were reached by rule-of-thumb procedures which included uncontrolled experimentation, observation, supposition, and occasional flashes of intuition.   Often the answers that came up were wrong. (After all, was— is!—the sea only ten cubits in diameter as stated in the quote above.) But then all this could be said about hiking over the trail-less wilds of Alaska as well.

So it was in this sense—the earlier, more empirical form of Geometry—that I was out tracing my own circle across the landscape. Though I was tracing a circular route, it was certainly not a circle in the Euclidean sense of the term. I couldn't even say I was tracing a circumferential route as I made my slow, methodical way around the Wolverine massif—which was a far bigger circle-like shape than I'd ever traced on paper in all my school years.

But though my tracks led a long way back—perhaps more than ten miles back, the way to the summit above, which marked the farthest point from the beginning and end of my circle, seemed longer yet—even though it was only three hundred or so feet above the snowfield I wallowed in. The way out to complete the circle was longer yet—maybe another ten miles.

The early practitioners of Geometry in Egypt and Babylon would've probably been content with my inexact estimates. But Thales of Miletus, one of the first great Greek teachers of Geometry, would not have been at all happy with my estimates. The natural world, however, does not often submit itself to such exact rules as those epitomized by Thales' postulates and theorems. First, I had no way of precisely measuring the distance I'd come—and still had to go. Second, the weather conditions which determine what's on the ground below as well as well as what's fallen from the sky above will always change the route and the time it takes to do that route.

Then, third, physically working outside is not the same as mentally working at a desk. It is difficult to remain objective when confronted with the terrible beauty and apparent randomness of nature—as opposed to handling a calculator and drawing compass.

Yet despite being in such a predicament through a lack of just such reasoning, I had no reason to complain. Things were still better than they were last time I'd gotten the urge to climb. Only a week before, after coming back to the spring of the valleys below after going up into the snowy heights of South Suicide Peak, I had promised myself not to hurry back into the mountains. The frigid and snow-blowing winds I contested with in that climb convinced me there was no reason to climb again soon.

"Wait until Spring really comes," I told myself.

Then less than a week later it seemed as though it was suddenly spring. Yes, there was still snow in the high country. As far as the eye could see there was snow, dazzling snow: snow sparkling like hard diamonds on the summits; snow shining like glass crystal along the ridges; snow as cold and hard as marble spilling down gullies and hanging in the glaciered cols; and there was even snow as soft and white as pearls, stretching across the valleys. Yet, despite all the cold whiteness covering the earth below, the air above was warm and colorful. Framed by a cloudless and brilliant turquoise sky, the sun spread its warmth in blinding sheets. And no wind blew. The air was as calm as a low tide beneath a full moon. I, for one, couldn't resist such a day.

Now I was in the middle of that day in the middle of a hike at the far side of a circular route that would eventually and inevitably—as long as I could keep moving—take me back to where I'd started.

Circles (or facsimiles thereof): they are more than just abstract creations of a logical mind. They are a part of every day of every life.

Driving to and from work, going to and from school while the circular sun and the circular moon floated through their circular trajectories above. Beyond them, in ever-widening circumferences circled the planets of the our single sun's solar system which moved in a bigger circle of many stars, which circled in yet bigger circles of galaxies and clusters of galaxies that, given enough time and energy, would circle back and forth forever in this entire universe's oscillating circle. By hiking around my minuscule circle of valleys, I was just doing my small part in that bigger scheme of things. Not that it made a difference to the bigger scheme of things; but at least it made me feel like I belonged.

Yet, though small, this circular route showed evidence of other circles—particularly the circle of seasons. It was especially evident in the season of transition I was hiking—and falling—through. Now, however, the transition wasn't very obvious. Wallowing in snow on that high face, with snow on all sides of me and even more snow as far as the eye could see, it seemed more like a winter day than a spring afternoon.

But though the snow was general all over the high country, it had not been a constant presence in the day. In fact, in the first few miles from where I had started back at the Prospect Heights parking lot, there was no snow to be seen anywhere. There wasn't even an abundance of mud from recent snow melt. The trail was only damp in spots.

Spring had definitely sprung forth down below. I heard it as I walked through a forest of greening leaf filled with a cacophony of bird songs. Squawking alto ptarmigans, mezzo jays and chirping soprano chickadees all joined in random song. Soon after, Campbell Creek, flowing fast and heavy with snow melt, added its own bass rumblings to the din. Then a marmot's call echoed down a slope like a distant clarinet. A squirrel chattered like a snare drum from a nearby spruce tree. It was a confusion of sounds that John Cage would've gladly spent all afternoon trying to put to paper or record on tape. I also saw spring in the abundance of buds pushing forth from the gray branches I walked amid and the first flowers and small shoots of various grasses pushing up through the soft, oozy ground below.

Farther up the trail though, on the Alpine meadows, spring was not nearly as evident. Despite the pied copses of birch and willow, here there were no signs of new green growth. All the grass lay matted on the soggy, shallow slopes, while the trail itself was a cold quagmire of half-frozen mud and running water. It was like walking up a slippery stream bed. It didn't help to walk up the stubbled earth on either side of the trail; it was just as wet. The whole hillside below Wolverine Peak seemed like one giant, saturated sponge. Soon, as would be expected, my shoes were also like two saturated sponges—very minuscule sponges compared with the mountain above, but, nevertheless, very cold sponges.

Higher still, patches of stale, dirty snow soon began to appear and disappear beneath my feet. I slid down and across the wooded hollow of the Middle Fork Campbell Creek once more and then climbed onto the open bluff where the Middle Fork Trail intersects with the Middle Fork Loop Trail. Here the former banks a hard left upstream on its way toward the still distant Williwaw Lakes while the later trail bears south around the front base of O'Malley Peak on its way to Glen Alps. I took the left hand turn up the valley.

Before long, the trail was winding through the tangled and twisting acres of Krummholz, that sturdy and stunted spruce that borders tree line. In the thick, green shadows, the snow, both on and off the trail, was becoming both deeper and more constant. Some of the snow in the shadows was still firm enough to walk over, but the higher and more open the country became, the more often I punched through it.

Step, step, punch. Step, step, step, punch. Step, punch. etc. etc.

Finally, after plunging thigh-deep into one more drift—which sunk me about neck deep into frustration, I decided it was time to put on the snowshoes I had tied onto my pack.

A small kinglet perched on a nearby branch sang to me as I sat in the snow strapping on my snowshoes. Accompanied only by the gurgling waters of Campbell Creek that drifted up through the tangled spruce, its bright song lifted into the otherwise still air. A single plane droned overhead and was gone. Yet through the tangled spruce the kinglet's song still drifted. No other sound could be heard. High above, telemarking tracks etched on the north slope of O'Malley gave evidence of other human voices that had been heard here recently. Rabbit tracks disappearing over a drift to my left and raven prints along the trail before me gave evidence of other wild life that had moved through. But for now, the kinglet and I were alone. Behind me, the single file of my tracks led back to the green, noisy valleys below, and the Anchorage Bowl beyond, with its constant blur of movement and din of sound.

Inevitably my circle would eventually lead me back to that bowl, just as all circles eventually lead back to where they were begun. No, it wasn't a perfect circle as defined by Euclidean Geometry. Nor was this the perfect circle that Ptolemy thought the planets and stars moved in around the earth. This was, instead, more like one of the ellipses that Copernicus calculated the planets (including the earth) moved in around the sun, and which all the heavenly bodies moved around each other.

Yet it was still a circle of sorts, and by tracing it I was imposing my own order on the landscape. I was not Thales formulating his theorems or Euclid toiling over his thirteen books or even Copernicus bending over his calculations. I was, instead, only one man walking up and back in a circle through a wild land. Yet just by being there—and, more importantly, by now writing about it and giving my being there a *theme*—I was creating a sense of order that had not been fixed on that piece of landscape of before.

> *It was her voice that made*
> *The sky acutest at its vanishing.*
> *She measured the hour of its solitude.*
> *She was the single artificer of the world*
> *In which she sang. And when she sang, the sea,*
> *Whatever self it had, became the self*
> *That was her song, for she was the maker. Then we,*
> *As we beheld her striding there alone,*
> *Knew that there never was a world for her*
> *Except the one she sang and, singing, made.*
> (From "Ideas of Order At Key West" by Wallace Stevens)

The sun beat down like a small persistent hammer on the back of my neck as I trudge up the long, broad snowfields that carpeted the valley floor. Heat rose off the nearby barren patches of tundra and rocks in shimmering waves. In time, the sun and its warmth would bring this high world to life. No doubt, there was already the throbbing of new life on those small patches of moss, weeds and lichen that stuck up through the snow like small olive and brown islands in a white sea. Somewhere in burrows beneath the snow I marched over were probably marmots, ground squirrels and voles ready to pop up after I passed and the snow fields melted away.

But though the earth was full of life, the land, despite the strong sun on this warm day on the edge of summer, was gray and bleak.

A small flock of Terns filled the sky with their screeching as I slabbed around the frozen, aquamarine waters of the Williwaw Lakes. But soon after, leaving the terns, the sleeping rodents, and squawking Ptarmigan behind me, I was climbing up toward the pass separating the Middle Fork from the North Fork of Campbell Creek. Tracking across the frozen lakes of the three broad steps that climb up to the pass, I kept one eye on the impressive, fractured, vertical face of Williwaw Peak towering to my right, and the other eye warily on the fractured ice at my feet. But nothing cracked; no water gurgled from below. No ground squirrel whistled at me. No bird sang. All was silent except for the crunch, crunch, crunch of my snowshoes and my own labored breathing.

After one last steep climb, I was at the crest of the pass, over 3,750 feet above sea level and looking far down into the next valley. I've been over this pass close to ten times, yet I always feel as though I'm seeing it for the first time whenever I am standing on its crest. Gazing once more down to the waters of Long Lake, almost 700 feet below, and the heights of the Tanaina-Koktoya ridge, rising close to 1,500 feet above the opposite shore of those waters to heights in excess of 5,000 feet, the sense of wonder was as new as the first time I'd stood on this same spot almost six years before.

Thales, Hippocrates and Euclid may have been great mathematicians, but all their calculations lack one very human aspect: time. Time, of course, has nothing to do with *pure* mathematics, which exists only in the vacuum of thought. But it has everything to do with the human condition. We are, after all, such tiny creatures who abide for but a day and then are gone, while the earth seemingly goes on and on. Then, of course, there's the night sky which humbles both the earth and us—and ever more so as it extends farther and farther away from us. Just before disappearing from sight entirely, at the outer fringes of the solar system, we must appear as nothing more than a dust mote drifting far out across the center of a wide sea. Soon after, as the dark sky extends father and farther away through countless centuries of light years, we disappear entirely into the vaster ocean of deep space.

On this single day on that wide ocean of time and space, both the lake below and the heights above were still largely frozen. But in the strong afternoon light of the May sun, they were thawing—and fast. Spring may be slow coming up this way, but it does eventually come.

Traversing a short way east along the crest, I soon found a steep, but not impassable, route to a glacial cirque below, the first step down to the valley below. From there, after a few cautious steps over stones, I slid down the remaining snow slope and was soon stomping across a lower snowfield toward Koktoya, the mountain I intended to climb. But before I could begin climbing that mountain, I still had to swing around most of the remaining upper bowl of the North Fork's headwaters. Only after that traverse, which meant toiling over one buttress and slabbing across another, would I be on the slopes of the mountain proper.

Now that I had found my way to the mountain, I still had to find my way to the summit. The southeast ridge, its jagged, Stegosaurus-backed crest outlined against the blue was not only a longer route, but with its rocky spires and snow corniced gullies, not the surest—or safest. The south face, on the other hand, streaked by dirty snow chutes lined by long rock ribs of scree and boulders, was more direct, although steeper. It seemed the more sure and safe route. I chose the south face.

Before slabbing over onto the south face proper, the snowshoes had to come off. In all the terrain I'd covered since breaking tree line over three hours before, I'd avoided slabbing across any steep slopes. Snowshoes are suited for climbing or descending fall lines, direct routes up and down ridges, or crossing shallow slopes. They are, however, extremely unstable when traversing steep slopes. Moving perpendicular to any slope, the claws beneath the feet are not able to confront the grade at a right angle. Instead the claws are parallel to the slope, rendering them virtually useless, wholly unable to properly grip the slope. What I was about to cross in order to get directly under the south face was at the worst possible angle for snowshoes. Despite having no crampons, it seemed—as usual—better to kick steps across the snowfield in front of me in my running shoes than try to waddle across it precariously in my snowshoes.

As it turned out, the snow was too soft to worry about. In the first fifty feet, I could easily kick into it for solid footing. In the next fifty feet, I could step into it for firm footing. In the next hundred feet, however, I could easily fall into it for lack of any footing. It was too soft to hold any weight, including my own and so I was left wallowing in wet, waist deep snow. It was too soft for even my ice ax to be of any use. The crust was just solid enough to allow me to pull myself up out of each hole. But as soon as I put my full weight on either foot, whoof! down I'd plummet again into the morass of wet powder.

All that was left to do was crawl as best I could over the top—though even that was barely possible. But I was not like a baby crawling across a clean, white floor. Instead, I was like a pig wallowing in a morass of bleached mud. Soon, I was huffing and puffing like a freight train, and stopping continually to get my breath.

I wondered if such snow was prone to avalanche. Suddenly I wasn't so tired. I also realized how far I was away from the haven of solid rocks on the far side of the snow. Finding a hidden reserve of energy—produced more by emotional reaction than physical combustion—I pulled and pushed my way through the last feet of deep snow.

When I reached the rocks, I was finally able to climb directly, but steeply, toward the summit. The scree in the gullies I started to trace upward were squirmy and slippery from the snow melt draining down. Consequently, they were even more laborious than usual to climb. So instead of scrambling up gullies, I began climbing over rocks, boulders and ledges that walled them in on either side, picking my route upwards with as much care as possible to avoid the snow and scree—though it was impossible to avoid it all. There was still the inevitable short, deep snowfield to cross and scree to scramble frantically over, but at least I was moving upward.

So I climbed until there was no more climbing to do and all the world all around me dropped away. I was at the summit.

This was the third time I'd climbed Koktoya's approximately 5,150-foot summit. On the first two climbs, however, I had reached the summit in the small hours of the morning, when all the world was steeped in darkness. This was the first time I'd been at the summit in daylight—and it was quite a view.

To the south, far below, I could see my own blue thread of tracks curling over the snow, around ridges and across the flats below the sheer west face of Mount Williwaw. Around the east side of its dominant mass could be seen Turnagain Arm peaking over Indian Pass, while around the other side of that mountain—the highest in the Front Range—could be seen the other sky-piercing summits of The Ramp, Hidden Peak, O'Malley, and Powerline Pass Peak.

To the west, the Tanaina Ridge, rising directly out of the notch a half mile below me, extended for over two miles across jagged-topped summits and over sagging rock walls directly toward the Anchorage Bowl and the bright waters of Cook Inlet. Yet still farther, beyond both Anchorage and Cook Inlet, at the far edge of sight, hovered the bright silhouettes of the Alaska Range with its well-known massifs of Denali, Foraker and Hunter stretched in a tight, high semi-circle to the west and north.

Immediately to the north, just on the opposite shore of deep set Tanaina Lake which glistened over 2,000 feet below, rose the long, broad mass of Temptation Peak, while to the east, above Ship Creek Valley which wound still farther below—close to 3,000 feet—loomed the long, rounded crest of the south ridge of Rendezvous Peak beyond which reached peak after crystal peak toward the tangled eastern horizon where they finally disappeared in a shimmering haze.

In the register I found the well-known names of Bob Spurr, Jim Sayler as well as Willi Hersman and Tim Kelley. Their names appeared three or four times, among the only four pages dating back to the early 1980s.

Obviously not too many people made it here, to the back side of the Front Range—or maybe it just seemed that way. After all, I hadn't seen anyone all day, despite it being an ideal sunny Sunday in late spring. Yet I knew that, in time, other people would arrive at this point. Perhaps Jim, Willi or Tim would come back here again. Perhaps they'd write their names below mine, wondering what it was like when I was here—as I was wondering what it was like when they'd been here. Circles intersecting circles as the gyres of time spin onward. Bob, who died the year before while climbing in Colorado, would not be back, though the mountain upon which he once scribbled his name remains.

> *A generation goes, and a generation comes,*
> *but the earth remains forever.*
> *The sun rises and the sun goes down,*
> *and hastens to the place where it rises.*

The wind blows to the south, and goes around to the north;
round and round goes the wind, and on its circuits the wind
returns.
All streams run to the sea, but the sea is not full;
to the place where the streams flow, there they flow again.
All things are full of weariness; a man cannot utter it;
the eye is not satisfied with seeing, nor the ear filled with hearing.
What has been is what will be, and what has been done is what
will be done;
and there is nothing new under the sun.
      (Ecclesiastes 1:4-9)

No, perhaps there is nothing new under the sun. But change makes it seem new. And no doubt change had occurred in me since last time I'd stood on this summit as well as to those who had climbed to this place both before and since my last coming here. But even change, in the larger sense, is not new. All change is circular: seasons, years, decades, and centuries and even millenniums come and go. Planets, stars, solar systems, galaxies, clusters of galaxies whirl in and out of sight. Maybe even the Universe itself is spinning, holding all of time and matter in its great embrace. Thus do the countless circles of matter and time in this vast phantasmagoria do, indeed, tie the great and small together both objectively and subjectively. For we also, as I reflected on Bob, also come and go—as I know I had to go. I still had a circle to complete, a place to return to and other rounds of responsibilities and work.

Perhaps then pure mathematics does have its applications—but this thought is not new. Mathematicians who have come after Euclid as well as other physicists, engineers and even astronomers have all discovered Euclid's postulates and theorems applicable to the natural world. Euclid, surprisingly enough, also has an application to hikers. The need for order, for a route that ends where it began is a product of Euclid's calculations—though it is not necessarily the result of objective reasoning as much as it is the result of subjective desire: the need to impose order on the unknown. Though Euclid has his place in my mind, it is Ecclesiastes that has its place in my heart. I just like to *feel* a part of the world I turn through more than I like to *know* I'm part of the world I circle over. Perhaps Bob who has completed the much larger circle of life—which is far bigger than any mere hike—could say better than I as to whether or not such a feeling is justifiable or just sentimental nonsense.

Leaving the crest of the summit, I passed over onto the west ridge. Following the ridge's corniced top, I kick-stepped directly down toward the notch until I reached a long snow slope dropping off the south face. From there, after dropping onto the snow, I half skipped and slid back down to the valleys below. Within a half hour, I was down off the steep snow and stomping across the still frozen—but very slushy—surface of Long Lake. Soon, though, I had to put on the snowshoes again to keep from sinking to my thighs.

Then the terns began their slow circling overhead. A few even dive-bombed me, screeching in my ear as they passed angrily by. But being so early in the season, long before their nesting, most were content to just fly menacingly overhead. By the time I reached the end of the lake, I had an escort of a whole flyer squadron of them hovering just off my shoulder. No doubt, they were just as happy to see me finally disappear over the rise in the tundra at the far end of the lake, as I was to leave them behind me.

Now all I had to do was walk out. It wouldn't be easy, though. Instead of descending directly down the valley to where it opened up into the Anchorage Bowl, I had to climb to the top of the ridge above me and to the left. Along the crest of that ridge, I would traverse to the trail's end that would, in turn, take me back to my car.

After a mile or two of hiking down the valley, I turned left and started to climb again. Having been out for over eight hours now, it wasn't as easy a climb as it would've been six hours ago. I had no choice, though. It had to be done. Kicking my way up across firm snowfields and pulling myself up and over matted tundra I climbed slowly but methodically. Sometimes I utilized a snow-filled gully if the snow was firm enough; at other times I climbed rock ribs if the rock was steady enough. Though I was climbing steadily, there were times, being too eager to reach the top of the ridge, that I didn't seem to be making any progress at all. It was like getting caught in a revolving door, or in a film loop.

Eventually and inevitably, I did reach a saddle on that ridge top. From there I could look down once more into the Middle Fork valley I had toiled up just that morning. But I was not going to close the circle of this hike just yet. There were still a few miles to hike before I would come full circle. Turning west down the ridge, I soon found a sheep trail on the southern slope of that rocky ridge just below the crest of the southern slope of the rocky ridge, and marched westward. Passing one flock of sheep, which eyed me nervously as I stepped below them, I marched over two more snowy pinnacles and finally, after one last, short climb, reached a single point where all the ridges converged on the sky— the summit of Wolverine Peak.

The early evening sun shone full on my face and the entire Anchorage Bowl lay before me. At my feet were the first indentations of the trail that would take me down off the mountain's broad west face into the woods far below and back to my car where this day's circle would finally be completed. People, dwarfed on the wide slopes, could be seen moving up and down the thin string of trail in the early evening's hazy light. Even at this distance, no one seemed to be hurrying, no one seemed eager to be anywhere but where they were. No one but me, that is. After almost ten hours, I was ready to go home. Despite the warm sun on my face and a city at my feet, there was nothing I wanted to do more than pass down across the quietly peopled slopes of the mountain above to the green and noisy valleys below—and home, the only place where any circle is ever truly completed.

Middle Fork Trail

Note: The Middle Fork Trail is a pleasant, relatively flat trail that leads up to the shores of the numerous Williwaw Lakes. But the lakes need not be the end of the trail. There is also the option of continuing over the pass just west of Mount Williwaw and down past Long Lake, following the North Fork of Campbell down valley to where a final climb up and over Near Point (or Wolverine itself) connects back to the beginning of the Middle Fork Trail (see Option A). Even this option, though, has other options, such as climbing Koktoya Peak, East and West Tanaina, Tikishla Peak and even Wolverine Peak. Like so many other hikes in the Chugach Mountains, the choices just seem to keep branching outward like the limbs of a sturdy and steadily growing tree.

Trail Location: The Middle Fork Trail begins at a fork in the Wolverine Trail about a mile from Prospect Heights parking lot in the foothills of the Front Range that dominates the eastern horizon above Anchorage. To get to Prospect Heights go east up O'Malley Road from its intersection with the Seward Highway. Follow O'Malley approximately 4 miles to Hillside Road. Go left on Hillside and then take the very first right onto Upper O'Malley Road. When this road ends at a T intersection, turn left onto Prospect Drive. Follow this for a mile to a stop sign. Bear left through the stop sign and in a few hundred yards, on the right, will be the entrance to Chugach State Park. The Wolverine Bowl Trail begins at the far end of the parking lot just to the right of an outhouse and sign board. Follow this 100 yards to a T in the trail. Go right at the T and follow for about a mile to where it descends a small valley, where it crosses the Middle Fork of Campbell Creek over a sturdy bridge and then slabs up the opposite slope.

At the top of this short climb, a sign marks the beginning of Middle Fork Trail on the right.

Trail Grade: The Middle Fork Trail is almost entirely within level 1, with only short sections that climb continuously enough to rank a level 2.

Trail Condition: The lower part of the trail, along an old jeep road, has good footing with only occasional muddy spots. The problem here is that the trail is often overgrown with willow and weeds, that often have to be pushed through like swinging doors for yards at a time. Farther up, after leaving the jeep road, the trail is very muddy until it emerges out of the trees onto the Alpine meadows below the southwest ridge of Wolverine. From here to the trail's second crossing of the Middle Fork, the trail alternates between being very wet and very dry. Even after crossing the bridge and climbing the shoulder on the opposite bank—at the top of which is an intersection with the spur trail that comes from Glen Alps (which is a shorter, though much muddier, alternate route to this point—the trail continues to have long stretches of swamp and mud. Only after winding through acres of krummholtz for the next mile or so, is the mud left behind. From here, the trail stays mostly high and dry on a shelf above the creek.

Trail Mileage: It is 7 miles one way from Prospect Heights to the first of the Williwaw Lakes for a round trip total of 14 miles, whereas the one way trip to the ninth and last lake located just up valley at the base of the west buttress of Mount Williwaw to the north is 8 miles for a round trip total of 16 miles.

Total Elevation Gain: It is a 1,585 foot climb to the first lake, and a 1,805 foot climb to the last lake.

High Point: It is 2,600 feet above sea level at the first lake and 2,820 at the last lake.

Normal Hiking Time: A fast hiker can make the round-trip in 5 to 6 hours whereas those with children or wanting to spend time savoring the going and coming should expect to spend anywhere from 7 to 12 hours.

Campsites: The best campsites are located on the tundra bluffs around the lakes themselves. But do bring a stove because fires are not allowed inside park limits.

Best Time: June to early October are the best times to sit by the rippling waters of the lakes. Though the lakes are frozen to silence in the winter, this valley is still a fine destination for cross-country skiers and snowshoers.

USGS Maps: Anchorage A-7, A-8 NE and SE.

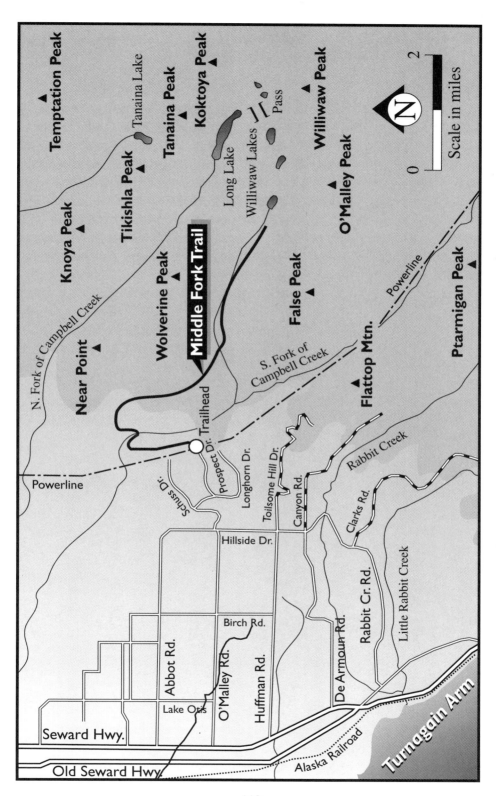

Temptation Peak ▲

Tanaina Lake

Tikishla Peak ▲

Tanaina Peak ▲

Koktoya Peak ▲

Williwaw Lakes
Pass

Williwaw Peak ▲

Knoya Peak ▲

N. Fork of Campbell Creek

Long Lake

O'Malley Peak ▲

Wolverine Peak ▲

Middle Fork Trail

Near Point ▲

False Peak ▲

S. Fork of Campbell Creek

Powerline

Ptarmigan Peak ▲

○ Trailhead

Prospect Dr.

Flattop Mtn. ▲

Rabbit Creek

Powerline

Schuss Dr.

Longhorn Dr.

Toilsome Hill Dr.

Canyon Rd.

Clarks Rd.

Hillside Dr.

Birch Rd.

Abbot Rd.

O'Malley Rd.

Huffman Rd.

De Armoun Rd.

Rabbit Cr. Rd.

Little Rabbit Creek

Lake Otis

Seward Hwy.

Alaska Railroad

Old Seward Hwy.

Turnagain Arm

N

Scale in miles

0   2

OPTION "A"

MIDDLE FORK TRAIL TO THE
NORTH FORK OF CAMPBELL CREEK

Trail Location: Follow the Middle Fork Trail up past the last of the Williwaw Lakes and then keep climbing up the pass to the north. (To get to Middle Fork Trail, see WALK-ABOUT GUIDE TO MIDDLE FORK TRAIL.) The trail-less climb rounds numerous "rosary bead" lakes on its way to the crest of the pass (3,750 feet). From here the route down to Long Lake is rather obvious. At the far end of the lake, continue down valley for another 2 to 2.5 miles before beginning the climbing to Near Point high on the left. From the top of Near Point, follow the trail back down to Prospect Heights.

Trail Grade: Middle Fork Trail varies between 1 and 2, with much more of the former than the later. The rest of the trip is almost entirely level 4, with only an occasional section of level 5 and possibly even a few moments of level 6 on the climb back up to Near Point. The trail leading down from Near Point reverts the hike back to levels 2 and 1, with only short sections of steep downhill hiking.

Trail Condition: There is no trail, but the open tundra over which most of the trip traverses makes for fine footing with only a few spots where scree or rocks are any hindrance at all.

Trail Mileage: The one way distance for the entire traverse is roughly 18 miles.

Total Elevation Gain: 3,550 feet if the chosen route ends with a climb Near Point, and almost 5,000 feet if the chosen route finishes by going over Wolverine Peak.

High Point: The pass below Williwaw is 3,750 feet above sea level, Near

Point is 3,050 feet above sea level and the summit of Wolverine Peak is 4,455 feet above sea level.

Normal Hiking Time: 7 hours to two days depending on the condition and ambition of the hiker(s).

Campsites: Too many good ones to count both around Williwaw lakes, up and over the pass as well as down most of the length of the North Fork of Campbell Creek. But please bring a camp stove because camp fires are not allowed inside of the park.

Best Time: June to September is the best time to make the traverse. It can be done in winter, but avalanches are a very real danger both in the pass and on the climb up the north side of Near Point.

USGS Maps: Anchorage A-7, A-8 NE and SE.

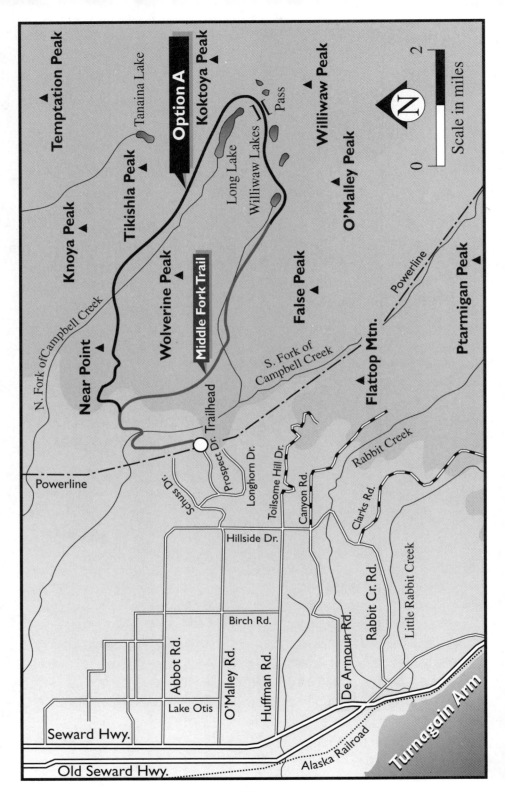

Temptation Peak

Tanaina Lake

Option A

Koktoya Peak

Pass

Williwaw Peak

Knoya Peak

Tikishla Peak

Long Lake

Williwaw Lakes

O'Malley Peak

N. Fork of Campbell Creek

Wolverine Peak

Middle Fork Trail

False Peak

S. Fork of Campbell Creek

Powerline

Ptarmigan Peak

Near Point

Flattop Mtn.

Prospect Dr. Trailhead

Longhorn Dr.

Toilsome Hill Dr.

Canyon Rd.

Rabbit Creek

Schuss Dr.

Powerline

Clarks Rd.

Hillside Dr.

De Armour Rd.

Little Rabbit Creek

Abbot Rd.

Birch Rd.

O'Malley Rd.

Huffman Rd.

Rabbit Cr. Rd.

Lake Otis

Seward Hwy.

Alaska Railroad

Old Seward Hwy.

Turnagain Arm

N

2

0

Scale in miles

Mount Willowaw from the ridge top near O'Malley Peak.

MIDDLE FORK TRAIL TO SHIP
CREEK OVERLOOK AND KOKTOYA PEAK

Trail Location: This option begins at the top of the pass between Williwaw Lakes and the Middle Fork of Campbell Creek and Long Lake and the North Fork of Campbell Creek. (To get there see WALK-ABOUT GUIDE TO MIDDLE FORK TRAIL and OPTION A above.)   From this pass, on a clear day, both the Ship Creek overlook and Koktoya Peak are visible off to the right. To get to the pass—and lose the least elevation in doing so—follow the ridge crest you are on to the right (east) for less than 100 yards until you can see two lakes below and to the left. Descend and pass around the left hand side of both lakes, crossing the second lake's outlet as close to the lake as possible. Once past the second lake, turn due east up the narrow, but wide and shallow alley way that leads up toward the top of the saddle. (One can also ascend directly over the large buttress that rises just to the left of this alley.) Nearing the top of the ridge after a steady .5 mile climb, bear left across the flats toward the lowest point in the saddle, which is located a few hundred yards to the north. From this overlook it is possible to look up and down the length of the Ship creek valley as well as gaze farther inland to the great peaks and perpetual snowfields of the inner Chugach. On a really clear day, one can even see as far as Mount Marcus Baker, the highest peak in the Chugach. One need not turn around here, though. With a little more effort— and a little more nerve—it's very possible to reach the summit of Koktoya Peak (which has an estimated elevation of 5,150 feet) located 3/4 miles up and to the left (north) of the saddle. Staying on the ridge crest, simply begin to climb.

As one gets higher, it will be necessary to skirt around a series of rock gendarmes and cliffs, but by shifting to the shallower slopes on the left, most of these potentially dangerous obstacles are easily avoided. There is also a considerable amount of scree to labor up and over. But with a little perseverance, the summit can be reached. The view is definitely worth the effort.

The return trip for both of these trips can be simply to retrace one's steps back up and over the pass and down past Williwaw Lakes to the Middle Fork Trail. More ambitious hikers may prefer to return by descending past Long Lake, and following North Fork of Campbell Creek down to where one can climb up over Near Point (which is also described in OPTION A).

Trail Grade: The hike from the high pass that separates the drainage of Middle Fork of Campbell Creek with the North Fork of Campbell Creek to the overlook entails mostly grade 4 climbing. The climb up to the summit of Koktoya, however, also rises to levels 5 with even some short sections of grade 6 climbing.

Trail Condition: The hike from the high pass that separates the drainage of Middle Fork of Campbell Creek with the North Fork of Campbell Creek to the overlook above Ship Creek is across mostly open tundra. The climb up to the pass does require crossing some long sections of scree, but none of these are steep enough to cause any real difficulty. The conditions underfoot on the climb up the summit of Koktoya, on the other hand, are very rough and rocky requiring a lot of use of the hands. It also has steeper, more difficult run-outs of scree to clamber up.

Trail Mileage: From the Prospect Heights parking area to the overlook it is 11 miles for a round-trip total of approximately 22 miles. From the Prospect Heights parking area to the summit of Koktoya is just under 12 miles for a round trip total of between 23.5 and 24 miles.

Total Elevation Gain: Hiking from Prospect Heights parking area to the pass above Ship Creek entails a total elevation gain of 4,750 feet. The same hike to the summit of Kokotya Peak has a total elevation gain of 5,400 feet.

High Point: The highest point on the hike to the pass above Ship Creek is at the pass itself, which is 4,455 feet above sea level. For those wishing to go farther, the summit of Koktoya Peak is estimated to be 5,150 feet above sea level.

Normal Hiking Time: The hike to the overlook and back (whether that way back is via the North Fork of Campbell Creek or the Middle Fork of Campbell Creek) should take anywhere from 9 hours to 3 days depending on the ambition and condition of the hiker(s) involved. The climb up the summit of Koktoya and back should take anywhere from 11 hours to 3 days depending, also, on the ambition and condition of the hiker(s) involved.

Campsites: There are plenty of campsites along the whole route. But for those looking for more scenic and remote (hence private), camping, try along any of the "rosary bead" lakes leading up the pass that separates the drainage of Middle Fork of Campbell Creek with the North Fork of Campbell Creek are recommended. The lakes just over the pass at the beginning of the climb up to the overlook are even more remote for those looking to really get away from it all. It is even possible to camp on the wide and flat Ship Creek overlook itself. Some snow tends to linger long up there—sometimes even into August—so there is usually a ready supply of water from which to draw.

Best Time: The best time to do either the hike up to the overlook or the climb up to summit of Koktoya is from mid-June to early September.

USGS Maps: Anchorage A-7, A-8 NE and SE.

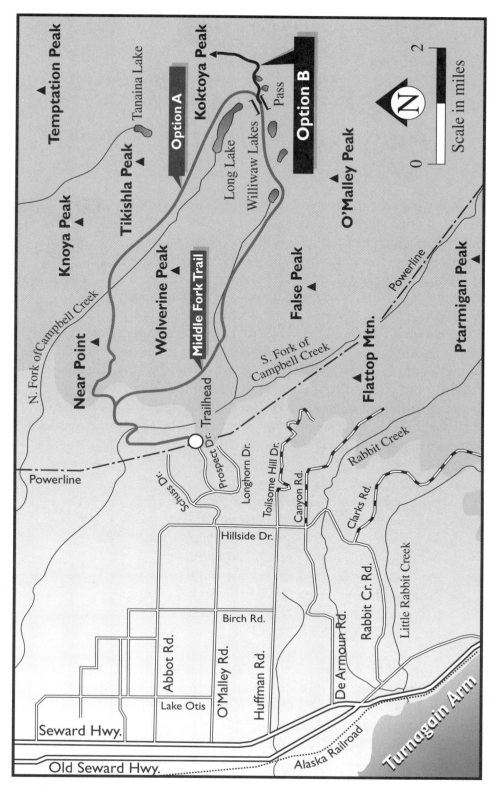

CHAPTER 7

Labor has it's Rewards-Sometimes

I wondered if this was how Sisyphus felt pushing the rock up that slope in Hades again and again, and yet again, as ordained he should for all time? With each step upward through the soft snow I drifted backwards a little bit. With each kicked step higher I slipped back half a step while the shadows of the wind-pushed clouds danced up and down the long slopes of snow around me. I, however, knew that my climb would eventually end. With a little perseverance and a lot of effort I would, in time, reach the top. Sisyphus, on the other hand, for all I knew, would never be finished. Long after I finished my climb, he would very possibly still be pushing that same rock up that same hill in the underworld, just as he has been doing for centuries without change. His labor is the same today as it was when described by Homer more than two and a half millennia ago:

> Then Sisyphos in torment I beheld
> being roustabout to a tremendous boulder.
> Leaning with both arms braced and legs driving,
> he heaved it toward a height, and almost over,
> but then a Power spun him round and sent
> the cruel boulder bounding down again to the plain.
> Whereon the man bent down again to toil,
> dripping sweat, and dust rose overhead.
> (The Odyssey: Bk. XI)

Nor had I been climbing that slope nearly as long as Sisyphus had been climbing his hill. Unlike Sisyphus, who has been climbing for centuries, I had started my climb less than an hour before, after hiking for less than a day. I had come out of the valleys just that morning. Leaving Glen Alps parking area, I had followed Powerline Pass Trail to the Middle Fork Loop Trail. Turning onto this second trail, I followed it down across

Campbell Creek and around the front of O'Malley Peak to where it intersected with the Middle Fork Trail. Turing right onto this third trail, I followed it all the way up-valley to Williwaw Lakes.

Finally, I had been hiking those trails in conditions not at all like the perpetual cold twilight of lifeless Tartarus in which Sisyphus toiled. Instead, all around me on the hike were signs of spring. New buds were already pushing their small green snouts up through the mud along the edge of the swamp-flooded trails. More tentative buds were clinging to the shelter of sun-warmed stones. Bird songs sounded from nearby trees. Farther up the valley, marmot whistles rang from brown tundra hummocks that rose like small islands above the runnels of water gushing out from beneath the scattered snowfields. Even as high as Williwaw Lakes the blue ice of the lakes was dissolving into wind-capped waves. The entire valley was peeling off its blankets of snow and frost and finally waking from its winter sleep, thus beginning another cycle of the seasons.

To a certain extent, every hike is another manifestation of the same cycles that the falling and rising of Sisyphus's rock represents. This is even more obvious in spring—especially if one seeks out the higher elevations. The trails I walked on, like the spring I walked through, only go so high in these mountains before they fade into rock and scree, and snow and ice. And when the trail petered out at my feet, so did the season. Trails, however, like the seasons, are not destinations in themselves as much as they are routes upon which the journey can be made to other destinations. A trail is not an end as much as it is a means to an end, a transition from one place to another—or one season to another.

Some mythologists conjecture that the endless rising and falling of Sisyphus's rock on that hill in the nether-world represents a similar natural cycle. The rock itself then becomes a sun disc and the hill he pushes it up time and time again is the vault of the sky. Such a reading only emphasizes the passage of time through which Sisyphus toils to push his rock up that hill in Hell. Through such symbolism, Sisyphus becomes a dark alter ego of the sun deity, making him a type of underworld Helios. If so, then it is a sun that moves up and down in a world forever devoid of life.

Perhaps this is what makes Sisyphus's punishment so cruel: The season through which he toils never changes. In Hades it is always gloomy and muted, like a windless, cold and cloud-darkened twilight in November. There is no hint of sunlight, no sense of warmth. Ovid in book IV of <u>Metamorphoses</u> refers to it simply as the "Stygian city, the palace of Dis, the dark one."

This was, so aptly stated, not much unlike the day into which I was ascending.

By the time I had toiled like Sisyphus, pulling my sliding feet up past the avalanche debris and embedded rocks of that high snowfield, up to the saddle between Koktoya Peak and Williwaw Peak, I had journeyed back into winter. Spring had fled, chased away by the wind that until then had only been visible in the fleeting shadows of clouds scudding across the snow at my feet. But I didn't know how strong the wind actually was until I crested the saddle and physically came face to face with it—and it nearly knocked me over! Suddenly what would've been nothing more than a strenuous climb up that ridge on any other day, became a cold, wind-battered ordeal. I was willing to embrace that ordeal. In part, because it would be short-lived. Even more so, however, for novelty of the climb itself. The uniqueness of where I was and when I was there made the climb worth *almost* any discomfort.

I would not, for one, have willingly submitted myself to the discomforts of Tartarus, or lower Hades, where according to the Sibyl in Vergil's <u>The Aeneid</u>, those who "dared horrid evil and reached what they had dared" were punished even worse. Aeneas is given an overpowering hint of what went on there merely by what he could see and hear as he is led by it.

> *Aeneas suddenly looks back; beneath*
> *a rock upon his left he sees a broad*
> *fortress encircled by a triple wall*
> *and girdled by a rapid flood of flames*
> *that rage: Tartarean Phlegethon whirling*
> *resounding rocks. A giant gateway stands*
> *in front, with solid adamantine pillars—*
> *no force of man, not even heaven's sons,*
> *enough to level these in war; a tower*
> *of iron rises in the air; there sits*

> *Tisiphone, who wears a bloody mantle.*
> *She guards the entrance, sleepless night and day.*
> *Both groans and savage scourging echo there,*
> *and then the clang of iron and dragging chains.*
> (VI. 725-38)

Fortunately, Aeneas has no reason to enter there. His journey through is down the fork in the highway that leads away from there and toward the twilight fields of Elysium. As they continue, Sibyl names many of those suffering in Phlegethon. Yet, though she does not mention Sisyphus by name, she does name his co-sufferer Ixion, with whom he is almost always paired, followed soon after by a paired description of their punishments.

> *And do not ask me what penalty,*
> *what shape of fate has overwhelmed their souls.*
> *For some are made to roll a giant boulder,*
> *and some are stretched along the spokes of wheels.*
> (VI. 816-19)

But regardless of what punishment the gods mete out to them, Tartarus is not a welcome place. 'Abandon all hope, ye who enter here" Dante would inscribe over its gate thirteen centuries after Vergil. For it is, as Milton says about Hell four centuries later in Paradise Lost, a "bottomless perdition" (I.47).

Waiting for the farther inland valleys to become more passable and the higher mountains of inland ridges to become climbable, I had been exploring the remote and lesser sought-out nooks and bumps of the Front Range—especially that range's far back ridge. More than any other valley or mountain in the Front Range, that back ridge has been my destination this spring. Like a medieval battlement, this impressive escarpment of rock, which extends for close to twenty miles from north to south, has an average height of more than 4,000 feet. Its lowest point is Powerline Pass at 3,550 feet, while its highest point is Mount Williwaw at 5,445 feet. In addition to Mount Williwaw, there are six more towering mountains of over 5,000 feet. From their various summits sheets of snow blow almost continuously in the high, cold winds that beat down upon them from the east and north. The wind, however, is all that passes the broad, two-mile-wide moat of the Ship Creek Valley which stretches along the entire base of the ridge and effectively separates the Front Range from the rest of the Chugach Mountains.

On this day I wanted to traverse the highest and most formidable section of this wall from the Koktoya saddle to Ship Pass, a distance of only about three miles. But what it lacks in distance, it makes up for in difficulty. For those three miles include climbs over Mount Williwaw, the tallest peak in the Front Range and The Ramp (5,250 feet) as well as, between these two summits, an exposed, jagged-toothed ridge that is easily one of the most challenging scrambles within shouting distance of Anchorage. It is also, with the addition of a nine-mile hike in and another six miles out, a remote ridge. I knew when I left the car that it would be a long day.

My long day had been begun by choice, whereas Sisyphus's long days, which followed one after another, for year after year and century after century, and even millennium after millennium forever and ever, were not endured by choice, but were a punishment from the gods.

Mythologists aren't quite certain why Sisyphus was condemned to endlessly push that rock up that hill in Hades. The poet-scholar Robert Graves seems to think it was for merely telling the River-god Asopus where Zeus, who had abducted his daughter Aegina, had taken the poor girl. For divulging this knowledge, Zeus, according to Graves in his two volume work <u>The Greek Myths</u>, "ordered his brother Hades to fetch Sisyphus down to Tartarus and punish him everlastingly for his betrayal of divine secrets." Another reason for his punishment may have been that, despite being a king of Corinth, he had accumulated much of his wealth by robbery and trickery, and often murdered unsuspecting travelers. In a land where hospitality was sacred, this was more than just a moral offense against his fellow humans, it was a sacrilegious effrontery to the gods themselves. So he was condemned to labor day after day for all eternity. For him, there was no longer a beginning, middle or end: there was just the rock and the hill and the slow, incessant passage of time.

Yet as I pushed my way up through the wind along a narrow sheep trail that led toward the summit of Mount Williwaw after already hiking and climbing for more than ten miles—past the last of the Williwaw

Lakes, over the pass leading into the North Fork of Campbell Creek and up that long, tedious snow gully to the thin, wind-blasted crest of that back ridge—I, too, felt the slow passage of time. Even after coming all that way, my long day felt like it was just beginning. Nor did I know what to expect between the summit of Williwaw and the Ramp. I had seen, straining my neck to look up from the shores of Williwaw Lake, the entire length of the ridge—and it did not look inviting. From down there, I could see along almost its entire length massive cornices hanging over the crests of near vertical snow couloirs that fluted downward. Between the cornices, pinnacle after pinnacle of stark, jagged-edged rocks rose in dark silhouettes against the windy, cloud-tearing sky.

After a short, steep climb up some last ledges and across some high, narrow snow fields, I was finally on the summit of Mount Williwaw. From here I was also at last able to get another look—this time looking down—the ridge I wanted to traverse. The Ramp looked temptingly close, only two air miles away. But the ridge in between did not foreshadow a speedy passage. I counted three 200-foot or more rock towers I'd have to climb up and over as well as dozens lesser, but no less sharp gendarmes to either get over or around. It would be, from what I could see, a time-consuming traverse.

After signing the register as apparently the first person to reach the summit of Mount Williwaw that year, I bid farewell to both the summit and (fortunately) the heavy wind and started down the broad scree slope that led to the crux of—and the reason for—this day's hike. Then, after crossing one last level saddle, I was following a sheep trail around the first tower and entering the maze of scree and rock that made up the ridge.

Soon I felt like one of those little bleeps in a computer game trying to wend its darting way through a labyrinth of corridors and tunnels, up ladders and down chutes to some final destination. More than a few times, I had to backtrack down off a ledge or yank and pull myself up some dusty gully of scree and crud, or even daintily step across a boulder where some couloir fell away at my feet in a dizzying plunge. At sea level I would have leapt over such boulders with carefree abandon. But poised over such exposure I stepped over the same boulders with careful deliberation.

There was just enough of both brain and brawn in the scrambling to make it invigorating; and more than enough of a kaleidoscope of views to make it intriguing—which was, in part, because it was so untamed. This was a place in its rawest state without a single trail threading between the rocks and where few people, despite its close proximity to the largest city in Alaska, ever come. The view to the east, across Ship valley to the high, snow-covered mountains that extended without break to the horizon, was intoxicating. The exposure to the west, as I stood looking down the vertical walls to the hanging glacier that gripped the lower slopes and out across the bowl to where the half-frozen, blue waters of Williwaw Lake could be seen beyond the couloir's broad outlet, was exhilarating.

For the most part, though, I stayed in the shade on the less exposed east flank of the ridge where I had more options of climbing up and down to get around the numerous rocks and ledges that blocked my way. Occasionally I had to cross deep stretches of snow or slide down scree, but very rarely did I have to turn around to find another way, whereas, to stay on the crest was to have few or no options. There was no way to climb across any portion of the vertical western slope to get around obstacles; the only way to go to the west was down, straight down—more than 2,000 feet straight down.

I knew, also, that if I had to retreat off this ridge for any reason, that my route would be down toward Ship valley. But if I could make it far enough along the ridge, I would not even have to go all the way to the valley's floor. Once last year I had followed a goat trail leading from Ship Pass to where it emptied out onto some cliffs, so I knew that if I went far enough, I could descend some gully and pick up that trail. When at last I could finally see that ribbon of trail two thousand feet below me on the gentler slopes of the ridge, I heaved a quick sigh of relief. Not only would it, if necessary, save me a considerable amount of time if I had to retreat off the ridge, but it also indicated that I was making progress.

But I had no intention of leaving the climb; nor did I want to finish the climb—not just yet. Unlike Sisyphus, I was content for the time being to labor among those stones along that high ridge. In fact, the sun-splashed ridge top was the most tempting place to be during the climb—despite the wind that swept over its crest from the west. Often I crawled up to the crest just to move for a few steps in that warm light. Nor was I the only living entity seeking out that light: A spider scampered across a boulder, a finch flitted across a narrow ravine ahead of me, and even two small purple mountain harebells shone like two gemstones in a waste of rock. So spring was finally reaching up here with her long, tentative fingers.

If Sisyphus's rock did represent the sun, then somewhere deep in the earth, that poor soul's efforts had once again pushed it to the top of that hill in Hades. Yet though Sisyphus's rock might be reaching its zenith, it did not alter his fate, or that netherworld where that fate unfolded. He and that world were outside the bounds of all natural cycles—including that of the sun itself.

Or maybe his sufferings made him oblivious to that cycle. Perhaps Sisyphus was the ancient Greeks' embodiment of *everyman*, the archetypal human creature that toils day in and day out in a seemingly endless, changeless routine. Through day after day, season after season and year after year in the constant rounds of life and death that are piled one upon another throughout a lifetime, he continues his labors. As Sophocles writes in his play <u>Ajax</u>.

> *Only the base will long for length of life*
> *that never turns another way from evil.*
> *What joy is there in day that follows day,*
> *now swift, now slow, and death the only goal.*
> *I count as nothing him who feels within*
> *the glow of empty hopes.*
> (1. 472-77)

This is, admittedly a very pessimistic—and, some may think, a very unGreek-like view of the world. Yet, though it may seem surprising, the Greeks were dearly in love with life. No one in the Greek world looked forward to death. Even the shade of great Achilles, when told by Odysseus on his journey to the Underworld that his fame was now immortal among the living and that even in Hades his "power is royal among the dead men's shades," could only answer scornfully,

> *"Let me hear no smooth talk*
> *of death from you, Odysseus, light of councils,*
> *Better, I say, to break sod as a farm hand*

> *for some poor country man, on iron rations,*
> *than lord it over all the exhausted dead."*
> (The Odyssey Bk. XI)

This, at first, seems antithesis to the usual depiction of Greek myths with their comely nymphs and quaint shepherds and their handsome gods and beautiful goddesses reclining on their pillowed couches, sipping purple wine from golden goblets on the sunny porches of their home on Olympus. But this sunny picture is actually the false one. The Greeks were a pragmatic people—they had to be, living in the harsh land where farming the stony steep hills was never easy and the nearby sea was always dangerous. Theirs was actually a very realistic view of the world, a result of what in Christian terms is told in the story of Adam and Eve's expulsion from Eden and, in the case of the Greeks, is told through the story of Prometheus's stealing fire from the gods: it is the human's knowledge of the world around him and the self-knowledge of his place in that world.

It is this pragmatic view of his world that resulted in the transcendent beauty, yet always humanistic quality of the art his culture bequeathed to posterity—and which, almost single-handedly, shaped all of western culture. Because for the Greeks, the struggle was everything. Whether it be Odysseus working his slow way home to Ithaca, Leonidas and his small band trying to stem the Persian tide at Thermopylae, Praxiteles chiseling a human form from a marble block, or Pythagoras coaxing natural law from the elements, the struggle was all. That alone gave meaning to life. The struggle gave them joy—albeit, a gritted-toothed joy that smiled less out of carefree happiness than grudging acceptance. This acceptance of what life held in store did have its rewards, however. As Aeschylus, the first great dramatist of western culture, states in his play Agamemnon.

> *God, whose law it is that he who learns must suffer.*
> *And even in our sleep pain that cannot forget,*
> *falls drop by drop upon the heart,*
> *and in our own despite, against our will,*
> *comes wisdom to us by the awful grace of God.*
> (176-80)

Of course, *most* of humankind would rather be happy than wise. But is happiness the same as joy? In writing of Greek drama, Nietzsche defined tragic pleasure as, "the reaffirmation of the will to live in the face of death, and the joy of its inexhaustibility when so reaffirmed." This affirmation only comes through the realization that there is dignity and significance in every human life. This alone brings joy. And in this joy is rooted the source of great art. As Euripides in <u>The Trojan Women</u> makes the old Trojan queen Hecuba say:

> *Yet had God not turned us in his hand*
> *and cast to earth our greatness,*
> *we would have passed away giving nothing to men.*
> *They would have found no theme for song in us*
> *nor made great poems from our sorrow.*

A hike, of course, has no tragic elements in it, and very rarely spawns great art, but anyone who goes on a hike must accept the conditions as they come and take pleasure in the joys that are given— which is sometimes nothing more than suddenly having the goal of the days' labor heave into view.

As I crawled to the top of one boulder, the summit of the Ramp suddenly seemed very close. I felt as though I could reach out over the gulf between it and me and touch it. But though close, there was still more climbing to do; and it was the most difficult scrambling yet with a lot of hand-over-hand maneuvering to get up, over or around the largest knobs I had yet encountered. And as the difficulty increased, so did my anticipation—which only made the summit seem farther and farther away. But the summit was not the next, the next, or even the next pinnacle on the ridge. The end of a journey always seems to be the longest part. I thought about watched pots that don't boil.

But finally, after one last, long pull up a slippery gully, I was at the summit of the Ramp. I have no idea how long the traverse took. Nor do I know what time it was as I stood on the summit. All I knew was that it was late.

According to Ovid, the only time Sisyphus ever rested was on the day Orpheus sang his way through the underworld in his ultimately failed attempt to bring his deceased wife Eurydice back to the world of the living. Then, mesmerized by the beauty of the sad minstrel's song, Sisyphus, like all the other inhabitants of Hades, momentarily forgot his suffering. Like his fellow sufferers Tantalus and Ixion, Sisyphus ceased from his endless toils and "climbed on his rock to listen" (Bk. X).

So did I, also momentarily, climb upon a rock to sit and gaze out on the world around me. Mists were drifting up over Ship Pass below me. The summit of O'Malley, more than a mile down the ridge directly in front of me, was haloed in silver light. Beyond it lay the calm waters of Cook Inlet. Disturbed only by sporadic fine mists of falling rain, it looked like finely pounded gold in the bright light of the sun that, after its long day, was resting beyond the mists and rain on the clouds that skirted the western horizon.

But I could not rest long—not yet. Like Sisyphus listening to Orpheus, my rest was only momentary. I had yet to go down, down to the valleys where I would find the trails that would carry me to home and rest, whereas Sisyphus had to return to his rock and his ongoing labors.

Some slow and dangerous ridge walking in the Front Range of the Chugach.

Middle Fork Loop Trail

Trail Location: This short trail, which connects Powerline Pass Trail with the Middle Fork Trail, begins just a little over a half mile from the start of the Powerline Trail just after that trail emerges out of the woods and turns down the wide road under the powerlines themselves. The sign that marks the beginning of this trail is less than a hundred yards down the road on the left hand side and is clearly labeled "Middle Fork Loop Trail."
The first part of this trail is all downhill to a bridge across the South Fork of Campbell Creek. From here it is all uphill to a fork in the trail. The right hand fork begins the climb up O'Malley Peak. The left fork, which is the Middle Fork Loop Trail, slabs around the front of O'Malley on a fairly level traverse to where, on a small, open knoll, it intersects with the Middle Fork Trail.

Trail Grade: This fairly level trail—with only one short climb up and out of the Campbell Creek basin—is a grade 1 hike from beginning to end.

Trail Condition: Though predominantly flat, this trail is, nevertheless, very muddy—especially along the flats on the north side of Campbell Creek. Anyone hiking this trail should expect to get sucked into any one of numerous mud holes in the trail itself or wet from the swampy tundra on all sides.

Trail Mileage: The distance from Powerline Pass Trail to this trail's intersection with Middle Fork Trail is just over 1.5 miles.

Total Elevation Gain: The total elevation gain, mostly due to the climb in and out of the creek basin, is approximately 150 feet.

High Point: The highest point reached along this trail is 2,150 feet above sea level at the fork in the trail just north of Campbell Creek.

Normal Hiking Time: The hike from Glen Alps parking area to the should take anywhere from 45 minutes to 2 hours depending on the condition and ambition of the hiker(s)—and how much care they take in the futile attempt to keep their feet dry.

Campsites: The best campsite is located on the small knoll where Middle Fork Loop Trail intersects with Middle Fork Trail. Wherever you camp, though, please bring a stove because campfires are prohibited inside park limits.

Best Time: This almost entirely level hike can, because of the minimal avalanche dangers along its length, be done any time of the year. It may even be one of the few trails that is best done in winter—if for no other reason than to avoid the mud and swamps of summer.

USGS Maps: Anchorage A-8.

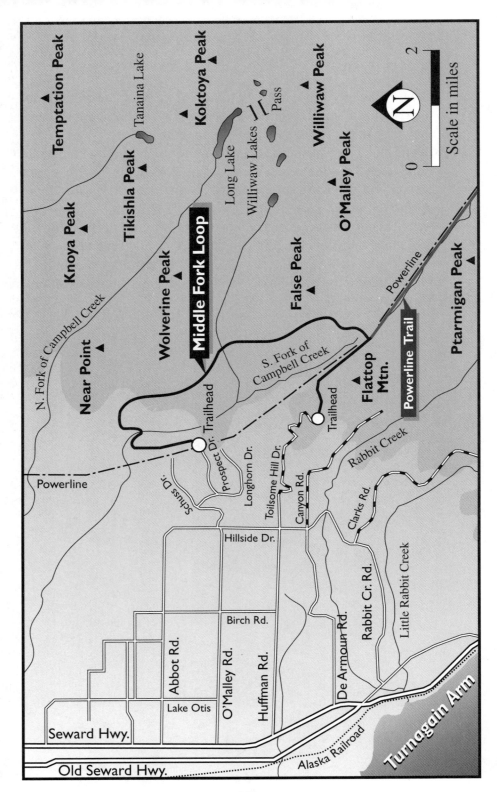

Approaching Peak Two with Ship Pass and Ptarmigan Peak in the background.

TRAVERSE FROM WILLIWAW PEAK TO THE RAMP

Note: This difficult hike is in included this book for two reasons: 1) to give an example of how many variations and options beyond the trails themselves are available in the Chugach Mountains (after all, a trail need only be the beginning of a hike, not the end); and 2) to include a detailed trail guide for the experienced back country traveler and ridge scrambler.

Be warned, however, that this particular variation is recommended only for those strong enough and experienced enough in rock scrambling to negotiate a long, spired and fluted, trackless ridge—and who do not suffer too extremely from vertigo. It is definitely not a trip for beginners or those out of shape.

Trail Location: Follow the Middle Fork to its end at Williwaw Lakes. (To get there, see WALK-ABOUT GUIDE TO MIDDLE FORK TRAIL.) From the lakes, there are two choices: 1) continue straight ahead into the great cirque below the south slopes of Williwaw or 2) continue climbing up and around to the left under the massive west face of Williwaw until the pass above the North Fork of Campbell Creek and Long Lake is reached.

In the first option, which only very experienced and fearless rock scramblers should attempt, the goal is to climb out of the cirque onto the wide plateau just below the summit cone of Williwaw. From here turn right, or south and away from the summit of Williwaw, and continue down the crest of the ridge to the summit of The Ramp.

In the second option, descend from the pass going east, cross in front of the rock glacier and the last steep buttress of the northwest ridge of Williwaw on the right and ascend the first wide gully to the long col between Williwaw to the south and Koktoya to the north. From this point turn right, or south and continue down the ridge, following a goat trail for as long as possible on the climb up and over Williwaw to where this route joins with option 1 on the wide plateau on the southern side of the summit cone.

From here, as in option 1, continue down the ridge to the summit of The Ramp. From The Ramp descend to pick up the Hidden Lake Trail (see WALK-ABOUT GUIDE TO HIDDEN LAKE TRAIL) which can be followed to Powerline Trail (see WALK-ABOUT GUIDE TO POWERLINE TRAIL) and back to Glen Alps parking area.

Trail Grade: From the end of Middle Fork Trail the grade of this hike slowly increases from a 4 up the pass, to a 5 on the climb to the ridge and a grade 6 along the entire length of the ridge to The Ramp.

Trail Condition: From soft tundra to scree, to rock scrambling and climbing—on which some may even find it desirable to have a rope for—this hike/climb has almost every condition underfoot imaginable. There may even be snow and ice in some sections depending on the amount on snow that dropped the previous winter.

Trail Mileage: From the parking lot at Prospect Heights via the cirque on the south side of Williwaw, the one way mileage to Glen Alps parking area is 18 miles, whereas the one way mileage via the north col of Williwaw is about 22 miles.

Total Elevation Gain: From the parking lot at Prospect Heights via the cirque on the south side of Williwaw, this hike entails a total climb of 4,300 feet, whereas via the col on the north side of Williwaw the total elevation gain is just under 6,200 feet. In the reverse direction, from Glen Alps to Prospect Heights, the first option entails a climb of just under 3,000 feet, whereas the second option entails a climb of 4,500 feet. Those choosing the first option should be made aware of the fact that the down climb into the cirque on the south side of Williwaw is very steep and dangerous and might be best avoided by opting for the longer—and relatively gentler—route over Williwaw.

High Point: On the first option, the highest point reached is 5,240 feet above sea level at the summit of The Ramp, whereas the highest point reached on the second option is 5,445 above sea level at the summit of Williwaw Peak.

Normal Hiking Time: Both options can be done in 1 long day or 2 shorter days.

Campsites: There are plenty of campsites around Williwaw Lakes, as well along the base of the cirque on the north end of the traverse, and there are plenty of campsites in the Ship Pass valley on the south end of the traverse, but there are no decent campsites along the traverse itself.

Best Time: This hike/climb is best done from June to September. Avalanches both in the ascending to the ridge and descending from the ridge are reason enough not to attempt this traverse during the winter months.

USGS Maps: Anchorage A-7 and A-8.

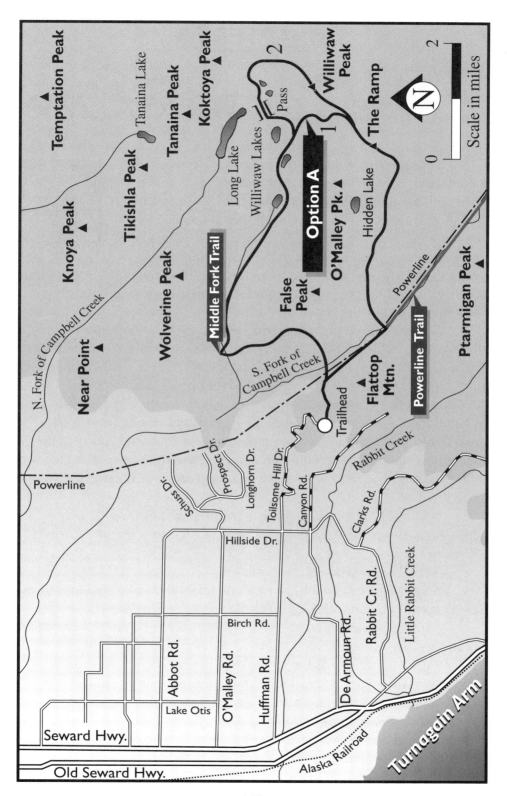

CHAPTER 8

Life is Meeting

Following a bear's flailed path down through wet, eyeball high grass, was not a usual part of my daily runs. Then nothing about this day's run was usual—including the fact that I wasn't even running at the moment. I hoped to be running again soon, though, as soon as I reached the road which was winding through the tree's 300 feet below me. In the meantime, I still had to get myself way down off this last steep, slippery, heel of the ridge I had been following from the summit of Wolverine Peak for the last two or more miles.

So far I'd been pierced by rain, pelted by snow, buried by the clouds and numbed by the wind. My fingers were white, my throat was dry, and I was wet to the bone. Yet, I had never strayed farther than seven miles from downtown Anchorage and never farther than three miles from the nearest road—such as the one now just below me. Regardless of how wet and numb I was, I knew I'd be all-right once I reached that road. From there, I still had a few more miles to survive before I reached the comforts of the car. That would seem easy, though—even easier than the short distance I had yet to climb down to the road. All I had to do was reach the road.

"Geez," I muttered, pushing myself under a wet log, "funny— ugh!—how the simplest trips—ouch!—can turn into some of the biggest adventures."

Then I slipped down some wet grass.

"Aghh! Isn't there a Murphy's law about that?" I asked myself as I picked myself up and stumbled onward.

"Well, if there isn't one—oof!—there oughta be one," I answered as I tripped over another weed-hidden log.

That's the nature of the mountains, though. Even the Front Range right above Anchorage is capable of transforming routine outings into novel experiences—which is what I'd been discovering for years. It's what I was discovering on this day as well.

All I intended to do was run to the top of Wolverine. It didn't seem dangerous or exciting; it was only a way to get in a nice long run in the hills before winter set in. A few changes in the weather and a couple of alternatives in the route, however, along with a handful of moments to stand and stare, had turned my long run into a longer and exponentially more interesting—and more dangerous—adventure.

It was over three hours ago that I parked the car at the pull out located at the north end of Campbell Airstrip on Basher Road. The air was chilly and damp when I got out of the car, but it didn't look or feel like rain. The high clouds were broken by scattered shafts of sunlight. The gray could even burn off and expose the deeper, sharper blue sky beyond.

I still harbored the hope of a blue day for the next hour as I wound through the maze of trails that meander slowly upward through Campbell Reserve to the higher trails of Hillside ski area just to the east. When I emerged from beneath the cover of trees after following Campbell Creek upstream to the gasline right-of-way that cuts at a right angle through Hillside, the sky was noticeably darker. Yet there were still occasional swathes of sunlight highlighting the autumn yellows of the nearby woods and hills. So there wasn't any need for worry—at least not yet. So far it was just like any other autumn afternoon run.

Even as I began laboring up the fall line of the gas line trail through Hillside, the idea of having to worry still hadn't crossed my mind. Despite the fact that the closer I got to the mountains, the heavier the clouds hung overhead, there was no danger; it was still just like any other October afternoon run. With my feet turning in smaller and smaller circles of steps as the trail got steeper and steeper, my hopes had still only sobered to the wish for at least a partially clear day. But the higher I got and the longer I was out, even these hopes began to dim. Finally, when the first drops of rain began plopping onto my nylon parka, even these last hopes were extinguished once and for all. So persistent—or pig-headed—had my hopes become, that I still had to look twice, however, to actually believe there were water drops beading on my arms and crackling on the hard earth and brown weeds at my feet.

Now, for the first time since getting out of the car, I began to worry. It was now obvious that the higher I was getting, the worse the weather was becoming. No longer was it quite like any other autumn afternoon run. It was starting to seem like an adventure.

I wondered what it was like 3,500 feet higher at the summit of Wolverine. If the weather was turning sour down here, it was probably even more unpalatable up there—and in the hour or more it would take me to reach the summit, the weather up there might very well become downright rotten.

For an instant I thought about turning around and retreating to the gentler weather below.

"Why? I can turn around anytime I want," I said to myself out loud. "I've come this far, so I might as well go up and at least have a look for myself."

Once I made that decision to continue, however, I knew my Irish pig-headedness would not let me stop until I reached the summit.

At the top of the gas line, I crossed one shallow ditch, turned left and jogged one hundred feet down the road where I turned right into the Prospect Heights parking lot. This is the trailhead for the climb to the summit of Wolverine, Williwaw Lakes, Near Point and the Glen Alps network of trails as well as an array of other trail-less and trackless ventures.

By the time I turned into the parking lot, the rain had abated—at least for the time being. The clouds had also lifted enough to see what lay ahead—and above—me. As I ran slowly past the twenty or so parked cars, I could see, beyond the end of the parking lot and over the first low, forested hillock to where the wide, western face of Wolverine slanted in a long triangular ramp up to its distant, mist-blurred pinpoint of a summit. Behind it, a dull, monotonous gray washed the whole sky, hiding all else from sight and mind. All that remained was just the solitary mountain in its gray frame of clouds, nothing else.

The dusting of snow which lay like scattered eider down on the highest few feet of the summit pyramid was evidence of winter's presence. I wondered if it was winter up there now, if the mist that obscured the summit was, in fact, falling snow. If so, then this was not going to be a normal autumn hike much longer.

Maybe that's good, I thought as I started running up the trail, better to meet winter now on my terms than later on its terms.

Later would be soon enough anyway—coming as it usually does by mid-October in South-Central Alaska. So I'd decided to meet it now while I still had some control over the choice.

With that decision, made, I was definitely committed. I was going to the summit. And that choice transformed a simple autumn afternoon run into an all-season adventure.

In five minutes I was across the bridge in the hollow of Campbell Creek and jogging up the opposite bank toward the junction with the Middle Fork Trail. Going straight at that trail junction—saving the other trails for other days, other hikes—I continued up the Wolverine Bowl Trail. Ten minutes later I took a sharp right off the main trail—which is, in fact, an old jeep road—and began climbing the steeper and narrower last three mile climb to the summit. Up through willow and alder, spruce and blueberry bushes, the trail ascended more steeply, narrowing toward tree line but always relentlessly going up.

Then the rain started to fall again, a little heavier than before. A cold breeze began to hum through the krummholz and low bushes I climbed between. A chill slithered like a cold snake down my spine.

A couple I passed—only the fourth and fifth people I'd seen so far—remarked about the weather.

"It's probably snowing up there," she said pointing.

"You're probably right," I answered, looking down at my bare legs.

"And it's probably cold up there, too," her boyfriend added.

I looked up at him. I didn't need him to tell me that, but I thanked him for his concern.

"I'll be all-right," I answered.

Then I looked past them up toward the dim summit that sloped up and away from us all.

Would I really be all-right?

"I can always retreat if it gets too bad," I told myself as I went huffing and puffing up the trail again.

"But you're too pig-headed an Irishman to retreat," I answered myself with a breath-labored brogue as I began picking my way with short, narrow strides around the rocks and roots that now hindered the footing on the yet steeper trail.

Cresting the low, central buttress that juts out above tree line from the face of the mountain like a huge jetty, I expected the high, harder winds to begin buffeting me at any moment. If I was cold now, any wind would only make me colder—perhaps even too cold to make the summit. "It would have to be pretty damn cold," my Irish genes answered, "after how far we've come and how little we have to go."

The argument was moot, though. The winds never picked up.

Even as I scurried along the crest of the buttress and began the last, steady climb to the summit ridge, the air remained calm.

But if the winds never picked up, the snow did begin to fall. Within six hundred feet of the summit, I was being pelted by the wet, sticking stuff. The snow soaked my parka and clung to my eyelashes. As I scrambled yet higher, it began turning the trail into a slippery white thread winding through the tufted tundra. I stopped running.

A hoot and a holler from above, though, told me that I was close to the summit. In another five minutes I was there: 4,455 feet above sea level. I wasn't alone. Nor did I expect to be alone, having heard the hoot and holler from above as I climbed the last few hundred yards to get to the summit. A couple, Tim Tucker and Carina Fisher, had arrived there a short time before me. Standing close behind him with her hands tucked underneath his parka to get warm, they stood as one on the highest point of the mountain gazing eastward farther into the mountains.

I hopped up next to them. Now instead of just the two of them, it was the three of us. Standing with our backs to Anchorage, we stood gazing farther into the cloud-darkened wilds of the mountains. Big, soft drops of snow fell on us and around us, covering the rocks we stood on and the mountains we looked out on as well as all the valleys below and melding us together.

Located right next door to the largest city in Alaska, Wolverine Peak is perhaps the second most frequently climbed mountain in South-Central Alaska—and maybe in all of Alaska. Only its nearby neighbor Flattop, located just a few mountains to the south, entertains more hikers and climbers per year than Wolverine. Not today, though.

I hardly noticed as flakes dripped down my face and clung to my bare legs. Other places, other responsibilities, and even other people that call for our attention, that compel each of us to turn away from the landscape before us and begin the long trek back down to the parking lot and home, were forgotten. All that mattered were the clouds, the snow, and the lands and the three people beholding them in all their terrible beauty.

Yes, it was winter up there, but no longer did I care about why or on whose terms the meeting was taking place. Precedence or dominance didn't matter. There was only the meeting, and, as Martin Buber, the twentieth-century Jewish philosopher and mystic said, "All life is meeting." Meeting, as Buber explains it, takes place on those rare moments when we don't address the world as *I-It* or *I-Them*—which are the ways we usually address the people and things we *experience* in our every day lives. The meeting are those rare times when we address the world as *I-Thou*.

There is no magic in relation. It is not an avoidance of the everyday world nor a selfish refusal to accept other forms of knowledge. It is not a form of escapism, solipsism or provincialism. On the contrary, it is all inclusive. Yet it is also a form of mysticism in the purest sense: it is a state of perception which results in a *reciprocity* between two entities.

> *I contemplate a tree.*
> *I can accept it as a picture: a rigid pillar in a flood of light. . . .*
> *I can assign it to a species and observe it as an instance, with an eye to its construction and its way of life. . . .*
> *I can dissolve it into a number, into a pure relation between numbers, and eternalize it. . . .*
> *Throughout all of this the tree remains my object and has its place and its time span, its kind and condition.*
> *But it can also happen, if will and grace are joined, that as I contemplate the tree I am drawn into a relation, and the tree ceases to be an It. . . .*
> *This does not require me to forego any of the modes of contemplation. . . .*
> *Whatever belongs to the tree is included: its form and its mechanics, its color and its chemistry, its conversation with the elements and its conversation with the stars—all this in its entirety. . . .*
> *What I encounter is neither the soul of a tree nor a dryad, but the itself.*
> (I and Thou 57-59)

Then Buber goes on to explain how relation, *actual* life and meeting are interrelated.

> *The basic word I-Thou can be spoken only with one's whole being.*
> *The concentration and fusion of a whole being can never be accomplished by me, can never be accomplished without me. I*

require a Thou to become; becoming I, I say Thou.
All actual life is encounter.
(I and Thou 62)

Or, to translate it slightly differently, *all life is meeting*.

Although I didn't know this when I first got out of the car, this meeting was why I'd come. This is the reason for all adventures. Whether the physical goal is achieved or not—whether a certain mountain is climbed, or that ocean is crossed, or that continent is traversed, determines only the material success of any adventure. Apart from this there can also be a spiritual adventure, and sometimes the success of one does not determine the success of another. They are, instead, usually diametrically opposed. As Emily Dickinson, a woman whose solitary life was full of *meetings*, wrote, "Success is counted sweetest by those that never succeed."

At other times, success and meeting are fused together in a great struggle. George Leigh-Mallory, the first great Everest climber who disappeared near its summit in early June, 1924 and was never seen or heard from again, perhaps said it best: "Have we vanquished an enemy? None but ourselves."

"None but ourselves," I repeated to myself. Only when struggling against great powers—like Mount Everest—do we realize how small and insignificant we truly are. In that humbling realization there can also be meeting.

Me. I had neither struggled greatly or failed grandly. Yet here I was in a time and a place of meeting. I felt very privileged.

Then I shivered. It was time to go.

Instead of taking the same trail down as I took up, I decided to take a different route. I retraced my steps only as far as where the trail turned off the summit ridge and continued down the broad west face. At that point, I continued straight on down the narrow ridge top. Jogging around rock outcrops and hopping down the still spongy tundra, I made fast time to the top of the deep notch that separates Wolverine from Near Point. Here the unstable and slippery rocks on the steep slope forced me to pick my way slowly down the long way to more level ground. From the bottom of the notch, I climbed up and around two more rocky knolls to the 3,000-foot summit of Near Point.

This is where I made my third and final decision that transformed the last vestiges of an outing into a full-fledged adventure. Instead of taking the Near Point Trail back down the parking lot, I decided to bushwhack straight down the west face of the mountain to the neighborhood of Stuckagain Heights. What a mistake!

"It shouldn't be too bad this time of year," Tim had said when I told him I might do it. But bushwhacking is bad all times of the year—it's just that it's worse some times of the year than others. I knew that, too, but it didn't make me alter my decision.

Yes, the late season did allow me to plan my routes better through the leafless copses of alder and willow. Yes, the devil's club and thorny bushes were not as far-reaching as they were at the height of summer. And, yes, there may have even been fewer animals sharing the criss-crossing game trails. But all these positive reasons only made the bushwhacking somewhat easier—which was still not very easy. The grass was still waist high or higher, downed trees and branches still tripped me up, and I still had to push through the green fir and spruce. On top of that, everything was dripping wet.

By the time I reached the road I was a drowned, bruised and a very cold rat. My legs were bloody and bruised, burs and branches hung from my hair and shoes, I was soaked from head to foot and chilled down to the core. It could've been worse, though—it might've been a much longer, colder bushwhack.

The worse was over, though. Now all I had was just a three mile jog back to the car—and it was all downhill. I was—both figuratively and literally—out of the woods. The adventure was over. Now it was just another autumn run again—at least for the time being.

No doubt, I would go back to the mountains soon and no doubt at some time, expect less than what I get, and so, no doubt, end up transforming another outing into another adventure. The Front Range has a way of doing that. The Front Range, however, does not always have a way of hallowing every adventure with a moment of meeting. That, I think, would be to expect too much. For meeting depends more on the disposition of a moment than the expectations of a day. But it is that lucky moment that can make the misery of the rest of the day worth it.

Wolverine Peak

Trail Location: The trail to Wolverine Peak begins at Prospect Heights in the foothills of the Front Range that dominates the eastern horizon above Anchorage. To get to Prospect Heights go east up O'Malley Road from its intersection with the Seward Highway. Follow O'Malley approximately 4 miles to Hillside Road. Go left and then take the very first right onto Upper O'Malley Road. When this road ends at a T intersection, turn left onto Prospect Drive. Follow this for a mile to a stop sign. Bear left through the stop sign and in a few hundred yards, on the right, will be the entrance to Chugach State Park. The trail begins at the far end of the parking lot just to the right of an outhouse and sign board.

Trail Grade: The first mile or so along the initially wide trail is grade 1 hiking. After crossing the bridge over the South Fork of Campbell Creek, it steepens to a grade 2 which it more or less maintains, with only occasional lapses back to level 1, for the next few miles. Even after beginning the climb proper at the sharp right hand turn at mile 2 and 1/3 from the parking lot, the trail only sporadically reaches the difficulty of level 3 with the exception of the final few hundred feet to the summit which is all level 3.

Trail Condition: In that the trail is mostly an old road, the trail conditions are usually excellent. There are some roots, rocks and mud between miles 2 and 1/3 and 3 miles and some sporadic scree and stones above tree line, but overall the footing is good too excellent.

Trail Mileage: The one way hike to the summit of Wolverine is 5.5 miles for a round trip total of 11 miles.

Total Elevation Gain: The hike to the summit of Wolverine entails a climb 3,340 feet.

High Point: The summit of Wolverine is 4,455 feet above sea level.

Normal Hiking Time: 5 to 7 hours or if you prefer to dawdle along the trail and linger over a long lunch at the summit on a nice day, 7 to 9 hours.

Campsites: There are no campsites along this trail to speak of, nor are they necessary considering this hike is usually done as a day hike. However, below tree line there are some meadows off the trail that could provide enough level ground to pitch a tent. But do bring a stove because campfires are prohibited inside park limits.

Best Time: Wolverine is definitely an all-season mountain. Most people hike it from June to September, but the adventurous can enjoy the hard change that winter brings to mountain if they are willing to put up with the usual winter winds and cold. If one stays on the trail, there is little avalanche danger, though it's still steep enough to warrant carrying an ice ax.

USGS Maps: Anchorage A-7, A-8 NE.

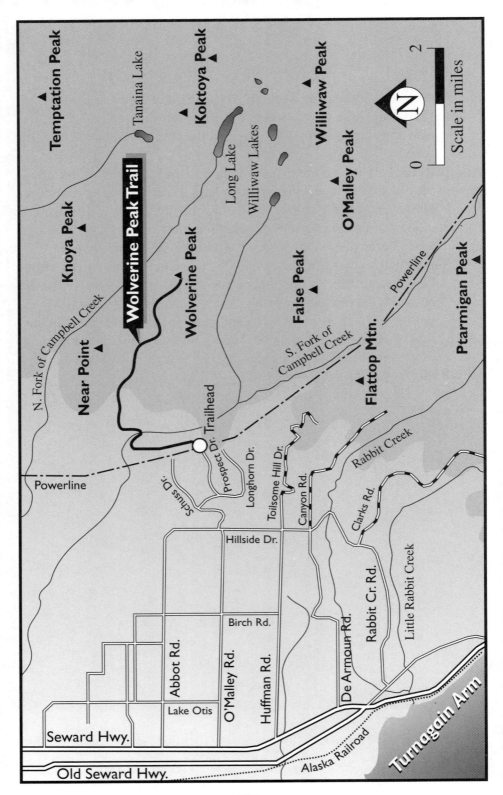

Temptation Peak

Tanaina Lake

Koktoya Peak

Williwaw Peak

Knoya Peak

Long Lake

Williwaw Lakes

O'Malley Peak

Wolverine Peak Trail

N. Fork of Campbell Creek

Wolverine Peak

Near Point

False Peak

S. Fork of Campbell Creek

Powerline

Ptarmigan Peak

Trailhead

Prospect Dr.

Flattop Mtn.

Longhorn Dr.

Toilsome Hill Dr.

Canyon Rd.

Rabbit Creek

Powerline

Schuss Dr.

Clarks Rd.

Hillside Dr.

Birch Rd.

Little Rabbit Creek

Rabbit Cr. Rd.

Abbot Rd.

O'Malley Rd.

Huffman Rd.

De Armour Rd.

Lake Otis

Seward Hwy.

Alaska Railroad

Old Seward Hwy.

Turnagain Arm

N

Scale in miles

2

0

On the ridge just east of the summit of Wolverine Peak with Mount
Williwaw in the background.

Near Point

Trail Location: To climb Near Point, simply follow the Wolverine Trail for the first two miles and where it takes a sharp right hand turn off, go straight ahead. (To get to Wolverine Peak Trail, see WALK-ABOUT GUIDE TO WOLVERINE PEAK.) In less than a mile, this trail will steepen as it begins to switchback up the southwest side of the mountain. From the beginning of the climb, it is a muddy-footed 1.5 mile climb to the top. (For another way to climb Near Point, refer to OPTION A of WALK-ABOUT GUIDE TO MIDDLE FORK TRAIL.)

Trail Grade: The climb up Near Point, which shares the first 2 and 1/3 miles of trail with the Wolverine Peak climb, is a level 2 to level 3 climb

Trail Condition: From where it separates from the trail up Wolverine Peak and up through the first switchbacks, the trail is dry and wide. The higher the trail goes, though, the muddier it gets as it climbs in and out of hollows. Once above tree line, however, the trail is dry once more and pleasantly open with good views of Anchorage, Cook Inlet and Knik Arm to the west and north. From the summit, there are additional views looking east deep into the Chugach to Long Lake, and the summits that rise above and beyond it.

Trail Mileage: The one way climb to the summit of Near Point is a little over 4.7 miles for a round trip total of just 9.4 miles.

Total Elevation Gain: The climb to the top of Near Point entails a climb of 2,050 feet.

High Point: It is 3,050 feet above sea level at the summit of Near Point.

Normal Hiking Time: 4 to 5 hours for most people or—for those with children or a lot of time on their hands—6 to 8 hours.

Campsites: There are no campsites along this trail to speak of, nor are they necessary considering this hike is usually done as a day hike. However, below tree line there are some meadows off the trail that could provide enough level ground to pitch a tent. But do bring a stove because campfires are prohibited inside park limits.

Best Time: Like Wolverine, Near Point is an all-season mountain. Most people hike it from June to September, but the adventurous can enjoy the hard change that winter brings to mountain if they are willing to put up with the usual winter conditions.

USGS Maps: Anchorage A-7, A-8 NE.

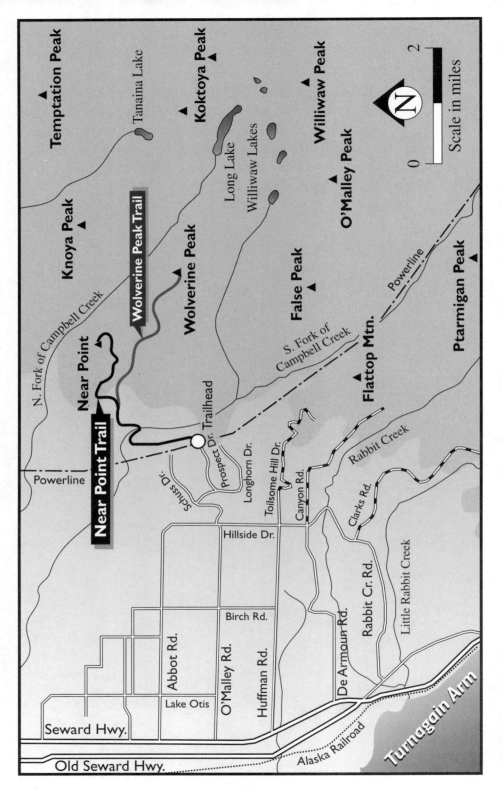

Temptation Peak

Tanaina Lake

Koktoya Peak

Williwaw Peak

Knoya Peak

O'Malley Peak

Long Lake

Williwaw Lakes

Wolverine Peak Trail

N. Fork of Campbell Creek

Wolverine Peak

Near Point

False Peak

S. Fork of Campbell Creek

Powerline

Ptarmigan Peak

Near Point Trail

Trailhead

Flattop Mtn.

Powerline

Prospect Dr.

Longhorn Dr.

Toilsome Hill Dr.

Canyon Rd.

Rabbit Creek

Schuss Dr.

Clarks Rd.

Hillside Dr.

Rabbit Cr. Rd.

Little Rabbit Creek

Birch Rd.

De Armoun Rd.

Abbot Rd.

O'Malley Rd.

Huffman Rd.

Lake Otis

Seward Hwy.

Alaska Railroad

Old Seward Hwy.

Turnagain Arm

N

2

Scale in miles

0

Summit break in the Front Range of the Chugach.

TRAVERSE FROM NEAR POINT TO WOLVERINE PEAK

Trail Location: The concept of this trip is simple: from the summit of Near Point (to get there, see "Trail Location" under WALK-ABOUT GUIDE TO NEAR POINT above), simply continue east along the crest of the ridge to the summit of Wolverine Peak. The ridge will narrow dramatically at times. This may require getting off the crest and slabbing to the right or left just below it, but none of these narrow sections are long or excessively dangerous. In less than 1/3 of a mile, the ridge will rise to go over one more summit (2,963 feet) immediately after which it will drop almost 300 feet to the base of the northwest buttress of Wolverine Peak. Climb directly up the face of the buttress to the ridge top. From the top of the buttress it a little over 1 mile up the ridge to the summit of Wolverine Peak.

　　　(This trip can, of course, also be done in reverse. In which case, the concept remains the same: simply stay on the crest of the ridge.)

Trail Grade: This trip fluctuates between grades 4 and 6. Surprisingly, however, the grade 6 climbing comes very early in the traverse, along the ridge top just to the east of Near Point. The climb up the face of the buttress leans toward being grade 5 while the last mile up the ridge is mostly grade 4 hiking.

Trail Condition: There's a little bit of brush along the Near Point ridge, but most of the traverse is rocky tundra with some scattered patches of scree. Once on the Wolverine ridge there is even a sporadic sheep trail to follow.

Trail Mileage: It is approximately 2.5 miles from the summit of Near Point to the Summit of Wolverine for a total of just under 13 miles to and from Prospect Heights parking area.

Total Elevation Gain: From Near Point to Wolverine Peak entails an elevation gain of almost 1,950 feet for a total elevation gain of 4,000 feet to and from the parking lot. In reverse, from Wolverine Peak to Near Point, the total elevation gain is approximately 500 feet for a total elevation gain of 3,840 feet to and from the parking lot.

High Point: The highest point on this traverse is at the summit of Wolverine Peak which is 4,455 feet above sea level.

Normal Hiking Time: From Near Point to the summit of Wolverine should take anywhere from 1-3 hours depending on the condition and ambition of the hiker(s) involved. This adds up to a round trip total of 7 to 12 hours to and from Prospect Heights parking area.

Campsites: There are no campsites to speak of, though it's certainly possible to pitch a tent almost anywhere on the saddle at the base of Wolverine Peak's northwest buttress. There is, however, no readily available water source here—the nearest being at least a half mile downhill on either side.

Best Time: This traverse is best done from early June to mid-September. Experienced snow climbers and mountaineers, however, may find this easily accessed traverse worthwhile to do any time of year.

USGS Maps: Anchorage A-7, A-8 NE.

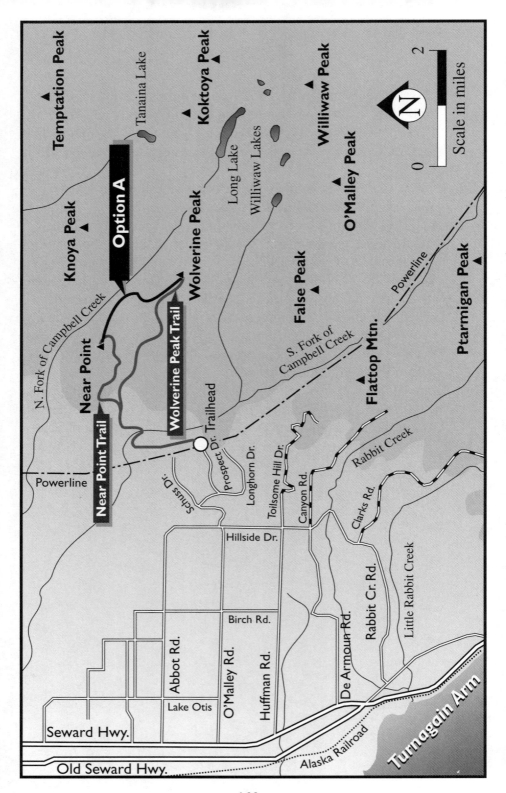

Temptation Peak

Tanaina Lake

Knoya Peak

Koktoya Peak

Williwaw Peak

Long Lake

Williwaw Lakes

O'Malley Peak

Option A

Wolverine Peak

False Peak

Near Point

N. Fork of Campbell Creek

Wolverine Peak Trail

Powerline

S. Fork of Campbell Creek

Flattop Mtn.

Ptarmigan Peak

Near Point Trail

Trailhead

Powerline

Prospect Dr.

Rabbit Creek

Schuss Dr.

Longhorn Dr.

Toilsome Hill Dr.

Canyon Rd.

Clarks Rd.

Hillside Dr.

De Armour Rd.

Rabbit Cr. Rd.

Little Rabbit Creek

Birch Rd.

Abbot Rd.

O'Malley Rd.

Huffman Rd.

Lake Otis

Seward Hwy.

Alaska Railroad

Old Seward Hwy.

Turnagain Arm

N

Scale in miles

0   2

Blueberry picking in the Bold Peak valley.

CHAPTER 9

The Ying and Yang of it

The rain froze to hard sleet as we stumbled upward, skirting the cracked, fluted spires and the massive, eroding columns of unstable rock that rose like the ruins of an ancient ransacked fortress along the crest of the summit ridge. The scree we slipped and clambered over was the crumbling masonry of those ruins. We  pulled our hoods tighter around our faces as the sleet continued clattering against the rocks above us and bouncing off the rocks below us.

"Only in Alaska," I heard Tucker mutter in front of me as he continued to pick his way through the shifting slope of boulders at his feet.

I only nodded in agreement, lifting my head up and down under my stiff hood with sober emphasis.

Tucker didn't notice that I hadn't answered—he didn't even turn around. Why should he? He didn't expect an answer. There are simple certain facts that are irrefutable.

In Alaska in the mountains anything is possible at any time of the year. Even though it was July 29, a day in the middle of Alaska's all-too-brief summer, that made no difference. Summer in Alaska, after all, is not a season as much as it is just a period on the calendar—a period which often has little to do with the mildness or severity of the weather. The conditions are simply not always dependent on what month it is in any given year. The distinction between the seasons and their weather becomes more blurred the farther one goes north in the state or the higher one goes up in the mountains. Once over 5,000 feet in the Chugach Mountains, for instance—which is where we happened to be—the condition can be any thing on any day in any season. So being somewhere high up on the summit ridge of Mount Tikishla was sufficient enough explanation for the severity of the weather of that particular day.

As Confucius wrote in <u>The Analects</u>, "If a man does not have long-range considerations, he will surely incur imminent afflictions." Confucius (551-479 B.C.), whose philosophy is more practical and ethical than it is religious, was speaking of preparation:

> *In all matters success depends on preparation; without preparation there will always be failure. When what is to be said is previously determined, there will be no difficulty in carrying it out. When a line of conduct is previously determined, there will be no occasion for vexation. When general principles are previously determined, there will be no perplexity to know what to do.*

The word prepare originates from the Latin word *praeparare*, meaning to equip. According to <u>The American Heritage Dictionary</u>, the primary meaning of the word *equip* is "to supply with necessities such as tools or provisions." For Confucius, *equipping* someone meant, furnishing that person with the mental qualities necessary for performance.

In any hike, it is, of course, important to be mentally prepared for any difficulties that may be encountered, but without physical preparation any mental preparation becomes moot—especially on any hike into the mountains of Alaska. We knew the *afflictions* that one can encounter in these mountains and, following the old Boy Scout adage of "be prepared," we *were* prepared—prepared for anything, from a blizzard in July to a flood in December. Carrying full day packs, we each had the food and gear to survive almost any conditions that swooped down from the sky above or reared up from the land below.

We also knew that the weather was not the only difficulty to contend with when climbing Tikishla. Though Mount Tikishla is easy to see from almost any vantage point in the Anchorage Bowl (it is the prominent spire on the ridge just north of Wolverine Peak), there is nothing easy about hiking to it or climbing it. Not only is it tall—its summit being 5,150 feet above sea level—but it is also far removed from any trailhead. Furthermore, there are no trails that come in close proximity to the mountain, nor are there any trails on the mountain to make the climb itself any easier. There's no human foot trail, game trail, or even a decent sheep trail anywhere on that mountain. It is, indeed, by

Front Range standards, an isolated mountain that takes a long time to reach and a difficult mountain that takes a lot of work to climb.

But just because the mountain is a little more inaccessible and more difficult to climb, and a little taller than most doesn't mean that it's not worth climbing. I'd actually stood on Tikishla's summit three times prior to this climb with Tucker. And just as varied as the times I'd stood on that summit, were the routes I had taken to approach that mountain. For though the mountain is a long, hard climb, there are as many ways to get to Tikishla as there are points on a compass. None of these approaches from any direction were, as would be expected, easy. All entailed long hikes and gains of many feet in elevation.

Tucker, Jenny and I boldly, but not very intelligently, had chosen to begin our climb from one of the farthest and lowest trailheads in relation to the summit. (Jenny, though, really can't be blamed. She, being a dog—an Australian Cattle Dog to be exact—was only an accessory to Tucker's and my not very intelligent decision.) From the corner of Muldoon and Tudor roads where we began, the summit is more than six and a half unswerving, straight-as-the-crow-flies miles away—miles which don't take into account a turn in the trail, a bend in the ridge, or the amount of climbing involved in getting to that summit. Not being crows, we had, from the moment we stepped out of the car, more than eight miles of trail and rough ground to cover and over 4,800 feet to climb to get to the top.

There was a blessing to the route Tucker and I had chosen, though. If you know how to find the way, a fine network of trails will eventually carry the hiker all the way to tree line—and even a little beyond—thus saving miles of slow, hard bushwhacking. For myself as well as for Tucker, such a trail was so precious that it might as well be paved in gold. To have a track already beaten through the lower forests and the higher brush was wellworth a few extra feet to climb and a few extra yards to walk—even if these extended into thousands of extra feet to climb and thousands of extra yards and even miles to walk. Bushwhacking to both of us was *that* time-consuming and *that* heart-breaking.

Not exactly up with the sun, we parked Tucker's van in the parking lot of the small shopping plaza at the far east end of Tudor Road at 10:30 on that July 29th morning at the height of summer, and crossed the road to the power lines that parallel the road. We then followed these powerlines due east for less than a mile to where they intersected with another line of larger, more potent power lines. Then we turned right (southeast) onto the dirt road that followed the broad right-of-way under these power lines up toward Powerline Pass.

We weren't going to Powerline Pass, though. Within a mile, just after passing the first gas line substation situated under the power lines, we turned sharply left onto a much narrower path which within a few steps ducked through a cave-like opening into the woods. We then followed this trail for less than a half mile to a gravel road. Turning left onto the gravel road, we walked for another two hundred yards or so to where another trail—which appears to be an old jeep road—diverged on the right. This was the trail up to tree line.

For an hour or more we followed this last and longest trail as it wound like a great coiling snake up through the forest. Yet for all its twists and turns, it still wound steadily upward to where the green, spangled hardwoods of the lower elevations gave way to dark spruce and bright birch which, in turn, gave way to willow and krummholz which, finally in their own turn, dwindled to the tufts of grass and sporadic brush of the treeless tundra on the summit of an open, rounded knoll. Some people know this knoll across the valley to the north of Stuckagain Heights as Ice Cream Cone and some people know it as Baldy. Whether either of these is an official name, I don't know. All I do know is that when Tucker and I reached the top of that rounded knoll, we were above tree line—which was all *we* needed to know.

Reaching tree line in the Chugach is always a major milestone. Even on this day, inspite of the long way we still had to go, it was definitely a milestone. For now we were at last on the threshold of the high mountains. From here the world rose wide and open before us. From this point upward there were only tundra slopes, rocky cliffs, snow-filled gullies and the single summit moving against the perpetual sky.

On rare, calm days the landscape above tree line opens up like a serene sixteenth-century Dutch landscape painting—something by Vermeer, Cuyp or van Ruisdael—with a serene blue sky bathing broad, sloping meadows and calm harbors in long, radiant rays of golden light. On more common days when the wind is up and the clouds are down, the landscape above tree line is more like a nineteenth-century Romantic painting—something by Turner, Delacroix or Bierstadt—with a raging ocean bursting against the rocky bastions of magnificent cloud-piercing summits.

Unfortunately, when we arrived above tree line, we found ourselves on the edge of one of those more common days of raging wind and billowing clouds. From as far as we could see to our left on the north to as far as we could see on our right to the south, we were confronted with the fearful beauty of Bierstadt's mountains wrapped in the stormy unrest of one of Turner's skies. And they were really close—not more than two hundred yards away. There, where the ridge rounded off a few hundred yards above us, a gray, soupy maelstrom of dark clouds hid almost everything beyond from human perception.

Not only that, but turning due east to follow the ridge as it arched up over that next rounded mound, we found ourselves heading right into the heart of that maelstrom. North to our left and south to our right, long slender ridges extended from the clouds like prows of mammoth rock jetties into the surprisingly clear Anchorage Bowl behind us. All that was visible in front of us, though, was the jagged, towering heights of a few high ridges and the spired summits of the highest mountains rising above that gray sea of turbulent clouds. It was a terribly magnificent sight.

It wasn't windy or violent as we toiled up the flank of the first knoll on the ridge. But the cold, wet mountain air that hit us head-on as we topped that first knoll gave us a not very subtle hint of what lay in wait in the clouds still above and beyond us. Suddenly late July felt like early October.

> *Teselu came to Confucius with evident anger in his face and said, "Does a gentleman sometimes find himself in adversity?" "Yes," replied Confucius, "a gentleman also sometimes finds himself in adversity, but when a common man finds himself in adversity, he forgets himself and does all sorts of foolish things."*
> (from The Life of Confucius by Szema Ch'ien)

In his work Tao-te Ching ("Classic of the Way and Its Virtue"), Lao-tzu (570?-490? B.C.), a contemporary of Confucius, preaches the same thing, only in a much more round-about way:

The Sage:
Manages affairs without action;
Preaches the doctrine without words;
All things take their rise, but he does not turn away from them;
He gives them life, but does not take possession of them;
He acts, but does not appropriate;
Accomplishes, but claims no credit.

This seemingly contradictory and other-worldly doctrine preached by Lao-tzu may, at first glance, seem the exact opposite of the matter-of-fact philosophy taught by Confucius. Yet Lao-tzu's mystic *Sage* has many similarities to Confucius's pragmatic *gentleman*. This becomes more apparent when Lao-tzu is approached through the writings of his spiritual disciple Chuang-tzu (370?-301 B.C.):

Thus those who say that they would have right without its correlate, wrong, or good government without its correlate, misrule, do not apprehend the great principles of the universe, nor the nature of all creation. One might as well talk of the existence of heaven without that of earth, or of the negative principle without the positive, which is clearly impossible. Yet people keep on discussing it without stop; such people must be either fools or knaves.

Or to put it in the terms of western Christianity, how can we know good unless we know evil? (This was the reason Adam and Eve *had* to eat the so-called forbidden fruit and fall from the garden.) Similarly, how could Tucker and I know a *good* day from a *bad* day, or a *dangerous* day from a (relatively) *safe* day unless we had experience of both? Having that knowledge was the only way we could have possibly prepared for the possibilities of what lay ahead. And we could only prepare properly by fully accepting—even expecting—any and all possibilities.

Both Confucius's gentleman and Lao-tzu's sage "apprehend the great principle of the universe" which is based on polarities—not to be confused with the western concept of opposites—which affects every life and which therefore, must be accepted without any qualifications or

173

reservations.

The moral man conforms himself to his life circumstances; he does not desire anything outside his position. . . . Finding himself in circumstances of danger and difficulty, he acts according to what is required of a man under such circumstances. In a one word, the moral man can find himself in no situation of life in which he is not master of himself.
(Confucius)

Tucker and I, finding ourselves in "circumstances of [possible] danger and difficulty," might have desired to conform ourselves to different circumstances, but we also knew that if we were going to climb Tikishla it was necessary to "act according to what is required" in response to the circumstances—however unfavorable and unwanted they may have been—or not only lose mastership of our lives, but maybe even our lives themselves.

Our first priority was to prepare our bodies—which was the easy part. Huddling behind a couple of boulders for protection, we began shuffling through our packs for wind suits, mittens and hats.

Next, and much harder, was preparing our minds.

"This isn't going to be much fun," Tucker remarked as he pulled on his wind pants.

I couldn't disagree with him.

According to Chuang-tzu, "not to allow external events to injure one's mind is called whole." This, however is much easier said than done. The weather, after all, determined not only our immediate moods, but could also easily alter the outcome of the entire day. Whether or not we could even climb the mountain was now in doubt.

Nature says few words:
Hence it is that a squall lasts not a whole morning.
A rainstorm continues not a whole day.
Where do they come from?
From Nature.
Even Nature does not last long.
(from the Tao-te Ching)

174

No, Nature, meaning the world we live in, will not *last long* in relation to the greater scheme of things. In that the sage is right. Squalls, however, do last *a whole morning* and rainstorms do continue the *whole day*—and may even continue for many days. Tucker and I had both experienced such squalls and rainstorms—and such snowstorms and blizzards as well.

"At least it's not raining on us," I remarked as we started once again up the ridge.

"No, not yet, at least," Tucker answered.

I wondered, thinking of Chuang-tzu, if that was the response of an *uninjured mind*.

Then the still, damp air was suddenly broken by the thudding blades of a whirring helicopter that swooped like a great bird of prey over the crest of the hillock above us. It descended in a rush over our heads, turned once and then climbed back over the summit mound above where it settled out of view as if it was landing. Suddenly forgetting the clouds gathered above us and the winds circling around us and even the climb still ahead of us, we lurched up the trail after it.

"Wow!" was all I heard Tucker marvel as he chased the helicopter up and over the next knoll.

'Amazing," was all I thought as I hurried up the hill behind him.

It's amazing, the ease with which modern man can travel, when he wants to, to even the most inaccessible and wild places. Here Tucker and I were, having plodded upward for two hours or more to reach a single point above tree line, the same point a helicopter, beginning more than five miles farther away, climbs in a matter of minutes.

I wondered if those inside the helicopter shared with Tucker and me the amazement regarding the time and place we had all come together. I wondered if they felt same overwhelming awe before the cloudy powers above us, the same fearful delight in scanning the rocky peaks around us, and the same satisfaction looking back on the clear valleys behind us. Or, I wondered, did their lack of effort to get to this place at the same time Tucker and I in any way lessen their appreciation of it.

I wondered, but I knew I'd never know the answer for sure. Appreciation is not a measurable commodity. Oh, one can say that one likes something while someone else may say he doesn't like that same something. But who can measure the abstracts such as like and dislike?

Elizabeth Barrett Browning may claim she can "count the ways" of her love, but can she? Can one measure love the way one measures a door frame or weigh a loaf of bread? And if two people exclaim their wonder at the same object, can one actually say that one person's appreciation is better than another's? One may shout his wonder louder or another may define his appreciation more eloquently, but does this make his wonder and appreciation greater than anybody else's?

And how does one measure and compare the different responses of various cultures? Lao-tzu, thought that silence was the best sign of appreciation. (He actually didn't even consider the written word adequate to convey his true regard or understanding of anything!) Westerners, on the other hand, show their appreciation in the concert hall by the amount of noise they make. Usually this is followed by a plethora of glowing words in the press.

It's true that many westerners also show their appreciation and wonder by silence. But this usually occurs only when they wish to show their appreciation for an inanimate plastic or graphic art work, such as a painting, sculpture or even a movie. Under these circumstances, usually a single, "Wow," or "Ahh," or, at the most, "Isn't that interesting," or "Isn't that beautiful" are considered sufficient praise. Silent awe is also the usual response to any natural wonder, whether it be in admiration of the panoramic landscape or in surprise to a wild animal. But just imagine if a live performance was greeted in a similar fashion. What would a musician or actor performing in Carnegie Hall or on Broadway think if a masterful and passionate performance was greeted by a room full of silence and a blank page in the news paper?

But no matter how wonder and appreciation are expressed, they are incalculable. Wonder as a concrete entity is elusive and ineffable and therefore, in the end, ungraspable. Attempting to measure and weigh it is as futile as attempting to understand the Tao through mere words:

> The Tao that can be told of
> Is not the Absolute Tao;
> The names that can be given
> Are not Absolute Names.
>   (from the Tao-te Ching)

I would like to believe, however, that the greater the effort, the greater the reward. It would seem only natural that the greater the physical and/or mental effort put into any task is rewarded by a corresponding amount of joy at the completion of that task, whether that task is painting a picture, writing a book or running a marathon, or even grocery shopping. In other words, satisfaction has a distinct correlation to time and effort; they are, in fact, mutually dependent.

Yet whether the greater and longer effort Tucker and I made to reach that high knoll made our appreciation and wonder of that wild landscape greater than the crew of that helicopter is, in the end, moot. None of us could pour our wonder into a cup to measure it or put it on a scale to weigh it. Yet we still felt it.

> *That is why it is called the Form of the Formless,*
> *The Image of Nothingness.*
> *That is why it is called the Elusive:*
> *Meet it and you do not see its face;*
> *Follow it and you do not see its back.*
> (from the Tao-te Ching)

Rushing ahead, anxious to find out what happened to the helicopter, I was just rounding the crest of the summit mound behind which it had disappeared when the whirring accelerated dramatically and the helicopter suddenly lifted over the hill's brow directly in front of me like a lugubrious raven. It hovered momentarily face to face with me, turned once and then darted downward over the sloping tundra into the bowl below. I have to admit, I envied the thrill of such a ride.

Another half hour of steady climbing brought Tucker, Jenny and me to the ridge top on the east rim of the huge hanging valley that cuts a great gaping hole in Tikishla's southwest flank. The rocks at our feet fell steeply to the broad, smooth meadow of the valley below only to rise more steeply and more dramatically to the Tikishla's southwest ridge proper. Somewhere in the clouds above and beyond that rose the yet invisible summit.

Yet, for a moment, how near or far the distance to the summit was didn't matter. We squatted on some rocks with the apparent intention of choosing a route, but that was just an excuse to drink in the mystery and magnitude of the scene. Tucker pointed to a flock of sheep moving against the darker slope a half mile below us. I saw a raven gliding against the lighter clouds a few hundred yards above us. From the depths of the valleys below there floated up to us the rhythmic but faint rumble of rushing water. From across the ridges above blustered the loud, but sporadic wind.

Yet neither the sights we saw nor the sounds we heard seemed quite real. Instead, the gossamer mists moving over the valley and threading across the opposite slope lent to the entire prospect the uncertainty of a dream. Then even that uncertain dream disappeared. As we sat and watched, greater masses of dark mist pushed over the northwest ridge up valley from us. They spilled in tumbling heaps into the valley below and began filling it quickly until the entire valley was nothing but a stirred cauldron of gray, heavy soup. In a matter of moments, everything but the slope immediately falling away at our feet was lost from view. Tucker gasped beside me.

At least by that time we had chosen our route. It may not have been the best of choices, but it was ours and based on the simple premise that we did not want to lose any of the elevation that we had already worked so hard to gain. What we decided was to slab across the slope we were on until we reached the north ridge at the upper end of the valley. From there we would climb that ridge's jagged back up to the summit ridge. It might not have been the easiest route, but it did seem the most expeditious—though in retrospect, I now wonder if that was so.

There was no time to wonder, however. We had chosen our route, and now being able to see no other, had no choice but to adhere to that choice.

Then it started to rain. As soon as we rose from our rocky seats, the first splattering drops were falling on our parkas and splashing in the dirt at our feet.

"Well, I see we don't have any choice about the weather either, do we?" Tucker smirked grimly.

Nature is unkind:
It treats the creation like sacrificial straw dogs.
          (from the <u>Tao-te Ching</u>)

This does not mean Nature is malicious or evil-minded. Nor does it mean that if Nature were not unkind, it would be kind. Instead it means that lacking kindness, it lacks all human characteristics. Nature is, in fact, impartial and impersonal in its workings. Like the old man who survives the cataracts, it merely, as the contemporary adage says, "goes with the flow." It goes with the flow of itself. Man, being part of the *li* of the Tao, must, also like the old man "go with the flow":

> *To adjust oneself to events and surroundings casually is the way of Tao.*
> (Chuang-tzu)

Well, I don't know if we were *casual* about adjusting ourselves to our surroundings, but we were certainly willing, as Confucius says, to *act according to what is required.*

Slabbing, or moving across a slope at an approximately right angle to its fall line, is never easy. It's hard on the ankles and on the sense of balance. The ankles have to bend sideways to accommodate the angle of the slope and allow the feet to fall flat-footed. This awkward stance affects the sense of balance as the body, in turn, tries to remain upright. The resulting gait can make the ankles throb in a very short time and cause the body to sway unsteadily from the very first step. The discomfort and difficulty is further increased if the slope is steeper or if the ground is uneven or unstable underfoot.

Luckily the slope we slabbed across above the valley was not exceptionally steep. It was, however, littered with unanchored boulder and gullies of loose scree which made for treacherous footing. The spitting, sporadic rain which had started almost as soon as we rose from our rest—and which would be just the first of many we would work beneath during the course of the day—only made matters worse. Not only were rocks loose, but now they would be slippery as well. These were not, to say the least, ideal conditions for traversing a slope.

We must have looked like a couple of late-night drunks weaving home from the local pub as we made our stumbling, slipping and sliding way across the ridge's face. It couldn't be helped, though. The slope was so slick and unstable that it was it was difficult to stay upright for any more than two consecutive steps. With every step the feet slipped and slid on the loose stones and slick mud. Nor could we pause for even a change of mind between steps. If we did, we'd be carried three or four feet downward by the loose-rocked slope. So we just kept moving and stumbling and bumbling across. Occasional respites were given by rooted tufts of grass from which we could catch a breath while looking out over the misty route ahead. But these small islands of firm earth were few and far between on the rocky currents of that shifting slope.

Our hair hung like wet string. Our breaths rose like fog. Our clothes clung to us in wet, dripping clumps. Our shoes were caked in mud.

"Ugh!" Tucker groaned as he slid off of a rock and landed on his rump in the wet dirt.

"Argh!" I answered as I slipped off some wet grass and stumbled two steps forward before falling on my hands to break my fall.

And still the rain continued to patter down around us:

The Heaven and Earth join,
And the sweet rain falls,
Beyond the command of men,
(from the <u>Tao-te Ching</u>)

Though *noisome* was perhaps a better word than *sweet* to describe our opinion of the rain, we both knew it was indeed *beyond the command of men*. Otherwise, we would've called on it to stop. As it was, it had been just another thing to prepare for beforehand and another thing to accept along the way.

Halfway across the valley a clearing wind disrobed the summit far above us of clouds and afforded us just enough time to double-check before we bent our heads once more to the rocks under our feet. The next time we looked up, the summit was once again hidden in clouds.

A half hour of lurching and lunging across the slope brought us— at last—to the saddle of the north ridge across which should've been seen the rising mass of Temptation Peak. But no peak was visible on this day. Instead, a swirling mass of clouds ebbed at our feet hiding the valley that should've been below us and the summit that should've towered above its far side.

"C'est la vie," Tucker said shaking his head.

We both knew the mountain was there. That we couldn't see it, didn't mean it didn't exist. It would have been nice to see it, but it was not to be. It was just another thing to accept on this day.

With no view to dawdle over, we turned once again to our climb.

Hand over hand over cold, wet stones and broken scree we climbed. Pushing ourselves up narrow gullies and pulling ourselves up muddy chimneys, clawing around outcrops and crawling across short cliffs, we moved upward without rest from our labor. Not until the steep ridge we were on finally intersected with the summit ridge and rounded off to a gentler grade did we finally take a quick rest from our labor.

But neither the rest itself nor the fact that we were on the summit ridge meant that we were even close to the end of our labor.

If anything, the climb became more labor intensive. For now, instead of using just simple brute strength, we also had to utilize some of the gray matter between our ears in deciding which one of the five or six rocky miters along that long ridge was the actual summit. Trying to decipher the proper perspective in the foreshortened ridge was difficult enough, but trying to do it through the fluctuating veils of mist of rain made it well-nigh impossible.

"Well, let's just keep climbing all of them until we're sure we're on the right one," I suggested. "There's got to be a marker or something on one of these to indicate the summit."

Jenny looked up at me and tilted her head.

"Well, if nothing else we'll know we're there when we're looking down on everything else."

Then Jenny turned to look at Tucker.

"Okay," Tucker acquiesced reluctantly.

We climbed the first pinnacle. It wasn't it. From it, though, we realized that we could skirt the second and try the third. Another spire farther down the ridge did appear taller than the third, but we couldn't say for certain. The only thing we knew for certain was we didn't want to do any more work than was absolutely necessary. So instead of skirting all the way down the ridge to that distant spire, we gambled that we were being deceived by some atmospheric sleight-of-hand and bypassed only the second spire. If the third spire wasn't it, then we'd try that more distant one.

According to both Confucius and Loa-tzu, preparation is primarily mentally planning ahead. But what we previously determine to say to a child who is late getting home can suddenly become sadly irrelevant if it's later learned that the child is late because he or she was in an accident. And a route we previously determine to take can suddenly become impassable if a bridge is out or an avalanche blocks the road. And what if none of the spires on the ridgetop ahead of us was the summit proper? External forces can, after all, disrupt any previously determined plans. Is it possible to prepare for such external chances and changes of fortune?

Confucius thinks so:

Being true to oneself is the law of God.
To try to be true to oneself is the law of man.
He who is naturally true to himself is one who, without effort, hits upon what is right, and without thinking understands what he wants to know, whose life is easily and naturally in harmony with the moral law. . . . He who learns to be his true self is one who finds out what is good and holds fast to it.

Learning to be true to oneself is, however, not easy. But it can, in the end, teach one to be true to the world to which we are so closely tied:

Truth is the beginning and end of material existence. Without truth there is no material existence. It is for this reason that the moral man values truth.
Truth is not only the fulfillment of our own being; it is that by which things outside of us have an existence. The fulfillment of our being is moral sense. The fulfillment of the nature of things outside of us is intellect. These, moral sense and intellect, are the powers or faculties of our being. They combine the inner or subjective and outer or objective use of the power of the mind. Therefore, with truth, everything is done right.

That, however, did not mean everything we were doing—or planning to do—was right. When Tucker whooped from the top of that third miter, however, I knew our gamble had paid off.

"There's a cairn up here!" He called down from the lip of the chimney I was still pulling myself up.

By the time I was mantling out of the chimney and onto the table top summit, he had also had found the plastic register tube lodged among the cairn's rocks. It was 3:15 p.m.

With no view to reward our labor, there was not much else to do but eat. So while Tucker ate a sandwich and watered Jenny from the cap of his water bottle, I munched a pop-tart and read to them various excerpts from the register.

From it we learned that Tikishla had first been climbed in 1966. The same entry went on to note the difficulty of bushwhacking up through the brush from Anchorage.

"And we thought we worked hard to get here," Tucker laughed through a mouthful of sandwich.

We also learned that if the register had in fact been signed by every group or person who reached the summit, then only eighty people had climbed Tikishla in the twelve years or so since 1980 when the register was first put in place.

"That's an average of only six or seven per year," I calculated quickly.

"And probably ten or twenty times that number of people climbed Flattop just last Sunday," Tucker answered.

"And how many people climb Flattop every year?" I asked. "Thousands? Tens of thousands?"

It was then, just as we finished that little mathematical comparison, that the light rain turned to heavy sleet.

"Oh well," Tucker shrugged.

Acceptance is also a form of preparation. It is assenting to the conditions, an acquiescence to the fact that whatever will be, will be. But this acceptance is not resignation. It is not throwing the hands up in despair. Instead, it is an acceptance of one's place. According to Confucius, the "moral man" lives a life that "is an exemplification of the universal order (*li*)":

> *Li is the principle by which the ancient kings embodied the laws of heaven and regulated the expressions of human nature. . .*
> *Li is based on heaven, patterned on the earth . . . . and through it everything becomes right in the family, the state and the world.*

Acceptance to such an order is not resignation. It is simply bowing of the will to a greater order, a submission of the ego to a greater whole.

But *li* is not simply an ideal social order. It is the principal order or organic pattern which governs the organic pattern of the entire universe. *Li* is not mechanical or legal order. Instead, it is the pliable order of nature which results in the patterns of flowing water, in the shapes of trees and flowers, in the forms of clouds, the tracings of rain, and the cut of snowflakes, as well as the movement of the sky above and the contour of the earth below. As Alan Watts points out in <u>Tao: The Watercourse Way</u>, "It was through the appreciation of *li* that landscape painting arose in China long before Europeans got the point of it. . . "

Chuang-tzu tells a story about an old man who falls into a cataract and yet somehow survives. When asked for an explanation as to how he survived his fall down the cascades and rapids of the cataracts, the old man replies,

> *No, I have no explanation. There was my original condition to begin with; then habit growing into nature; and lastly acquiescence in destiny. Plunging in with the whirl, I came out with the swirl. I accommodated myself to the water, not the water to me. And so I am able to deal with it after this fashion. . . . I was born upon dry land. . .and accommodated myself to dry land. That was my original condition. Growing up on the water, I accommodated myself to the water. That was what I meant by nature. And doing as I did without being conscious of any effort so to do, that was what I meant by destiny.*

Can one prepare oneself to do as much—or as little? Probably not to the extent that the old man did. Tucker and I certainly weren't as resigning to the land as the old man was to the water. Still, all day long we had tried to accommodate ourselves to the conditions that came and went around us:

> *Therefore the Sage travels all day*
> *Yet never leaves his provision-cart.*
> (from the <u>Tao-te Ching</u>)

This is not resignation. It is simply acceptance.

But that didn't make the hail stop. Nor did it prevent us from suddenly becoming much colder than we'd been a moment before. The time had come to make a hasty retreat—at least as hasty as we could. For we were even slower climbing down from the ridge then we were going up. First, there was still scree to slip and trip over. Second, the bellowing wind and clattering sleet that now blew over the summit heights pushed us back and forth like a big, malicious hand as we tried to make our way down the rocks.

"I'll be happy when we're out of this," I yelled to Tucker through the stinging gusts.

"Yeah!" he yelled back.

That's why, when reaching the end of the summit ridge, we didn't continue backtracking down the northwest ridge we had come up earlier. Instead we dove directly down into the hanging valley we had so carefully avoided earlier. The elevation we had squandered on the way up we were now happy to lose—and the faster the better.

It was a slippery, wayward-footed descent down the valley wall, but once on the soft grass of the gently tilted valley floor, the walking was easy and even invigorating.

Only Jenny seemed eager for more climbing as she chased a flock of sheep up and down the slopes behind us.

As we neared the end of the hanging valley and turned west toward the city to begin slabbing down the slope above the North Fork of Campbell Creek, it began to rain again. Wet and cold not only from top to bottom and side to side, but also from front to back, we had little choice but to keep moving. Nor when the rain stopped did we feel any warmer. Instead, saturated by the wet grass we slipped and tripped through, we actually got colder and colder the more we walked. We didn't stop. That would have been pointless. And anyway, we could now see the rounded top of Ice Cream Cone at the end of the ridge whose flank we stumbled along as well as the trail that would take us home dropping off its side into the woods below.

Our ankles ached from the side-stepping on the steep slope. Our sodden running shoes kept slipping out from beneath us in the wet grass. If one had squeezed our bodies, we probably would have squelched like a couple of sponges and disgorged a few gallons of water onto the earth below. Yet suddenly, inexplicably it all seemed hilariously funny. I don't remember what Tucker said to me—something absurdly mundane about the weather—but I found it ludicrously and spectacularly funny. I was laughing so hard at one point that I had to bend over to ease the pain in my stomach. Tucker looked back once in rather disgusting amusement, only to find that the mood was highly contagious. In a matter of moments, after I had tried vainly to explain the humor that so affected me, Tucker was also doubled over in the same fit of hysterics.

This didn't make our walking any easier or faster, but it eased the pain. Eventually, however, the gray sky and wet world subdued our mirth. But not before we were once again standing on the rounded top of Ice Cream Cone. Then the cold rain began to fall once again.

We were done with the rain, though. We were done with the sleet. We were done with the rocks and scree. And we were done with the cold wind and clouds that blew over us, around us all day, and seemingly even through us as we toiled over the bare heights above. We were done with it all. We had had enough. It was time to go home:

> Retire when your work is done,
> Such is Heaven's way.
> (from the Tao-te Ching)

It was time to return to the month of July from which we'd come, to return to the warm, wooded valleys below where the wind was but a harmless noise overhead and the rain was but a gentle pattering on the shoulders. Yes, there was something to be said for the comforts of the valley, especially after coming from the rigors of the mountains.

And it didn't take long to cross the border between the two. In less than a hundred feet below the summit of Ice Cream Cone, the rain stopped. Less than a hundred feet later, we ducked under the green canopy of the wet trees already sparkling in broken sunlight and entered once again into the company of the soft summer season they harbored. It was a change, as Confucius might say, we were more *prepared* for than we had been for anything else that day. But that sounds too formal. For we were really just two people happy to be getting in out of the rain.

Dusk settles over Long Lake in the Front Range of the Chugach Mountains. The city of Anchorage and Knik Arm are just visible in the lighted distance.

Tikishla Peak

Trail Location: The trail to Tikishla via Ice Cream Cone (which is often also referred to also as Baldy) begins in the Chugach Foothills subdivision in East Anchorage. To get to the trailhead, take East 36th Avenue east from Muldoon Road, turn right on Pioneer Drive and follow it until winds its way to Klutina Drive, a dead end street on the right. Park anywhere near the chain link fence at the end of this road without blocking access through the fence. Please also try to be considerate to the people in the neighborhood by not parking on their lawns or blocking their driveways.

Immediately after passing through the gate, turn left onto the right-of-way of the first set of powerlines overhead. Follow these to larger set of powerlines and turn right on their larger, wider right-of-way. Now follow these larger powerlines south-southeast toward the small, fenced in electrical station that can be seen about a half mile up the powerline right-of-way. Just beyond this station there is a small trail opening on the left leading into the woods. Take it. Follow this trail for another five minutes or so until a tank trail is reached. (This is an obvious reminder that you're on Fort Richardson military reservation land. If you haven't taken the time to notify them about your itinerary—in case of military maneuvers taking place in the area—the tank road should also cause a small—very small—pang of guilt.) Go left on the tank road for another five minutes or so before turning onto the first trail on the right. This is the trail up to Ice Cream Cone or Baldy.

Follow this trail as it winds steadily upward through the various levels of altitudinal woods until, just a few yards above tree line, the summit is reached . From here, follow the undulating crest of the ridge east and upward until another steady climb brings you to the rim above the hanging valley beyond which rises the summit of Tikishla. From this point you can go up the ridge a short way to climb Konoya (4,600 feet) before continuing on to Tikishla (or returning home if you so desire). Another choice is to descend directly into the valley and begin climbing Tikishla proper. These choices, among others, are at your beck and call.

Trail Grade: Except for the first mile or so past the tank roads, which are mostly 1, the trail to Ice Cream Cone and past it to where the trail finally ends is a grade 3. The traverse of the hanging valley rates a 4, which rises to 5 for most of the climb up the mountain proper. The summit ridge, however, rates a 6.

Trail Condition: The trail for the first mile or two until the final turn off the tank road is flat and wide. The remainder of the trail up to Ice Cream Cone and up to the first knoll beyond is sometimes muddy and overgrown below tree line in a few spots. The footing on the rest of the trail to the top of the ridge is good to excellent. In fact, only high on the mountain proper does the scree begin to make the going exceptionally difficult. This is especially true on the slab across the summit ridge, where the whole slope seems to shift beneath the feet with every step.

Trail Mileage: The one way trip to the summit of Tikishla is over 9 miles for a round trip total of 18 to 19 miles.

Total Elevation Gain: The hike to the summit of Tikishla entails an overall climb of over 5,000 feet.

High Point: The summit of Konoya Peak is 4,600 feet above sea level and the summit of Tikishla is 5,150 feet above sea level.

Normal Hiking Time: A strong hiker and climber can get up and back to Tikishla inside of 10 hours. Most people, however, should expect to spend either 1 very long day or even 2 days to make the round-trip.

Campsites: The best would be in the hanging valley between Konoya and Tikishla peaks. Depending on the wetness of the season or the amount of snow that fell the previous winter, water is usually present in the valley.

Best Time: Due to the avalanche dangers, June through September are the best months for this climb. However, if one is knowledgeable about snow conditions and is a capable winter traveler, any time of the year is an opportune time to climb Tikishla.

USGS Maps: Anchorage A-7, A-8 NE.

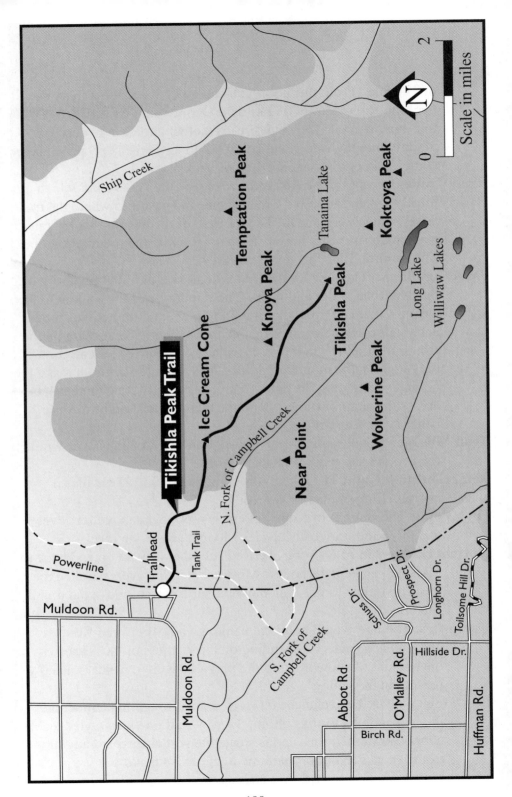

Tikishla Peak Trail

Ice Cream Cone

Ship Creek

Temptation Peak ▲

Knoya Peak ▲

Tanaina Lake

Tikishla Peak ▲

Koktoya Peak ▲

Long Lake

Williwaw Lakes

N. Fork of Campbell Creek

Wolverine Peak ▲

Near Point ▲

Trailhead

Tank Trail

Powerline

Muldoon Rd.

S. Fork of Campbell Creek

Schuss Jr.

Prospect Dr.

Longhorn Dr.

Toilsome Hill Dr.

Abbot Rd.

O'Malley Rd.

Hillside Dr.

Birch Rd.

Huffman Rd.

N

Scale in miles

0   2

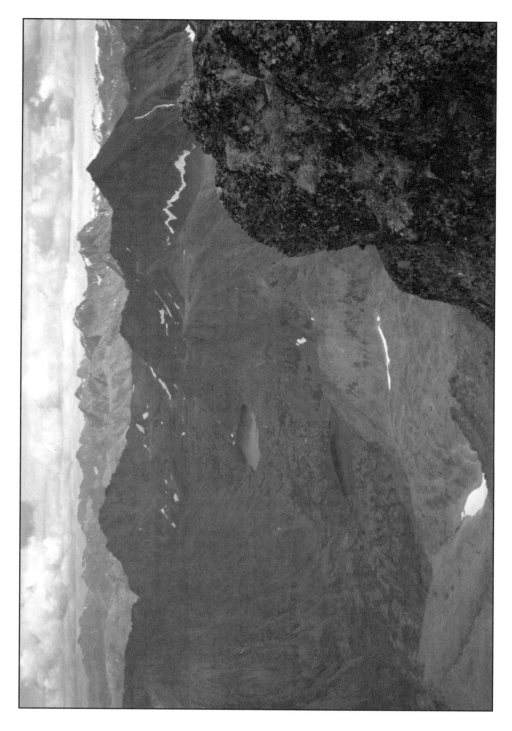

Series of 'rosary bead' lakes leading up to pass between the Middle Fork and North Fork of Campbell Creek in the Front Range of the Chugach.

OPTION "A"

TIKISHLA PEAK VIA NEAR POINT

Trail Location: This route begins at Prospect Heights parking area. To get to Prospect Heights go east up O'Malley Road from its intersection with the Seward Highway. Follow O'Malley approximately 4 miles to Hillside Road. Go left and then take the very first right onto Upper O'Malley Road. When this road ends at a T intersection, turn left onto Prospect Drive. Follow this for a mile to a stop sign. Bear left through the stop sign and in a few hundred yards, on the right, will be the entrance to Chugach State Park. The trail begins at the far end of the parking lot just to the right of an outhouse and sign board.

From the parking lot, follow the trail to the top of Near Point by simply following the Wolverine Trail for the first two miles. Where it takes a sharp right hand turn off up the mountain proper, go straight ahead. In less than a mile, this trail will steepen as it begins to switchback up the southwest side of the mountain. From the beginning of the climb, it is a muddy-footed 1.5 mile climb to the top.

From the summit continue along the broken trail that follows on the ridgetop until the hollow just below the massive buttress of Wolverine's northwest ridge is reached. This is the most suitable spot for descending to the North Fork of Campbell Creek far below to the left or north. After crossing the creek, continue up the long, wide hanging valley that rises up toward the convergence of the northwest and south ridge of the mountain. Either of these two ridges provide access to the summit still far above.

Trail Grade: The trail to the top of Near Point is a 2 to 3. But beyond this, despite the long descent to the North Fork of Campbell Creek, the conditions pass through a 4 and then slowly rise—with the gain in elevation—through 5 all the way to where a rating of 6 is reached along the summit ridge.

Trail Condition: The trail up to Near Point is, for the most part, along a wide, dry homestead road. Only on the summit pyramid itself does the trail become narrow and often very muddy. Once above tree line, however, the trail becomes dry again. The rough trail leading from Near Point down the ridge is just that: rough with lots of short, rocky ups and downs.

With the exception of the brush that borders the North Fork of Campbell Creek, the trail-less traverse across to Tikishla itself is on firm and often fragrant and flowery tundra. Once the climb up the mountain begins in earnest, though, expect scree and rocks to soon become a hindrance; and expect them to become more of a hindrance the higher up you climb.

Trail Mileage: It's a 9 mile hike from Prospect Heights to Tikishla Peak for a round trip total of 18 miles.

Total Elevation Gain: Including the climb up Near Point, expect to climb at least 5,000 feet during the course of this hike.

High Point: It is 5,150 feet above sea level at the summit of Tikishla.

Normal Hiking Time: This hike can be done in 1 long day, but most people take a more leisurely 2 days to complete it.

Campsites: The valley through which runs the North Fork of Campbell Creek has many wonderful spots for camping, as does the hanging valley that rise out of it into the broad, flat basin below Tikishla's northwest and southwest ridges.

Best Time: Both the north slope of Near Point and the high ridges of Tikishla are extremely dangerous in the winter due to avalanches, therefore it is best to undertake this hike from June to September. This warning should deter even those experienced in winter travel from doing this trip. However, if any one feels they absolutely must do this trip, it is strongly suggested that they exercise extreme caution—especially on the seemingly innocent north slope of Near Point.

USGS Maps: Anchorage A-7, A-8 NE.

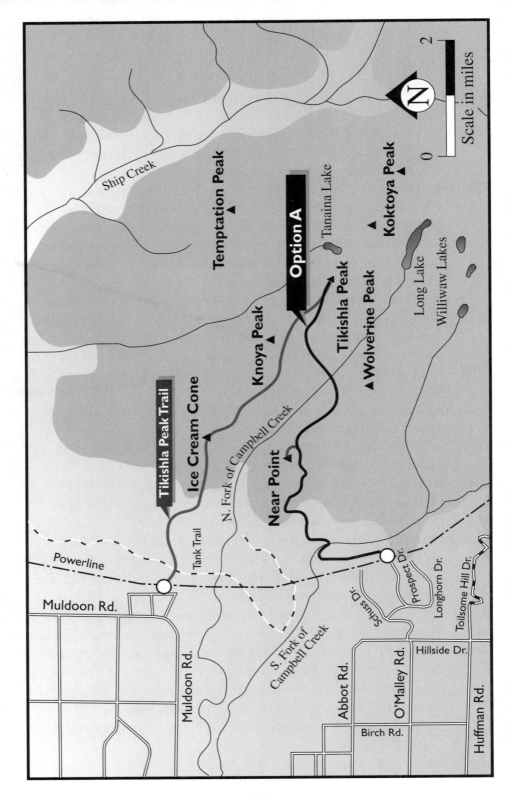

Scale in miles

N

2

0

Ship Creek

Temptation Peak ▲

Option A

Tanaina Lake

Koktoya Peak ▲

Knoya Peak ▲

Tikishla Peak ▲

▲ Wolverine Peak

Long Lake

Williwaw Lakes

Tikishla Peak Trail

Ice Cream Cone ▲

N. Fork of Campbell Creek

Near Point ▲

Tank Trail

Powerline

Prospect Dr.

Muldoon Rd.

Muldoon Rd.

S. Fork of Campbell Creek

Schuss Dr.

Longhorn Dr.

Toilsome Hill Dr.

Abbot Rd.

O'Malley Rd.

Hillside Dr.

Birch Rd.

Huffman Rd.

Evening on the Bold Overlook Trail.

TIKISHLA PEAK VIA MIDDLE FORK TRAIL

Trail Location: Follow OPTION A of WALK-ABOUT GUIDE TO
MIDDLE FORK TRAIL to lower end of Long Lake. Continue
down the valley until a suitable approach to Tikishla Peak can be
seen up the right hand (north) ridge. (Do not climb too early
because there is no easy way along the ridge from East and West
Tanaina peaks to Tikishla Peak—but than again, East and West
Tanaina are also spectacular destinations.) If one wants to be
absolutely sure about a route up to the summit, continue down
valley until the huge hanging bowl on the southwest side of the
mountain opens up above and to the right. Once in the bowl,
continue up the ridge to the east (right) and on to the summit.
After the climb resume OPTION A by coming out over Near Point
back to Prospect Heights.

Trail Grade: After leaving Middle Fork Trail, the route's grade rises to a
trackless 4 going over the pass and down the valley. Grade 5 is
reached with the climb up Tikishla, the topmost of which is
difficult enough to raise the grade to a 6.

Trail Condition: With the exception of Middle Fork Trail, the route is
almost entirely on dry and gravely tundra. Only on the summit
ridge of Tikishla is the footing difficult because of the loose rock
slope.

Total Mileage: This traverse is a 21 to 22 mile hike, which includes the
climb up Tikishla along with the hike up the Middle Fork and
down the North Fork of Campbell Creek.

Total Elevation Gain: This hike entails an overall climb of 4,285 feet,
including the 2,135 foot climb over the pass above Williwaw
Lakes as well as the 2,150 foot climb from Long Lake to the
summit of Tikishla.

High Point: The pass between Williwaw Lakes and Long Lake is 3,750 feet above sea level. The summit of Tikishla Peak is 5,150 feet above sea level.

Normal Hiking Time: This climb can be done in 1 very long day by the sturdy of heart and strong of limb, or 2 or 3 days for those wishing to keep a more leisurely pace.

Campsites: Almost anywhere along the route there are campsites with both wonderful views and plenty of nearby water. Remember, however, campfires are prohibited inside of park limits, so make sure you bring a stove.

Best Time: Due to the avalanche dangers both in the pass and on Tikishla Peak itself, the best times for this extended hike is anywhere from June to September. Those well-versed in reading snow and well-experienced in winter climbing and camping can, of course, attempt it any month of the year.

USGS Maps: Anchorage A-7, A-8.

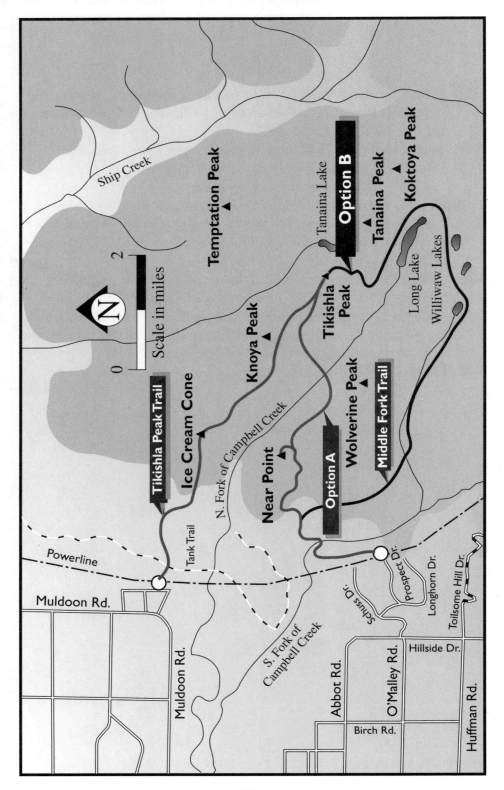

Ridge walking in the Front Range of the Chugach Mountains.

CHAPTER 10

Hidden Ways

It didn't feel like the day marked on the calendar. Instead, it felt as though we were the farthest we could possibly be from the sun. Whether we were at the bottom of the earth in late June, in the darkest, coldest, and shortest days of that hemisphere's winter, or in the same season of the northern hemisphere's year didn't matter. It felt like either of these—as well as any other day close to the dead center of the coldest season in the darkest days of the year in any of the harshest places imaginable on this planet. It just wasn't like the day it was supposed to be.

How could it feel any different with the north wind blowing so hard and the snow falling so thick? And no way for us to avoid them? The wind was blowing from what seemed like everywhere, driving sharp pellets of snow across our faces and into our eyes. Icicles hung from any strand of hair sticking out from under my balaclava. Frost clung in white sheets to the arms and belly of my nylon parka. And snow dangled in lumpy clumps from the laces on my shoes and backs of my mittens. We didn't stop, though. Nor did we think about turning back. Instead we just kept clawing methodically up. Slowly, slowly, despite the snow and wind, we continued scrabbling up the crusted slope until all that remained was just a few last feet of wind-curled drifts between us and the frozen, still hidden summit of Temptation Peak.

The Almighty—we cannot find him.
(Job 37:23)

For all intents and purposes, it seemed like winter. Appearances can be deceiving, though. For though we were cold, the wind and snow couldn't be blamed on it being the shortest day of the long year. Nor could we say we were at the mercy of any day in the cold-blooded month of January or that we were being subjected to the malice of a heartless day in February, or even the irascibility of a blustery day in March. We couldn't blame it on any day in any of those months. Because it wasn't even winter. It was, instead, the Autumn Equinox, the first day of fall. Though hard to believe, the season of summer had come to an end just the day before. Now here we were in a blizzard! Yes, it was hard to believe.

> *Can you find out the deep things of God?*
> *Can you find out the limits of the Almighty?*
> *It is higher than heaven—what can you do?*
> *Deeper than Sheol—what can you know?*
> *Its measure is longer than the earth, and broader than the sea.*
> (Job 11:7-9)

Yes, appearances can be deceiving—but we had no one to blame but ourselves:

> *For ye suffer fools gladly, seeing ye yourselves are wise.*
> (2 Corinthians 11:19)

I was the fool, though. So I had to either suffer myself gladly or revile myself for my own foolish presumptions.

After all, it wasn't that we hadn't been warned. It was already two weeks since the first snow had draped the shoulders of the highest ridges like a white cape. In addition, it had only been two days since another snowfall had buried the entire Front Range in a white shroud all the way down to tree line and below. So it didn't shock either of us that it was snowing again. It was, nevertheless, terribly disconcerting—and very humbling. Neither was there anyone to blame but me for us being where we were. I was the one who had decided to climb despite the new-fallen snow. I had also decided to continue climbing up and out of the valleys below despite the gathering storm clouds over the mountains. Yes, it was all my fault—because Jenny is a dog, an Australian cattle dog.

Admittedly, she's not much to look at with her short legs, stocky torso and the dingo patch over one eye, but she has enough stamina to have reached the summits of many 5,000-foot peaks in the company of her owner Tucker and me. She's even climbed to the top of a few of these summits in the deep of winter. And she goes on these climbs willingly. She's so willing that I'm tempted to believe that she may be as fond of hiking as she is of her food bowl—as preposterous as that may sound.

But even she has her limits, and this snow storm may have been one of them. When she lifted her head to me through the blowing snow and tilted it as if to question the methods of my madness, I actually began to wonder if maybe I had gone too far this time. Yet all I could do was shrug my shoulders and apologize to her for my rash judgment.

It just hadn't seemed like winter when we got out of the car about 10:30 that morning down near the corner of Muldoon and Tudor roads. Nor did it seem like winter despite the glazed, frozen puddles we skirted around as we hiked up the access road under the power lines we followed for the first mile or so of walking. Nor did the frost-whitened grass and wilted devil's club in the forest off the powerlines' right-of-way make it seem any more like winter. Even when we reached the first sporadic patches of snow huddling under the protective shadows of the spruce and fir trees that lined the muddy trail at higher elevations, it was still hard to believe winter was so close. In fact, I was so unwilling to believe in winter's closeness that I was just wearing a turtleneck and running tights.

> *Faith is the substance of things hoped for, the evidence*
> *of things not seen.*
>> (Hebrews 11:1)

My faith, however, was not wholly blind. After all, I could still look up and see—and feel—the shining sun. That alone made it hard to believe in winter's arrival. The sun has a unique way of dispelling all doubts when it lays its hand warmly on the shoulder. Even on the coldest days in the harshest winds, the sun is a reassuring presence. It can make even the most experienced of hikers and climbers as gullible as newborn babes. And this day was no different. Shining down from a cloud-vacant sky, it certainly had me believing that winter was still many months and many latitudes away:

> *Let no man deceive himself. If any man among you seemeth to be*
> *wise in this world, let him become a fool, that he may be wise.*
> *For the wisdom of this world is foolishness with God.*
>> (1 Corinthians 3:18–19)

When we reached the top of Ice Cream Cone a little after 11:30, however, winter suddenly didn't seem so far off. First, there was the obvious presence of the snow at our feet. It wasn't deep and it wasn't old, but it was there. But an even more obvious harbinger of winter was the wind. It was a wind that not only—as on almost every climb above tree line—could be felt, but it could also be seen. It could be seen in the bent, snow-crusted grasses and leaning brush. It could also be seen in the small, whirling cyclones of snow, as well as in the wind-carved furrows that zigzagged through the deeper snow across the hilltop. It was a wind that looked cold—and certainly was. I immediately pulled on wind pants over my running tights.

Upon reaching the top of the next knoll, I was still following the same route that Jenny, Tucker and I had taken to climb Tikishla almost two months before. Unlike on that summer day, however, I now had to push my feet up through crusted drifts of snow. A few months on the down hill side of the Summer Solstice was all it took for the high hills above Anchorage to slide back into the conditions of winter. It was obvious, too, that the higher we got the more wintry it would become— which was not very comforting considering the summit of Temptation was still more than 3,000 feet above us:

> *The fear of the Lord is the beginning of wisdom.*
>   (Psalms 111:10)

The beginning of wisdom, however, is not the same as being wise—and there were many reasons on this climb, I was learning, for me to wish for at least a little bit of wisdom.

The deceiving weather was one reason. Another reason was the mountain itself. With an elevation of 5,350 feet, Temptation is—give or take a few inches—the same height as Koktoya and only superseded in height by the 5,445-foot-high Mount Williwaw in the Front Range of the Chugach. What makes Temptation even more of a challenge is that it is as remote as it is high, being not only far away from any easy access but also hemmed in on almost every side by other ridges and peaks. It is like a castle keep whose turrets are just visible over the outer castle walls that surround it. Nevertheless, despite all the barriers around it, Temptation has, like Tikishla, as many possibilities of approach as there are directions.

Having already climbed the mountain from the north and south on other days both alone and with others, on this day I was taking Jenny up the longest and highest of any approach route to the mountain. Despite the wind and the crust-drifted snow we were pushing through, I—as yet—had no reason to regret that choice.

At the top of the next knoll, instead of continuing due east up the ridge toward Tikishla, we descended northward, bounding and tripping down through the snow that lay over the bent but unbroken grass and brush. Having never had a chance to freeze before the first snow, the growth beneath us still had the bounce of green wood. It was so green, in fact, that the branches that popped up in our passing were still heavy with crisp leaves. Was it possible that nature was even deceiving itself about winter's presence, thinking that maybe it was just a momentary whim of the powers that be, a short aberration in the normal cycle of seasons?

The powers that be are ordained of God.
(Romans 13:1)

In Proverbs, the narrator speaks of "three things which are too wonderful for me, yea, four which I know not" (Proverbs 30:18). Yea, there's a fifth thing that is too wonderful for me: weather in Alaska.

At the base of the knoll, we immediately began another ascent toward the lowest saddle in the next ridge that still separated us from the Temptation valley. It was not the most direct route (that involved an almost 2,000-foot climb over the ridge to the northeast), but it was the easiest, which I assumed would also make it the fastest. I assumed wrong.

The thick growth beneath the snow which had put a bounce in my step on the descent off the last knoll now was sunk too deep on this short ascent. It was like walking on a very old and very worn spring mattress. It became very tiring in a very short time. With Jenny dogging my heels (no pun intended), I tried following the fresh tracks of a moose to save the strain of breaking trail, but they only led me into deeper brush with too long strides. After one last lunge across a tufted hillock, I finally threw up my hands and pointed northeast toward the barren ridge line above.

"We're going that way, lassie!"

So without any deviation of direction, we climbed in a beeline for the brush-less heights. The ascent might have been steeper than going up the vale below but as soon as we climbed out of the brush it also became vastly easier. After only ten minutes of steady climbing, Jenny and I were over the crest of the ridge and looking more than 1,500 feet down into a deep valley. Far down the valley to the left (west) could be seen the snaking ribbon of Arctic Valley Road. Winding up to the ski area, it was clearly visible against the distant snow-covered woods on the ridge. Far up the valley to our right (east) was a tremendous couloir hemmed in by snow-streaked rocks and higher rolling summits. These were not our destinations though, so they didn't command my attention (or Jenny's, for that matter, who was busy nipping at a scuttling leaf a few feet farther up the ridge) the way the massive ridge directly across the valley did. Slowly and circuitously, that bald, humped ridge led the eye slowly upward, over round, nameless outcrops and false peaks sulking under new snow, around ravines and above trackless, shallow gullies streaked by recent avalanches and black-ribboned rock falls. But it didn't stop there. Instead, it led the eye higher yet past jagged spires and mist-obscured cliffs and up and across the barren wind-blown snows of a wide, steep meadow until they finally reached the immense preponderance of Temptation's summit, beyond which could be seen nothing but the clouded sky. It was an impressive sight.

Sing to him, sing praises to him, tell of all his wondrous works!
(Psalms 105:2)

Wondrous, yes. But on this day, not very inviting.

Yet even as my eyes rested uneasily on that single point against the gray sky, a movement far below made me turn. No matter how puny and distant, movement—which means life—on a winter landscape always catches the eye. Maybe it's like being drawn to like. Maybe it's the loneliness of the place. Or maybe it's just the novelty of motion in an otherwise still world. I'm not sure what it is, but the eyes always notice another life—another consciousness in flux—no matter how near or far it is.

So I turned and looked and, lo and behold, far below, trudging slowly down the fall line of the valley were two pack-laden figures. Plodding slowly through the snow along the bank of the creek far below, their presence was totally unexpected, yet very welcome. I was going to holler a hello. But I got no farther than opening my mouth. Something about the place and time prevented me from speaking—never mind yelling. It was simply too quiet a day, too remote a place. And anyway,

205

who was I to intrude on their apparent solitude? What good would it
have done other than selfishly declare my presence? Still, when one of
them stopped and seemed to look up toward the ridge I was on, I couldn't
restrain from waving my arms wildly over my head in greeting. I don't
know if I was seen or not. Nor would I ever know:

Our paths were in opposite directions—theirs down the valley and
mine up the valley. Yet though I wouldn't see them, I might be able to
claim their broken trail for my own use.

"Just think, Jenny, we're going to have trail. How about that?"

She turned her head to look up at me. I don't think she cared one
way or another.

Still, I wasn't in that much of a hurry to converge with their trail.
I certainly wasn't going to charge straight down to the valley floor just to
follow their footsteps. That would've meant more climbing up valley.
Jenny looked up at me, waiting. Finally, after a few more moments'
thought, and a few more glances around the jagged rims of the valley, I
was ready to go. Instead of descending straight to the trail, I decided that
it might be better for us to slab down and across the ridge in the direction
of Temptation. That way we would join the trail at an angle farther up
valley. It seemed like a good plan, at least at the time.

The Lord knows that the thoughts of the wise are futile.
(1 Corinthians 3:20)

Not that I am wise—but that didn't necessarily make my plan any
less futile. Still, it didn't appear to be a bad plan. For the time being it
actually appeared to be a good plan. But only time would tell.

Plummeting down through the snow and brush, half-running and
half-sliding, we stumbled at last through some low fir trees onto their
trail. The only problem was that their trail soon led where I couldn't
follow: straight across one of the widest possible crossings of the creek.
They must've been wearing some high, waterproof boots which easily
kept their feet dry—no matter what they stepped in. I, on the other hand,
was only wearing an old pair of running shoes (with lots of socks, and
more in my pack) which made such a wet crossing unthinkable unless I
wanted frozen feet. So Jenny and I had to plod reluctantly upstream to
find a passable bridge of rocks. It was more than a half mile, but just
above a confluence in the creek, we came upon some ice-glazed stones

that gave us some footing to the opposite shore.

> *Ask, and it will be given to you; seek, and you will find;*
> *knock, and it will be opened to you.*
>   (Matthew 7:7)

In another two hundred yards we *were* knocking on the door of the U.S. Army-maintained Upper Snowhawk Cabin.

There was no answer, so I took the liberty of entering. Positioned at another confluence of the creek we had followed with another stream descending from the mountains and ridges far up the valley, this clean, well-lighted place would've pleased even Ernest Hemingway. Six-sided with numerous windows to look out at the world and numerous shelves—some with emergency food and equipment and others with straight-stacked books and magazines—and bunks to accommodate any and all who seeks shelter within, this cabin is always a welcome place of rest—whether in the coming or going, or no matter how long or short the stay.

We certainly weren't going to stay long—but that's because we couldn't stay long. The hour was late and already the summit was floating in and out of steadily darkening clouds. Time was suddenly of the essence.

> *Lord, make me to know mine end, and the measure of my days,*
> *what it is; that I may know how frail I am.*
>   (Psalms 39:4)

Within fifteen minutes, after another time-consuming search for a crossing over the second creek, we were toiling up the southwest ridge of the mountain proper.

"We're finally here," I muttered to Jenny as she pushed up through the snow beside me. "It took some doing, but we're finally on the mountain."

Nosing up through the snow beside me, she didn't seem impressed.

"At least on a trail," I continued, gesturing at the footprints we were once again able to follow after abandoning them earlier at the first stream crossing.

That didn't seem to impress her either.

"Well, we'll be able to turn around soon," I finally conceded. With that, she at last looked up.

> *. . . all things are possible to him that believeth.*
>   (Mark 9:23)

After a slow, slogging ascent, we rounded off onto the high, flat ridge that hides the dark glacial tarn nestled far below it and the dizzying, rocky confusion of the north ridge that rises up directly from its opposite shore. Without any visible outlet, the lake on this cold, gray day lay frothing with foreboding mists in its deep basin like Grendel's foul, swampy lair, while above us, still seemingly hours away, hovered the ghost of the wind-haunted summit.

Yet though the summit was a lot closer than it appeared—another illusion of the clouds—the wind and snow didn't make it much easier to reach. Thankfully, those who had gone before had kicked some solid steps in the hard-packed snow.

> *How beautiful upon the mountains are the feet of him that*
> *bringeth good tidings. . .*
>   (Isaiah 52:7)

Winding between the broad, frozen meadow on my right and the rocky spires and cliffs high above the tarn on my left, the steps led upward. Visibility lessened as they led higher. Clouds swirled around us and the snow clung to our eyelashes and frosted our hair. My parka was wind-blasted white and my feet were balls of caked rime. I must have looked like a walking snow ghost—I know Jenny did.

When the steps reached the older, harder snow higher up the mountain, they became less frequent. Either the snow had been too hard to kick steps into, or the steps they had kicked out were now covered by drifting snow; it was hard to tell for sure. All I knew was that they were, except for an occasional tracing of a boot print in the crusted snow, almost entirely gone. This lack of good steps wouldn't have mattered much except for the fact that as we climbed higher and higher, the slope was getting treacherously steep.

> *Be sober, be vigilant; because your adversary the devil, as a*
> *roaring lion, walketh about, seeking whom he may devour.*
> (1 Peter 5:8)

The last few feet to the summit had me literally clambering up on all fours while the snow and wind darkened all but the small gray space through which we moved.

Yes, appearances can be deceiving. The only reason I knew we were at the summit was a small cairn at the crest of the ridge and the vertical drop that fell away into boiling clouds just beyond it. Huffing and puffing, I sat back and pulled Jenny up beside me. It seemed we had arrived.

> *I have fought a good fight, I have finished my course,*
> *I have kept the faith.*
> (2 Timothy 4:7)

"Hard to believe, eh, lassie," I said hugging Jenny's snow-clad body with my right arm, "that yesterday it was still summer."

She only cocked her head at me in response.

"All things considered, though, I guess we're lucky to be here," I concluded for the two of us.

> *The race is not to the swift, nor the battle to the strong, neither yet*
> *bread to the wise, nor yet riches to men of understanding, nor yet*
> *favour to men of skill; but time and chance happeneth to them all.*
> (Ecclesiastes 9:11)

But it was not a day to enjoy the view—what little view there was—or even to bask in our small success. It was not a day to linger at all. Instead, with the wind filling our ears and the snow pelting our faces and the clouds swirling around us, it was a time to get down off the mountain as soon as possible. So after quickly signing the register, and shoving my numbing fingers back inside my mittens, we turned to the obscured valleys below. It was 4 p.m.

Fortunately snow, which makes a slope much more difficult to go up when it's there, conversely makes the same slope much easier to go

down. Half-slipping and half-sliding, half-skiing and always off balance I
started down the mountain while Jenny did nosedives into the drifts
beside me. With such a hell-bent descent through the snow, we were
hiking toward Snowhawk Cabin far before we would've been if there had
been no snow—a blessing for my cold hands and feet.

To Jenny, though, it didn't matter. She actually seems to like
snow, which is something I'll never understand.

> *Is it by your wisdom that the hawk soars, and spreads his wings*
> *toward the south?*
> *Is it by your command that the eagle mounts up and makes his*
> *nest on high?*
> (Job 39:26-7)

She leaps through it like a porpoise, squirms under like a clam,
and wallows in it like a pig. She seems indefatigable in her contortions.

Reaching the cabin, I shared two Pop-Tarts and my water with
Jenny before leading her out into the snowy afternoon for the long
journey home. For that journey, however, I chose a different way than the
one we had come. It was a route with more obstacles, including more
elevation gain and loss in steeper and longer climbs. But what it
complicated through difficulty, it more than made up for in quickness.
For according to the map, it was also the most direct route back to the car:

> *Lead me, O Lord. . . make thy way straight before me.*
> (Psalms 5:8)

By 7 p.m., after one long frustrating hand-and-foot scramble up an
icy gully that led out of the Temptation valley and a heavy-footed slog
over the next low knoll, we were back on the crest of Ice Cream Cone.
But the scene before us had changed. Any clouds seen over the
Anchorage Bowl earlier had dispersed. Only the sun, shining full upon
my face and across the length and breadth of the city below, remained.
Beyond the city, Cook Inlet lay calm beneath the quiet gaze of Mount
Susitna, which was already skirted in the first mists of the evening. Even
the more distant peaks of the Alaska Range were but tranquil silhouettes
against the orange sky.

Thou art clothed with honor and majesty, who coverest thyself with light as with a garment, who hast stretched out the heavens like a tent, who hast laid the beams of thy chambers on the waters. . .
(Psalms 104:1-3)

To the north, Denali thrust its mighty head and shoulders through a thin veil of clouds, while to the south, the Kenai Peninsula was already shrouded with the coming night. The entire prospect was so quiet and benign that I thought I had walked into the midst of one of William Wordsworth's poems. Only behind me did a dark, storm-clouded sky, moving menacingly behind the immovable, marble white ridges, disturb the peace.

. . . who makest the clouds thy chariot, who ridest on the wings of the wind, who makest the winds thy messengers, fire and flame thy ministers.
(Psalms 104:3-4)

"Snow," I said out loud to no one in particular. "Winter's here already—and I don't think it's just a matter of appearance." The all too recent memory of my numb feet and hands back up at Temptation's summit were real reminders that, yes, winter had already arrived in these upland hills and mountains. Regardless of what day it was on the calendar, winter was here to stay.

"It's only a matter of time," I said, turning to Jenny who was resting in the snow nearby. "At least we still have a choice, though, eh lass?"

And I had made my choice. I was going back to autumn.

So I turned my face once more to the blazing sun and started my descent into the flaming trees below. I knew that this season of golden transition would only linger for a few weeks more until winter followed me down the same path.

Temptation Peak

Trail Location: The trail to Temptation via Ice Cream Cone (which is often also referred to also as Baldy, begins in the Chugach Foothills subdivision in East Anchorage. To get to the trailhead, take East 36th Avenue east from Muldoon Road, turn right on Pioneer Drive and follow it until it winds its way to Klutina Drive, a dead end street on the right. Park anywhere near the chain link fence at the end of this road without blocking access through the fence. Please also try to be considerate to the people in the neighborhood by not parking on their lawns or blocking their driveways.

Immediately after passing through the gate, turn left onto the right-of-way of the first set of powerlines overhead. Follow these to larger set of powerlines and turn right on their larger, wider right-of-way. Now follow these larger powerlines south-southeast toward the small, fenced in electrical station that can be seen about a half mile up the powerline right-of-way. Just beyond this station there is a small trail opening on the left leading into the woods. Take it. Follow this trail for another five minutes or so until a tank trail is reached. (This is an obvious reminder that you're on Fort Richardson military reservation land. If you haven't taken the time to notify them about your itinerary—in case of military maneuvers taking place in the area—the tank road should also cause a small—very small—pang of guilt.) Go left on the tank road gain for another five minutes or so before turning onto the first trail on the right. This is the trail up to Ice Cream Cone or Baldy.

This trail winds steadily upward through the woods until the summit is reached just a few yards above tree line. At this point, stay on the ridge proper, following it up over the next knoll. From here, instead of continuing up the ridge to Konoya and Tikishla, bear left (northeast) off the ridge and descend into the valley. Follow this valley up to the low saddle to the north. The crest of the saddle will provide a magnificent view of—at last—Temptation Peak itself as well as the valley that has to be crossed to reach it. Upper Snowhawk Cabin should also be visible just up valley from the convergence of two streams. Head for the cabin. It's a long descent into this valley and, after all the elevation that has been gained to this point, no one wants to give any of it up, but the only way to the mountain is down. After the first stream is crossed and the cabin is reached, the route continues right up to the base of the southeast ridge—which is the large buttress extending toward the cabin.

The base of the ridge is where the real climb begins. There's nothing extreme about it, though. All it takes is work. It's also difficult to get lost on this climb. Simply stay on the crest of the ridge up past the hidden tarn to the summit ridge. From here it's best to stay just to the right of the rock cliffs and spires that tower far above the tarn's basin. If one doesn't stray too far out onto the wide, open slopes to the right or try to maneuver through the rocks on the left, the summit will soon be reached.

Trail Grade: Except for the first mile or so past the tank roads, which are mostly 1, the trail to Ice Cream Cone and past it to where the trail finally ends is a grade 3. The climb up through to the saddle as well as the rest of the way to Upper Snowhawk Cabin rates a 4. Only when the climb up the southwest ridge begins does the route rise to a level 5, at which it stays all the way to the summit.

Trail Condition: The trail for the first 1 to 2 miles to the final turn off the tank road is flat and wide. The remainder of the trail up to Ice Cream Cone and up to the first knoll beyond is sometimes muddy and only overgrown in a few spots. The footing for the hike across the tundra, though, can vary from being almost brush free in late May and early June to being spongy and overgrown by late August—or covered with snow by mid-September. The conditions in the next valley also vary from season to season, though there always seems to be at least some brush that has to be pushed through. The footing on the climb itself, however, is almost always firm with only a few skids of scree to cross or climb near the summit.

Trail Mileage: One way from the subdivision to the summit of Temptation is about 11 miles for a round trip total of approximately 22 miles.

Total Elevation Gain: The net gain in elevation during the course of the hike from East Anchorage to the summit is approximately 5,100 feet, but this does not include the additional 1,000 feet or so that is lost—and therefore has to be won again—between the top of Ice Cream Cone and Temptation Peak valley.

High Point: It is 5,350 feet above sea level at the summit of Temptation Peak.

Normal Hiking Time: This hike should take1 to 2 days, depending on the strength and ambition of the party.

Campsites: Besides Upper Snowhawk Cabin, the entire valley between Tikishla Peak and Temptation Peak is rampant with choice camping sites. If you do choose to use the cabin, it would be a good idea, considering they were built and are maintained by the military, to get permission by calling the Military Police on Fort Rich.

Best Time: The best months of year to climb Temptation Peak are from June to September. Those with adequate cold weather experience will also enjoy making the long trek to this peak in the deep days of winter.

USGS Maps: Anchorage A-7, A-8 NE.

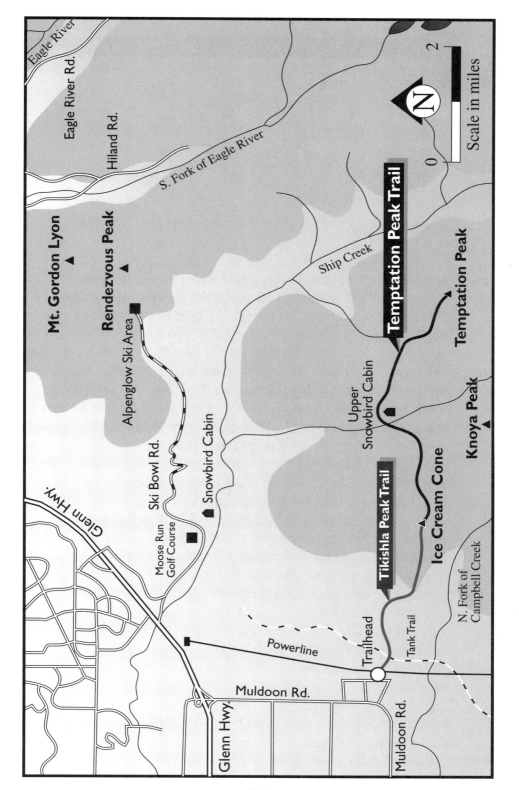

215

TEMPTATION PEAK VIA ARCTIC VALLEY ROAD

Trail Location: The trailhead to this little known way to the base of Temptation Peak is located off of Arctic Valley Road. To get there, drive north from Anchorage on the Glenn Highway to the Arctic Valley Road exit, which is the first exit after the Muldoon exchange. (Southbound traffic should take the Fort Rich exit and, following the signs to Arctic Valley, go left at the top of the ramp and continue straight for 1.5 miles to the T intersection with Arctic Valley Road.) Follow Arctic Valley Road for just under 1.5 miles past the golf course. After passing the golf course, a marked right hand turn on the first small hill in the road will lead to Snowhawk Cabins. Follow this gravel road for less than a 100 feet to the first Y intersection and go left and continue until the gate is reached. Park here on the outside of the gate. (It's a good idea to phone the Military Police on Fort Rich to let them know not only that you're parking here, but also, as a matter of courtesy, where you plan to hike. After all it is military land.)
Once through the gate, continue hiking up the road to the damn, cross and follow the trail as it rounds the first large buttress on the ridge to the right and turns into the Snow Hawk Creek valley. The trail continues up valley paralleling Snow Hawk Creek all the way to Upper Snow Hawk Cabin at the base of Temptation.

Trail Grade: This relatively gentle climb is a grade 2 hike for almost its entire length.

Trail Condition: As would be expected of any trail that hugs a valley floor, there is mud and rocks and some brush to negotiate for almost its entire length.

Trail Mileage: The one way trip from the gate to Upper Snow Hawk

Cabin is about 5.5 miles for a round trip total of 11 miles. The summit of Temptation Peak is roughly 3 miles from the cabin for a round trip total to and from the gate of 17 miles.

Total Elevation Gain: The hike to Upper Snow Hawk cabin entails a climb of almost 2,300 feet, whereas the climb from the parking lot to the summit of Temptation Peak is almost 4,800 feet.

High Point: Upper Snow Hawk Cabin is 2,650 feet above sea level, whereas the summit of Temptation Peak is 5,350 feet above sea level.

Normal Hiking Time: The hike to and from the cabin can take anywhere from 4 to 8 hours. Extending this time to 2 days, however, would allow hikers to enjoy the clean and comfortable solitude of the cabin for a night. The hike to and from the summit of Temptation Peak, on the other hand, can take anywhere from 1 long day to 2 slightly more leisurely days.

Campsites: Both the Lower Snow Hawk Cabin, located a little over 2 miles along the trail, and Upper Snow Hawk Cabin are open. It would be a good idea, though, considering they were built and are maintained by the military, that any one wishing to use these cabins get permission by calling the Military Police on Fort Rich.

Best Time: June to September are the best time for this hike. And though the hike to Upper Snow Hawk Cabin can be done in the winter on snowshoes or skis, the avalanche dangers on Temptation Peak itself should make any one think more than twice about climbing it during the winter.

USGS Maps: Anchorage A-7 and A-8.

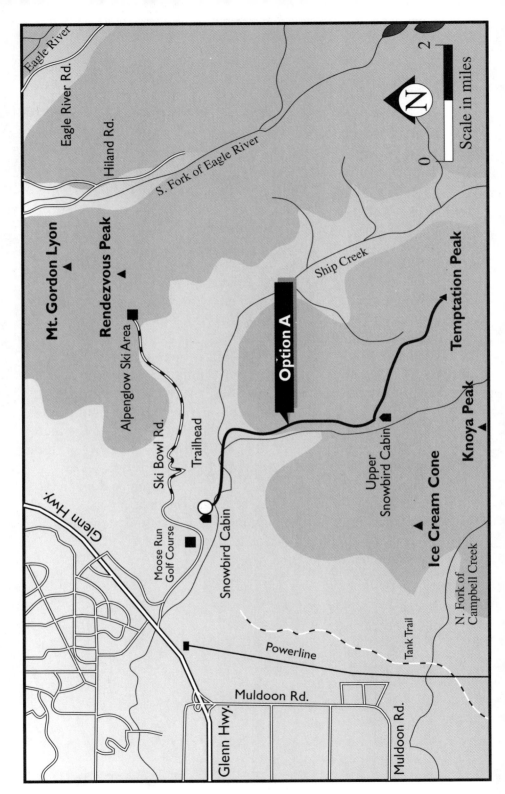

Above Ship Creek valley looking toward Temptation Peak and the Front Range of the Chugach Mountains.

TEMPTATION PEAK VIA SHIP CREEK TRAIL

Note: This route, which begins on the Ship Creek end of the Arctic Valley to Indian Pass Traverse, is so muddy, wet and overgrown with brush on the approach march, that it's difficult to even call it an option. But what it lacks in ease, it more than makes up for in wildness. Want an adventure, this is it. Beware, however: People suffering from hypothermia and exhaustion have had to be rescued from this area at the height of summer. So exercise caution. (If you do choose this route to Temptation, beware of climbing out of the Ship Creek valley too early in order to avoid the rock-spired and chimney fluted north ridge proper—which should not be attempted unless you have a rope and the ability to use it. My friend Alan and I were up there once—without a rope—and were forced into making a hasty retreat when the drastic exposure along those knife-edged heights made it too dangerous to go on.)

Trail Location: This route begins on the Ship Creek, located at mile 6.5 on Arctic Valley Road, the first exit off the Glenn Highway northbound after Muldoon (southbound traffic from Eagle River should take the Fort Rich exit). Follow this road 6.5 miles up past the golf course to where it becomes gravel. A little more than a half mile below the Alpenglow Ski Area, which is where the road ends, there is a parking area on the right which marks the Ship Creek trailhead (elevation 1,950 feet). This trail, which is the beginning of the popular 21 mile winter traverse to Indian, should be followed into the muddy and brushy base of the valley. Continue up valley until, first, a suitable way across Ship Creek is found, followed by, second, a route of ascent can be found up to the high ridge on the right (west) side of the valley south of the

220

first hanging valley and north of Koktoya Peak. (Do not start to climb too early for fear of having to contend with the technical demands of Temptation's north ridge.) Once up the ridge, the walking conditions will be substantially better across the long traverse to the summit.

Trail Grade: This route has some grade 1 only at the very beginning after which it jumps to levels 4, 5 and 6 as first heavy brush and mud, followed by a long climb up and across the heights to get to the summit.

Trail Condition: Everything from deep mud and a stream crossing to tundra and scree.

Trail Mileage: The one way hike from Arctic Valley Road to the summit of Temptation is about 10 miles for a round trip total of approximately 20 miles.

Total Elevation Gain: The net gain in the climb from the floor of Ship Creek valley to the summit of Temptation Peak is roughly 4,300 feet.

High Point: It is 5,350 feet above sea level at the summit of Temptation Peak.

Normal Hiking Time: This hike should take anywhere from 1 to 2 days depending on the condition and ambition of the hiker(s).

Campsites: Bugs and mud make camping in Ship Creek valley in the summer a very trying experience, though it can be done. In the winter, however, it is a delightful place to be.

Best Time: There is no best time to do this hike and climb. Summer is muddy, buggy and brushy, whereas winter, when the valley will be solid underfoot, presents avalanche dangers up above. If perchance, however, the snow comes late some year and the temperatures are still cold enough to freeze the swamps and bogs, then that is the best time for this hike.

USGS Maps: Anchorage A-7.

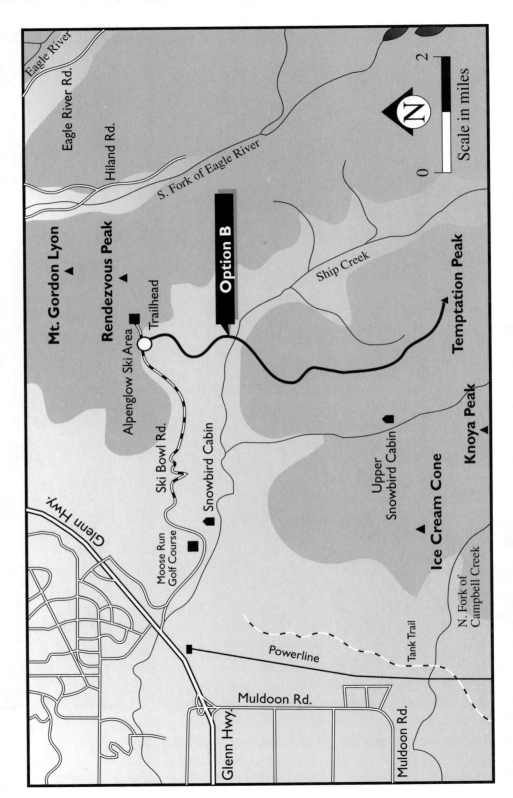

Eagle River

Eagle River Rd.

Hiland Rd.

S. Fork of Eagle River

N

Scale in miles

0   2

Mt. Gordon Lyon ▲

Rendezvous Peak ▲

Option B

Trailhead

Alpenglow Ski Area ■

Ship Creek

Temptation Peak ▲

Ski Bowl Rd.

Snowbird Cabin ◆

Upper
Snowbird Cabin ◆

Knoya Peak ▲

Glenn Hwy.

Moose Run
Golf Course ■

Ice Cream Cone ▲

N. Fork of
Campbell Creek

Powerline

Tank Trail

Muldoon Rd.

Glenn Hwy.

Muldoon Rd.

On the ridge across the valley from Temptation Peak.

CHAPTER 11

The Democratic Mountain

"So what are we looking at?" Sophia asked.

We were looking at so much that I didn't know where to begin.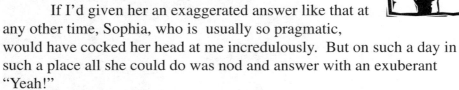

"Everything," I finally answered.

If I'd given her an exaggerated answer like that at any other time, Sophia, who is usually so pragmatic, would have cocked her head at me incredulously. But on such a day in such a place all she could do was nod and answer with an exuberant "Yeah!"

It did seem that we were indeed looking out on everything as we stood in windy sunlight on the summit of Rendezvous Peak. And if it wasn't everything, it was at least all of South-Central Alaska—and then some.

Directly below us to the east flowed the South Fork of Eagle River. Beginning downstream to the north, we could see where the ribbon of South Fork flowed over the mouth of this upper valley into the deeper, wider Eagle River valley far below to our left. Then turning clockwise to our right, we could follow its flashing ribbon back up valley to where it drained out of the shimmering waters of Eagle Lake and Symphony Lake that lay like sparking foil around the massive, rocky bases of Cantata, Calliope and Eagle peaks. Beyond both the upper and lower ends of the creek, we could raise our eyes to spired rows of peak after peak of snow-covered summits and long, undulating ridges that extended on and on into the wild heart of the Chugach all the way to the misty horizon.

When we half-turned to look back over our shoulders to the right again, our eyes passed over the long, level ridge that separated the South Fork of Eagle River from the Ship Creek drainage that emptied into the Anchorage Bowl behind and which, when we followed it upstream, stretched for close to fifteen miles, climbing slowly up and out of sight around the bulk of the jagged Front Range to where, somewhere just out of view, it reached the crest of Indian Pass. Beyond that it was seven more miles down to the gray waters of Turnagain Arm. But though we couldn't see the waters of Turnagain Arm itself, we could see the mountains rising on its far side and stretching, like those to the north and east of us, all the way to the far horizon.

Turning right again until we were facing west, we could just barely peek around the northernmost corner of the solid-walled Front Range to see the northernmost neighborhoods of the Anchorage Bowl, with its myriad of people and perpetual hustle. Still looking west, beyond the city were the surrounding cold waters of Cook Inlet across which rose the long, dominant silhouette of Mount Susitna. Then beyond even that, as if at the far end of the world, rose the diamond summits of the perpetually snow-covered Alaska Range.

Finally, completing the circle, we could turn north once more, and look over the near summit of Mount Gordon Lyon, and across the waters of Knik Arm, and then across miles and miles of muskeg, dark forests, trackless tundra and shining lakes to the crystal form of Denali, the Great One itself, standing alone in those northern wastes against the blue sky.

Yes, it did seem like everything. But to look at all of this "everything" from the top of Rendezvous Peak did not take much effort. Yet compared to the number of people who toil up Flattop, Wolverine Peak and Bird Ridge, not many people climb this mountain—even though it's a more scenic climb than the first, a shorter climb than the second and a less steep climb than the third. It's the ignored gem in the crown.

What makes the mountain so precious, however, is not just the view from the summit. It's true value lies in the fact that almost anyone with at least a modicum of time and effort can enjoy that view. Rendezvous is the most democratic of mountains.

First, as Michael Meek, one of the members of our party pointed out at the end of the hike, "it's so accessible." After all, it took us only a half hour to drive from midtown Anchorage to the base of the mountain.

Second, once we were out of our cars and looking up, we had numerous choices as to how to climb the mountain. I myself had climbed Rendezvous Peak from virtually every direction: up the ski trails on the west flank of the mountain, which was the most popular way; from the South Fork of Eagle River on the east side of the mountain, which was

225

also popular; up from the long, undulating ridge that extended southwest from the mountain, which was the longest, most scenic way; and even up from the brushy and boggy Ship Creek valley to the south, which, for good reason, was the least popular way. (I myself am not in a hurry to slog through those mosquito-infested swamps and woods again.)

Being on the western side of the mountain, however, did not necessarily restrict us to going up the ski slopes. Even from the parking lot, we had three or four choices: we could take the most obvious route, which led directly up the ski slope to the summit; or we could follow a dirt road that led up the western ridge line from the army's ski facilities on our right; or we could climb the ridge behind us and follow its crest in a big arc to the north and east over Mount Gordon Lyon and up to Rendezvous; or, last but not least, we could follow the valley up to the saddle between the two peaks on our left and from there turn right up to the summit.

None of these routes were too difficult or dangerous for us to climb. There were no steep ledges or cliffs to climb up—or fall from—on any of the routes. But each did have advantages and disadvantages. The first was the shortest, but steepest route that followed the public ski facility's chair lift straight up the fall line of the mountain. The second was the least wild route, following the access road of the army's ski area up past ski tow posts and chair lift towers and along old fences, and by a sundry of bits and pieces of scrap metal, broken chairs and other such clutter and debris that can be found in any ski resort anywhere. The third route, on the other hand, though spectacular, was by far the longest and perhaps, for that reason alone, not the best choice for the group I was leading—half of whom had never climbed a mountain in Alaska—if they'd ever climbed at all. So I chose the last route—which was also the easiest.

Along with Sophia, I had with me seven adults ranging from Elena and Bethany, who were nine and ten years old respectively, to George who was sixty-three. There were also three dogs in the party, the smallest being Dozer, a Pomeranian who was no bigger than a size 12 shoe box. But what Dozer lacked in size he more than made up for in energy. All afternoon, he darted up and down our straggling line in a futile attempt to herd us.

Not to belittle Dozer's best efforts, but it should be pointed out that it's difficult to get lost on Rendezvous Peak despite the numerous ways to the summit. Being the unofficial guide for this outing, I chose to take not only the easiest route, but also the most difficult route to get lost on. Taking a more gradual route up the back side of the mountain (as opposed to a direct assault up the steep face of the ski slopes), we only had to follow the shallow, and sometimes muddy trail out of the upper parking lot to where it begins to parallel a stream all the way up the valley to the saddle between Gordon Lyon and Rendezvous.

Of course, it didn't take long for our party of ten to get strung out all up and down the trail. From the end of the line, I could easily see the kids and dogs darting ahead. Behind them came Sheenagh, who'd done quite a bit of walking in her native Scotland, followed by Sophia. Not far behind them moved the group of Michael, Douglas and Cathy, and a short distance behind came the last group, Bruno, George and I.

It didn't matter if we got separated, though. No one was going to get lost—not on this mountain in this valley. The valley was so narrow and so short and so free of growth that nobody was ever out of sight— especially if everyone stayed on the trail that wound up the gut of the valley. And no one was about to leave the trail for the steeper climbs on either side of the valley. Instead everyone was taxed hard enough just climbing the grade of the trail itself. So I wasn't worried as the line of people stretched farther and farther apart, becoming a longer and longer snake, the farther we went up the valley.

Only when Bethany and Elena disappeared over the head wall of the valley was anyone in the group out of sight. That, however, did not mean anyone was about to get lost. On the contrary, even after reaching that saddle between Rendezvous Peak on the right and Mount Gordon Lyon on the left, it was still difficult to get lost—mostly because the overlook at the saddle had too good a view to leave in a hurry.

This overlook, which hung far above not only the South Fork of Eagle River but also above the much deeper Eagle River beyond it, as everyone reaching it discovered for themselves, was a great place for a break. In fact, when at last, taking up the rear, I came up to join them, not a single person turned toward me. Instead they all just sat there facing outward taking in the view.

"What a great spot," Cathy said as she clicked a picture.

"Indeed," Sheenagh answered, refusing to take her eyes off the view before her, as she groped blindly with one hand behind her for her water bottle.

"I would have never thought it was here," someone else said.

Some even thought this was reward enough.

"Why go on?" Bruno asked.

"Because we don't have any choice," I said pointing up the trail that led up the mountain that was now back over our right shoulders.

There, chasing each other up the long, final climb up summit cone, were Bethany and Elena. Already halfway up the steep slope, the two of them were nothing more than two colorful dots against the tundra.

"Look at 'em go!" Sheenagh called.

"Like a couple of little mountain goats," Sophia added.

"I think we should follow them," I suggested.

Bruno shrugged in acquiescence.

"And I think we should follow them right now," I added, not wanting them to get too far out of sight when the trail began to circle around the back side of the mountain to the left.

A few minutes later, after packing and shouldering our waist packs and back packs, we were all on the trail again and climbing toward the summit. Five minutes after that we were as strung out on this section of the trail as we had been below. In five more minutes we were following Bethany and Elena around the back side of the mountain. And after five more minutes, and a final short scramble up a few rocks—along with a few irritable questions as to how much farther and a few breathless complaints about how hard it was—we were all on the summit, basking in a view which was even better than the view from the saddle below.

"So here we are," George, between labored breaths, exclaimed dramatically as he stepped onto the level top just ahead of me, the last person in the group.

Yes, we had all made it to the top. The mountain was indeed democratic.

"Well, that wasn't so bad," someone said.

And suddenly all the time and effort of the climb were forgotten. Within literally moments, one would've never thought that we'd labored 1,500 feet up the side of a mountain to get where we were. The only proof of how far we'd climbed was how far we had to now look down to see the cars—that and the fact that we could also see from the Kenai to

Denali. We had, indeed, come a long way up.

How far we'd come, though, was only one reason we could see so far. Another reason we could see so far in all directions was simply that Rendezvous Peak is relatively isolated by Chugach standards. Except for Mount Gordon Lyon, the nearest summit is at least four to five air miles away. Nor is it the low end of a long ridge like Flattop or Bird Ridge, or closely hemmed in by taller mountains like Wolverine Peak. It is, instead, the high end of a long ridge that is separated from *all* other higher peaks (except Mount Gordon Lyon) by not only wide river and creek valleys but also by Knik Arm and Cook Inlet.

All these facts combined to make us feel as if we were standing not only on a mountain, but a mountain that seemed much taller than it actually was. After all, it's not many mountains that allow the eyes to gaze in any of the four principle directions and see all the way to the horizon. And on this blue, cloudless day that was exactly what we were able do.

Even the most novel situation, however, becomes common with time. It was no different with us. After the wonders of where we were and what we could see began to become familiar, people began to turn to more worldly affairs. Bruno, who had been a ski instructor on the slopes below, harked back to those memories, while Douglas fed the ever-energetic Dozer and Sheenagh watered her dog McKinley out of a canteen. Cathy, meanwhile, sat with eyes closed, face turned upward into the warm sun. If it weren't for the view on all sides, we could have been just a group of people waiting for the next bus. Then we all gathered for group pictures on the rock outcrop of the summit. As cameras began to click, Sophia promised to get a flag embossed with the name of the restaurant where we all worked.

"We'll call ourselves the Villa Nova Expeditionary Party," Sheenagh suggested.

"Yeah, and then when the expedition's done, we can start the party," Bruno laughed.

"I can't believe we forgot the wine," George added as an afterthought.

"It's down there," Sophia said, pointing down the ski slope to where the cars were parked 1,500 feet below us.

"Along with the coolers," Michael added.

"I guess that means it's time to go," I concluded.

With the food and wine beckoning from where they were stashed in the cars far below, the group began to slowly straggle in ones and twos off the summit.

Of all the ways to the top of Rendezvous peak, I don't know of one that is particularly dangerous. By most mountain standards they can actually be considered safe. There are very few places one can fall and sustain much more than a bruise anywhere on the mountain. But that's not always true about coming down the mountain—or any mountain, for that matter. Most mountaineering accidents occur on descents when fatigue and momentum easily succumb to gravity—even on the easiest of slopes.

So as we took our leave of the summit and started down the steeper west slope of the mountain, I was a little concerned. Being the last one off the summit, I scrutinized each person in the group for signs of weariness, watching whether or not he or she moved too slowly or stumbled too easily. I was worried that someone—particularly the inexperienced members of the party (which was just about everybody!)—might not even notice his or her own fatigue and, consequently, get seriously hurt in some way. But I wasn't worried for long.

Fatigue, however, was obviously not the problem as we began our pell-mell and scattered descent down the gully just below the summit. And suddenly, instead of worrying about fatigue, I was worried about overeagerness. But even that worry didn't last for long. Everyone, despite being in a hurry, was in control of each step. They were as surefooted as sheep. From above, they actually looked like a flock of sheep fanning out across the slope in search of graze. But that's only what they looked like because their focus had changed.

Now instead of searching for food, they were searching for snow. For despite the warm August day, there were still thick sheets of snow filling the lower gullies of the mountain. And, of course, it was to the highest and biggest patches of this lingering snow that the group gravitated. Below, other patches extended like a string of raindrop pearls down almost the entire length of the gully.

There's nothing like a little bit of snow to turn a group of sober adults into reckless kids. I watched as the first of the group—Bethany, I think it was—plunged into the first and highest patch of snow. Landing fanny first, she whizzed downward with Elena close behind. Bouncing onto the short patch of grass at the bottom of the first snow patch, they picked themselves up and flung themselves down the next. Behind them, the rest of the group was following suit, hurling themselves onto the snow with utter, playful abandon. Foot skiing and fanny sliding, they made their fast, happy way down the snow-filled gully. Their hoots and screams of pleasure were already filling the air when I jumped onto the first snow field and began skiing, tripping and plunge-stepping down after them.

And so, all the way down the mountain, sliding and slipping from one scattered snow field to another, we stumbled and tumbled our way toward the parking lot, filling the air with screams and laughter, while the dogs barked and howled in pursuit.

Only at the end of the last snow patch were the screams of pleasure transformed into cries of surprise as more than one person crashed through the thin snow at the lowest tip of the snow-field and fell into the cold melt water cascading below.

"Yeeoww!!" I heard Sophia scream.

"Owweeh!" Michael hollered next as he splashed into the water behind Sophia.

Some of the first in the group who couldn't stop in time got their feet wet, some got their rear ends wet. Luckily those of us at the back of the pack were well warned, in time to skirt off the snow just before it broke off into that cold run-out.

But it didn't matter much who was wet and who wasn't. No one was going to die from it—not on this mountain on this day. With the sun out, the day warm and the cars less than a half mile away, they would only suffer from a little bit of ribbing at worst.

But even the ribbing had stopped by the time, a half hour later we were lounging in the parking lot, tailgates down, coolers of food ready and the wine and beer opened or uncorked.

Sheenagh raised her glass in a toast from the lounge chair she had brought just for this moment.

"I wonder if it gets any better than this?" Bruno asked in mock imitation of the TV commercial.

One had to indeed wonder if it did get any better.

The sun warmed the cool earth below and the mountain shimmered in the dappled sky above, and everything was good.

"Here's to the powers that be for giving us such a fine day on such a fine mountain," I toasted in answer to Sheenagh's raised glass.

But the democratic mountain above would not—could not—stay the same. Today this was a hiker's mountain. Soon, in a matter of weeks, though, it would become a berry picker's mountain. Then, other people, new faces would come and plunk themselves down in the heart of one of the berry patches that clutter the mountain. Children would gorge themselves, filling hands with a gob of berries and stuffing them into their mouths while the juice trickled down their chins. Young couples would gather them for a later snack on the top of the mountain, while a small bevy of elderly women would carry buckets of berries home to be cooked and jarred as preserves or baked into a pie. Then, only weeks after that, it would become a skier's and snowboarder's mountain. Groups of teenagers, fresh out of school for the day and families out for the weekend would liven the whitened slopes above with their rainbow ski suits. Ski and snowboard tracks would carve the snow into gently curving lines disrupted by an occasional shaded divot where this or that person slipped or stumbled. And at night, from almost anywhere in the Anchorage Bowl, the lights of those high slopes would give evidence of other people pursuing other lives. For in the end Rendezvous Peak is more than just a hiker's mountain—even though that's what it's always been for me.

But no matter what the reason for going to the mountain, Rendezvous seems to be able to accommodate all in its own fashion. It doesn't ask for too much effort to get to its summit, nor does it ask for too much caution to return unscathed. Nor does it ask for much skill or knowledge to do either. But though it doesn't ask for much, it gives much in return.

It is the ignored gem in the crown, and yet it's not autocratic in its rule. It is, instead, democratic in habitation and disposition. It's a mountain that is not at all biased towards age or ability, or even temper or means. Yet it offers a view from its summit to match that of the gods on Mount Olympus.

"Yeah," was all Sophia could say at the time. Maybe that's all that needs to be said. (But that seems to say it all.)

Glissading down a snow-field in early July on Rendezvous Peak.

Rendezvous Peak

Trail Location: The normal route up Rendezvous Peak begins at the
Alpenglow Ski Area located at the upper end of Arctic Valley
Road. To get to the ski area go north on the Glenn Highway from
downtown Anchorage to the Arctic Valley Road exit, which is the
first exit after Muldoon Road. (Those coming from Eagle River
will want to take the Fort Richardson exit and follow the signs to
Arctic Valley.) Follow this road straight past Moose Run Golf
Course on the left and the driving range on the right. Continue
driving upward as the paved road gives way to gravel and begins
to traverse back and forth as it winds ever upward to its very end
at the parking lot of Alpenglow Ski Area. The mountain directly
above you to the east with the ski lifts on it is Rendezvous Peak.
From the parking lot (2,550 feet), there are any numbers of ways
to reach the summit. The most obvious ascent is to follow one of
the ski lifts up the slope, but I don't think these are the best or
most scenic ways to climb the mountain.

The most scenic route—as well as the most gradual ascent begins
by following the trail that parallels the stream up the wide valley
northeast (left) of the parking lot. This eventually leads to a high
saddle (3,468 feet) which overlooks the South Fork of Eagle
River. From this saddle, there is access to both the unnamed
mountain to the left as well as Mount Gordon Lyon, the summit
across the shallow tundra valley directly below the saddle to the
north.

To continue up Rendezvous Peak follow the broken trail that leads
up the relatively steep slope to the right to the summit.

This may be the best way up the mountain, but that does not
necessarily mean it the best way down. On a clear day, the
parking lot is visible 1,500 feet below and any which way one

wants to take to get to it is safe and easy—and often lots of fun, especially if there's a short snow-field or two to help hurry the descent.

Those looking for a change from the normal route may want to try the ascent from the South Fork Trail off of Hiland Road (to get to the trailhead of this route please refer to the next chapter). About a quarter to a half mile up the South Fork Trail there is an unmarked trail that climbs directly up the shallow gully to the top of the ridge. From the top of the ridge (which is a favorite spot for many "ridge-runners"), it is a short traverse over to the back side of Rendezvous Peak.

Trail Grade: The trail grade for the entire climb varies from 2 to 3 all the way to the summit.

Trail Condition: There may be some muddy spots along the trail that leads up the valley from the parking lot, but other than that it is a dry and brush free climb.

Trail Mileage: The mileage from the parking area to the summit is approximately 1.75 miles. Depending on the choice of descents, however, the round trip total will vary from 3 to 3.5 miles.

Total Elevation Gain: The total elevation gain in the climb to the summit of Rendezvous Peak is 1,500 feet. The total elevation gain in the climb to the summit of Mount Gordon Lyon is only 100 feet more at 1,600 feet.

High Point: The summit of Rendezvous Peak is 4,050 feet above sea level. The summit of Mount Gordon Lyon is approximately 4,150 feet above sea level.

Normal Hiking Time: A total of 2 to 5 hours will be all that's needed for just about any body to get up and down Rendezvous Peak.

Campsites: None—but none are needed.

Best Time: Any time of year is a good time to climb Rendezvous Peak. In the winter, however, it's a good idea to stay on obvious wind-blown ridges to avoid any possible avalanche dangers.

USGS Maps: Anchorage A-7, B-7 SW.

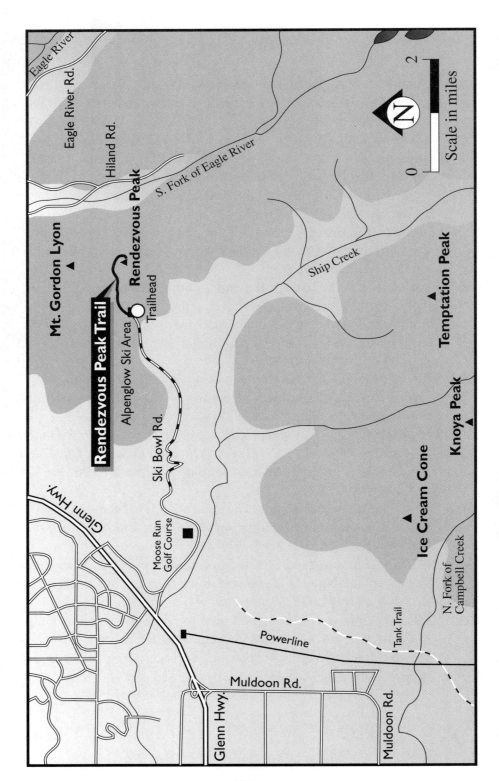

Rendezvous Peak Trail

Mt. Gordon Lyon ▲

Rendezvous Peak ▲

Trailhead

Alpenglow Ski Area

Ski Bowl Rd.

Moose Run Golf Course

Eagle River

Eagle River Rd.

Hiland Rd.

S. Fork of Eagle River

Ship Creek

Temptation Peak ▲

Knoya Peak ▲

Ice Cream Cone ▲

N. Fork of Campbell Creek

Tank Trail

Powerline

Glenn Hwy.

Muldoon Rd.

Glenn Hwy.

Muldoon Rd.

N

0 — 2

Scale in miles

236

Looking south down across the Front Range of the Chugach from Rendezvous Peak.

RENDEZVOUS PEAK
VIA THE SOUTH FORK OF EAGLE RIVER

Trail Location: To get to the trail head at South Fork of Eagle River drive north on the Glenn Highway out of Anchorage to the Eagle River Loop Road/Hiland Road exit located seven miles past the Muldoon Road exit. Turn right at the end of the exit onto Eagle River Loop Road and in only one tenth of a mile turn right again onto Hiland Road (or Hiland Drive). In another 3.5 miles take the right-handfork at the end of state maintenance of the roadway. This is still Hiland Road. In another 1.5 miles take another right-handfork, still staying on Hiland Road, and continue following it for less than half mile to where it descends to cross the South Fork of Eagle River. Approximately 1.5 miles from the river crossing take a right onto South Creek Road. This road will descend and re-cross the river. Just beyond the river, turn right onto the appropriately named West River Drive and follow this road to the park entrance a short way up on the right.

On a normal weekend day in the summer, what little parking space available is full to overflowing. If this problem occurs, park along the side of the road without blocking driveways or local traffic. The people who live in the area would appreciate it.

To get to the trail up to Rendezvous Peak, follow the trail to Symphony and Eagle lakes up past the boardwalks to where it begins to turn down valley and level off. Soon on the right will appear an unmarked footpath leading straight up toward the ridge. (This is the first trail intersection you will reach on the South Fork of eagle River Trail.) Follow this unmarked trail into a deep trough in the crest of the ridge above where another trail which

238

continues north and south along the top of the ridge intersects with it at a right angle. Turn right (north) onto this new trail and climb toward the next summit along the ridge's crest. (If this side trail along the ridge top is not found, it is also possible to simply bushwhack to the top of the ridge. It's hard to get lost—just pick a route up the slope and climb straight to the crest.) At the top of the ridge, stay on the trail and continue down ridge toward the double summit of Rendezvous Peak. The trail will go right between the two cones. The cone on the right—without the ski lift terminal—is the true summit.

Trail Grade: From the parking lot on West River Drive to the top of the ridge this hike rates a level 3. Surprisingly this level drops to levels 1 and 2 on the hike along the ridge crest to the summit.

Trail Condition: Despite the fact that these are un-maintained trails, they are almost always in fine condition with little brush and few rocks to hinder the hiking—this is due to the fact that the route is almost entirely above tree line.

Trail Mileage: The round trip from West River Drive to the summit of Rendezvous Peak and back is roughly 4 to 5 miles.

Total Elevation Gain: The climb from the North Fork of Eagle River to the summit of Rendezvous Peak entails a climb of 2,150 feet.

High Point: It is 4,050 feet above sea level at the summit of Rendezvous Peak.

Normal Hiking Time: The round trip to and from the summit of Rendezvous Peak should take anywhere 2 to 4 hours depending on the condition and incentive of the hiker(s)

Campsites: None to speak of. The top of ridge is a fine place for a picnic, however.

Best Time: late May to early October are the best times to do this hike. It can be done in the winter, but be very wary of avalanche conditions on the ascent to the ridge top.

USGS Maps: Anchorage A-7, B-7 SW.

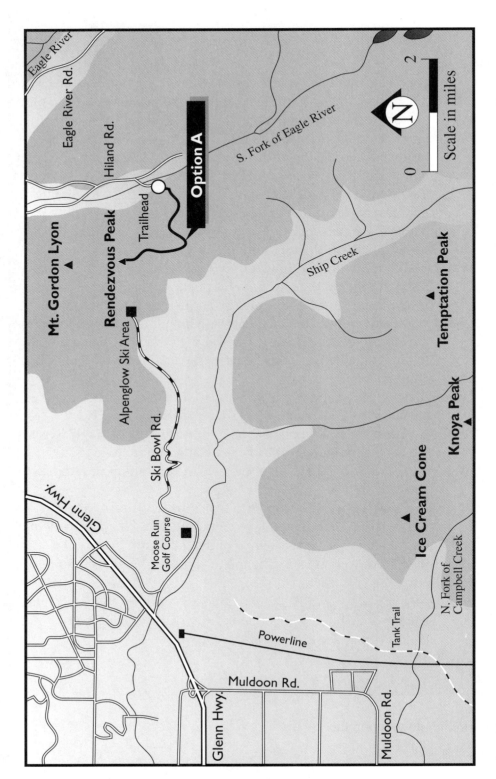

Mt. Gordon Lyon

Rendezvous Peak ▲

Eagle River

Eagle River Rd.

Hiland Rd.

Trailhead

Option A

S. Fork of Eagle River

N

2

0

Scale in miles

Ship Creek

Temptation Peak ▲

Alpenglow Ski Area

Ski Bowl Rd.

Knoya Peak ▲

Ice Cream Cone ▲

Moose Run Golf Course

Glenn Hwy.

N. Fork of Campbell Creek

Tank Trail

Powerline

Glenn Hwy.

Muldoon Rd.

Muldoon Rd.

240

Looking down upon the South Fork of Eagle River to Eagle Lake from Rendezvous Peak.

TRAVERSE OF ARCTIC VALLEY SKYLINE

Note: For the time and effort this traverse around the uppermost rim of Arctic Valley takes, it is easily one of the most scenic traverses in not only the Front Range, but also, arguably, in almost the entire Chugach Mountains. Not only is it a short drive from Anchorage, but it also a (relatively) short hike. Many could do it in an afternoon. In that afternoon—*if* it's a clear—they will see to the north, beyond the Talkeetna Mountains, Denali, the highest peak in Alaska, as well as its satellite peaks Foraker and Hunter. To the west will be seen Mount Susitna and the Alaskan Range along with numerous volcanoes. To the south is Kenai Peninsula, while to the east and south are the near Chugach Mountains.

Trail Location: This traverse begins at the southernmost end of the Fort Richardson ski resort area. To get there, park at the Alpenglow Ski Area. (To get there see WALK-ABOUT GUIDE TO RENDEZVOUS PEAK.) From here, backtrack back down the road only a hundred feet or so and go under or around the gate into the military resort area. Go down the parking lot to the farthest end and look for a dirt road that goes up the southernmost side of the ski slope. Follow this road up the skyline of the ridge past the uppermost towers of various rope and chair lifts. Just past the highest chair lift, there is a small dip in the ridge. Just up the other side of this dip is the summit of Rendezvous Peak.
From the summit of Rendezvous Peak, the safest route is to backtrack back into the dip and circle around the back side of the summit of Rendezvous to the north on a narrow trail. (Do not mistake this small trail for the larger, wider trail that continues down the ridge to the southeast). Once on the north side of the summit cone, an obvious trail follows some orange boundary

markers down to the saddle between Rendezvous Peak and Mount Gordon Lyon. From this saddle, follow the trail up the opposite side toward the summit of Mount Gordon Lyon. The last few feet are a little rough underfoot, but the view will be worth it. From the summit of this peak, one can either descend directly back to the parking lot by back-tracking back down to the saddle just climbed from and turning down the valley from there or, if one wants to do a true traverse, stay on the skyline and continue down the ridge to the military fort (being careful not to trespass on the grounds of the fort itself). Because the road leading down to Arctic Valley Road on the far side of the fort is government property—and posted with vary adamant No Trespassing signs—it is best not to continue any farther along the ridge crest. Instead descend one of the dirt roads on the east (left) side of the ridge that drop back down to the parking lot below.

Trail Grade: The trail grade for the entire traverse goes back and forth between levels 2 to 4. The first road walking up the skyline is grade 2, followed by grade 3 up to the summit of Rendezvous Peak. It is also a grade 3 hike from the summit of Rendezvous Peak back down to the saddle and halfway up to the summit of Mount Gordon Lyon. From where the trail largely disappears just below the summit of Mount Gordon Lyon and all the way around to the fort it is a level 4 hike after which, once on the road again, it is level 2.

Trail Condition: There may be some muddy spots on the roads on either end of the traverse, and there may be some rocks to clamber over near the summit of Mount Gordon Lyon, but other than that is largely a dry and brush free climb.

Trail Mileage: The mileage from the parking area all the way around the uppermost rim of the valley is almost 6 miles. This includes the road across the parking lots at the beginning of the hike and the .5 mile hike up Arctic Valley Road at the end of the hike..

Total Elevation Gain: The total elevation gain during the course of the traverse is approximately 2,900 feet.

High Point: The highest point reached along the entire traverse is at the summit of Mount Gordon Lyon which is approximately 4,150 feet above sea level. The summit of Rendezvous Peak is 4,050 feet above sea level.

Normal Hiking Time: Depending on the condition and ambition of the hiker(s), 2 to 7 hours will be all that's needed for most people to circle the ridge-line.

Campsites: None—but none are needed.

Best Time: The best time of year to do this traverse is from early June to mid-October. Because of the avalanche danger on the slopes between Rendezvous Peak and Mount Gordon Lyon, it is not recommended to do this traverse as a winter hike.

USGS Maps: Anchorage A-7, B-7 SW.

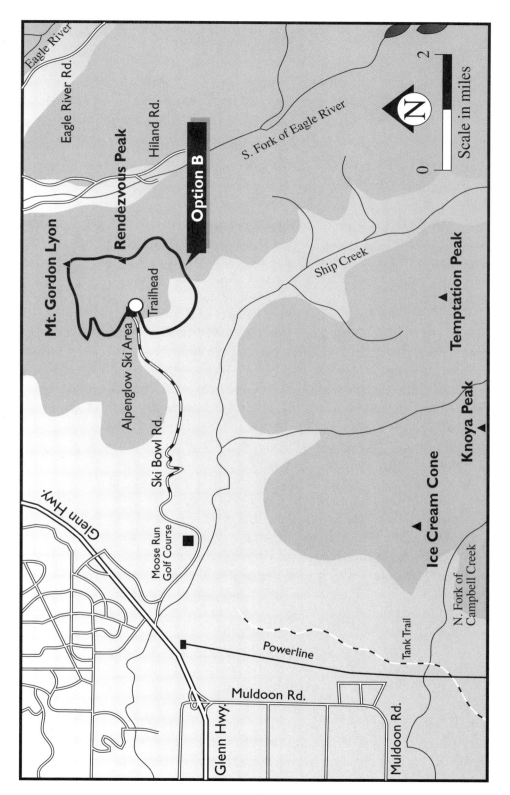

Eagle River

Eagle River Rd.

Hiland Rd.

Rendezvous Peak

Option B

S. Fork of Eagle River

Mt. Gordon Lyon

Trailhead

Ship Creek

Alpenglow Ski Area

Temptation Peak

Ski Bowl Rd.

Knoya Peak

Moose Run Golf Course

Ice Cream Cone

Glenn Hwy.

N. Fork of Campbell Creek

Powerline

Tank Trail

Muldoon Rd.

Glenn Hwy.

Muldoon Rd.

N

0   2

Scale in miles

245

CHAPTER 12

Consistent Contrast

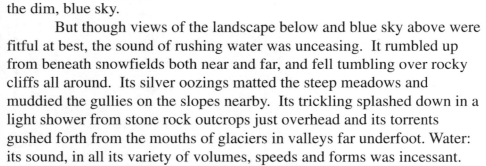

Through the listless, chilling mists sporadic glimpses of nearby slopes of moraine and shattered stone, crumbling rock faces and snow-choked ravines came and went. Higher up and farther away, when the mists parted just long enough, there came into view an occasional ridge or wide buttress rising into the finality of a towering summit. In the rare moments when the mists thinned long enough and far enough away, there was nothing to see above and beyond that summit but the dim, blue sky.

But though views of the landscape below and blue sky above were fitful at best, the sound of rushing water was unceasing. It rumbled up from beneath snowfields both near and far, and fell tumbling over rocky cliffs all around. Its silver oozings matted the steep meadows and muddied the gullies on the slopes nearby. Its trickling splashed down in a light shower from stone rock outcrops just overhead and its torrents gushed forth from the mouths of glaciers in valleys far underfoot. Water: its sound, in all its variety of volumes, speeds and forms was incessant.

Water, the life-giving blood of the dying winter, was moving everywhere, and it was always moving downward—down to the fields and forests far below which were already rich with the fresh sproutings of spring. There, the valleys were green and golden with life. There, the sun of May and the rains of June, along with the snow melt from the mountains above, had elbowed winter aside.

The contrast between the fitful views of the landscape and the unceasing sound of water, was just one contrast of many that I passed in and out of on this long day's climb. For though it was spring in the valleys below, it certainly wasn't in the mountains. Climbing alone on a narrow ridge 5,000 feet up through the broken mists and among the jagged summits I was still in the heart of winter. For in truth, up there among the rocky crags and snow-choked ravines, winter never passes. It never leaves those heights, but takes only short, restless naps at which times the sun steals quietly over the ridges and summits, melting the snow and warming the rocks for but a few moments until winter wakens again and strides forth from ridge to ridge and summit to summit, trailing behind him his cape of mists and snow and blustering winds.

So though it was sunny and summery in the valleys below, winter still moved in the strong breezes and the damp mists that blew and curled about the heights above where I was climbing. This, however, did not mean that I was ready to come down from those heights yet. For somewhere still above me was that summit moving in and out of the mists. It was a summit I wanted to reach—even though it seemed, as the day progressed, to become more inaccessible both by distance and design.

That, however, was just one more dichotomy in the day. Ever since I'd left the car at the trailhead to the South Fork of Eagle River Trail more than four hours before, small and large contrasts had diffused and divided the day. Some of these contrasts I expected; others were pleasant surprises; and still others were just minor inconveniences; while still others were major obstacles—like the mountain itself. Both the time it was taking me to climb it, and the conditions I was climbing in had come as surprises—which were fast turning into major obstacles.

For close to two hours now I'd been climbing the northwest ridge of Cantata Peak. During that time, I'd encountered so many changes in weather and conditions that it was hard to believe I was still on the same mountain now as when I started. Around every turn, I'd been met by changes in weather and terrain until the world above was so different from the world below that it was difficult to believe they were even attached to one another. But mountains are like that: they create their own contrasts. They also create contrasts in the landscape surrounding them— and in that inconsistency, at least Cantata Peak was consistent.

> *Do I contradict myself?*
> *Very well then I contradict myself,*
> *(I am large, I contain multitudes).*
> (from "Song of Myself" sct. 51 by Walt Whitman)

Located at the upper end of the South Fork of Eagle River, this peak's dominant massif not only commands the eye, but also controls much of the valley's moods. First, it divides the headwaters of the two major tributaries of the South Fork of Eagle River, each of which is different from the other in both environment and ecology. To the east of the mountain, the largest of the two tributaries flows out of the rock and snow wastes of Flute Glacier—the closest glacier to downtown Anchorage—into the cold, milky waters of Eagle Lake. Mostly barren, this tributary's upper valley is the home of a few hardy sheep and sturdy ravens. To the west of the mountain, the second tributary flows out of a lonely glacial cirque located high up in a secluded valley directly below Cantata's back side. But unlike the first tributary, this one immediately drops into greener and lusher valleys before emptying into the warmer, bluer waters of Symphony Lake. With more food sources and higher air temperatures, this valley is home to a large variety of wildlife including marmots, song birds and foxes as well as more sheep and ravens and larger birds of prey such as hawks and even a few eagles.   Second, these two valleys, in turn, each harbor unique types of plants and wildlife. But though these creeks and the lakes they flow into are unique, once they flow out of the lakes, they become one and the same when they mingle to form the waters of the South Fork of Eagle River which, in turn, flows down into the larger waters of Eagle River, which in turn yet again, flows into Knik Arm and on into the waters of Cook Inlet and the Pacific Ocean beyond.   Yet, though the waters become one and the same, they still differ from the land they pass through as creeks, streams and river, and the continents they border as inlets, seas, and oceans. But then even the waters themselves differ from each other in a myriad of ways: glacier-fed streams versus aquifer-fed brooks, cold versus hot springs, fresh versus salt water, and the various currents that circle through the numerous oceans that all have their distinct dispositions and plant and animal life. From the mountain tops above to the sea bottom below, the world is composed of contrasts. They are a fundamental aspect of creation.

> *In the beginning God created the heaven and the earth.*
>   (Genesis 1:1)

Contrariety is, in fact, what separates order from chaos and underlies all of creation. From the moment God divided the light from the darkness and brought about the evening and morning of the first day, the contrasts between night and day, dry land and seas, sun and moon, the different seasons, and the various beasts of the sea, land and air, have defined the physical world. Once the human creature was able to think beyond the merely physical world, contrariety has also defined the moral world—as symbolized by the tree of the knowledge of good and evil.

Though I'd read Genesis, I was, however, unaware of the more subtle contrasts in the environment of this particular valley simply because I'd never been here before. As a newcomer here, the contrast between this valley and all the other valleys I'd ever hiked up and down or climbed in and out of was overwhelming enough. Everything was new to me—which made everything all that more dramatic. Just the sense of discovery in being on a trail that was unique to my experience was striking. But then I had also had a tremendous sense of discovery and anticipation in just driving to this new trail. For in all my years of hiking and climbing in the Chugach Mountains, I'd never once set foot in the valley of the South Fork of Eagle River.

Consequently, that sense of discovery was very real on this warm Saturday morning as I drove up the long and winding way of Hiland Road. Neither did it diminish in any way as a little before 9 a.m. I slowly began jogging up the boardwalks built through the trees and over the bogs in the first quarter mile of trail. Indeed, it only increased when I climbed out of the trees and reached the sunlit bench the trail traversed whose top the trail traversed for more than a mile. It was there that a panoramic view of the length and breadth of the valley and its bordering mountains stopped me, awestruck, in my tracks.

I had seen pictures of this valley in various books, but nothing could be compared with what it was like to actually—and finally—be there. Expectation and actuality: just another contrast in the day:

> *I know not anything more pleasant, or more instructive, than to compare experience with expectation, or to register from time to time the difference between idea and reality. It is by this kind of observation that we grow daily less liable to be disappointed.*
> (from a letter by Samuel Johnson published in Life of Samuel Johnson by James Boswell)

I was far from disappointed. On the contrary, I was wonder

struck, perhaps not unlike how the later poet John Keats felt when he first read Homer. In that poem he alludes to Balboa (whom he mistakenly calls Cortez) looking on the Pacific Ocean for the first time with looks of *wild surmize*. No doubt, I must have had the same look on my face as I looked out across that valley that was as new to me as the Pacific Ocean was to those early New World explorers.

On a very mundane level, you could say that I felt like the (proverbial) kid in a candy store discovering all sorts of sweets for the first time. I was so eager to look around that I stumbled over my feet two, three, maybe four times as I descended to cross the foot bridge over the South Fork, climb back up to the low bench on the opposite side and turn up the valley proper. By the time I had passed beyond the last sporadic fir and willow trees and into the wide open valley beyond, I had tripped two or three more times.

I was speechless with awe. The only words I could utter were "Ahh!" and "Oooh!" and "Wow!" I think the closest I came to forming a complete sentence was to tell myself, "Look at that!" Fortunately, I was alone on the trail. If anyone saw me in this state, with glazed eyes and gaping mouth, they probably would've harbored serious thoughts about my mental capabilities. If at that moment I had been able to look at myself in a mirror, I probably would've thought the same.

On either side of the broad valley, the meadowed slopes rose gently to rounded lower ridge tops above. Beyond those ridgetops hovered higher, rockier spurs and summits. A few last remaining snowfields sparkled like inlaid pearls in some of the high gullies and over some of the high meadows over which they still lay. In contrast to that high snow, the alpine meadows around me were green and pink with the first growth of the early season and buzzing with the work of bees and the songs of birds. A gentle north wind stirred the brush on either side of the trail while the river murmured ceaselessly just below me to the right. Not even the frequent mud puddles and boggy patches in the trail could dampen the mood—though they literally dampened my feet.

But this was just another contrast in this day of contrarieties. The valley was full of contrasts. High and low, near and far, they defined the landscape of this lower valley as much as they defined the tributary valleys that surrounded the mountain towards which I was hurrying. They also defined me.

The human creature, after all, is what it is both by dint of the contrasts that created him and the contrasts which he, in turn, created. The mountains of the world, such as those that surrounded me, have been largely responsible for some of those natural and artificial contrasts. It is the mountains that did—and do—give birth to the waters that run to the sea. Whether causing the rain or snow to fall, glaciers to form, creeks to run or warm and cold air masses to flow, they have helped form and perpetuate life—including human life.

Humankind—instinctively at first—reciprocated by paying homage to the mountains. Throughout human history—and pre-history—the mountains, however obviously physical they are themselves (which anybody who has attempted to ascend them or circumnavigate them knows only too well), have been the source of much abstract thought. Many religions and myths have their sacred mountains, some of which, such as Mount Meru in Tibetan mythology and the heights of Asgard in Norse mythology are myths themselves. Other mountains, however, such as Mount Everest, known to the local Tibetans and Nepalis as Chomolungma which means "Earth Mother Goddess"; Mount Kailas, which is sacred to both Buddhists and Hindus, the latter believing it is the birth place of the god Shiva, the great destroyer and restorer of worlds; Muztagh Ata in the Pamirs, which means "the father of the snow mountains"; Mount Ararat in Turkey, which is also traditionally reputed to be the place where Noah's ark came to rest after the deluge; as well as Mount Katahdin in Maine and even Denali in Alaska have all been—and still are—considered sacred by the native Americans who live around them. There are also the nine sacred mountains of Chinese mythology, the four sacred mountains of Buddhism, and the five holy mountains of Taoism, all of which play distinct roles in these religions' rites and doctrine.

In addition, the Kunlun Mountains in China, Mount Olympus in Greece, and Mount Fuji in Japan, to name but three well known locations, were once thought to be homes of the gods. Mountains are considered places where humankind and deity had met, such as in the story of Moses on Mount Sinai. Consequently, that mountain is sacred to three of the world's major religions: Judaism, Christianity and Mohammedism. Some religions have also made the tops of mountains places of worship. For instance, on the summit of Mount Athos, a sacred mountain of Greek

251

Orthodoxy, there is a small stone chapel dedicated to the Transfiguration of Christ. At other times, if a culture's resources and population were great enough, or no mountain was readily available, they built their own mountain. (Another way of bringing the mountain to Mohammed if Mohammed won't go to the mountain.) These artificial mountains—usually centrally located in a city and topped by a temple—then became the places of worship and sacrifice. The best examples of these costly mountains are the ziggurats of the Sumerians and Babylonians, and the pyramids of the Aztecs, Mayans and Incans. Sometimes the place of worship, however, is transformed, through arrogance, into a place of confrontation with the deity, as occurs in the myth of the Tower of Babel—a story which every mountain climber should perhaps take to heart.

I certainly did—especially after deciding why I had come to this valley. For I had come to explore the valley, not just "smell the roses." Never having been here before, however, I didn't know exactly what specific part of the valley I was going to explore. Only after climbing the first half mile or so of trail up to that first open bench did I realize exactly what my destination was to be: the one mountain that dominated the entire upper end of the valley. It wasn't the tallest mountain in sight, nor the most formidable. I didn't even know its name. It was, however, the most obvious. Furthermore, the lower slope of the mountain arched upward like a stately ballroom staircase from the imperial days of Old Vienna. This magnificent means of ascent could not easily be refused.

The broken summit ridge silhouetted in the high mists far above that lower grand staircase, though, was not nearly as inviting. Aloof and cold, that narrow, upper rocky ladder looked ready to deny any and all ill-prepared and ill-equipped climbers who challenged it—like me. I wondered if I could climb even the lowest cliffs of that high ridge.

Without contraries is no progression. Attraction and repulsion, reason and energy, love and hate, are necessary to human existence.
    (from "The Marriage of Heaven and Hell"
    by William Blake)

I didn't wonder long. In a matter of moments I had made my decision.

With only a fanny pack stuffed with a wind suit, some hard candies, a Snickers bar and a pocket-sized notebook, I was certainly ill-equipped for any Alpine assault. But that didn't make me any less willing; it just meant I had to be more discreet. "At least remember," I muttered to myself, "they say discretion is the better part of valor. Don't be afraid of being a coward."

Around 10 a.m., about six miles from the trailhead, I crossed over the drainage at the north end of Eagle Lake and scampered up onto the acres and acres of crushed stone piled here by some glacier centuries ago. From cairn to cairn I made my uneven way to where, eventually, the trail follows the crest of the narrow moraine ridge that separates the murky glacial waters of Eagle Lake from the clear turquoise waters of Symphony Lake. Just another contrast in the world around me.

Halfway down the moraine ridge, between the calm waters below and the dark mountain above, a couple with their two dogs had established their single-tent camp. Greeting me warmly as she sat on a camp stool facing the mountain, the woman was kind enough to help me name that mountain.

"Where are you going?" she asked.

"I'm going to try to climb this mountain here," I answered, pointing upward, "though I'm not even sure what it's called."

"Well, that's easy to find out," she said, "I'll get the map." And she turned to go to the tent behind her as one of the dogs sniffed at me warily from behind.

"Careful," she warned over her shoulder, "he's a secret nipper."

Not wanting my day to end prematurely and ignominiously because of a dog bite, I turned to face the accused canine. We stood eyeballing each other in mutual distrust until its mistress returned.

From the map I learned that the mountain before us was called Cantata; and that its summit was 6,410 feet above sea level. That meant that I still had close to 4,000 feet to climb, if climbing without rope or partner was even feasible.

I gulped involuntarily.

Some anthropologists claim that among most prehistoric peoples, the process of naming the objects and beings in their world was a primary goal. It was a sign of their intellectual and cultural maturing. "To name it is to know it." In such a way the world becomes a little more familiar and even comprehensible. But this naming of objects and other creatures also implied the acceptance of differences between themselves and what they were naming—just as a growing child learns to name and differentiate objects in his or her world. Humankind was quickly learning that the world was composed of contraries: what was good to eat, what was bad to eat; which animals were dangerous, and which were harmless, which seasons were good for hunting, and which were good for gathering; and thousands of other small and large differences that made up the creation around them, and which established their place in that creation.

In time, humankind learned to follow the passage of the sun and moon, and the different stars marking the changing seasons, which often meant migration or travel from one pasture or hunting ground to another. Even after humankind first learned to harvest the fruits of the earth and establish permanent settlements—which later became villages, towns, and, after many centuries, great cities—the stars and the seasons were still vitally important in determining when to reap and sow, and when to trade and even when to go to war. Through observation and sympathetic action, humankind established its place in that cycle and, in turn, its relationship to that world—a relationship based upon their limited knowledge of the contraries of that world.

Now, with progress and knowledge, this fundamental relationship to the world has largely been lost. Oh, we still like to know the name of the street we're driving on, or the name of the person we're conversing with over white wine at some dinner party, or sometimes even the name of that cluster of stars rising up over the far horizon. Such naming, however, has more to do with idle curiosity or the desire for physical comfort than with the need for spiritual understanding and tribal survival. It has become a means of mastering and manipulating the world instead of comprehending and conforming to its mystery, which is precisely what a large part of the world was to prehistoric and ancient humanity: a mystery. To live in that mystery the people of those long ago times used their limited—but always expanding—knowledge of their surroundings to create a world picture in which all things co-existed as part of one great whole. In that great whole everything and every being was unique in its own way, because they all had a specific function in that great whole. Therefore, for early humankind the contrasts of the world were necessary if life as they knew it was to prosper. Humankind now, however, uses the contrasts of the world mostly as excuses for having to conquer and control all that is different instead of trying to understand and accept those differences which are a natural—even desirable—product and manifestation of creation.

> *Glory be to God for dappled things—*
> *For skies of couple-color as a brinded cow;*
> *For rose-moles all in stipple upon trout that swim;*
> *Fresh-firecoal chestnut falls; finches wings;*
> *Landscape plotted and pieced—fold, fallow, and plow;*
> *And all trades, their gear and tackle and trim.*
> *All things counter, original, spare, strange;*
> *Whatever is fickle, freckled (who knows how?)*
> *With swift, slow; sweet, sour; adazzle, dim;*
> *He fathers-forth whose beauty is past change: Praise him.*
> ("Pied Beauty" by Gerard Manley Hopkins)

Not that I want to imply, now that I knew its name, a mystical relationship between myself and Cantata Peak as ancient man would have assumed; but then neither did I want to master the mountain as modern man would have desired. I only wanted to know if I could climb it. That was the only mystery that really concerned me at the moment—even if I had to climb thousands of feet before I would be able to solve that mystery.

The density of the contour lines on the map the woman and I held between us suggested that the peak was inaccessible from almost every direction. But that grand staircase of a slope rising up before us still looked inviting. It also seemed cowardly to allow a map to decide whether I could climb Cantata or not. There are, after all, some things that one has to discover for himself—and I was intent on discovering for myself whether or not I could climb this mountain. Only thus would I be able to reconcile for myself the possible contrast between what the map implied and the mountain actually was. For I wanted to know more about this mountain than just its name.

By 11 a.m. I had slabbed up and around a low knoll at the base of the mountain and had begun my ascent up the grand staircase. Up over scattered snowfields, matted meadows and loose scree I picked my way.

I stopped and drank out of a spring so cold that it gave me a headache and continued upward toward the heights that towered above me. Those heights did not now, however, seem as inaccessible as they had from the lakes below. No route that I could see so far seemed impossible—unless I wanted to make a fruitless attempt to climb the monumental gendarme that guarded access to the base of the northwest ridge.

The climb was, in distinct contrast to what I expected, easy, almost boring. I began to shed my doubts like an unwanted skin as I climbed higher and higher. At the top of the staircase, I bore right (southeast) up a narrowing, rock-strewn gorge and then turned left, and up again. Soon I was up and around what I thought were the final steps of the high, narrow northwest ridge and very close to the summit. Now far above the valleys below, I expected the summit to come hovering into sight at any moment. (I thought I was that close.)

Eagerly, I followed a wide gully up over the top of the grand stairway and turned east. Then, less than a hundred yards later, I scurried up the back side of a small knoll. At the top of the knoll I looked up—and stopped dead in my tracks. I didn't stop because I was close, though.

On the contrary, I stopped because I was unnerved. This was my first look at the summit since far down the trail, and I expected a close and welcome view of it, but I got neither. For not only, (again) in contrast to what I expected, was I still far away from the summit—*very* far away—but also in contrast to what I'd already climbed, the way to that summit was much more difficult. In fact, if what I saw before me was actually as difficult as it looked, I was not about to get much closer to that summit than I was now. For rising between me and that summit and dominating the entire eastern horizon from north to south was the long, and very dangerous looking, upper west ridge of the mountain. Only at the far upper end of that ridge, up past the crumbling gullies, formidable rock faces, splintered spires, and dizzying cliffs and ledges, could I make out the barely discernible summit itself, half hidden in thin clouds.

Only moments before, I'd been very confident of reaching the summit. Now, however, as I gazed up the length of that knife-edge ridge to the still oh-so-far-away summit, I was, like Dante at the gates of Hell, ready to abandon all hope. But I wasn't ready to abandon the climb—at least not yet.

It belongs to the imperfection of everything human that man
can only attain his desire by passing through its opposite.
(from The Journals of Søren Kierkegaard)

I sat down on stone and chewed on a hard candy while I collected my thoughts and pondered my options—which weren't many. All that was obvious was that I was either just finishing or just beginning this climb. And since I didn't want to give in to the former impulse just yet, I sat and studied the ridge. The route did look difficult—to say the least—but on increased scrutiny it didn't look entirely impossible. Yes, the ridge was just a stegosaurus back of rock plates rising above me in a continuous series of towers, outcrops and cliffs interspersed with steep gullies and deep chasms. None of those towers or cliffs on closer look, however, seemed obviously insurmountable and none of the gullies or chasms appeared impassable—but none of these obstacles seemed safe, either. The climb, if it was even possible, would not be easy.

The only thing, in fact, that made me think the climb truly possible was the sheep trail leading across the saddle fifty feet or so below me and up into the maze of rock and gullies of the ridge where it soon disappeared. In my experience, I've never been on a sheep trail that served anything more than a functional purpose: goats don't climb mountains "because they're there"; nor do they have dead-end trails to what a highway sign would label "scenic vistas"; and they certainly don't go over the summits of mountains unless they have no other choice. No. In my experience Dall Sheep—and mountain goats—establish a trail for only one reason: to get from point A to point B by the most effortless and expedient route. They do not choose their routes—or destinations—for amusement or aesthetic fulfillment. Their motives are always strictly governed by necessity.

So, I thought as I slowly continued to suck at the hard candy in my mouth, the sheep's utilitarian motives just might benefit my recreational ambition. With that line of reasoning and a small spark of hope, I stood up, girded my (proverbial) loins, and strode down and across the short saddle to the rocks rising beyond. But such purposeful striding didn't last long—only as long as it took me to reach the bottom of the first bastion of rocks on the ridge. This is where my assault of the mountain's highest and most formidable defense works began.

Admittedly, in the scheme of things, it was an assault of little or no consequence to the world at large. Some might even think it futile, like Charlie Brown's ongoing attempt to kick a football held by Lucy. This assault had no malicious intentions, though. If any violence was to occur, it would be to me, and me alone, and solely because of me.

The danger and the desire in climbing, however, are often so intertwined that it is difficult to separate one from the other. One climbs because it is exhilarating; it is exhilarating because it is dangerous; therefore one climbs because it is dangerous. This syllogism doesn't hold true in all cases, but it holds true in many. Why the danger is exhilarating, though, is difficult and, ultimately, futile to explain. But then perhaps one shouldn't try to logically justify an adventure that satisfies the gut so completely.

> *Opposition is true friendship.*
> (from "The Marriage of Heaven and Hell"
> by William Blake)

For it was both intimidating and invigorating, and often just plain frightening, as I climbed hand over hand up the sharp boulders, squeezed around menacing towers, or crawled over ledges above dizzyingly high cliffs. Many's the time I lost track of the trail I was trying to follow as I slowly made my way upward. More than once I also had to descend to find another, perhaps safer (a relative term, at best, in this instance) route up—if such a route did exist. And every time I lost my way or had to change direction I doubted again if I'd ever stand upon the summit.

Neither did the gathering clouds make me any more confident of my prospects. They did, however, put the summit out of sight and, hence, out of mind, for at least a few minutes. The clouds also put out of sight and mind most views of the high ridges and mountains around me and the deep valleys below. I began to concentrate more on the climb itself. There were even moments when I forgot why I was climbing.

Never once, however, did I forget that I was alone, which actually made me cautious. I thought twice about every move up, down or around any obstacle the ridge confronted me with simply because I was alone. Because if I twisted an ankle, or worse, and were unable to move, it would be a long time before anyone would find me. Oh, I'd taken the precaution to let people know where I was, and thus leave some semblance of a verbal trail behind me in my passing; but it would be a long time before anyone even began to think that I was overdue. So I climbed cautiously because of the safety factor. I also climbed cautiously simply because I was nervous. For, safety aside, I, for one, tend to be more confident when climbing with others, no matter where I am or what I am doing. In the company of others, the darkness hides fewer dangers, the sea harbors fewer denizens, and the heights foster fewer fears.

Yet though alone and aware of every danger, including the often more dangerous business of coming down, I still climbed. By stops and starts, and twists and turns, and even by going down as well as up, I was still moving toward the summit, though the summit seemed to get no closer. Not being able to either sense it or see it, I had stopped even thinking about the summit. All my concentration was bound with each immediate move and maneuver: how to get up the next rock or across the next gully. I had coalesced with the climb, climbing only for the climbing's sake—and enjoying it immensely. Not for long, though.

> *Most men pursue pleasure with such breathless haste*
> *that they hurry past it.*
> (from Either/Or, vol I by Søren Kierkegaard)

Not that I "hurried" past the moment intentionally. Simply by the process of continuing to climb, I had no choice but to move beyond it. For after pulling myself up the scree of one gully and peering over its lip, I was struck awake by a sight that broke my trance of concentration. For there, on the low saddle at the top of the next gully, was a rock cairn, a pile of stones stacked one on top of the other to mark the way.

I felt like Robinson Crusoe discovering the footsteps in the sand on the beach of the island where he was castaway. I had to look twice to believe my eyes.

"Goats don't make cairns," I said to myself out loud and with enough conviction to believe myself. "Somebody's been here before . . . and that somebody's marked the way. At least I can't imagine anybody marking the wrong way. . . . So this must be the way."

And so it seemed to be. Because from the top of the cairn's gully, the trail crossed onto a broad, steep scree slope at the top of which, well above and beyond one last serrated wall of stones, was what looked to be the summit silhouetted against the mid-day clouds. Then, as if on cue, the clouds began to break up, skitting this way and that as a strong, clearing breeze blew in from the north. Soon what seemed to be the summit stood out all the more clearly above.

I kept my excitement in check, though, until I could be certain. I had, after all, at least climbed enough to know how deceiving summits can be. I knew from experience how true summits can hide easily behind three or four or more false summits, each of which, upon climbing, reveals another, higher, "summit" beyond it. I knew what it was like after climbing three or four such "summits" to feel all the anticipation of success dwindle with each passing "summit". I'd felt the heart sink lower and lower as I continued to climb higher and higher, struggling past false summit after false summit, until finally reaching the actual summit brought more relief than joy.

So I climbed with guarded heart. Up across the loose scree I made my slow way, scaring a few sheep simply by my presence; and then up through the serrated rock until there was only me and the ridgeline above me etched against the now clear sky. Then, just like that, it was done: I had reached the summit. The time was 1 p.m.

The spire of Eagle Peak (6,955 ft.) rose before me to the east, partially hidden by lingering mists and partly, in turn, hiding the panorama of snow-covered peaks, bending glaciers and blue sky behind it that went on and on as far as the eye could see. In the same manner, the sheer, snow-covered face of Calliope Mountain (6,810 ft.) to the south, also obscured almost any view of the nearer mountains behind it as well as the Kenai Peninsula far beyond.

In every other direction, though, the eyes were carried downward over shorter summits, to rounded ridges, soft valleys and the turquoise waters of lakes and tarns, including Eagle Lake and Symphony Lake directly below me to the north. In a large semi-circle those blue waters and green valleys girded three sides of the mountain I looked down from. Yet though being so near, they did not seem a part of the same world as the mountain from which I was looking down. The waters were too blue and too yielding, the valleys too green and too teeming with lushness and life to be of the same world as the mountain I stood atop:

When the stars threw down their spears
And watered heaven with their tears,
Did he smile his work to see?
Did he who made the Lamb make thee?
(from "The Tyger" by William Blake)

Yet for being so high with such extensive views, it was eerily quiet. It was so quiet that except for the scrape of my sneakers over the rocks and the flap of a loose strap on my pack, all I could hear was the pounding of my heart. I sat down to watch the afternoon mists skirt over nearby ridges. A soundless jet dodged in and out of the clouds far above.

Then the clouds began to close in and the next thing I knew, I was fumbling for my windbreaker to stave off the cold. The cold wouldn't be staved off for long, though. And with the cold came the mists, which were soon rolling thickly enough around me to obscure most of the views. There was no longer any reason for me to stay. It was time to eat the Snickers bar I carried with me and be gone.

I've carried Snickers bars on almost every hike I've ever gone on for as long as I can remember. First, on the hikes my father took me and my younger brother Robert on when we were finally deemed old enough to go with him and our older brothers Terry and Tim for an overnight hike in the White Mountains of New Hampshire. Every summer after that, we made at least one trip north to the mountains. On every one of these expeditions, Snickers bars, along with Chunkies, were our unofficial snack food. Having such snack foods was, in my young mind, reason enough to go anywhere, especially if it meant having all I could eat. Though the body has grown since then, the mind hasn't and still rejoices in the justifiable indulgence of Snickers bars on every hike. Since coming to Alaska, I've replaced Chunkies with Pop Tarts (which may be a case of switching from one type of junk food to a "junkier" junk food). I do, however, still carry at least one Snickers bar with me on every outing both as a tribute to the memory of those early days of hiking with my father and brothers, and also simply because I still prefer a Snickers bar to every other candy bar, bar none. So as a tribute to the past and the satisfaction with the present, I lingered on that lone summit and ate my Snickers bar.

And suddenly the barrier between past and present was broken.

Once again I was but a child on Mount Chocorua in New Hampshire, or a boy resting at the top of the Boot Spurr on Mount Washington farther north in the Presidential Range, or a teenager on Mount Mansfield in Vermont with my cousin David, or perhaps somewhere high in the Great Smokey Mountains that straddle the border of Tennessee and North Carolina or in the Wind River Range in Wyoming or any one of the many places I'd wandered in the long years of hiking that now crowded in around me. There was no difference between past or present, no contrast to be made between what was and what had been. There was only the here, the now, and the always. And it remained so for as long as it took me to eat my candy bar.

Then as a final offering to the powers that be in those barren heights, I stood and passed water. It hissed and steamed on the cold rocks at my feet while the clouds continued to close in around me. Then I turned to the valleys below.

I had no desire to go down the way I'd come up, though. Instead I wanted a way that would not only seek out new country. I also, I'll admit, wanted to avoid the ridge I'd just climbed.

Well, the route I chose did pass through new country, but it wasn't—as I was to discover—any less dangerous. My plan was to first slab southwest for a few hundred yards down the ridge I'd just climbed. Then I'd turn due south and down into the glacial cirque between Cantata and Calliope. Once at the shore of the tarn at the bottom of the cirque, I'd turn west and, following the tarn's outlet stream down into the lusher, lower valleys below, which I'd then, in turn, follow around the base of the mountain back to the lakes and the trail I hiked up that morning. The scree slope dropping off the summit did extend down a long way and made it appear that the route would get me off the mountain easily; but as I got lower, it suddenly started to look like it wouldn't get me down at all. For after I'd skidded my way down the broad, slippery slope to where it became fragmented by fifty- and sixty-foot high rock ribs that extended down the flank of the mountain like ancient jetties on a beach, my way came to a dead end. It seemed that all I had done was give up the serrated ridge with its teeth of sheer ledges for a steep, shifting slope fluted by narrow gullies.

No matter what narrow corridor of scree I tried to descend, it only dropped a hundred yards or so before dumping its load of scree—and almost me—over a vertical ledge to the cirque below. Soon, instead of descending to the southwest, I was shifting backwards towards the southeast, clambering up and down one dusty gully after another in search of a way down. Soon it seemed like the only way to get down was to climb up to the summit again, which was an idea I both dreaded and loathed. Five, six, seven scree corridors I slid down only to have to crawl back up. My throat was dry and gritty from the dust I kicked up; my hands were chapped and swollen from grabbing the sharp rocks, and my shoes were filled with dirt and pebbles, but I had little choice but to persist.

Then, at long last—and very close to where the cirque turned around at its far eastern end and climbed toward the summit of Calliope—I pulled myself over one last short rib and, with a sigh of relief, found myself looking down a gentle scree slope all the way down to the valley floor below. Dropping myself onto the scree, I plunged, stepping and sliding downward with a loud "whoop!" that echoed off the hanging glaciers and snow-plastered walls all around me.

Very shortly I was kicking my way across the snow-covered valley floor below. A few minutes later, at 2:30 p.m., I was picking my way through the broken ice and snow along the thick ice-sheeted shore of the cirque's lake. Then a few more minutes after that, I popped out of the small fissure at the end of the lake where its overflow of frothing gray waters of melted snow and ice spilled into the green of the valleys below. By three o'clock, after plunging down some last sporadic snow fields, I was back on firm, level ground.

Back here, behind Cantata and surrounded by ridges, spring was slow in coming. The grass was still matted and brown, the first flower shoots were just pushing up from the wet earth, and the branches of the few trees in sight were only now breaking forth with red and green nodes of what would someday be bright leaves. It wouldn't be long, though, before spring would blossom forth.

Yet even the potential green of this valley was good enough for me. The day had come nearly full circle. I had climbed into winter; now I was happy to return to spring. In contrast to how I felt at the beginning of the day, I had enough by the end of the day of rocky summits and snow-filled cirques. Now all I wanted to do was walk through green fields and hear the sound of rushing waters.

The beginning, middle, and end of the birth, growth, and
perfection of whatever we behold is from contraries, by
contraries, and to contraries; and whatever contrarity is, there is
action and reaction, there is motion, diversity, multitude, and
order, there are degrees, succession and vicissitude.

(from The Expulsion of the Triumphant Beast, "First
Dialogue" by Giordano Bruno, sixteenth-century
Italian philosopher)

Pushing my way through the low brush I passed a solitary tent on a low bluff. Then I rounded the last wide bend of the mountain base. Soon I was picking my way up over the broken boulders above Symphony Lake. The wind whistled in the rocks around me. Two white terns skimmed over the blue waters below.

By 3:30 p.m. I was on the moraine between Symphony Lake and Eagle Lake and passing the tent where the woman had shown me the map that morning. This afternoon, though, no one was home.

"They must be off exploring somewhere," I thought. "Yes, a time for rest and a time for play."

Ten minutes later I stepped off the last glacial moraine near the far end of the lakes and started down the boggy trail.

Various people passed me going the other way: people with packs, people with children; and one lone person with a dog. Two women out for an early evening hike were absorbed in conversation, and hardly looked up when I greeted them in passing. Plunging through the mud and marshes on the trail with less and less care as I got closer and closer to the end, I crossed the South Fork, climbed up onto the opposite bench into the brilliant sunshine of the late afternoon. The long light stretching over the valley was green and gold. The sky above was turquoise.

Stepping up on a rock, I admired the view for a few moments. That morning, this valley had been a blank on the map for me. Now, after nine hours of hiking and climbing, I had filled in at least some of that blank. That was just one more contrast in this day of many contrasts. When I came back again, maybe in another month or another season, there would be other changes to notice, other contrasts to compare with this day—maybe even another sunset like this one to admire. That was reason enough to come back.

But for now, it was time to go home. Bidding the valley good-bye for now, I stepped off the rock and once again headed down the trail. Ten minutes later, with the last of the sun's rays slanting over my shoulder, I was back at the car. It was a few minutes after five and I had a powerful thirst, a sunburned face and shoes full of mud and stones, but no complaints. I had actually done what I wanted to do.

Two hours later I was playing dinner music at Villa Nova Restaurant, but I was having trouble concentrating. My mental lapses, however, weren't due to bruises or fatigue. Instead my inability to concentrate was simply due to the fact that though I had changed modality, I had not entirely changed persona. My body may have conformed to responsibility, but my mind was still moving amongst the images and memories of the day. It was still up amongst the knife-edge ridges and looking out from the misty summit of that one mountain or pushing through the green grasses and striding between the waters of the lakes in the valleys below it. Already they were commingling in the memory, becoming one and the same in the experience of the long day that was now behind me.

> *We delight in one knowable thing, which comprehends all that is knowable; in one apprehensible, which draws together all that can be apprehended; in a single being that includes all, above all in the one which is itself the all.*
> (from <u>Cause, Principle, and Unity</u>, "Fifth Dialogue" by Giordano Bruno)

Now if only I could make more knowable the music at hand. . . . Sometimes you never come down from your mountain entirely, no matter how much time or distance has passed.

South Fork of Eagle River Trail

Note: Though the trail only goes to and from the lakes, the valleys that surround the lakes and feed the lakes with their constant gifts of water are worth the effort it takes to explore them. The peaks above, though all difficult to climb, (sometimes requiring the technical expertise of an experience mountaineer) are also worthwhile exploring in their own right. Fact is, there are simply too many side trips to create separate guides for them all. So instead, I will only mention the possible options of (A) climbing up to the Overlook above Eagle River, (B) climbing up to the tarns located in the hanging valleys to the southwest of Symphony Lake, (C) trekking the long way back to the glacial cirque that lies in an alpine wonderland between Cantata Peak and Calliope Peak, and (D) traversing around Eagle Lake to the base of Flute Glacier whose waters feeds the lake from the east via a series of impressive waterfalls. Climbers may prefer summits to lakes, of which there is no dearth—and they are all noteworthy for the effort it takes to climb them as well as the views they offer from their summits. Cantata Peak (6,410 feet), the most obvious mountain in the center of the valley, along with Eagle Peak (6,955 feet) to the left or east of it and Calliope Peak (6,810 feet) behind it as well as Flute Peak (6,610 feet) at the head of Flute Glacier are the most spectacular climbs. But Triangle Peak (5,455 feet), Mount Ewe (6,250 feet) and Hurdy-Gurdy Mountain are also all exhilarating climbs—as are numerous other unnamed peaks and ridges that tower over the valley. All of these mountains, however, with the exception perhaps of Triangle Peak, are difficult and dangerous climbs and beyond the ability of most casual hikers—and therefore beyond the scope of this book.

Trail Location: To get to the trail head at South Fork of Eagle River drive north on the Glenn Highway out of Anchorage to the Eagle River Loop Road/Hiland Road exit located seven miles past the

Muldoon Road exit. Turn right at the end of the exit onto Eagle River Loop Road and in only one tenth of a mile turn right again onto Hiland Road (or Hiland Drive). In another 3.5 miles take the right-handfork at the end of state maintenance of the roadway. This is still Hiland Road. In another 1.5 miles take another right-handfork, still staying on Hiland Road, and continue following it for less than a half mile to where it descends to cross the South Fork of Eagle River. Approximately 1.5 miles from the river crossing take a right onto South Creek Road. This road will descend and re-cross the river. Just beyond the river, turn right onto the appropriately named West River Drive and follow this road to the park entrance a short way up on the left.

On a normal weekend day in the summer, what little parking space that's available is full to overflowing. If this problem occurs, park along the side of the road without blocking driveways or local traffic. The people who live in the area would appreciate it.

The trail begins on the boardwalks that climb into the woods at the south end of the parking area.

Trail Grade: The only climb of any substance on this trail is in the first half mile from the parking lot, as the route climbs up onto a shelf high above the valley after which it descends to cross the river in two miles. This part of the route rates a level 2. From this point on, however, it is a low, steady uphill with only slight changes in elevation which, in turn, make the rating level back and forth between 1 and 2.

Trail Condition: For the first 5 miles, the trail is predominantly dirt with some rocks. After crossing the river, hikers will encounter quite a few muddy spots on even the sunniest of days. As one nears the lakes the dirt with some rocks slowly reverses itself to rocks with only some dirt as the trail begins up and across a great moraine of boulders. The trail across this slow-footed section is marked by sporadic cairns. But the uncertainty of the footing among the loose rocks should concern the hiker more than the certainty of the trail's direction.

Trail Mileage: The one way hike from the trailhead to the half-finished cabin on the isthmus between Symphony Lake and Eagle Lake is approximately 5.5 miles for a round trip total of 11 miles.

Total Elevation Gain: The hike from the trailhead to the isthmus between the lakes entails a climb of just over 900 feet.

High Point: It is 2,650 feet above sea level on the isthmus between the two lakes.

Normal Hiking Time: Runners and skiers who use this trail for training can probably make the round trip to and from the lakes in roughly two hours. Normal hikers, depending on ambition and conditioning, should expect to spend anywhere from 4 to 8 hours.

Campsites: There are many campsites all up and down the valley—with some especially scenic ones up near the lakes or even beyond the lakes. But because no fires are allowed inside state park boundaries, please be sure to bring a stove.

Best Time: Any time is a good time for this trip. But if it is attempted in winter, beware of the winds that blow up and down this valley with fierce and destructive power which makes frostbite more a danger than avalanches.

USGS Maps: Anchorage A-7.

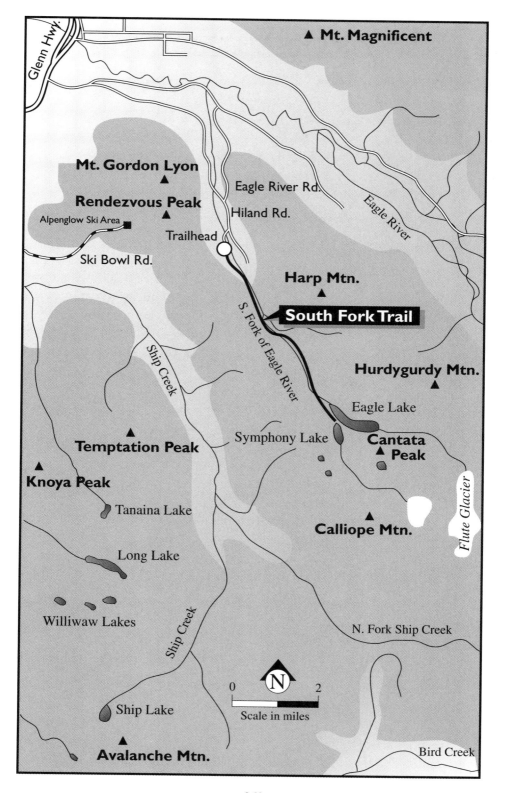

EAGLE RIVER OVERLOOK

Trail Location: The "Overlook" is actually a 5,130 foot peak located on the back ridge above the deep hanging valley located to the north above the South Fork of Eagle River. To get there, follow the South Fork Trail for approximately 2 miles to where it crosses the bridge over the South Fork. (To get to the South Fork Trail, see WALK-ABOUT GUIDE TO SOUTH FORK TRAIL.) About .5 mile up the trail from the bridge, the trail will turn right and continue up valley. Instead of following this main trail, however, look for a dim trail that leads up to the hanging valley above. (The Parks and Recreation Map refers to this trail as "Hanging Valley Trail".) Though it is certainly not the best of trails, being steep and largely overgrown, it is good enough to get one through much of the lower brush and up into the higher, clearer alpine country above. If the trail is lost at any time, look for game trails to follow while still staying in the gut of the valley. Higher up where the valley swings right, look for a place to cross the creek and begin climbing the open slope toward a saddle located high on the ridge above. But don't just charge in a straight line toward the high ridge. Instead, the easiest route up this final slope is to first climb to the lower saddle on the ridge line to the left and from there turn right and up the buttress of the ridge to the higher ridgelineabove. From here, the view into the Eagle River Valley far below and the mountains beyond is nothing short of breathtaking. But the view is even better from either the 5,065 foot summit to the right or the higher, 5,130 foot Overlook to the left—both of which are easily reached from the saddle.

Trail Grade: The first miles of this route along the South Fork Trail are grade 2 hiking. Once one leaves the main trail, however, the grade quickly rises (with the elevation) through grade 3 on the lower part of the Hanging Valley Trail, grade 4 when that trail peters out and, for the final push up to the high saddle, grade 5 hiking.

Trail Condition: The South Fork Trail is wide, though somewhat rocky in spots. The rustic Hanging Valley Trail is, on the other hand, sometimes muddy and largely overgrown. Higher up on the ridge, there is some scree to clamber up and some boulders to wind through and over, but overall the footing is relatively good compared to most climbs above tree line in the Chugach.

Trail Mileage: It is 2.5 miles from the trailhead to junction with the Hanging Valley Trail, and approximately 3.5 miles from the there to the saddle just below Overlook for a total of 6 miles one way— which means a total of 12 miles for the round-trip.

Total Elevation Gain: The total elevation gain from the trailhead to the Overlook is roughly 3,150 feet.

High Point: The highest point reached on this hike is 5,130 feet at the summit of the Overlook.

Normal Hiking Time: The round trip to and from the trailhead should take anywhere from 7 to 12 hours depending on the condition and ambition of the hiker(s).

Campsites: There are some campsites in the South Fork valley, but the best can be found high up in the hanging valley where there is both plenty of water and (usually) plenty of solitude. But because no fires are allowed inside state park boundaries, please be sure to bring a stove.

Best Time: The best time to do this hike is from mid-June to mid-September. It can also be done in the winter as a ski tour. Some skiers, in fact continue right over the pass and down into Eagle River. But everyone who does this trip should be *very* wary of avalanches on the climb up to the Overlook. It is a steep, and therefore, very dangerous slope when covered in snow.

USGS Maps: Anchorage A-7.

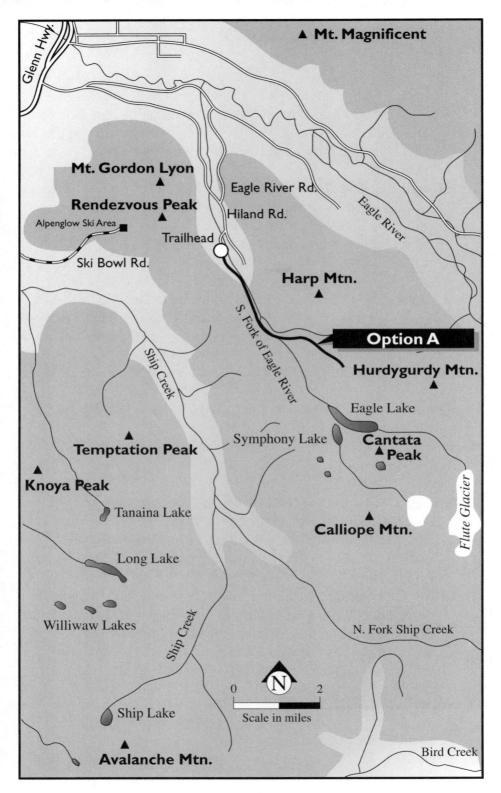

▲ **Mt. Magnificent**

Glenn Hwy.

Mt. Gordon Lyon ▲

Rendezvous Peak ▲

Eagle River Rd.

Hiland Rd.

Eagle River

Alpenglow Ski Area ■

Trailhead ○

Ski Bowl Rd.

Harp Mtn. ▲

S. Fork of Eagle River

Option A

Ship Creek

Hurdygurdy Mtn. ▲

Eagle Lake

Temptation Peak ▲

Symphony Lake

Cantata Peak ▲

▲ **Knoya Peak**

Tanaina Lake

Flute Glacier

Calliope Mtn. ▲

Long Lake

Williwaw Lakes

Ship Creek

N. Fork Ship Creek

0 ▲N 2

Scale in miles

Ship Lake

▲ **Avalanche Mtn.**

Bird Creek

Heading south on the ridge between the South Fork of Eagle River and Ship Creek.

TARNS ABOVE SYMPHONY LAKE

Trail Location: The scenic, but contorted landscape around these two tarns located roughly a mile to the south of Symphony Lake in a hanging valley up to the right are a fine destination for anyone interested in natural science as well as those interested in simply exploring a unique landscape. To get to this hanging valley, hike the South Fork Trail all the way to its end between Symphony Lake and Eagle Lake. (To get to the South Fork Trail, see WALK-ABOUT GUIDE TO SOUTH FORK TRAIL.) From here, continue down the isthmus between the lakes to the end of Symphony Lake. A ghost of a trail circles around the end of Symphony Lake into the brushy valley beyond. The brush is never so thick, however, as to hide one's destination from view. Pick a way along game trails or any other openings in the brush while slanting toward the most obvious hanging valley that can be seen up and to the right. At some point the creek leading into Symphony Lake will have to be crossed, which will usually mean wet feet. Once across the creek the brush will begin to thin out as one climbs out of the valley into the more open tundra above which, in turn, soon gives way to rocks and moraine that have to be scrambled over and through before the tarns are finally reached. After the tarns are fully explored, more ambitious hikers may even want to climb to the wide plateau on ridgetop above. The effort will not go un-rewarded as from up there one can bask in magnificent views of both the North Fork of Ship Creek as well as the Ship Creek Valley itself with the back side of the Front Range rising up beyond it.

Trail Grade: The first part of this trip along South Fork Trail to the lakes is a grade 1 to 2 hike. From the end of Symphony Lake, the grade climbs to level 5 simply because of the substantial amount of bush-whacking required to get across the valley. Surprisingly, the hiking reverts to level 4 once one climbs out of the brush and begins the final climb to the tarns—but this is because that last climb is neither too long nor too steep. Those wishing to climb beyond the tarns up the ridge above will once again encounter grade 5 hiking because of the length and steepness of the ascent.

Trail Condition: The South Fork Trail is, despite some mud and rocks, easy to negotiate. Only when one leaves the isthmus between the two lakes does the footing begin to become more treacherously difficult to follow—not only because of the brush, but also because of the rocks hiding in the brush. Much of the valley crossing can also be muddy and marshy—especially after a heavy rain. This is followed by a rocky climb up to the tarns over sometimes treacherously unstable boulders.

Trail Mileage: The mileage to the end of the trail between Symphony Lake and Eagle Lake is 5.5 miles. From there it is another 1/2 mile around to the end of Symphony followed by another 1 mile or so bush-whacking and climbing to the tarns for a one way total of just over 7 miles which adds up to a 14 mile round trip to and from the trailhead.

Total Elevation Gain: The total elevation gain from the trailhead to the upper tarn is approximately 1,800 feet.

High Point: The highest point reached on this hike is just over 3,500 feet at the shore of the upper tarn—and just under 4,500 feet for anyone who climbs to the plateau on the ridge top beyond.

Normal Hiking Time: This hike should take anywhere from 4 to 9 hours depending on the ambition and condition of the hiker(s) involved.

Campsites: There are many campsites all up and down the valley—with some especially scenic ones up near the lakes. Beyond the lakes it is mostly too brushy and wet to pitch a tent. There are, however, more than a few level spots to pitch a tent on the shore of either tarn. But because no fires are allowed inside state park boundaries, please be sure to bring a stove.

Best Time: The best time for this hike is from early June to late September. It can also be done—and maybe even with less effort because of the lack of bush-whacking involved—as a ski tour or snowshoe hike in the winter as long as one stays away from the steep-sided ridges that can let loose an avalanche at any given moment.

USGS Maps: Anchorage A-7.

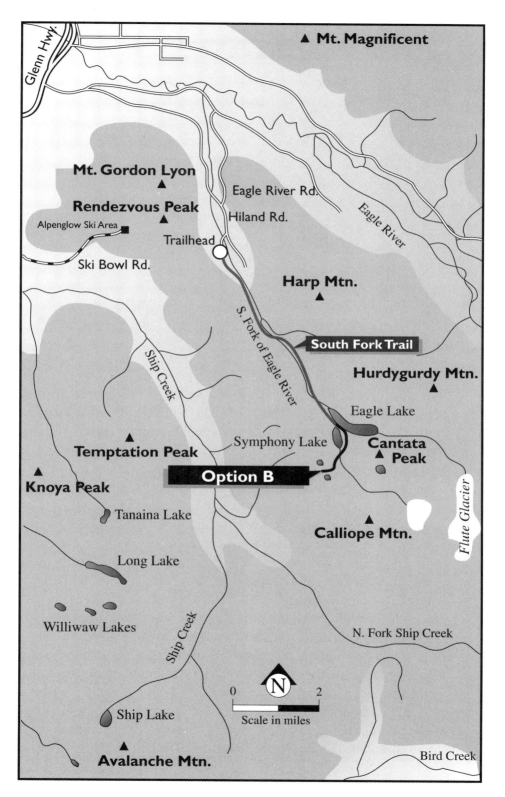

▲ Mt. Magnificent

Glenn Hwy.

Mt. Gordon Lyon ▲

Rendezvous Peak ▲

Alpenglow Ski Area

Eagle River Rd.

Hiland Rd.

Eagle River

Trailhead

Ski Bowl Rd.

Harp Mtn. ▲

S. Fork of Eagle River

South Fork Trail

Ship Creek

Hurdygurdy Mtn. ▲

Eagle Lake

Temptation Peak ▲

Symphony Lake

Cantata Peak ▲

Knoya Peak ▲

Option B

Tanaina Lake

Calliope Mtn. ▲

Flute Glacier

Long Lake

Williwaw Lakes

Ship Creek

N. Fork Ship Creek

Ship Lake

N

0   2

Scale in miles

Avalanche Mtn. ▲

Bird Creek

OPTION "C"

GLACIAL CIRQUE
BEHIND CANTATA PEAK

Trail Location: The cirque behind Cantata Peak surrounded as it is by massive peaks and tumbling snowfields, is uniquely alpine—so alpine, in fact, that one would swear they were over 10,000 feet above sea level instead of just a mere 3.900 feet above. To get there, hike the South Fork Trail all the way to its end between Symphony Lake and Eagle Lake. (To get to the South Fork Trail, see WALK-ABOUT GUIDE TO SOUTH FORK TRAIL.) Then continue down the isthmus between the lakes to the end of Symphony Lake. A ghost of a trail circles around the end of Symphony Lake into the brushy valley beyond. (The brush is never so thick, however, as to hide one's route from view.) Staying as high as possible, slab down the left-handside of the valley, keeping the creek always below you and to the right. The going is not particularly easy as there are many rocks to scramble over and occasional gullies to scamper in and out of, but with a little perseverance one will eventually get around the corner of the valley to where the brush begins to thin out. Here, the creek descends through a series of stunning waterfalls from above. Follow these waterfalls back up through a narrow opening in the ridge above to where just beyond lies the cirque. From here, climb along the shore on the left or out onto the moraine up on the right. Truly ambitious hikers—if they're not tired enough yet—may even want to continue up the back side of the cirque to the pass leading south. From the top of this pass, it is not too difficult a climb up the right-handridge line to the summit of Triangle Peak (5,455 feet).

Trail Grade: The first part of this trip along South Fork Trail to the lakes is a grade 1 to 2 hike. From the end of Symphony Lake, the grade climbs to level 5 simply because the substantial amount of bush-whacking required to get up the valley. Surprisingly, the hiking reverts to a gray area between levels 4 and 5 once one begins the final climb up alongside the waterfalls to the cirque. Those wishing to climb beyond the cirque up to the summit of Triangle Peak will once again encounter strict grade 5 hiking with possibly even some short stretches of grade 6 scrambling.

Trail Condition: The South Fork Trail is, despite some mud and rocks, easy to negotiate. Only when one leaves the isthmus between the two lakes does the footing begin to become more treacherously difficult to follow—not only because of the brush, but also because of the rocks hiding in the brush. Much of the traverse up the valley will also be hard on the ankles—simply because of all the side-hilling that has to be done. The final climb up to the cirque, though steep, has excellent footing almost all the way. Those wandering across the moraine above, however, should exercise care on the treacherously unstable boulders.

Trail Mileage: The mileage to the end of the trail between Symphony Lake and Eagle Lake is 5.5 miles. From there it is another 1/2 mile around to the end of Symphony followed by another 2 miles or so bush-whacking and climbing to the cirque for a one way total of just over 9 miles which adds up to a 18 mile round trip to and from the trailhead.

Total Elevation Gain: The total elevation gain from the trailhead to the cirque is approximately 2,200 feet.

High Point: The highest point reached is approximately 3,800 above sea level at the cirque itself.

Normal Hiking Time: This hike should take anywhere from 6 to 14 hours depending on the ambition and condition of the hiker(s) involved.

Campsites: There are many campsites all up and down the lower valley—with some especially scenic ones up near the lakes. Once beyond the lakes the available camping spots become more sporadic, though there are one or two spots farther upstream near the base of the waterfalls. There are even one or two spots on the few plots of tundra along the cirque above. But because no fires are allowed inside state park boundaries, please be sure to bring a stove.

Best Time: The best time to do this hike is from mid June to mid-September. It is not recommended as a winter trip simply because of the avalanche danger on the final climb to the cirque as well as at the cirque itself.

USGS Maps: Anchorage A-7.

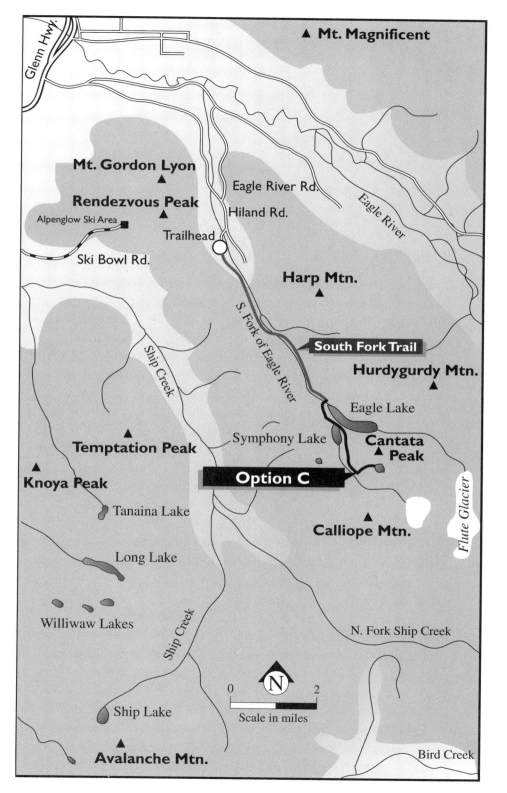

Mt. Magnificent

Glenn Hwy.

Mt. Gordon Lyon

Rendezvous Peak

Alpenglow Ski Area

Eagle River Rd.

Hiland Rd.

Eagle River

Trailhead

Ski Bowl Rd.

Harp Mtn.

S. Fork of Eagle River

South Fork Trail

Hurdygurdy Mtn.

Ship Creek

Eagle Lake

Temptation Peak

Symphony Lake

Cantata Peak

Knoya Peak

Option C

Tanaina Lake

Calliope Mtn.

Flute Glacier

Long Lake

Williwaw Lakes

Ship Creek

N. Fork Ship Creek

Ship Lake

0   N   2

Scale in miles

Avalanche Mtn.

Bird Creek

A WALK-ABOUT GUIDE TO

OPTION "D"

BASE OF FLUTE GLACIER

Trail Location: Though it is difficult to get to, Flute Glacier, the nearest full-sized glacier to downtown Anchorage, is well worth the effort. To get there, hike the South Fork Trail all the way to its end between Symphony Lake and Eagle Lake. From here, continue down the isthmus between the lakes to the end of Eagle Lake. A ghost of a trail circles around the end of Eagle Lake into the brushy valley beyond. At the end of the lake, one enters the first of three (what my friend Tucker calls) "antechambers" which are interesting and distinct sections of the hike that clearly define periods of the glacier's retreat back up the valley—and which are separated by long, steep shelves over which tumble great waterfalls. Thefirst antechamber extends from the end of the lake and is largely along the braided flood plains of the creek. There is no definite way to get up this section of the route as the braids are always changing course and re-routing themselves from season to season. The important point is just to continue upstream as best you can. Just try to follow the stream. At the upper end of this first antechamber, the stream narrows enough to make walking along it quite easy, and enjoyable. To get up and out of the first antechamber, cross over to the north (left hand) side of the stream and climb the scree slope high up to where a sheep trail slabs through the creeks' opening into the second antechamber. This antechamber is nothing more than a pleasant walk upstream across mud and rock flats to the base of the next shelf. Again, stay to the north (left hand) side of the creek as you climb this shelf up past the gorge of the creek and into the third and final antechamber with its piles of moraine and rubble beyond which lies the great expanse of the glacier itself. From here it is possible to climb into anyone of the nearby valleys or up onto any of the lower ridges from the tops of which one can look down onto the glacier as well as look up to the higher peaks all around.

Trail Grade: The first part of this trip along South Fork Trail to the lakes is a grade 1 to 2 hike. From the end of Eagle Lake, however, the grade climbs to level 4 simply because the substantial amount of bush-whacking required to get up the valley. Surprisingly, the hiking reverts to a mostly level 4 the higher one gets up the valleys, despite the steep climbs leading into and out of each antechamber.

Trail Condition: The South Fork Trail is, despite some mud and rocks, easy to negotiate. Only when one leaves the isthmus between the two lakes does the footing begin to become more treacherously difficult to follow—not only because of the brush covering much of the first part of the trail leading along the lake, but also because of the rocks hiding in the brush. Once out on the flood flats of the creek, the hiking becomes decidedly easier, but also decidedly wetter. Many's the time one will have to take off his or her shoes to wade across a particularly wide braid or pool. Higher up, however, where the creek narrows, the walking actually becomes easier, though steeper. And once above the first waterfall, the walking becomes even easier—much of it being over hardened mud flats or imbedded rock fields—and remains so, with little scree and no brush to contend with all the way to the base of the glacier.

Trail Mileage: The mileage to the end of the trail between Symphony Lake and Eagle Lake is 5.5 miles. From there it is another 1 mile around to the end of Eagle Lake followed by another almost 3 miles or so bush-whacking and climbing to the base of the glacier for a one way total of just over 9.5 miles which adds up to a 19 mile round trip to and from the trailhead.

Total Elevation Gain: The total elevation gain from the trailhead to the base of the glacier approximately 3,800 feet.

High Point: The highest point reached is approximately 4,300 above sea level at the base of the glacier itself.

Normal Hiking Time: This hike should take anywhere from 8 to 16 hours depending on the ambition and condition of the hiker(s) involved.

Campsites: There are many campsites all up and down the lower valley—with some especially scenic ones up near the lakes. Once beyond the lakes the available camping spots become more sporadic, though there are one or two spots farther upstream near the base of the waterfalls. Not until one reaches the tundra above the first waterfall are any substantial and obvious campsites available. It is even possible to camp right at the snout of the glacier—as well as on any one of the nearby patches of tundra. But because no fires are allowed inside state park boundaries, please be sure to bring a stove.

Best Time: The best time to do this hike is from mid June to mid-September. It is not recommended as a winter trip simply because of the avalanche danger not only on the steep climbs around the waterfalls but also the danger of avalanches from the high, steep mountain sides which loom constantly overhead the entire way up the valley.

USGS Maps: Anchorage A-7.

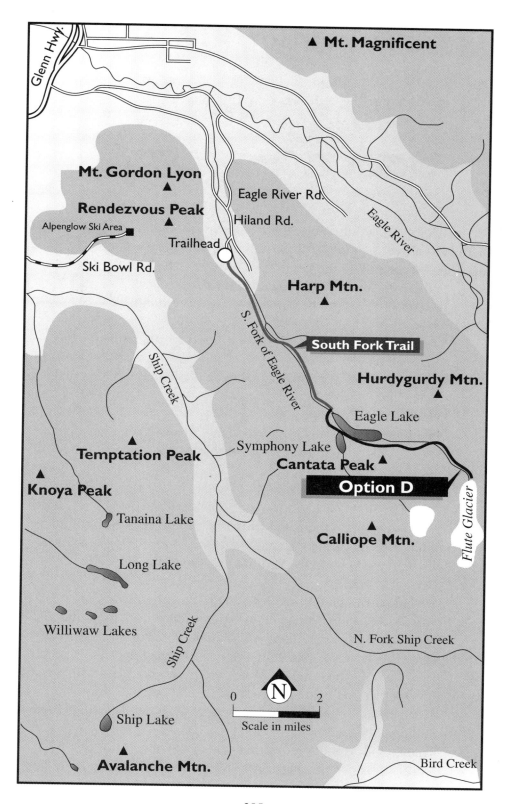

Glenn Hwy.

▲ **Mt. Magnificent**

Mt. Gordon Lyon
▲

Rendezvous Peak
▲

Alpenglow Ski Area ■

Trailhead ○

Ski Bowl Rd.

Eagle River Rd.

Hiland Rd.

Eagle River

Harp Mtn.
▲

S. Fork of Eagle River

South Fork Trail

Hurdygurdy Mtn.
▲

Ship Creek

Eagle Lake

Temptation Peak ▲

Symphony Lake

Cantata Peak ▲

Option D

▲
Knoya Peak

Tanaina Lake

Calliope Mtn. ▲

Flute Glacier

Long Lake

Williwaw Lakes

Ship Creek

N. Fork Ship Creek

0   **N**   2

Scale in miles

Ship Lake

▲
Avalanche Mtn.

Bird Creek

CHAPTER 13

What Would Socrates Say?

"Help!" the faint voice called. All eyes turned to where the voice emerged out of the dark, deep copse of alders just off the trail to the left.

"Where are you?" Georgia called back.

Two or three alder tops in the middle of the stand shook wildly.

"Is it a bear?" someone else in our group whispered nervously, thinking the worst.

By this time we were moving through the long grass to the edge of the hollow the alders filled.

"Help!" the voice called again.

Only then did we suddenly realize that this was obviously not a cry of fear.   "Ahgg! Help me move this thing!" the voice called a third time.

That was no bear.

"Dick Griffin?" I asked myself as much as the voice below. With that, I stuck my head into the alders only to be confronted by a roll of chain link fence being pushed up and out of them—and right toward me. Beyond the big bale loomed the familiar gray-haired head.

"Dick, it is you!"

"Yeah, and I'm glad to see you," he huffed at me.

With Susan's help, I dragged the roll of fence back up to the trail.

"Now," said Dick, hoisting his red pack on behind us, "you can help me carry it." It was as much an order as a request.

"How far?" I asked, hoisting one end to my shoulders with Susan picking up the other end behind me.

"To Dishwater Creek," he answered, "I'm fixing the bridge there with some Eagle Scouts."

"Thank God," I muttered, as we started down the trail.

Georgia looked at me with a tilt of her head and perplexity in her eyes as if to question my sudden relief.

"Well he could've said the Visitor's Center," I explained with a quick shrug.

After all, Dishwater Creek was only a few hundred yards away—we could actually see it spilling from the ridge nearby—whereas the Eagle River Visitor's Center was still close to nine miles away.

"We thought you were a bear," Debbie said to Dick.

He stopped and looked at her. Neither scowling nor smiling he answered: "You've got too vivid an imagination."

Perhaps. But then we'd been discussing books for most of the morning, so our imaginations were working overtime. Still, regardless of sometimes creating real fears out of mere apparitions—or, by the opposite token, sometimes concealing real dangers behind mere daydreams—I, for one, would much rather carry a book or a few poems in my head than a bale of wire over my shoulder, as I was doing now! Not only are the words and ideas of books and poems weightless, but they often make the miles shorter than they seem—which can't necessarily be said about a bale of wire over the shoulder. And not only can books and poems, and music and drama, for that matter, be described, discussed and quoted along the trail, but given the right mind confronted with the right stimuli, they can even be created. For many writers, poets and composers throughout history have utilized walking—purposeful walking, just like we were doing up until meeting Dick—as a stimulant to their creative work.

Though Socrates frowned on what he considered the frivolous activity of poets and writers, he did believe that both the mind and body should be exercised constantly. But this exercise should not be undertaken for personal use—like the writing of books, poetry or music. For Socrates, the mind and body should be exercised for strictly utilitarian purposes.

As I toiled along under my end of that bale of wire, I wondered if Socrates would've been proud of me. After all, at least now I was doing something more "useful" with my time than merely walking through the woods. I was putting my physical ability to work for some common good. For according to Socrates, only when the mind and body are functioning at their maximum abilities can the whole person be of any benefit to the formation of his ideal state. It is for this reason that again and again throughout his work <u>The Republic</u>, Plato quotes Socrates insisting that music and gymnastics be the primary subjects studied in his Republic:

> *Let us describe the education of our men. . . . What then is the education to be? Perhaps we could hardly find a better than that which the experience of the past has already discovered, which consists, I believe, in gymnastic, for the body, and music for the mind.*
> (bk. 2)

Thus are the body through gymnastics and the mind through music both exercised to their fullest capabilities. A worthy goal to be sure, and one that is not foreign to the world of poets and other writers of fiction—even if Plato didn't have much use for them in his Republic. A number of poets and writers throughout history have exercised their bodies and minds to the fullest. Sometimes, like Aeschylus who fought at Marathon, poets and writers used their physical ability for the good of the state. Aeschylus's valorous contribution to the state as being one of those brave few on the plains of Marathon who beat back the first great Persian invasion of Greece warranted such merit that his epitaph makes no mention of his poetic greatness.

> *Aeschylus, the Athenian, Euphorion's son, is dead.*
> *This tomb in Gela's cornland covers him.*
> *His glorious courage the hallowed fields of Marathon could tell,*
> *and the long haired Mede had known of it.*

George Gordon, Lord Byron, one of the most famous poets—and one of the most notorious of men in Europe during the early nineteenth-century—died at Missolonghi on April 19, 1824 at age 36 while taking part in the war for Greek independence against the Turks. But his death was not in vain: Later that year, in October, Greek forces, still in mourning over Lord Byron's death, nearly annihilated an Ottoman army at Mitylene. But more often than not, most poets undertook physical exercise for personal benefits—as we had been doing up until the moment I hoisted that bale of wire onto my shoulder.

Our party of four had already come about nineteen miles from the beginning of the Eagle River Trail on the other side of Crow Pass to where we were surprised by Dick. For most of that time, we'd been talking—and talking mostly about books. To now labor under a bale of fence like a beast of burden for any distance was certainly not conducive to such conversation—or any other conversation, for that matter. Neither was it my idea of a good time at this point—or, in addition, at any other point. Our intention was to do the trail in a single day. For that one day we'd shed the responsibilities of home and work and just walk. And we'd walk unburdened by even the necessities of overnight travel. Now carrying a bale of wire only replaced one burden with another. Not that I wouldn't have helped Dick—I'd do that anytime he asked. Still, I was happy he didn't need my help for too long. After all, I'd much rather carry on a conversation during a hike—especially one about books—than carry a heavy load on any hike.

The only time silence had prevailed over our little group was in the first miles of the hike when at 8:15 a.m. we first started climbing up through the cold shadows of the morning toward Crow Pass. Carrying just fanny packs, we walked gingerly up over the frozen ground trying to generate some semblance of heat in our bodies.

"Is it always this cold this early in the morning in Alaska?" Debbie Turillo, a nurse from Vermont who was up for a summer residency, asked.

"Sometimes it's colder," Georgia Gustafson answered with a laugh.

"And sometimes it's even colder than that," Susan Holloway, the last of our group added with a smile.

It would only be natural to assume that such a state of physical discomfort rarely results in a state of mental inspiration. But such an assumption would, more often than not, be wrong. Physical effort—and the various levels of discomfort and pain that accompany it—often sparks the imagination. Perhaps it's the result of the mind's attempt to disassociate itself from the body; or perhaps it's caused by the mind's fuller realization of the body's presence. Either way, what's certain is that the mind and body establish a unique union during periods of high physical stress that has resulted in many great pieces of writing.

This is particularly true when that physical effort takes place in any natural setting—as the Italian poet Petrarch (1304-1374), one of the first mountaineers in history, discovered. Petrarch was one of the first people ever to climb a mountain for sheer pleasure and write about it— thus establishing a genre of writing that has continued without decline to this day. But unlike most people who hike and climb today, this fourteenth-century poet, living in a world hovering between the Middle Ages and the Renaissance, could not simply enjoy the hike for what it was: an exhilarating day in the mountains. This cleric-humanist found metaphors—which he often extended to great lengths—in everything living and dead. In a long letter to his father written in 1336, soon after he and his brother climbed Mount Ventoux located in the Provence region of France, he transformed the simple effort of climbing into an allegory of the soul struggling toward God:

> *At every step I thought, if it cost so much sweat and toil to bring the body a little nearer to heaven, great indeed must be the cross, the dungeon, and the sting which should terrify the soul as it draws nigh unto God, and crush the turgid height of ignorance and the fate of man.*

Nor should we smirk at such thematic material. Petrarch was one of the most esteemed men of letters and learning in his day. Considered the first modern poet, his development of the sonnet form influenced the works of numerous English Renaissance poets, many of whom, like Sir Thomas Wyatt (1503-1542) and Sir Henry Howard, Earl of Surrey (1517?-1547), made translations of his works. Even major poets such as Chaucer, Spenser, and Shakespeare freely acknowledged their indebtedness to the older master. And who knows? Perhaps part of Petrarch's poetic greatness was a result of his walking and climbing, both of which could've been a partial source of both his rhythmic language and inspirational thought—as in the quote above.

Unlike Petrarch, the physical discomfort we felt from climbing in the cold morning did not result in any great moments of inspiration. Instead, it only made us move our feet faster up the frozen trail. Up through the trees, we could see the summits around the pass washed in golden sunlight. We hurried towards them like flies drawn to a light bulb, wanting only to stand in the warm light—no allegory intended.

An hour later, however, after climbing out of the willow and grass below onto the switchbacked, flower-spotted tundra above and finally cresting the south side of the pass by a Forest Service hut, the sunlight we'd seen sparkling from the nearby summits below was all gone. The pass—as usual—was under a mist of clouds. The wind, also as usual, was blowing hard at its crest. Luckily, though, it was out of the south and at our backs out of the south as we crossed over to the north edge of the pass and its dramatic overview.

From here, we could look out over the turquoise ice of Raven Glacier that filled the high, jagged valley to the right. That was impressive. But what dominated the landscape was what lay directly below us to its left. There, channeled by two high ridges on either side, stretched the entire Raven Creek valley. Winding down over the dark mounds of moraine to the tundra below, it fell away in a pale green swath toward the distant, forested valley of Eagle River beyond which rose another, greater, bastion of rocky, snowy summits.

This was one of the highlights—if not the highlight—of the whole trail. Debbie, perhaps because she was from out of state, sensed this immediately. She wanted a group photo by the wind-downed marker at the pass itself with the cold mass of the glacier and mountains behind us. Then, shivering in the intensifying wind, we started down over the moraine toward the distant green of the valley below.

Once off the last moraine and beyond the roaring, frightening depths of Raven Gorge, we allowed gravity to take over. Half walking, and half jogging, we effortlessly glided down the now smoother trail.

On our long, winding way down to the river, we passed three groups tottering under heavy packs. Watching them labor under their loads—their portable homes away from home—made me momentarily wonder if the camping was worth the effort of the hiking. I thought about asking them, but at the time it seemed presumptuous, so I just gave them a smiling "good morning" as we skipped on down the trail.

We weren't trying to prove anything. We weren't trying to be like Jack London who, being a great swimmer, sometimes used this physical ability to win a bet or discharge a dare—usually when he was drunk, which was quite often. Nor were we trying to be like Ernest Hemingway, whose machismo played such a large part in his personal identity, and who often used his hunting, fishing—and even female—conquests as a source of pride and a basis for bragging. We weren't out for trophies, bragging rights, or even to win a bet or dare.

We weren't even trying to be like Byron who swam the Hellespont one night to prove the literary point that Leander from Greek mythology who lived in Abydos could've swum across the same body of water to clandestinely meet his lover Hero, a priestess of Aphrodite who lived at Sestos, a town on the opposite shore as well as prove his own physical prowess. Unlike Leander, Byron swam the channel during the day, thus having no need to follow a lamp like the one Hero lit every night in a tower to guide her lover. Also unlike Leander, Byron's one swim ended successfully whereas Leander's continuous crossings of the Hellespont ultimately did not. According to the myth, one night a storm blew the lamp out and Leander, unable to find the shore, drowned. When Hero found his washed-up body at the base of her tower, she, no longer wishing to live, threw herself from its balcony. We were just out for a long day's walk, though I did transgress those simple bounds once.

Having been up and down and back and forth along every foot of this trail many times, using it to begin trips and finish trips, access nearby mountains and ridges, connect passes, and even utilize as an emergency exit, I'd never done it end to end in one hike. Today I was going to do just that.

"There's a first time for everything," Susan answered me very flatly when I told them. I was put in my place.

It was obvious that we were out simply for a little fun, a little conversation, and (maybe) some insight. It was no place and time to prove anything.

All up and around the mile-wide trough of the valley mountains rose into the midmorning sky. Those rising directly above us on either side were still streaked with dirty snow or scarred by avalanches. Others—especially those we could see hovering on the far horizon beyond the mountains we moved toward down the valley—were girded by permanent landscapes of snow and ice. Above Yukla, towering far above the Eagle River valley we moved down towards, transparent banners of clouds flapped in a high, cold wind. It made me shiver just looking at it.

Gustav Mahler, one of the great composers of the late nineteenth century, was always inspired by his wanderings in the mountains. He was especially inspired when those wanderings took him up among the crags and summits of the high peaks—like those we looked at on our hike. Retiring to his summer estate in the Austrian Alps after a busy season of conducting various orchestras and organizing numerous opera houses, he would settle down to a regime of doing nothing but composing. Yet there was always time for hiking in the hills and higher yet into the mountains beyond. For Mahler, the exertion and solitude of these long hikes or climbs were a constant source of inspiration for his large-scale musical creations. (Despite the angst of many of his works, Plato might still have been content to see how Mahler combined "gymnastics", or physical exercise, and music in his life's work.)

The names of various movements in Mahler's symphonies attest again and again to the effect these walks had on his music. The very first movement of his First Symphony, subtitled "Titan" (completed in 1888 and first performed in Budapest the following year), is inscribed in the autograph score "Spring and no ending." The second movement of the same symphony is based on the song "Over the field I went this morning" from the collection Lieder eines fahrenden Gesellen (Songs of a Wayfarer) which he composed in 1884. In the Third Symphony, the themes of the first movement in the autograph score are titled "Pan Awakes," "Summer Marches in—Procession of Bacchus." The second and third movements of the same symphony are inscribed "What the flowers in the meadows tell me" and "What the animals in the forest tell me." The fourth movement, darker in tone, is inscribed "What the night tells me." After a fifth movement, follows the sixth, which is inscribed "What God tells me" thus completing the journey that for Mahler begins in nature and ends in God—an evolutionary journey that for Mahler represented all that man is and could hope to be. The significance is that it begins in the wild woods and fields of nature, not in the cities or books of humankind, and ends high in the mountains on the very edge of the sky.

In 1907, the same year Mahler lost his eldest daughter Maria Anna to diphtheria, he was diagnosed with a heart problem. "Relax. Do not exert yourself," the doctors ordered him. It was virtually a death order for Mahler who so loved to hike and climb. How stricken he was by this cruel prohibition can be heard in his Ninth Symphony. In that work, Mahler took his own irregular heart beat and made it the rhythmic basis of the tragic first movement. It is especially prominent in the passage for solo timpani that takes place, significantly, about halfway through the movement. It was Mahler's farewell to the world. As his fellow composer Alban Berg wrote to his future wife after playing through this first movement, "The first movement is the most heavenly thing that Mahler ever wrote. It is the expression of an exceptional fondness for this earth, the longing to live in peace on it, to enjoy nature to its depths— before death comes. For he comes irresistibly. The whole movement is permeated by premonitions of death. . . ." Bruno Walter, another close friend of the composer who conducted the first performance of this work, agreed. In his book, Gustav Mahler, he wrote, ". . . the first movement grew to be a tragically moving and noble epitome of the farewell feeling." But Walter sensed the mood of farewell even more in the last movement. It is in this wide, achingly sweet slow movement, that, Mahler, as Walter hears it, "peacefully bids farewell to the world."

Indeed, it was Mahler's farewell. This work, Mahler's Ninth Symphony, was completed on April 10, 1910. Just over a year later on May 18, 1911, Mahler was dead.

Though death has quieted the man, Mahler's love for and humility before the mountains he wandered amongst lives on in his music. But this love and humility are not consistent in tone. They can, paradoxically, be both grand and pathetic—and, surprisingly, often at the same time. However, it is this very same paradoxical mix of moods which is—not surprisingly—more or less what every wanderer among any mountains has felt at one time or another.

But though Socrates believed that music should be one of two primary subjects taught in his Republic, he would've shunned this paradoxical mix of moods found in Mahler's music. For Socrates believed that only those specific types of music using those categorized modes (scales) that invoked moods only beneficial to the state should be taught and played. All else, regardless of how satisfying to the individual listener, should be shunned.

Perhaps, by extension, Plato and Socrates would also expel mountaineers and explorers from their ideal state. Not only are they too independent and egotistical, but even among these men who are out to stand on the highest peaks and reach the most difficult places, the odd mixture of emotions found in Mahler's music is also present. George Leigh-Mallory, who in 1924 may have been the first person to ever climb

Everest (he never returned to tell about his exploits), wrote a profound and moving thesis on the poet Shelley while attending Oxford. Perhaps it was because of this sensitivity of soul that, despite his great abilities and accomplishments—or perhaps because of them, he was humbled by the mountains he challenged. Even when he reached the summits, his pride could of accomplishment could not overcome his humility:

> *Is this the summit, crowning the day? How cool and quiet! We're not exultant; but delighted, joyful; soberly astonished. . . . Have we vanquished an enemy? None but ourselves. Have we gained success? That word means nothing here. Have we won a kingdom? No . . . and yes. We have achieved an ultimate satisfaction . . . fulfilled a destiny. . . . To struggle and to understand—never this last without the other; such is the law. . . . We've only been obeying an old law then? Ah, but it's the law . . . and we understand—a little more. So ancient, wise and terrible— and yet kind we see them; with steps for children's feet.*
> (Alpine Journal, c.1917)

These words were written just after he reached the summit of Mont Blanc by the difficult route via the Col de la Brevna. They are words of a man who read profusely and profoundly. Later, on his various expeditions to Everest, Mallory always carried philosophy and poetry books. Often late at night, high on the cold mountain's flanks, he and his fellow climbers would read to each other out of these books while the fierce stars crackled in the cold sky that stalked just outside the thin walls of their puny tents.

"So what are you reading?" Susan asked me as we tumbled down into the long grasses of the lower elevations.

"Well, I just finished Killer Angels by Michael Shaara," I answered. "I've been tending toward more and more historical fiction lately. What about you?" I asked in return as a ptarmigan flung its wing-flapping self across the trail just ahead of us.

We stopped to watch it disappear into the brush on our left.

"Well, I'm between books right now," she answered as we once again began our quick shuffle down the trail. "Do you have any recommendations?"

"Boccaccio's fun," I suggested, "or maybe Homer?"

"How about something a little more contemporary?"

So the discussion moved forward to such moderns as <u>Grendel</u> by John Gardner, as well as well as other works by the likes of Gabriel Garcia Marquez, Umberto Eco, Cormac McCarthy and Milan Kundera. Though the landscape changed continually while we walked, the topic of reading did not. Not even when we ducked below tree line for the first— and last—time since the other side of Crow Pass. From here all the way to the Visitor's Center, the trail would be in the trees. But though the inspiration of the high, remote mountains above was partially blotted out by the thin canopy of spruce, birch and hickory we now hiked beneath, the talk of books went on. Only when the physical discomfort overwhelmed all other thoughts did we momentarily forget everything else.

"I've never been so cold,'" said Debbie as she tried to shake some life back into her cold, leaden feet after crossing the frigid, glacier-silted waters of Eagle River. Georgia had been trying to mentally prepare her for the crossing for four miles, but the reality was—as always when it comes to cold water—much harsher than any forewarning could describe.

Now all we had to do was follow Eagle River downstream for thirteen miles through the woods. Hiking in the opposite direction, north to south, along the Eagle River Trail would've entailed more elevation gain, but there would've always been something to look forward to— especially the pass which would've come, as it should, near the end of the hike. This day, it seemed as though the hike was already over—even though we still had thirteen more miles to walk. They were scenic and wild miles, but in comparison to the way we'd come, they were anticlimactic—even boring. Not only were we now almost entirely in the woods, but it was predominantly flat—monotony for the body as well as the mind. We started to dawdle.

To walk up and down hill is less wearying than to walk on the flat.
(Aristotle)

I started reciting poetry to myself to pass the time. It was not, however, my own poetry. I was not like that most famous of ancient poets, Homer (fl. 850 B.C.), who made a living carrying his own "books" around in his head and reciting them to the many ruling class patrons who had the time and inclination to listen. Nor was I one of the troubadours and trouveres wandering from court to court in Medieval France and Burgundy, ready to sing my songs for the residing aristocracies' pleasure—and reward. Nor was I some Nordic bard chanting his alliterative runes in the fire-warmed mead hall of some great, gold-giving and bracelet-bestowing Norseland king, or one of the composing-singing members of some acting troupe moving from village to village to perform any one of the many Miracle Plays that were popular in fourteenth-century England. Nor was I even some old Irish harper moving through the desolate wastes of his Cromwell-devastated homeland in search of some now lost lord or clan head to pluck his rusted strings for his heart's ease.

No, I was just a simple, silent reciter of other poets' rhymes and lines. I was like some ancient jongleur singing an old, tired song on the dirty steps of some decrepit town's fountain. Or I was like some poverty-stricken hurdy-gurdy man, grinding his wheezing instrument in weary accompaniment to his old voice as he plied his way from small village to village along the dusty, narrow back roads of nineteenth-century Europe. The only difference was that I did not recite my poems out of necessity. I did not utter verse for gain or notoriety—only to pass the time as we made our long way through the woods.

Still, to each his own. To me, these woods were not very interesting—especially after being in the open heights back on the other side of the river. To anyone else from any other place—like Debbie, for instance—such woods would probably be a source of wonder. For some, they may have even been a source of inspiration. After all, this type of landscape—long valleys of stream-filled woods and forests and narrow meadows and fields clutching at the bases of the high, barren crags that leaned overhead—was only slightly less tame than that which inspired Wordsworth, who, like Mahler, was another composer who found inspiration in the wild places near his home.

Unlike Mahler, however, who was inspired to write music when he hiked or climbed, Wordsworth composed poems wherever he walked. Whether he wandered in his beloved Lake District, or all over England and Scotland on one of his many walking tours, he "wrote" poems in his head. One such poem is the famous "Lines Composed Above Tintern Abbey," first conceived during a walking tour with his sister Dorothy along the River Wye. Nor did it have to be a unique or special walk that produced such lines. Even if that walk was just the twelve-mile round-trip to get his mail at Grasmere, poetry was sure to be "written" along the way. No matter what time of year and what the destination, the cadence of his steps became the rhythm of his verse. In such a way did he truly combine mind and body in every creative effort of every one of his great poems.

Then when he got home or wherever he happened to be staying that night, he would take the time to either dictate them to his sister Dorothy—who was, in turns, his muse, guide, confidante, first critic, and even co-author—or write them out on paper himself, cutting, adding and revising as he worked. But all this "home" work of the night was just to put the creations of the day into some semblance of a finished form. For all intents and purposes, when he sat down at the end of his walk, the poem was a complete entity in his head. As one of the ancient Greek playwrights answered when asked how one of his plays was coming along, "It's all done. All I have to do is write it down."

Perhaps if Socrates had known Wordsworth's method of creation, involving as it did the combined efforts of both mind and body, that philosopher from Greece might have even allowed the English Romantic poet into the Republic. For, on the whole, Socrates—at least according to Plato—did not have much use for poets in the Republic. He found them full of great words; however, they were words they themselves did not fully comprehend—if they understood them at all!

> *So I soon made up my mind about the poets too: I decided that it was not wisdom that enabled them to write their poetry, but a kind of instinct or inspiration, such as you find in seers and prophets who deliver all their sublime messages without knowing in the least what they mean.*
> (Plato quoting Socrates in <u>Apology</u>)

For Socrates, the creation and recitation of poetry was an untruthful diversion that took men's energies away from the pragmatic job of running the state. He considered poets charlatans, if not liars, who wrote or recited about everything without understanding anything. Even as philosophers, they were blind to the true, profounder meaning of even their own words. (But then, on the other extreme, neither did Plato have much use for mathematicians, either. As he says in bk. 7, "I have hardly ever known a mathematician who was capable of reasoning." So at least he did not discriminate in his disregard.)

Percy Bysshe Shelley would, of course, have disagreed with Socrates entirely—but, ironically for the same reason. In his famous treatise "In Defence of Poetry" published in 1822, Shelley agreed that poets do not understand the words they speak, but only because they were not necessarily uttering their own thoughts. In Shelley's opinion (albeit a very biased opinion, because he himself was a poet) the poet is oracular in nature. Because he is "the happiest, the best, the wisest, and the most illustrious of men," he is, in essence, the medium through which speak the moral and ethical—and very much alive—ideals of the universe. This union with the greater powers that be make him not only a worthwhile citizen, but an exemplary leader:

> *Poets are the hierophants of an unapprehended inspiration; the mirrors of the gigantic shadows which futurity casts upon the present; the words which express what they understand not; the trumpets which sing to battle and feel not what they inspire; the influence which is moved not, but moves. Poets are the unacknowledged legislators of the world.*

Just after passing along a secluded beaver pond, we passed three more pairs of hikers lumbering along under heavy loads in the woods along the river. One pair was laboriously negotiating one section of trail that is so roughly cut among the rocks and roots along a steep bank above the river that ropes and ladders were put in to aid hikers. We stepped past them gingerly with a friendly "good afternoon." They gave us a big smile and a "hello" in return.

It was obvious they were having a good time, but I wasn't envious.

Perhaps, seeing that we were only carrying fanny packs, they were a little worried about our safety. But there was no need—especially now that we were out of the high country and in the woods. Down here, all a relatively fast walker needs is a light pack on the back to satisfy the body's needs—and perhaps a few poems in the memory to supply the mind's needs.

Diversions for the mind weren't always necessary despite being largely surrounded by trees. There were still many views of massive mountains and plummeting waterfalls to gaze out upon through the low or thin canopy or while crossing a meadow or stream—and they weren't always what one would call "quaint". Looking up and out of the rock-piled gorge between the twin giants of Yukla Peak (7,535 feet) and Eagle Peak (6,955 feet) rising on the west and east side of the river respectively was—as always—a little unnerving. The perpendicular cliffs overhead, crumbling ever so slowly into rubble and dust seemed to actually lean in over our heads.

"It's almost claustrophobic," Debbie said in mild disbelief. These mountains were nothing like the predominantly rounded, wooded domes of her native Vermont. I think she was slightly relieved to finally get out from beneath their harsh shadows.

Farther on, we heard a woodpecker thrumming from afar while game hens and marmots crisscrossed the trail and rocks nearby. Then, of course, we had the ever-present flies and mosquitoes to swipe at as well as the possibility of bears to think about, so there was plenty to hold our interest. Like the best travel writers, we didn't have to create imaginary works of word or music; all we had to do was observe and remember— like Herodotus.

The ancient Greek Herodotus (484?-425 BC)—like every travel writer that followed him—made a book of what he observed and remembered. But his wasn't just any book. His travels, travels which, like ours, entailed nothing more than observing and remembering—only on a much larger scale—resulted in one of the great monuments of western literature. Known as the "father of history," Herodotus created a written work after his many years of wanderings, which provides anyone who reads it with a vast, panoramic view of virtually the entire ancient Middle East. For wherever he went, whether to Samos, Asia Minor, Babylonia, Egypt, Greece, or Italy, Herodotus listened and remembered. He met great kings, practiced little-known customs, and walked over much terrain and through many a variety of climate, and always heard stories—stories of both the near and far, and the living and dead—and remembered it all.

Sometimes he got his knowledge firsthand; at other times,

secondhand. Yet like any good scholar, he did not take everything he heard or even saw verbatim. His famous work, simply called <u>History</u>, is full of qualifiers and diverging views and opinions. But by including even doubtful information—which for Herodotus meant anything to which which he was not eyewitness himself or got from a reliable source—his book became the most complete picture of the ancient world available, narrating the customs, legends, history, and traditions of many of the peoples of that long-ago world. The Lydians, Scythians, Medes, Persians, Assyrians, and Egyptians, as well as, of course, all the peoples and tribes that make up the vast conglomerate of city-states, kingdoms and towns of Greece itself were all described. In addition to these nonfictional peoples, Herodotus also indulged in discussions of fictional and mythological personages and peoples such as Midas and the Hyperboreans.

Eventually Herodotus coalesced all this material about the people and places of Asia into background material for what would become his main theme: the armed conflicts between the Greeks and the Persians that shaped not only Herodotus's ancient world—but the entire history of the western world that followed. But whether Herodotus intended his travels to serve such a utilitarian purpose when he first set out, I can't say. No one knows. But somewhere along the way—or soon after arriving home—the great historian found his purpose. Socrates would've been proud of him.

The old sage, however, might not have been so proud of us. About an hour later, after dropping Dick Griffith and his bale of fence amid a troop of Eagle Scouts at Dishwater Creek, we hurried on through the woods unburdened by all purposes other than that of walking. The finish didn't seem so far away now. It seemed closer yet after we scurried up the short climb onto a bench above the river and started down the last miles of spruce-lined, cobbled trail.

This was the type of trail that Beethoven, another wanderer who composed while he walked, would've felt at home on. Much like Wordsworth, he took most of his creative walks close to home, the only difference being that Beethoven's home in the major metropolis of Vienna was much tamer than Wordworth's home in the Lake District. Just to get out of Vienna and walk one of the countless paths or narrow roads that wove through the nearby countryside where he might perhaps visit one of the local rural taverns was enough of a pedestrian journey for Beethoven.

It is said that the famous "brook" theme in the first movement of his Sixth Symphony is the sound of the shaded Schreiberbach, a stream in the Wildgrube, a narrow, green valley just beyond the village of Heiligenstadt—one of Beethoven's favorite ambulatory destinations. Even to this day it is still referred to as the *Beethovengang* (Beethoven Path). Not surprisingly, almost every one of the symphony's themes and ideas—even that of the rustic band's attempt at music-making—can be traced to the countryside and villages near this famous vale.

Within two miles, we were passing cleaner and more neatly dressed people out walking casually through the woods. Dressed in pressed slacks, clean, colorful shirts and blouses, sometimes wearing sandals, deck shoes—one lady even had on heels—carrying casual V-neck sweaters and even suit coats caped over their shoulders beneath their well-coifed heads of hair, they looked like models from an Eddie Bauer's catalog. Next to them, we, in our dirty clothes and ripped, muddy sneakers and with our sweat-stained faces, appeared like vagabonds.

But our short day of vagabonding was nothing compared to the lifelong travels of Ibn Battuta (1304-1377). In his first twenty-four years of wandering, which took him from Egypt to Siberia and from the Levant to Sumatra, he saw more of the known world than anyone before him. Though comprehensive, his narrative about where he went and what he saw, which he first began writing in 1349 at the insistence of the Sultan of Morocco, is disjointed. Maybe he was in a hurry to get on the road again. Still, just the fact that Battuta was on that road for close to half a century—during which time he reputedly walked more than 75,000 miles—makes his long, sprawling tale worth reading. After all, even if he remembered just half of what he saw in his one lifetime, that would still probably be more than most of us would remember after five lifetimes.

"We must be getting close now," Susan said when we finally stepped on to the pristine, wood-lined and gravel-paved trails that surround the Visitor's Center. These short trails—or "nature walks"—that drop down to the river before circling back to the center have informative billboards, viewing decks and many benches to help people learn about and look at some of the flora and fauna in the area.

"Yeah, we're close," Georgia said, reminiscing about the Crow Pass Race, "Now we start counting park benches. . . There should be two.

Oooh, and it was so hard to run past them last year. All I wanted to do was lie down on every one."

I guess you can hike—or run—a trail too fast sometimes.

Then we passed a third park bench.

"Oh," Georgia laughed again, "I forgot this one. But I probably wanted to lie down on this one, too!"

A few steps later we strode up into the bright, midafternoon sunshine to the visitor center's back porch where we all could—and did—sit down. That night we would even sleep in our own beds.

With a sigh of comfort, I pulled off my dirty shoes. They were old, worn and thin before I started, with rips along both sides and thin-soled from many miles. Now they were older, more worn, and thinner—and very muddy. I didn't even want to ride in the same car with them. I tossed them in the nearest trash container.

"Look!" called Susan, turning to Georgia and Debbie, "his first traverse of the trail and we worked him so hard that he had to throw his shoes away!"

There was no arguing that.

But though the shoes could be discarded, the memories of the day could not. Like every other writer who's ever been inspired by the natural world around him, I had walked, observed—and now I would remember. No great symphony like those of Beethoven's or Mahler's would come of it; nor any great poems like those of Homer, Wordsworth or Byron; and not even any outstanding history or travel book like that of Herodotus or Ibn Battuta. All that would come of it would be these few lines about how four people passed but one day of our all-too-short lives hiking together along a trail somewhere in the mountains of South-Central Alaska. That would be memory enough.

Eagle River Trail

Trail Location: The northern terminus of the Eagle River Trail is just behind the Eagle River Visitor Center at the southern end of Eagle River Road. To get there from Anchorage take the Eagle River Loop/Hiland Road exit at mile 10 on the Glenn Highway. Go straight past the Hiland Road turn-off at the first set of lights and continue on the Eagle River Loop Road for 2.6 miles across Eagle River to the intersection with Eagle River Road. At this intersection go right, and follow Eagle River Road for almost 11 miles—a wonderfully scenic 11 miles, I might add, up the gut of the Eagle River valley—to the Visitor Center. To get to the trail from north, take the Eagle River exit at mile 14 of the Glenn Highway, and cross back over the highway. Then take a right onto Eagle River Road—look for the sign with an arrow indicating the Visitor Center—and follow this road for just over 12 miles to the trailhead.

The first mile or so of the trail itself can be a little confusing because of various other trails that connect and cross the main trail. The two ends of the Rodak Nature Trail, a .6 mile loop, are the first trails that enter the main trail from the right. The first right-handturn doubles as the Albert Loop Trail—a 3.2 mile round-trip—as well. Less than a mile further the other end of the Albert Loop Trail crosses the main trail at a right angle. After this, the right-of-way of the Eagle River Trail remains fairly obvious despite some other lesser trails that criss-cross it. Just go straight past all these other trails and few or no difficulties will be encountered.

The southern terminus of the Eagle River Trail is located at the dead-end of Crow Creek Road out of Girdwood. To get there drive south from Anchorage for 37 miles on the Seward Highway to mile 90 and turn left—or north—onto Alyeska Highway. Two miles up this road, Crow Creek Road diverges from the main road on the left. Follow this road for five miles over a bridge, after which take the right-handfork and continue uphill for one more mile to the end of the road at the parking area. The trail begins at to the outhouse at the far end of the parking area.

The trail is generally easy to follow for the first three miles up to Crow Pass. There are a large number of criss-crossing trails that have been formed by people finding their own way up and over the tundra. But the main trail is easy to pick out from all these eroding trails—and should be followed to limit further erosion on these lesser trails.

The hike up to the pass is not only resplendent with views, but also rich with history, for the trail follow the old Idtarod Trail, and also passes the ruins of the Monarch Mine (at mile 1.7) as well as the remaining paraphernalia of other mining efforts up near the pass. If one perseveres up to the pass itself, the mesmerizing waters of Crystal Lake will be found reflecting the craggy peaks and glaciers hanging from the slopes above while a mile or so beyond the pass one can gaze long and hard at the frozen turquoise mass of Raven Glacier descending slowly from the vast snowfields that lie beyond the ridges silhouetted against the dark blue sky.

Trail Grade: The Eagle River Trail from the Visitor Center to the river crossing is mostly level but because it is rough underfoot it deserves a rating of 2. From the river to the top of Crow Pass, because of its long slow ascent rates a 3—which, if it wasn't for the trail, would rise to a level 4 during the final climb to the pass because of the steep and rocky climb. The descent from the pass to the parking lot on Crow Creek Road reverts back to level 1 with only short sections of rocky footing that would rate a 2. If you plan to bushwhack the 2.5 miles to the mouth of Eagle Glacier from where the trail crosses the river, expect to encounter nothing but heavily vegetated level 4 hiking. The side trip to the base of Raven Glacier also rates a 4 because of the unstable footing.

Trail Condition: Only a few miles of this 28 mile long trail offer ideal hiking conditions. This is not ,however, to say that the hiking is poor. Instead, it is simply a rugged, only sporadically maintained trail. On the first ten to thirteen miles out of Eagle River, expect rocks underfoot and often weeds up to the waist. Later, where the trail slabs just above the river, the trail is rocky and muddy with short steep sections and down which have been built ladders and slung ropes to make the going easier and less dangerous. After the river crossing there are fewer rocks and no short steep sections—despite it being one long, steady climb—but there is usually a lot of mud and, after late June, very high grasses that are often so thick it's difficult to see the trail at your feet. As one gets higher up the valley the grasses shorten and the rocks return. One can also plan on having to cross at least one snow-field in the last mile or two of climbing to the pass. After the pass is reached, however, the trail—except for some muddy spots up over the crest and a few loose-rock sections in the first mile of the descent— becomes very tame and easy on the feet almost all the way to the parking lot.

Trail Mileage: It's a 28 mile traverse from one end of the trail to the other.

Total Elevation Gain: Hiking the trail southbound from Eagle River Visitor Center entails a total elevation gain of 3,250 feet, with a lot of little ups and downs along the first 13 miles along the river before—after crossing the river—making the one big climb up to the pass. On the other hand, hiking the trail northbound from Crow Creek Road entails only 2,200 feet of elevation gain— almost all of it in the first 4 miles to the top of Crow Pass.

High Point: The highest point reached along trail is 3,550 feet above sea level at the crest of Crow Pass.

Normal Hiking Time: It all depends: the entire traverse can be done as a day hike by almost anybody with some ambition; many people, however, take 2 or 3 days for the sheer enjoyment of it. Shorter hikes are the 8 mile round trip to the Perch from the Visitor Center which takes anywhere from 3 to 6 hours and the 8 mile round trip to the summit of Crow Pass from Crow Pass Road which takes from 4 to 7 hours—and a little bit longer if you decide to hike the extra mile through the pass to the overview of Raven Glacier— which is well-worth the little extra effort.

Campsites: There are numerous campsites all along the entire length of the trail. Along the river itself are three or four cleared and designated campsites. While there are no official campsites across the river, there are numerous areas to pitch a tent all the way up to the pass. And at the top of the pass there is a Forest Service A-frame cabin which is available for public use. (Reservations for use of the cabin can be obtained through the U.S. Forest Service, the address of which can be found in Appendix 2.) There is also a Public Use Cabin on the Eagle River Trail within 1.5 miles of Eagle River Nature Center and a Yurt on the Albert Loop Trail. (Reservations for both of these huts can be made through Eagle River Nature Center, the address of which can be found in Appendix 2.)

Best Time: Avalanches are a very real and very common danger in the first four miles to the top of Crow Pass from Crow Creek Road so its best not to venture on the south end of the trail in the winter. And while most people prefer to take to the trail in the summer months, the trip from the northern end of the trail is safe any time of year for hiking, skiing, and snow-shoeing.

USGS Maps: Anchorage A-6, A-7.

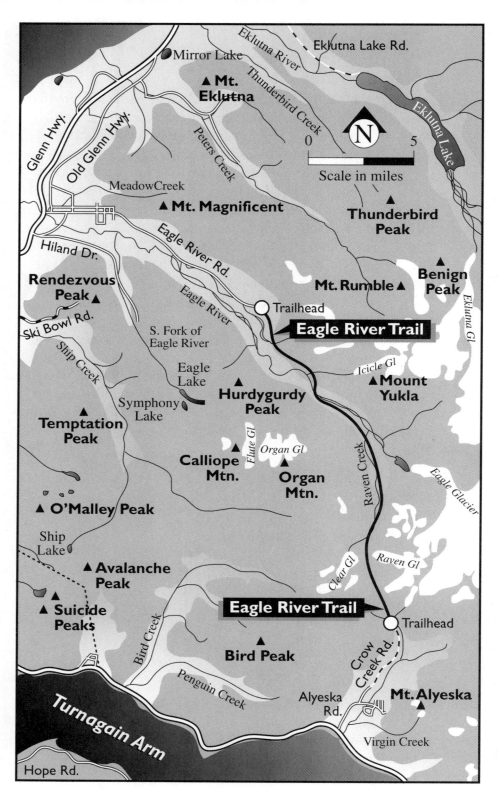

Looking back down Raven Creek to the Eagle River valley from the top of Resurrecdtion Pass.

Rodak Nature Trail

Trail Location: This scenic, educational trail begins at the Eagle River Visitor's Center, which is located at the very end of Eagle River Road in Eagle River. (To get there, follow the directions in the WALK-ABOUT GUIDE TO EAGLE RIVER TRAIL.) It is currently run by a non-profit "Friends" who have not only made the cabin into a small museum of exhibits pertaining to the surrounding area, but have also set up binoculars and scopes on the back porch for scanning the nearby mountains and slopes for wildlife. During the summer months, the group also schedules hikes and outdoor seminar, many of which take place along the Rodak Nature Trail and the Albert Loop Trail. Anyone wishing to hike alone, however, need only pick up one of the maps of the nearby area which are available for asking in the cabin.

To get to the Rodak Nature Trail, follow the Eagle River Trail from the back of the center for 100 yards to a trail junction. This junction marks the beginning (and end—for its a loop trail) of the Rodak Nature Trail. Bear right and follow the trail down toward Eagle River. Along the way, look for the interpretive signs that explain the geology, ecology, glaciology, zoology, and botany of the area. In a short distance, after crossing the two ends of an old road bed, the trail reaches a junction with the longer Albert Loop Trail coming in on the right. Soon afterwards, the trail reaches a viewing deck spanning a stream that, during the right season, hosts a small salmon run. The wetlands beyond, formed in recent years by local industrious beavers building their dams and hutches (which can be seen by looking both up and down stream from the deck), has made it a ideal spot to go bird-watching for various water fowl as well as eagles and various small mammals. From this point, the trail climbs in a gentle slope back to a second junction with the Eagle River Trail. At the junction, turn right to return back to the Visitor's Center.

Trail Grade: This short, wide and gentle trail never rises above Grade 1 from end to end.

Trail Condition: This trail is wide and flat with few rocks and roots to obstruct the footing. It is, in fact, easy enough to be able to scan the woods and wildlife nearby without having to worry too much about where the feet are stepping.

Trail Mileage: The entire loop to and from the Visitor's Center is 0.6 miles in length.

Total Elevation Gain: In either direction, the total elevation gain from end to end on this loop trail is less than 150 feet.

High Point: The highest point reached along the loop is, surprisingly, at the Visitor's Center itself where the elevation is almost precisely 500 feet above sea level.

Normal Hiking Time: Depending on how much reading of signs, watching of wildlife, or just meditating over the movement of water in any one of the streams one passes near or over, this trail could take anywhere from 15 minutes to 1.5 hours.

Campsites: There are no campsites along this short trail. However, the viewing deck may be a nice place for a long picnic or a short snack. There is also a Public Use Cabin on the Eagle River Trail within 1.5 miles of Eagle River Nature Center and a Yurt on the Albert Loop Trail. (Reservations for both of these huts can be made through Eagle River Nature Center, the address of which can be found in Appendix 2.)

Best Time: The best time to hike this trail is anywhere from early June to late September.

USGS Maps: Anchorage A-7 NE.

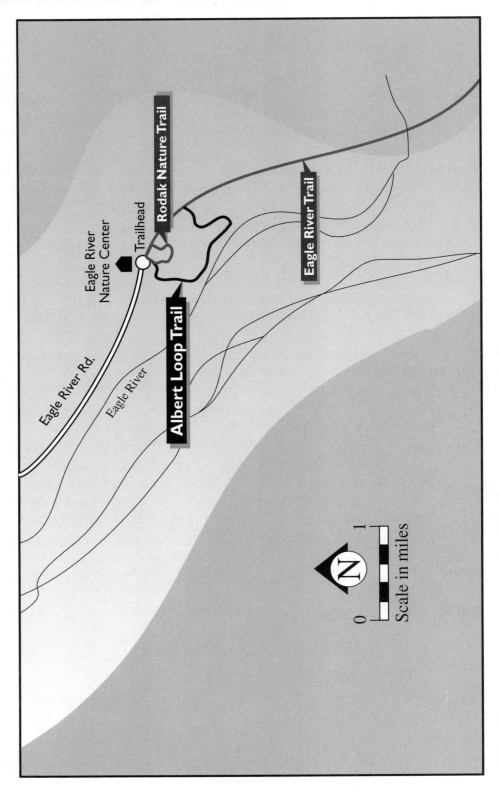

Eagle River Nature Center

Trailhead

Rodak Nature Trail

Eagle River Trail

Albert Loop Trail

Eagle River Rd.

Eagle River

N

Scale in miles

0   1

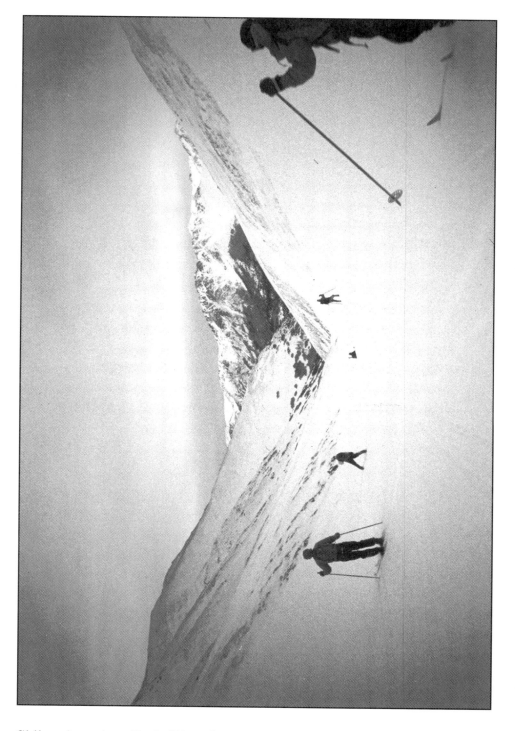

Skiing down into Eagle River in late December.

Albert Loop Trail

Trail Location: This short, scenic trail begins, like the Rodak Nature Trail, at the Eagle River Visitor's Center, which is located at the very end of Eagle River Road in Eagle River. (To get there, follow the directions in the WALK-ABOUT GUIDE TO EAGLE RIVER TRAIL.) It is currently run by a non-profit "Friends" who have not only made the cabin into a small museum of exhibits pertaining to the surrounding area, but have also set up binoculars and scopes on the back porch for scanning the nearby mountains and slopes for wildlife. During the summer months, the group also schedules hikes and outdoor seminar, many of which take place along the Rodak Nature Trail and the Albert Loop Trail. Anyone wishing to hike alone, however, need only pick up one of the maps of the nearby area which are available for asking in the cabin.

To get to the Albert Loop Trail, follow the Eagle River Trail from the back of the center for 0.7 miles (passing the two ends of the Rodak Nature Trail) to Four Corners trail junction. This junction marks the beginning of the Albert Loop Trail. Turn right and follow the trail down across two or three streams and past a Boulder Field Interpretive Area to the bank of Eagle River. Once at the river, the trail drops onto the gravel bar along the river's edge and turns right and down stream. This section of the trail is often flooded, however, because of the industrious activity of the same beavers who have altered the ecology along the Rodak Nature Trail. There is an alternate trail through the woods above the river bank. Follow the posts that mark the trail along the gravel bar until reaching a sign that points to where the trail climbs the embankment and re-enters the woods. It continues to parallel Eagle River for over a quarter mile before turning right

314

and climbing gently up and away from the river. After crossing over numerous small streams, this trail connects the with the first part of the Rodak Nature Trail, which can be followed either way (with the left-handway being the shortest, though not by much) back to the junction with the Eagle River Trail where a left-handturn soon brings into sight the Visitor's Center.

Trail Grade: This easy, but scenic trail is a consistent Grade 1 from end to end.

Trail Condition: Though not quite as smooth or gentle as the Rodak Nature Trail, this trail is still generally easy on the feet. the most difficult walking for many may be along the gravel bar which can be as soft and squishy underfoot as a tropical beach.

Trail Mileage: The entire loop to and from the Visitor's Center is 3.2 miles.

Total Elevation Gain: The total elevation, regardless of the direction this loop is traveled is approximately 150 feet.

High Point: Like the Rodak Nature Trail, this loop is unique in that the highest point reached is almost precisely 500 feet above sea level at the Visitor's Center itself.

Normal Hiking Time: Depending on how much sight-seeing in the wood or sun-bathing along the gravel bar one wants to do or baby-sitting along the entire trail one has to do, this loop can be hiked in anywhere from just under 1 hour to well over 3 hours.

Campsites: There are no campsites along this short trail. However, there are numerous places—especially along the gravel bar on sunny, flood free day—to enjoy a long picnic or a short snack. There is also a Public Use Cabin on the Eagle River Trail within 1.5 miles of Eagle River Nature Center and a Yurt on the Albert Loop Trail. (Reservations for both of these huts can be made through Eagle River Nature Center, the address of which can be found in Appendix 2.)

Best Time: The best time to hike this trail is anywhere from early June to late September.

USGS Maps: Anchorage A-7 NE.

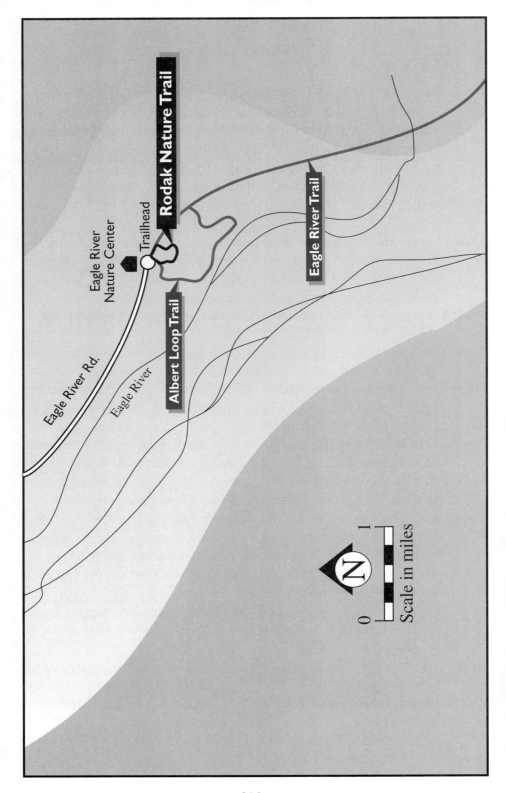

Eagle River Rd.

Eagle River Nature Center

Eagle River

Trailhead

Rodak Nature Trail

Albert Loop Trail

Eagle River Trail

N

Scale in miles

0   1

Raven Glacier as seen from the Eagle River Trail just north of Crow Pass.

CHAPTER 14

Christmas But In Name Alone

"It's beginning to look a lot like Christmas," I kept singing breathlessly over and over again like a broken record as I continued toiling up the ridge. It didn't matter that I couldn't look very far; the fifty or sixty feet I could see in any direction did look like Christmas. The entire landscape was whitened with freshly fallen snow. That didn't make me feel very festive, though. On the contrary, I was more frustrated and astonished than anything else. After all, it was late June, only a week past the solstice. We were supposed to be as far away from Christmas as the midday's sun is from the midnight's moon.

"It's beginning to look a lot like Christmas," I sang again as I continued plodding up the whitened ridge, the plump snowflakes falling drolly about me.

I stopped in my tracks. "But it's not supposed to look like Christmas!" I blurted out, kicking the snow with my right foot.

Now if I had been out far or deep, say in the Brooks Range to the north or in the Wrangells to the east, I might have been more willing to accept snow in June. If I'd been in the Alaska Range I would have even expected snow. But I was not out far or deep in any direction. Instead, I was less than ten air miles from downtown Anchorage climbing toward the 5,070-foot summit of Vista Peak high on the ridge above Eagle River. On a clear day this ridge is clearly visible from many miles away in either direction on the Glenn Highway, as well as from most parts of Anchorage. Naturally, one would assume that the opposite was true: that from the ridge one could see most of Anchorage as well as far beyond. Not on this day, though; not while the snow was falling.

As I slipped and tripped my way up the wet, frosted rocks on the west ridge of Vista Peak the visibility was no more than fifty feet. Yet though the visibility was poor, I knew that somewhere far below me to the left flowed the waters of Peter's Creek and far below me over a lower ridge to my right flowed Eagle River. So I was not so much lost as just slightly confused.

I wasn't confused enough, though, to forget where I was going. For my goal was quite simple: to circumnavigate the Meadow Creek Canyon somewhere below me to the right by traversing the ridge I was on to the head of the valley and then return on the lower ridge to my south, following it as far as I could before descending into the canyon itself and pushing my way out through the expected brush and brambles to the nearest road. Along the route, according to the map, rose four summits of more than 4,000 feet and three of more than 5,000 feet so I knew when I started that it wouldn't be an easy day. I didn't know, however, that it would be a snowy day.

"It is beginning to look a lot like Christmas," I sang halfheartedly yet again. I tried to repeat the bit of melody again, but the words died on my lips.

I shook my head in disbelief.

There had been, of course, no hint of snow in the air as I drove out of Anchorage that morning. On the contrary, after two days of rain and clouds, the weather seemed to be clearing. Streaks of sunlight were breaking through the tattered clouds and the mountains were shaking off their veils of mist. The day, in short, looked auspicious. But now what I'd seen that morning seemed days, even weeks ago. As I continued to kick upward through the snow, I wasn't even sure if it was still the same month, or even the same season.

Yet only a few hours before, when I began hiking from the gate at the end of Golden Eagle Drive high above Eagle River, the day had still seemed promising. Nor did it seem any less so as I followed the dirt road up past an abandoned mine, and on up the fall line of a long, gentle canyon to the open slopes above. Not only did the sky appear to be clearing overhead, but the route was also clear underfoot. Sporadic trails made it easy enough to make my way across the level, spongy tundra to the base of the first peak. Then there were even a few footpaths to follow up the serrated ridge line to the first summit, Black Tail Rocks (4,446 ft.).

The summit, however, was where the promising day started to disintegrate around me. First, it started to rain. It wasn't much of a rain. It was more an aggravating, spitting mist than a malicious, hard-driving rain. Still, pushed and pulled by squirrelly gusts of wind across the rocks,

I found it difficult to keep my balance. Even worse than the unsteady footing, though, was the veil of clouds that came with the rain. Dropping with a heavy thud that obliterated all visibility but for the hundred yards or so of ridge top sloping down before me, they made route finding iffy at best. Luckily, the veil had not dropped low enough to prevent me from going under it. By the time I reached the saddle between Round Top and Black Tail Rocks, I could once again see for miles—or at least almost. Behind me to the left, sporadic sunlight could be seen gleaming off Cook Inlet while behind me to the right were the dots of homes and black threads of roads that made up Eagle River. Far to the north, I could even make out the base of Denali shining gold and turquoise far beyond the thick layer of clouds that continued to hang ponderously overhead.

Then conditions worsened: the rain changed to sleet. With my head down as I pushed ahead into the wind, I didn't see the change. But I heard the change as the plopping of soft rain became a pattering of hard sleet on my anorak. It wasn't exactly music to my ears.

But by the time I rounded the ridge and reached the summit of Round Top (4,755 ft.) the hard pattering had given way to a soft brushing. It was now snowing; and it was accumulating rapidly. Even worse, there was no hint of it letting up or slowing down: Not one rent in the clouds above, not one ray of light on the earth below disturbed the homogenous gray backdrop of the world I moved through. Nor did a single ripple of wind rise to push the slate clouds aside as I traversed the few hundred yards out along the low ridge to the summit of Round Top (4,755 ft.). After backtracking along those same yards to where I would follow the main ridge south, there was still no change. The clouds and snow seemed destined to stay.

But at least the blanket of clouds had still not settled very low. Less than 400 feet below the summit of Round Top I had managed to slip out from underneath them. From there it was easy to trace my route ahead across a low saddle to where the bulk of Vista Peak rose into the clouds overhead. So while I might get cold and wet, I was not going to get lost—just occasionally displaced.

Vista Peak, as seen from Anchorage, is the obvious, slightly askew gable-roofed peak above Eagle River. To me, it's always looked like a relatively easy climb. But when even the gentlest slope is slick with snow, there are no easy climbs. It took me a half hour to climb the last five hundred feet over slippery, snow-covered rocks and slick, slushy tundra to the summit. My effort did not go unrewarded, though: The snow slowed to a stop, and the clouds began to lift. Slowly, as the veil of clouds parted, green, water-gushing valleys began to appear at the ridge's base. Much closer, wild pink and yellow flowers, half covered with small blobs of snow, began to sparkle in the filtered sunlight at my feet. It looked like it was going to clear after all.

But by the time I was climbing over the slippery and unsteady rocks of the next peak, the clouds had dropped—again—like a weighty, worn stage curtain. Once again I was surrounded by slate-gray folds of mists. The valleys below disappeared again. Nearby mountains disappeared again. Then the snow began to fall again.

Nor did the snow give any hint of abating as I clambered down the steep back side of this fourth peak and began toiling up what I presumed was the north ridge of the fifth and last, long humpbacked summit. For with the conditions deteriorated to a worse state than they were before, it was difficult to make out my exact location. Not only was the visibility less—having dwindled to less than fifty feet—but the snow was also accumulating faster. The wind was also blowing harder, more consistently.

"Christmas in July!" I muttered. "Humbug!"

Crouching down on the lee side of a large boulder, I pulled out my map. Without this map, I would've had only the vaguest idea of where I was. As it was, with the visibility so limited, the map still allowed me to make only educated guesses at best. And as best I could tell, according to the map, I had to cross over this last summit to reach the upper end of the canyon. From there, it looked like I had to stay on the ridgetop as it swung down to the right. So all I had to do was stay on the ridgetop. I turned and half rose to peek over the rock I was hiding behind.

"Easier said than done," I told myself as the wind and snow hit me in the face.

Squinting into the whiteout before me, I tried to find the summit, but it was hidden entirely by the close clouds. It was up there, somewhere, though. All I had to do was keep climbing and eventually I'd reach it—eventually. The problem was that the slope was so long and gradual that when I finally started to move, it was sometimes difficult to even tell if I was going up. Only when, as it seemed, I was nearing the top, did the slope get more pronounced. But with the wind blowing in my face and the ground slick beneath my feet, it still seemed to take much longer than it should have.

When, after a long, windy climb I finally did reach the summit—or what appeared to be the summit—I thought about descending immediately off the ridge's flank to the warmer valley below. I even went so far as to trip my way down the rocky slope to look out from underneath the clouds' thick layer. The end of the valley I was circling around was less than a half mile below me. So I was actually still on my route.

"Amazing," I said, shaking my head.

What was even more amazing was that the opposite ridge I wanted to follow out was actually bathed in sunshine. That view convinced me I should continue on my route as planned. So letting pride overcome discretion, back I climbed into the clouds.

The wind and snow seemed to take a malicious pleasure in my return and battered me continuously—so much so that I almost regretted my decision to go on. My fingers numbed and my nose whitened and the footing was anything but steady. Finally, however, after twenty minutes of cold, snow-blinding hiking I dropped off the end of the ridge below the clouds. Moments later, I was practically running across the tundra to get out from underneath the sleet and snow. Fifteen minutes after that, after climbing over the first two knobs on my return trip on the opposite ridge, the feeling returned to my fingers and nose. Soon after that even the rain petered out.

But the sun I'd seen sparking on this ridge less than a half hour before was now gone. Instead it was now shining on the ridge I had just traversed. There, on the ridge where only an hour or two before I had been hiking and climbing through a snowstorm in the clouds, the snow had stopped and the clouds were gone. All that remained was the newly fallen snow shining like wet abalone in the sunlight. In contrast, where I stood now, where only a half an hour before the sun had been shining, the ground was as dull as muddy coal beneath a high canopy of dark clouds.

My only consolation was that at least I was no longer being snowed or rained upon. Then, of course, it started to rain—again. Across the valley, meanwhile, the high ridge I'd come off was still sheathed in brilliant sunshine. It was very disheartening. If this was the power above's idea of retribution for my hubris, I was sufficiently humbled.

Luckily, it was only a feeble rain that soon ran out of energy. Pulling myself up the wet grass and steep rocks to the summit of Mount Magnificent (4,285 ft.) I even began to believe it was going to clear. From this, the highest point on this ridge, I gazed down on a world of exhaling mists and dissipating fogs. Columns of sunlight rolled across Eagle River Valley, revealing the movement of rush hour traffic along the wet streets, the bright lights of malls out toward the Seward Highway and the outlying grids of neighborhoods. Soon even Anchorage and Cook Inlet came into view, emerging out of the low-lying clouds and shining in the wet light of the early evening. It seemed like another world—to which I would soon have to return. Closer, the clouds were beginning to lift off the summits around me. If it wasn't for the long day behind me, I would've been reluctant to leave the high country opening up around me. The hour was late, though. The holiday—if you can call it that—was over. It was time to go home.

But now instead of weather making the going hard for me, I made it hard on myself. I didn't do it intentionally, of course. The result was the same, though. For instead of simply crossing Canyon Creek below and climbing back up to the low point along the ridge just below Black Tail Rocks and only a short distance from the mining camp near where I had started that morning, I decided to simply descend into the canyon and follow the creek out. I could easily see the road I wanted to get to; it wasn't very far. And having been on a trail further down the valley a few years ago on a walk with a friend, I also assumed there would be a trail.

But there wasn't a trail. Instead I walked into a trail-less tangle of wet undergrowth reaching up to my waist and overgrowth stretching over my head. Scratched at by nettles and devil's club, grabbed at by dripping willow and spruce, and sucked in by bogs and sinkholes, I muttered and cursed my slow, stumbling way forward.

First it was Christmas in July, now it was July in Christmas. In the matter of a few hours I had somehow traveled from an arctic waste to a tropical abundance. It made no difference to the ease of travel, though—both were anything but easy.

Then, to make matters worse, it began to rain again.

"Bah, humbug!" I muttered again as I pulled my hood up over my head.

323

But there was at least one consolation. Though I was cold and wet, the sun was shining on the wet, green world around me. The grass was sparkling like a field of emeralds about my feet; the leaves were twinkling like branches of diamonds around my head. With the cold rain behind me and the warm sun before me, I was slowly—and finally—winding my way out from beneath the clouds.

Then, looking behind me, I was greeted not just by gray clouds, but also by a shining rainbow. Arching across the valley, its blend of colors was as vivid and clean as a still wet oil painting. For a moment it even made me forget the snow, the rain, and even the bushwhacking. Only for a moment, though.

When I finally stumbled out of the jungle of brush into civilization I found myself on private property at the end of a long private drive. Brush and private property: two good reasons not to come down this way again. I made a mental note: "If I ever come this way again. . ."

No doubt, I should've avoided coming down the valley. The other route would've been easier. I should've just crossed the valley and made the thousand foot climb back up over the ridge. It would've saved me a lot of trouble. Should've, would've, should've, would've: all words of hindsight that did me no good, because it simply didn't matter now. But when I finally came out on the road, that mattered—that's all that mattered.

Standing on the clear, dry road, I turned one last time to look back up the valley I had worked so hard to come down. The snow had stopped. The rain had stopped. Even the clouds were dispersing. Only the rainbow remained, arching peacefully across the span between the two ridges I had traversed.

"I wonder," I mused out loud to myself, "if the rainbow, as with Noah of old, meant no more rain and no more floods?"

For a moment longer I stood facing the rainbow and thinking.

"Fat chance," I finally muttered.

Then I turned to walk back up the road to where my car was parked.

Descending the trail off of Baldy with the Anchorage Bowl in the distance.

Black Tail Rocks and Roundtop

Trail Location: Though this is not an officially recognized trail in Chugach State Park, it is one of the more popular trails. To get to the trailhead, drive north out of Anchorage to the Eagle River Loop/Hiland Road exit. Turn right onto South Eagle River Loop Road at the end of the ramp off the highway and continue on this road for 3.5 miles across the river, and through one set of lights. As the Loop Road swings left, West Skyline Drive will be on the right. Turn onto West Skyline Drive and follow it on its winding and twisting way to the very end where there will be a gate. Park here without blocking the gate. The area beyond the gate is private property but the owners do not take umbrage at hikers passing over their land—as long as they don't abuse the privilege. From the parking area, there are two choices of trails. The first, up alongside Meadow Creek itself, begins by following the road straight ahead past the gate. In less than a mile an abandoned farm and mine will be reached. Here, take a right-handturn up into a road/trail that is often heavily canopied with overgrown alders. In just over a mile of sometimes relatively steep hiking, this road/trail will eventually lead to the crest of the broad plateau below Black Tail Rocks. This route is the more gradual of the two, taking over two miles to climb 1,600 feet. The second route which leads up and over "Baldy" can be found in OPTION A below. To climb Black Tail Rocks from the plateau, it is best to follow the faint trail up the right-handslope, continuing to traverse across the top of the ridge to the summit. Round Top is another mile of mixed rock scrambling and tundra hiking along the ridge to the north/northwest.

Trail Grade: The Meadow Creek route up to the plateau rates a level 1 to 2. The climb from the plateau to the summits of Black Tail Rocks rate a level 3-4 with one or two very short sections of level 5 along the crest of the summit ridge.

Trail Condition: Both the Meadow Creek and Baldy routes can be muddy—and hence slippery—both during and just after a rain. But if the weather has been at all dry, expect excellent footing. The footing is also good to excellent across the plateau and even up most of the way to the summit of Black Tail Rocks. Only along the crest of the ridge is there any serious scree or rocks upon which to trip or twist an ankle.

Trail Mileage: The one way hike to the summit of Black Tail Rocks via Meadow Creek is 5 miles for a round trip total of 10 miles, whereas one way to the summit of Round Top is 6 miles, for a round trip total of 12 miles.

Total Elevation Gain: Total elevation gain from West Skyline Drive to the summit of Black Tail Rocks is 2,750 feet. To climb Round Top as well increases the total elevation gain to 3,470 feet.

High Point: The summit of Black Tail Rocks is 4,446 feet above sea level and the summit of Round Top is 4,755 feet above sea level.

Normal Hiking Time: Both summits can be climbed in anywhere from 5-9 hours.

Campsites: There are numerous places to camp both in the Meadow Creek valley as well as higher up on the plateau—where there is a small tarn on the northern side that can be used as a water supply. Because it is private property bring a stove to avoid having to chop any wood.

Best Time: Because of avalanche dangers on the mountains themselves—and even a little bit in upper Meadow Creek—it is best to do this hike from late May to early October.

USGS Maps: Anchorage B-7 SW and SE.

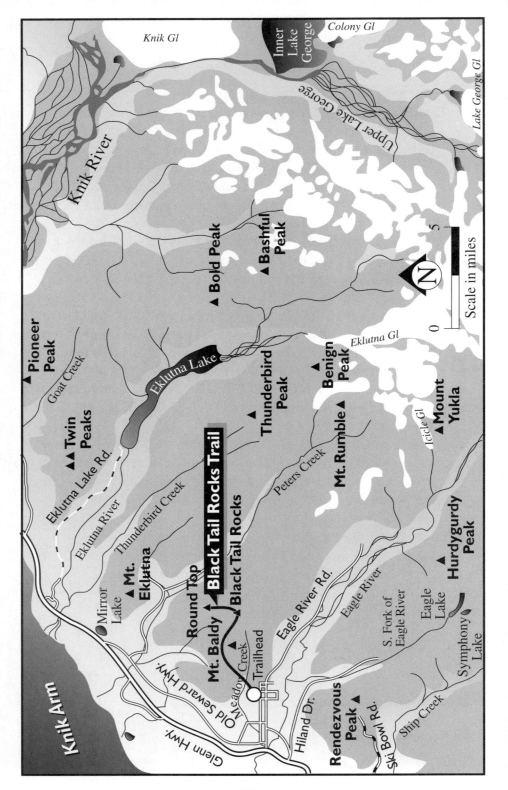

Knik Arm

Knik Gl

Colony Gl

Inner Lake George

Lake George Gl

Upper Lake George

Knik River

Bold Peak ▲

▲ Bashful Peak

▲

Pioneer Peak ▲

Goat Creek

Eklutna Lake

Eklutna Gl

▲ Twin Peaks ▲

Eklutna Lake Rd.

Eklutna River

Thunderbird Creek

Thunderbird Peak ▲

Benign Peak ▲

Icicle Gl

Mt. Rumble ▲

▲ Mount Yukla

Black Tail Rocks Trail

Black Tail Rocks

Peters Creek

Mirror Lake

Mt. Eklutna ▲

Round Top

Mt. Baldy

Eagle River Rd.

Eagle River

Hurdygurdy Peak ▲

Meadow Creek

Trailhead

S. Fork of Eagle River

Eagle Lake

Symphony Lake

Old Seward Hwy.

Glenn Hwy.

Hiland Dr.

Rendezvous Peak ▲

Ski Bowl Rd.

Ship Creek

N

Scale in miles

0   5

Looking toward the Eagle River valley from the plateau just below Black
Tail Rocks.

BLACK TAIL ROCKS AND ROUNDTOP
VIA BALDY

Trail Location: This second route up to Black Tail Rocks is actually
more popular than the Meadow Creek Route—probably because
the reward of good views are, though harder won, achieved
quicker than on the first route. The beginning of this route begins,
like the Meadow Creek route, at the very top of West Skyline
Drive above Eagle River. (To get there see WALK-ABOUT
GUIDE TO BLACK TAIL ROCKS AND ROUND TOP.)
This route, like the Meadow Creek route, also goes through the
gate. Instead of following the road to its end, however, it turns
uphill within 20 yards of the gate, climbing past a radio tower and
on upward to the summit of what is known locally as "Baldy"
(3,038 feet). Then a walk along the crest of the ridge, with
Meadow Creek below on the left and Eagle River much farther
below on the right, comes to an eventual convergence with the
Meadow Creek route on the broad plateau below Black Tail
Rocks. This second route requires much more work in that it only
takes a mile to make the same elevation gain as the Meadow
Creek Trail, but what it takes in effort, it certainly makes up for in
views.
To climb Black Tail Rocks from the plateau, it is best to follow the
faint trail up the right-handslope, continuing to traverse across the
top of the ridge to the summit. Round Top is another mile of
mixed rock scrambling and tundra hiking along the ridge to the
north/northwest.

Trail Grade: Whereas the Meadow Creek route up to the plateau rates a
level 1 to 2, the Baldy route rates a 2 to 3 because of its steeper

and more strenuous ascent. The climb from the plateau to the summits of Black Tail Rocks rate a level 3 to 4 with one or two very short sections of level 5 along the crest of the summit ridge.

Trail Condition: Like Meadow Creek, the trail up and over Baldy can be muddy—and hence slippery—both during and just after a rain. But if the weather has been at all dry, expect excellent footing. The footing is also good to excellent across the plateau and even up most of the way to the summit of Black Tail Rocks. Only along the crest of the ridge is there any serious scree or rocks to labor up or over.

Trail Mileage: The one way hike to the summit of Black Tail Rocks via Baldy is 4 miles for a round trip total of 8 miles, whereas the one way hike to the summit of Round Top via Baldy is 5 miles for a round trip total of 10 miles. For novelty, though, one may choose to go up Meadow Creek and down Baldy—or vice versa—for a round trip of 9 miles to Black Tail Rocks and 11 miles to Round Top.

Total Elevation Gain: Total elevation gain from West Skyline Drive to the summit of Black Tail Rocks is 2,750 feet. To climb Round Top as well increases the total elevation gain to 3,470 feet.

High Point: The summit of Black Tail Rocks is 4,446 feet above sea level and the summit of Round Top is 4,755 feet above sea level.

Normal Hiking Time: Both summits can be climbed in anywhere from 5-9 hours.

Campsites: There are numerous places to camp both in the Meadow Creek valley as well as higher up on the plateau—where there is a small tarn on the northern side that can be used as a water supply. Because it is private property bring a stove to avoid having to chop any wood.

Best Time: Because of avalanche dangers on the mountains themselves—as well as on the steep west slope of Baldy—it is best to do this hike some time between late May and early October.

USGS Maps: Anchorage B-7 SW and SE.

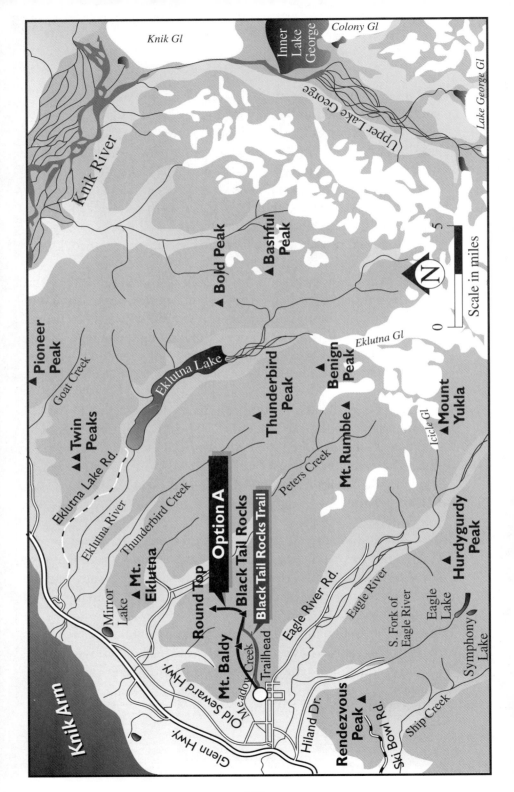

Knik Gl

Colony Gl

Inner Lake George

Upper Lake George

Lake George Gl

Knik River

Pioneer Peak

▲ Bold Peak

▲ Bashful Peak

▲

Goat Creek

Eklutna Lake

Eklutna Gl

▲ Twin Peaks

Eklutna Lake Rd.

Eklutna River

Thunderbird Creek

Thunderbird Peak

▲

▲ Benign Peak

▲ Mount Yukla

Icicle Gl

Mirror Lake

▲ Mt. Eklutna

Peters Creek

Mt. Rumble ▲

Round Top

Black Tail Rocks

Option A

Black Tail Rocks Trail

Mt. Baldy

Meadow Creek

Trailhead

Eagle River Rd.

Eagle River

Hurdygurdy Peak

▲

S. Fork of Eagle River

Eagle Lake

Old Seward Hwy.

Glenn Hwy.

Knik Arm

Hiland Dr.

Rendezvous Peak ▲

Ski Bowl Rd.

Ship Creek

Symphony Lake

N

0   5

Scale in miles

332

Near the summit of Black Tail rocks.

CHAPTER 15

The Comfort of Goodly Company

Stepping over slippery rocks and threading through thorny thickets, I picked my way up the braided stream bed as fast as I could in the face of a damp, raw, nose-reddening head wind. In front of me rose sharp, weather-beaten ramparts of rock. Behind me lay acres of soft, summer-thickened tundra. Below me frothed the heavy, milky glacial waters rushing from those rocks above to that tundra below. And all around me, wherever I looked, the landscape was tinted by autumn's variety of colors.

The world was in flux. The world is always in flux. Age to age, century to century, year to year, and season to season the world is always in a state of change. Even from day to day it is in a state of alteration: day to night and night to day, and all the variety of weather that each day can bring make the manifestations of passing time as constant as time itself.

> *The sun came up upon the left,*
> *Out of the sea came he!*
> *And he shone bright, and on the right*
> *Went down into the sea.*
> ("The Rime of the Ancient Mariner"
> by S.T. Coleridge, 25-8)

On this particular day of the countless that have come and gone through time, I was beginning to wonder if there was enough time left in it—enough daylight to see by—to get where I wanted to go. Considering how long it had taken me to reach where I was, there probably wasn't enough time. For unlike the Mariner who looked upon a sun getting higher and higher as he moved south, I looked upon a sun getting lower and lower as it moved south. I almost—in spite of all the ensuing hardships he endured—envied the Mariner sailing toward the summer of the equator, while I was left behind in the approaching winter of the Arctic. Already, despite being only mid-August, the days were getting noticeably shorter, the nights obviously longer.

Above my left shoulder, the awesome west buttress of Mount Rumble loomed in and out of the broken clouds. Its tortured preeminence quelled any and all misconceptions about going on. It was simply too late on this shorter day of the late season to consider hiking almost four miles more, and climbing another 2,600 feet to the 5,100-foot pass on the mountain's back side.

Already the gray day was dimming around me. A few scattered rays of sunlight splashed gold across nearby rocks and on the crags overhead. The few shadows they cast were long and dark.

Getting out of the wind a short time after leaving the stream bed below me, I sat down on a large stone and took a short drink. Then I took the time for a longer think.

My plan had been to circumnavigate Mount Rumble. First, I would follow the headwaters of Peters Creek back up the west side of Mount Rumble toward one of the many snouts of Eklutna Glacier that push out of the deep, cold recesses of the inner Chugach. Before reaching that land of ice, however, I would turn right—east—and climb up to the 5,100-foot pass, the lowest point on the high, southwest ridge of the mountain. From there, I hoped to descend to the stone glacier on the east side of Mount Rumble and follow its drainage out to where I could pick up the Peters Creek Trail again. Then, all I would have left was the long walk out.

This trip was not be, however. There was simply too little time with still too much to do.

"C'est la vie," I complained, looking up at the dark rocks looming over my head.

Sometimes things just do not work quite as planned.

Then it started to rain—and not just a little. After one or two preliminary drops, it turned into a downpour. Now it was definitely time to go. A moment later, when I was hurrying back down the way I'd come, the wind picked up.

And now the storm blast came, and he
Was tyrannous and strong:
He struck with o'taking wings,
And chased us south along.
      (41-4)

Moments before I had been sitting beneath dry, scattered sunlight. Now I was leaning into a horizontal deluge. And it all happened so fast.
    "Amazing, " I muttered, with not a little bit of disgust.
    The quickness of the change was amazing, not the change itself. The change wasn't even surprising. It was disconcerting, disheartening, and discomforting, but not surprising. Change is to be expected. It is the only constant in this world.

The sun now rose up on the right:
Out of the sea came he,
Still hid in mist, and on the left
Went down into the sea.
      (83-6)

Neither was the rain very surprising. This summer the rain had been almost as constant as change. At least part—if not all—of every hike or climb I'd undertaken this year had been spent in the companionship of rain. At first, its company was refreshing. Warming the air with the pungent smell of new growth, it greened the woods and blossomed the fields I walked through. It was also exciting to be there when it mysteriously shrouded the upland ridges, allowing only an occasional glimpse of nearby cliffs and distant summits still draped by wet and dirty sheets of the late season snow.

And through the drifts the snowy clifts
Did send a dismal sheen:
Nor shapes of men nor beasts we ken—
The ice was all between.
      (55-8)

Back in late May or early June, when we sometimes labored over the still barren highlands, the rain would playfully loosen layers of last winter's snow and push them into the valleys below. It never let me see these avalanches, though. Instead, from somewhere beyond the thick fog and mist that surrounded me, I would only hear the muffled crack of snow sloughing off the ridge. This would be followed by a louder and louder whoosh as it slid downward. After that, sometimes a loud rumble would follow as if the snow mass had been catapulted from some high rock bastion before crashing to the earth below. Or sometimes there would just be a fading-away whisper of the snow as it slid steadily down a long chute before spreading in a large lethal fan across the valley somewhere below.

Admittedly, the rain was wet and cold, but the novelty of those spring days more than made up for any discomfort. As always, though, things changed. First, spring began moving into summer. Then, as the spring days began to fade, the novelty that accompanied them began to wear off. In turn, as the novelty wore away, the uncomfortable aspects of the rain became more and more obvious. Soon there was not a trace of novelty remaining in the situation. It had all been washed away. All that mattered then was the cold and wet.

This wouldn't have been so bad if the rain had faded with the passing of time as well. Unlike the days of spring and the novelty of those days, however, the rain didn't disappear or fade away or diminish. On the contrary, it remained the only constant in the ensuing weeks. Some weeks it was heavy, some weeks it was light, but every week it was still there, still falling. That's what was so surprising: unlike every other being and thing, it seemed unaffected by the passage of time.

> *Day after day, day after day,*
> *We stuck, nor breath nor motion;*
> *As idle as a painted ship*
> *Upon a painted ocean.*
> (115-18)

Being idle in the warm, dry doldrums, however, might have seemed a luxury compared to always hurrying through a cold, wet rain.

It was always raining. Every week I went out hiking or climbing,

it was raining. It wouldn't rain Tuesday through Saturday, but come
Sunday and Monday—the only days I could go—the sun would dim, the
clouds move in, and soon it was raining again. Of course, I cannot say
that this lack of change pleased me. On the contrary, it was getting pretty
old in its constancy.

I was starting to feel like that character in the comic strip <u>L'il
Abner</u> with the little black cloud constantly hovering over his head. I
don't remember his last name, though, except for the fact that I recall it
didn't contain a single vowel. I do remember, however, that he was
always bent forward, walking with urgent hurry. A permanent frown was
etched upon his lips. And always, only a foot or so above his head, there
hovered that small black cloud. I always felt a tinge of sadness for him.

Now, weeks into the wet summer, I was just like him, walking
under the same constant cloud, with the same sad urgency. I wondered if
this was how Noah felt after thirty-nine and a half days in the ark; or
Jonah after three days in the belly of the fish; or how Odysseus felt after
clinging to a single spar for three days and nights while the storming seas
crashed over him before he finally struggled to land; or like Beowulf
struggling against storms and monsters in his seven days' swim with
naked sword in hand in the northern sea; or like a rat who's spent too long
a time in a drain pipe.

I was starting to look for webbing between my toes when I took
off my shoes. I was standing in front of the mirror more and more often,
twisting my head around to see if gills were opening up behind my ears.
And I had this urge to move my arms like I was doing the breaststroke
when I walk. I was also spending more time in pet shops standing in
front of the aquariums. I looked for seaweed salads on the menus of
restaurants. I was even waking up in the middle of many nights with a
craving for plankton.

Now here it was raining again, coming down in blinding, cold
sheets. The day was a washout. I looked skyward in frustration. It
seemed that all my days were destined to be clouded by rain.

"I wonder if the sun will ever shine on me again," I sighed with
resignation.

And the coming wind did roar more loud,
And the sails did sigh like sedge;

And the rain pour'd down from one black cloud;
The Moon was at its edge.
   (318-21)

The day hadn't started off so dismally, though. When I got out of the car a little after nine that morning the sky was a clear, seamless blue. The sun shone like a great gold disc in the still air just above the eastern peaks. A few minutes later I was hiking beneath the brightly lit canopy of trees that overhung Peters Creek Trail. Spangles of sunlight darted back and forth with every slight breeze.

The trail, being an old fire road, was wide, mostly level and dry. It looked like it had never rained here at all. Even the approaching autumn seemed distant. For though the late season was evident in the blazing, decaying underbrush, the trees above were still green with summer warmth. Occasionally small stands of evergreen trees sifted the morning sunlight into smoky strands. These dark masses of isolated conifers, however, stood in dark contrast to the much more numerous acres of dappled paper birch through which the road was cut. In row after row of black and white clarity they extended on either side of the road. Yet these rows of trees weren't all that was pleasing to the sight. Through their sparkling tops could sometimes be glimpsed the hazy shoulders of nearby mountains squared against the thin, blue sky.

Such a bright, open trail was not to last long, though. First, in less than two miles, the trail dropped off the main fire road onto a narrower, shadier track. Dewy grass took the place of gravel roadbed as the trail wound down over a stream and up around the next low ridge's shoulder. Then it dropped a short distance more before turning to parallel the rushing waters of Peters Creek. From this point on, the trail would always be within sound of the creek's varying voices. But though the creek would be a constant companion, the cooler, rustic road the trail had become would not.

For upon crossing the boundary of Chugach State Park after nearly four miles of old-road walking, the trail immediately became both rougher and harder to follow. No longer could I look around me as I hiked. Now my eyes had to watch my feet as the trail bent sharply around roots, through mud holes and over rocks.

Nor was the trail the only thing that was changing. The weather was too—and, like the trail, it was not a change for the better. First, thin wisps of clouds began straggling out of the south, hiding the blue sky behind a worn and dirty beige sheet. Then a subtle breeze began to whisper in the long grass at my feet and in the heavy branches of the black spruce trees at my head. It softly swept the sweat from my brow in passing before drifting down the valley behind me, mixing its murmuring with the mumbling of the nearby creek.

I didn't pay these changes much mind, though. The mists seemed too slow and thin to drop any rain, and the breeze seemed too small and weak to carry any storm. Meanwhile, the mountains above still towered cloud-free on all sides.

"Perhaps by late tonight or early tomorrow the rains will come," I thought. The forces around me didn't seem cataclysmic enough to bring them any sooner. "And I'll be long gone from here by then."

The powers that be, however, had other ideas—on both accounts. First, the trail began to deteriorate rapidly. I lost it twice in a meadow of neck-high grass. If it wasn't for the vantage points offered by the hollows of matted grass where moose had bedded down for the night, I might be there yet. I wished I had a machete in hand as I stumbled through the last of the grass toward the haven of the next copse of cottonwoods. The trail faded to nothing after the next two stream crossings. Only by picking out a logical route over the next hillock or through the next field was I able to link up with the fragments of remaining trail again. It was a game of cat and mouse. Even once out on the tundra, free of the lowland trees and grasses the trail was still—if not more—difficult to follow. For here, where few hikers had ever come, there was virtually no trail at all. Nor in the featureless meadows was there any logical route to follow. Finally, after futilely wasting a half hour looking for the trail in the last copse of trees, I gave it up and simply made a beeline for where I wanted to go.

> *The air is cut away before,*
> *And closes from behind.*
> *Fly, brother, fly! more high, more high!*
> *Or we shall be belated:*
> *For slow and slow that ship will go,*
> *When the Mariner's trance is abated.*
> (424-9)

"At least," I consoled myself, "though the trail may be getting worse, the views are definitely getting better."

Mount Rumble now impressively dominated the entire head of the valley as I, a tiny dot on the landscape, moved across its front. At a diagonal to my right rose the shattered east ridge of Peeking Mountain. Beyond it, lining the upper reaches of the valley that extended back behind Mount Rumble, other 6,000- and 7,000-foot summits ranged beneath the shifting mists.

It was disheartening, though, to see a fresh frosting of snow sprinkled like powdered sugar over their highest reaches. The change of seasons had already begun.

"Winter comes early up here," I sighed.

That's when I noticed that the shadows at my feet had disappeared and the earth around me had darkened. The wind was also now more difficult to face. The ridge to the south, beyond Rumble's broad right shoulder, which only moments before had been clear, was now suddenly bannered with clouds. Both above and below me, the day was changing, moodily turning against me.

It had not turned entirely, though. The wind might have buffeted me as I crossed below Rumble's fierce visage, and the trail might have been lost to me in the weedy tundra, but there was still daylight left in the graying sky. There was even the outline of the sun, though dull like a still half-buried plate of ancient tarnished bronze, still visible over the western heights. So there was no reason not to continue my climb around Rumble—at least not yet.

The problem was I still had miles to go before I could even begin to climb. First, beginning right at the base of the shelf I was on, there was well over a mile of swampy tundra to cross before I could even begin my way around the back side of the mountain. From there, I had to follow that narrow valley for three or four miles more before reaching the base of the specific gully which led up and over the pass. Then, even from there, it was still more than a mile climb up to the pass itself.

I looked up at the sky. Then I looked across the swamp in front of me. Then I looked up at the sky again.

And soon I heard a roaring wind:

> *It did not come anear;*
> *But with its sound it shook the sails,*
> *That were so thin and sere.*
> (309-12)

Far above me I could just make out a flag of mist extending out from the summit. I watched it intently for a number of quiet seconds.

Finally I just shrugged.

"Well, I'm not going to get there by standing here," I said.

So coming down off that last low—and dry—shelf, I started across the wet lowlands. Soon my shoes were squishy with water as I lunged from tussock to tussock, often sliding off one or missing another one and landing with a *squash* in the mushy ground below. At the creek bed, I turned left upstream into heavier brush. Then there were two crossings of milky glacial streams to make in the face of a now strong, clothes-snapping wind. To avoid the brush, I slipped and tripped my way right up the center of the rocky, braided creek bed. The snow-capped ridges far above me were now but dim outlines in the tattered clouds when I next glanced up from my bent, wind-leaning hike. But even then I wasn't ready to turn back—not yet.

Then, finally, I was around the shoulder of the mountain and climbing steeply toward the pass dimly outlined far above. Following the path of a herd of goats now lingering on the slopes above me, I began climbing rapidly, breathlessly, eager to get behind some ledge or ridge out of the wind's way.

When I was finally out of the wind, I sat down on that rock to think. That's when it started to rain. It didn't come down in a haphazard drizzle or soft drops. Neither did it come in spits and sputterings. The change was far more dramatic. After just one or two preliminary drops, it began coming down in horizontal sheets, plastering the grasses against the slope and pushing me to cover.

> *The thick black cloud was cleft, and still*
> *The Moon was at its side;*
> *Like waters shot from some high crag,*
> *The lightning fell with never a jag,*
> *A river steep and wide.*

(322—26)

It was time to go home. So, driven by the wind and rain off the shoulder of that high mountain, I turned homeward with hurrying, almost running, steps. Nor did I slow down as the wind and rain continued to push me out across the wet tundra to the woods beyond. Once again, the trail came and went below my feet, and once again I lost it at stream crossings and in high grass. I didn't stop to look for it, though. Neither did I stop to eat or drink or put on a warmer coat. None of that mattered now.

Now all that mattered was speed. For now, in addition to surviving the rain and wind, I also had to outrace the impending night. If I lost the trail, I just kept heading down valley. If I was blocked by a stream, I just stomped right through it. Farther down valley, as the rain and wind continued and the darkness increased, I found the trail again. But I didn't stop and rejoice. I didn't even stop to catch a breath. There was no time, not on this night with the wind and rain at my back and no stars overhead.

> *Like one that on a lonesome road*
> *Doth walk in fear and dread,*
> *And having once turn'd round, walks on,*
> *And turns no more his head;*
> *Because he knows a frightful fiend*
> *Doth close behind him tread.*
> (446-51)

All I wanted to do was reach the four-mile mark in the trail where it once again became a road. From there, I knew I could make it out regardless of the weather or time of day. Everything else was a blur as I descended single-mindedly down the darkening trail. But just before I reached the road, the rain lightened and the wind died down. Things seemed to be finally changing for the better.

Then, to my amazement, a shadow loomed up out of the trees.

"Alan?" I asked in disbelief.

"Shawn," he answered.

Alan had told me he might follow me down the trail once he got out of work, but I never really expected to see him—especially this late and in such conditions. I was, nevertheless, relieved to see him. Having been shortsighted enough not to bring a flashlight, I was thankful that Alan had been farsighted enough to bring two. So what could've been a very slow and nervous five-mile ordeal suddenly became an almost pleasant hike with a friend along a well-lit trail beneath what was now a gentle rain.

It no longer mattered that it was night and it was raining or that winter was already settling on the rocky heights above. It no longer even mattered that all the possibilities of the morning had come to naught. All that mattered was that something in this world of constant change seemed, at least for a moment, constant.

> *O sweeter than the marriage-feast,*
> *'Tis sweeter far to me,*
> *To walk together to the kirk*
> *With a goodly company! —*
> (601-4)

Or, on this particular night, hiking with "a goodly company" out to the remote road where our cars were parked.

The author on the rock glacier between Mount Rumble and Benign Peak.

Peters Creek Trail

Note: Peters Creek Trail is a very straightforward—and very decrepit—trail. But its shortcomings as a walkable and sometimes even findable trail are more than made up for by the area it accesses. The upper valley of Peters Creek, dominated by the gargantuan mass of Mount Rumble, is one of the most terribly beautiful in the Chugach—especially if one has the energy and makes the time to circumnavigate the mountain. Glaciers, gloomy, spired summits and eerie moonscapes of muddy ice and tumbling slopes of shale will repay all the effort it took to not only walk the trail itself, but explore beyond its last foot of maintained tread.

Trail Location: Drive north on the Glenn Highway from Anchorage to the Peters Creek Exit at mile 22. At the end of the ramp, take a right. (If you're coming from the north on Glenn Highway, go left at the end of the ramp and drive back over the highway.) In less than a hundred yards, you will merge with Old Ski Road which should be followed as it curves around and turns into Ski Road right after it passes Temple Road on the left. Ski Road will continue for another quarter mile to where it ends at a T intersection with Whaley Avenue. Go left on Whaley and drive for less than a quarter mile and take another left onto the appropriately named Chugach Park Drive. Follow this winding road for almost two miles to its intersection with Kullberg Drive. Go left on Kullberg Drive and in only a hundred yards or so go right onto Sullins Road. Sullins will switchback up the hillside. After passing a number of other roads, take a right on Malcolm Drive and continue straight uphill to the trailhead which will be directly in front of you as Malcolm swings up to the left.

Trail Grade: Peters Creek Trail can be divided into two, or even three sections, each of which has a different grade. The first 5 miles of trail along an old road is level 1. The rougher trail which follows does not have any dramatic ups or downs, but the rough footing and generally poor condition of the trail earns it the grades of levels 2 with sections with seemingly no trail which equates it to a level 4. Then once on the tundra in the upper valley where it is difficult to find any semblance of trail, the level rises to a consistent 4.

Trail Condition: As already stated, the first 5 miles because they are on an old road, are excellent for walking: wide, weed-less and smooth. The next 4 miles, however, are rooty, rocky, and weedy which makes for very poor and slow walking—even though the trail is virtually level. At stream crossings its difficult to find the trail on the opposite shore, and on the tundra there is neither marker nor cairn to guide the uninitiated hiker. Consequently this is one trail upon which I would recommend carrying a map so if you lose the trail—which I have done on numerous occasions in the upper valley—you can find your own way out and back. Of course, rougher conditions should be expected by anyone who walks off the end of the supposed trail at the base of Mount Rumble. The 5,000-plus-foot pass behind Mount Rumble is, though spectacular, a very difficult scramble—especially from the east. (See OPTION A—CIRCUMNAVIGATION OF MOUNT RUMBLE below for this trip.)

Trail Mileage: One way from the beginning of the trail to the base of Mount Rumble is roughly 9 miles, for a round-trip total of 18 miles.

Total Elevation Gain: From trailhead to trail's end, the total elevation gain is only 800 feet.

High Point: The elevation at the end of the trail at the base of Mount Rumble is approximately 2,500 feet above sea level.

Normal Hiking Time: To do the entire trail out and back should take anywhere from one very long day for even the most persistent and athletically gifted hiker to two days for the more leisure inclined walker. However, for those who want to spend time exploring the valleys and peaks of this secluded alpine wonderland, even three or four days might not be enough.

Campsites: Outside of the private property that borders the trail in the first miles, there are abundant unofficial campsites farther up valley. I personally recommend somewhere in the valleys on both the east and west side of Mount Rumble. Both valleys have plenty of running water and plenty of scenery.

Best Times: The trail because it is so level in such a wide valley, is a wonderful hike any time of year. However, the scramble around Mount Rumble and any other climbs in the upper valley should be done only between June and October to avoid danger of avalanches.

USGS Maps: Anchorage B-6, B-7 and A-6.

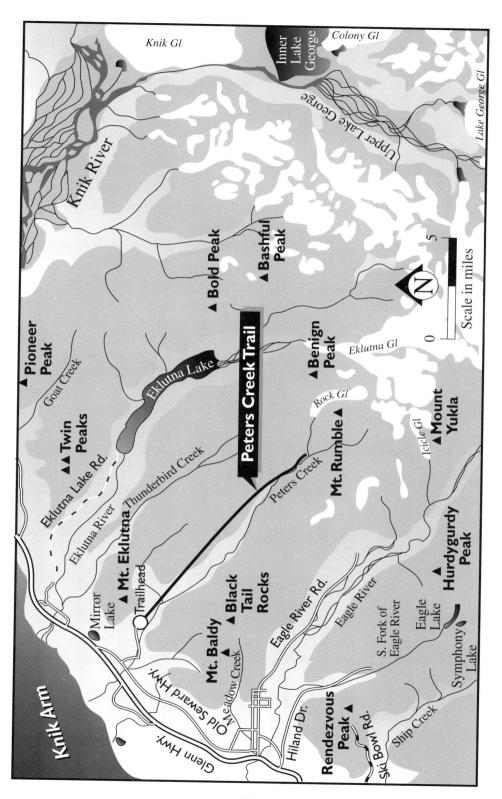

Knik Arm

Knik Gl

Inner Lake George

Colony Gl

Lake George Gl

Upper Lake George

Knik River

Bold Peak ▲

Bashful Peak ▲

N

Scale in miles

0   5

▲ Pioneer Peak

Goat Creek

Eklutna Lake

▲ Benign Peak

Eklutna Gl

Peters Creek Trail

▲▲ Twin Peaks

Eklutna Lake Rd.

Eklutna River

Thunderbird Creek

▲ Mt. Eklutna

Rock Gl

Mt. Rumble ▲

Peters Creek

Icicle Gl

▲ Mount Yukla

Mirror Lake

Trailhead

▲ Black Tail Rocks

Mt. Baldy ▲

Meadow Creek

Eagle River Rd.

Hurdygurdy Peak ▲

Eagle River

Eagle Lake

S. Fork of Eagle River

Symphony Lake

Glenn Hwy.

Old Seward Hwy.

Hiland Dr.

Rendezvous Peak ▲

Ski Bowl Rd.

Ship Creek

MOUNT EKLUTNA

Note: Mount Eklutna, towering high above Mirror Lake just north of Peters Creek on the Glenn Highway, is one of the most scenic spots in the Chugach. It does take some effort to reach the summit, but the climb is well worth it. On a clear day, one can look out over the Knik Arm to the Talkeetna Mountains and Denali, while to the west and southwest can be seen Mount Susitna and the Kenai Peninsula. Then, of course, to due south and east can be seen ridge upon ridge and summit after summit of the Chugach Mountains.

Trail Location: To climb Mount Eklutna, begin at the Peters Creek Trail. (To get there, see WALK-ABOUT GUIDE TO PETERS CREEK TRAIL.) Within a few hundred yards of the beginning of the trail, look for a side trail that climbs the embankment on the left. (This side trail is very easy to miss because it is not obvious in the embankment at eye level because footsteps in the soft dirt are often obliterated by rain and snow melt. Only at the top of the embankment is the trail at all obvious. There, a break in the lip of the embankment and a cut in the woods are the clues to the trail's beginning. But they take a sharp eye to find.) If you have not found the trail within a half mile and find yourself emerging from the woods into an open area, you've gone too far. It's time to back track and look more carefully.

Once on the trail, keep following it upward through the trees. Though not steep at first, it soon takes on a more laborious angle. Near tree line, the trail will begin climbing a deep-grassed, shallow gully. At the top of this gully, the trail begins to round off onto the a wide, tree-less plateau on the ridge top. To the left (northwest) is an overlook that stands high above Mirror Lake. To the right, and still 800 feet higher, and just beyond two false summits, is the summit of Mount Eklutna (4,110 feet). The 360 degree view from the summit is well-worth the effort it takes to climb it.

Trail Grade: The climb up to Eklutna Peak can be divided up into 2, maybe 3 sections of varying difficulty. The first section, the short way along the Peters Creek Trail, is, by far the easiest section. Being along an old road, it is a level 1 hike. Once up and over the embankment and onto the rougher trail that leads upward, the grade quickly rises through level 2 in the early going to level 3. Once above tree line, where the trail peters out on the ridge top, the level rises to grade 4.

Trail Condition: As already stated, the first few hundred yards along the Peters creek Trail, because they are on an old road, are excellent for walking: wide, weed-less and smooth. The next 2 or so miles to the top of the ridge are much rougher. Being both narrow as well as overgrown, it is also, because it is not an officially maintained trail, often blocked by fallen branches and logs. Up higher, closer to tree line, it is also often very muddy—and therefore slippery. Surprisingly, though, it is relatively free of rocks. Once up on the firm, usually well-drained tundra, the walking becomes much firmer and easier again. On rainy days, however, one should be careful n the moss covered rocks, which can suddenly become treacherous underfoot.

Trail Mileage: One way from the beginning of the trail to the plateau on the ridge top is approximately 2 miles. From there, it is another 1 mile to the summit of Mount Eklutna, for a total one way trip of 3 miles and round-trip total of 6 miles.

Total Elevation Gain: From trailhead to the summit of Mount Eklutna, the total elevation gain is approximately 3,200 feet.

High Point: The elevation at the summit of Mount Eklutna is 4,110 feet above sea level.

Normal Hiking Time: To do the entire hike to the summit of Mount Eklutna and back should take anywhere from 8 to 14 hours depending on the condition and ambition of the hiker(s).

Campsites: Because much of the land surrounding the first few miles of the Peters Creek is under private ownership, it is not advisable to camp in the lower elevations. Nor is it easy to find a level campsite anywhere along the rough trail leading up to the ridge top. For those who are adamant bout camping out, however, the top of the ridge above Mirror Lake is an ideal spot. Just be sure to carry up enough water up with you

Best Time: This hike is best made from mid-June to late September. Furthermore, because of the extreme avalanche conditions on the steep, upper slopes, it is not recommended at all as a winter hike or climb.

USGS Maps: Anchorage B-7.

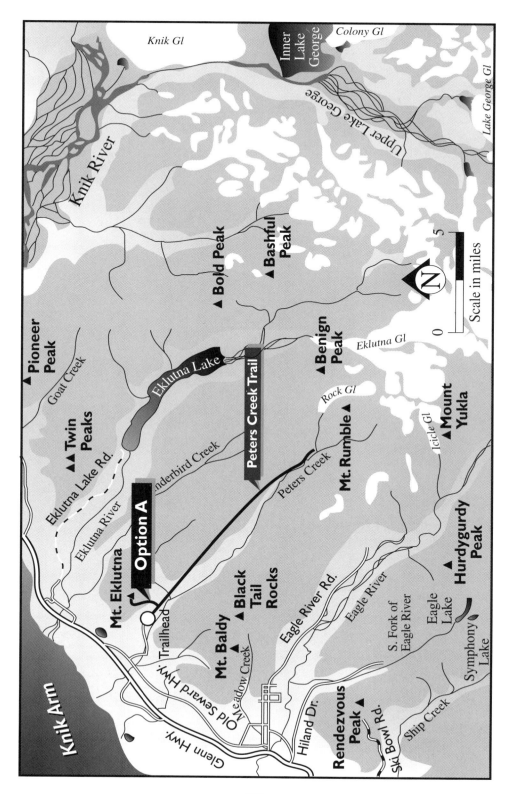

CIRCUMNAVIGATION OF MOUNT RUMBLE

Trail Location: This adventurous hike begins where the Peters Creek
Trail ends on the tundra below the precipitous north face of Mount
Rumble. (To get there, see WALK-ABOUT GUIDE TO PETERS
CREEK TRAIL.) From the end of the Peters Creek Trail, continue
around the right, or west side of the mountain, following Peters
Creek through brush and brambles around toward the back side of
the mountain where the slopes leading up to the left are gentler. At
this point, begin to look for the left-handtributary of Peters Creek
and follow it up slope. The pass, over 2,500 feet above the creek's
confluence will become more visible as the climb lengthens. The
last half mile is up steep and unstable scree.

At the top of the pass, descend directly down the steep scree slope
before you to the valley's floor. Follow this rock covered glacier
back out, swinging in a wide left-handarc, back to the front of
Mount Rumble where the Peters Creek Trail can be rejoined.

This circumnavigation can also be done in the opposite direction,
but it's not recommended. The half mile climb up the final scree
slope to the top of the pass is excruciatingly tiring. Not only is the
slope steep, but the scree is very unstable—much more so than the
other side. It's so unstable, in fact, that the more one moves, the
farther back down one seems to slip.

Trail Grade: Anyone who has the ambition to circumnavigate Mount
Rumble should expect to encounter levels 5 and 6 for the entire
trip.

Trail Condition: The lack of any trail to follow on this trip means that
the conditions are, at best, poor. Expect lots of bushwhacking
through alder and willow and tall-grassed meadows both in

following Peters Creek in on the west side of Mount Rumble as well as in the last mile or so back to rejoin Peters Creek Trail on the east side of the mountain. In between is scree, boulders and some very steep climbing. One can also expect snow to linger on both sides of the pass sometimes right into August.

Trail Mileage: The one way traverse from the end of Peters Creek Trail, over the pass and back to the trail is roughly 10 miles. The round trip, then, from the parking lot over the pass and back is 28 to 30 miles.

Total Elevation Gain: The circumnavigation up and over the pass entails a climb of almost 2,700 feet from the end of Peters Creek Trail. The total elevation from the trailhead to the top of the pass is, therefor, close to 3,500 feet.

High Point: The pass behind Mount Rumble is just under 5,100 feet above sea level.

Normal Hiking Time: The hike to and from the trailhead over the pass should take from 1 very long day to 3 days. Even from the end of Peters Creek Trail, the 10 mile circumnavigation should take the better part of a long day.

Campsites: The valleys on both sides of the pass have plenty of places to pitch a tent. But would-be campers on the east side of the pass would probably be more comfortable if they camped only once they got off the frozen moraine of the upper valley.

Best Time: The best months to do this traverse are from June to September. The extreme avalanche danger on both sides of the pass should make any one think twice about doing this trip in the winter. And after a winter of heavy snow, it might be wise not even to consider doing this trip until mid-July.

USGS Maps: Anchorage A-6 and B-6

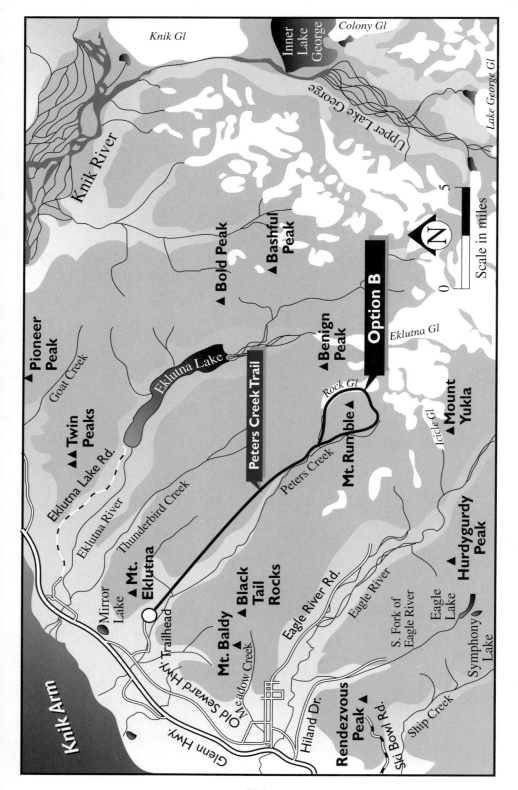

Knik Gl

Colony Gl

Inner Lake George

Upper Lake George

Lake George Gl

Knik River

Bold Peak ▲

Bashful Peak ▲

Option B

Benign Peak ▲

Eklutna Gl

Pioneer Peak ▲

Goat Creek

Eklutna Lake

Peters Creek Trail

Rock Gl

Mount Yukla ▲

Icicle Gl

Twin Peaks ▲▲

Eklutna Lake Rd.

Eklutna River

Thunderbird Creek

Mt. Rumble ▲

Peters Creek

Mirror Lake

Mt. Eklutna ▲

Trailhead

Black Tail Rocks ▲

Eagle River Rd.

Hurdygurdy Peak ▲

Mt. Baldy ▲

Meadow Creek

Eagle River

S. Fork of Eagle River

Eagle Lake

Old Seward Hwy.

Glenn Hwy.

Hiland Dr.

Ski Bowl Rd.

Symphony Lake

Rendezvous Peak ▲

Ship Creek

Knik Arm

N

Scale in miles

0   5

356

Loocking across the Front Range of the Chugach Mountains from the summit at South Suicide Peak.

CHAPTER 12

Taking Stock

Through cracks in the autumn canopy above, the sunlight streamed noiselessly earthward and splashed silently on the dirt floor of the forest and trail. What it lacked in sound, though, it more than made up for in sight. Through the prism of the changing leaves, it fell in diamond, sapphire, ruby, emerald and amethyst crystals of light. They were so bright that I had to squint as they floated in the warm air around me and splayed across the cool ground at my feet.

Meanwhile, up and over the edge of the deep ravine where I sat drifted the sound of churning water. There, almost one hundred feet down, the sun-flecked waters of the creek flowed softly toward the sea. Unlike the urgent days of the spring long past, though, the waters now seemed to be in little or no hurry to get anywhere. Nothing, in fact, seemed to be in a hurry.

It was Indian Summer.

Usually by mid-September, the Alaskan landscape was wet and dank. It wasn't even unusual to see the first dusting of snow on the high peaks in the gray sky. This year, however, was different. For once, we were having an Indian Summer like I recall from my days of growing up in New England when the long-rayed sun of September, after melting the mists of morning, would rise to warm the maturing earth. Fruits would ripen on still green vines and branches and corn and grains would still stand unharvested in golden fields. Even up until the third or fourth week in September, we'd still be mowing the lawn every week while the leaves in the trees just started turning color. Perhaps they'd reach their full blaze of color by mid-October, or, if the warm days lingered longer, maybe not until Halloween.

Now, for the first time I could remember in my few years here, an Indian Summer had come to South-Central Alaska. Though we were well over halfway through September, no frosts had whitened morning lawns or fields. The nights were, at worst, cool, while the days were always warm. Not only that, but no rain—the chilling bane of Alaska autumns—had fallen. Nor had any sobering snow fallen on the mountains above. Instead, almost every day the deep turquoise sky continued to reign overhead. Only the long shadows of the south-sinking sun gave any hint of the late season. But that hint seemed largely ignored by virtually everyone and everything. Summer simply didn't seem to be in a hurry to leave.

I was even in less of a hurry to get up from the bench I sat on as the summer seemed to be packing up and leaving South-Central Alaska. Unlike the season, however, I had far less to travel. I also had no obligations.

Thunderbird Falls is not a long trail. Nor does it provide access to any high or remote country. It is not, in short, a trail from which adventures generally start. This does not, however, make Thunderbird Falls Trail any less meaningful or important as a trail. It simply means that it serves a different function than many of the longer, deeper trails in the Chugach.

This is a trail, for instance, to which I always bring family and friends when they come to visit. It is also a trail to which I go when I need time to think—"take stock" an old Vermont friend used to say. It's a place for thought, not for adventure.

Here I can turn my brain off to the world. I can wander thoughtlessly up the wide, flat trail; or I can mindlessly stand and listen to the roar of the waters of Thunderbird Creek as it drifts slowly up from the ravines and gorges below; or I can simply sit on one of the few benches scattered along the length of the trail for no other reason than to watch the world go round without me. In short, it is a place I can slow down, "take stock."

It's also a place to wonder. This wonder is not to be confused with pondering about the family, thinking about work, or even planning a schedule or vacation. It is simply wondering—wondering what lies beyond the here and now. This direction of thought does not come easily. For it's only after turning my brain off to the world that I can open my mind to wonder. Yet it happens to me a lot along this trail. Even in my least ambitious moments on this trail, whether I'm walking on the wooded trail, standing above the gorge, or sitting at the falls themselves, I begin to wonder. It's not forced or enticed to occur; it just happens. And when it comes, I can't help but wonder.

It starts with what is below, behind or beyond what I can immediately see or hear around me. Is that ridge accessible from here? Can I get above treeline by following that bench? How far and how high is it to Thunderbird Peak from here? I will ask myself as I stand and stare. Thus do I attempt to connect and intersect the various lines of the here and now.

This mental puzzling, in turn, leads to other questions, other puzzles with more nebulous answers than the solid mountains overhead and the firm valleys underfoot can ever provide. How deep is the sky? How long has it been here? What other people have come here and asked the same questions? What brought them here? What brought me here?

Then the mystery of this life and these times comes upon me. I begin to wonder how the various and sporadic lines of the here and now intersect with the larger plane that extends into the past and future. I know, however, that no matter how many times I turn this larger puzzle around in my mind or flip it up and down in my thoughts none of the answers to it are forthcoming—at least not in this lifetime. Yet I also know that despite being unfathomable and unanswerable, the solving of this larger puzzle is the bigger—and maybe only goal—of idle wonder, or "taking stock," no matter how much we try to evade the issue.

Such wonder is often spawned in places beside such rushing waters. I think of Marcus Aurelius beside the Danube River, of Percy Bysshe Shelley beside the River Arve and William Wordsworth beside the River Severn, and of the countless holy men of the East that have continued to sit for forty centuries or more with hands folded and eyes closed in meditation along the shores of the 1,850-mile-long Indus River as it makes its journey from the high, wind-swept plateau of Tibet to the warm flood plains of the many-channeled delta that empties into the warm Arabian Sea. Mostly, though, I think of Heraclitus and the beginnings and endings of all things. I think of the burden of trying to reconcile the what has been, what is, and what will be with the what could've been, what might be and what could be.

Then a shadow moves across my eyes and the thoughts are gone. I shake my head. After looking up and down the trail one more time, I turn my face back to the warm sun. Then, like Snoopy in a cool breeze on a hot summer day, I shut my eyes to the long, breathless light. I feel a half smile, also like Snoopy's, rising to my cheeks

Sometimes just taking stock of the here and now is enough.

Descending a rocky outcropping on a high ridge.

Thunderbird Falls Trail

Trail Location: Thunderbird Falls Trail is located just off the Old Glenn Highway near Eklutna. To get there, take the Glenn Highway north out of Anchorage to the Thunderbird Falls Exit just past milepost 25 and continue bearing right down the ramp. The parking area for the trail is on the right under .5 miles from the exit and just before the Eklutna River bridge. Southbound traffic can take the Eklutna Exit at milepost 26 on the Glenn Highway, cross back over the highway, at which point continue on the Old Glenn Highway past Eklutna Lake Road and over the Eklutna River bridge to the parking area just beyond it on the left. The trailhead is located at the edge of the parking area.

Trail Grade: This trail is a grade 1 hike.

Trail Condition: Wide and flat with virtually no rocks and few muddy spots if any, this trail will be easy underfoot for almost everybody. There are even strategically placed benches for anyone needing a rest, or just an excuse to sit and look.

Trail Mileage: The one way hike to the falls from the parking area is 1 mile for a round trip total of 2 miles.

Total Elevation Gain: The hike in entails a climb of 200 feet, whereas the hike out entails climb of 140 feet.

High Point: The highest point reached on this short hike is 330 feet above sea level on the low ridge just before reaching the viewing decks at the falls themselves.

Normal Hiking Time: This hike should 1 to 2 hours depending on how much lingering and looking one cares to do.

Campsites: None.

Best Time: The best time to do this hike is from May to October when the falls aren't frozen. But even in the winter, when the cold can transform the liquid falls into a fluted tower of turquoise and green ice, this trail is relatively safe.

USGS Maps: Anchorage B-7 NE.

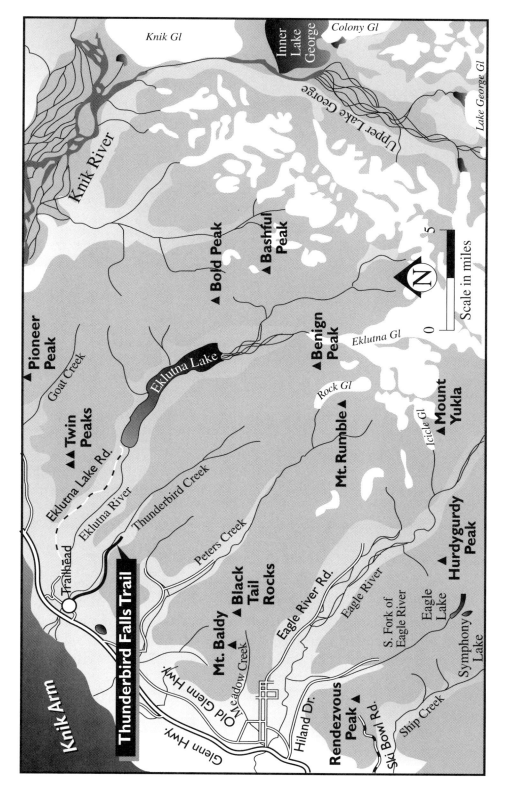

Knik Gl

Colony Gl

Inner Lake George

Upper Lake George

Lake George Gl

Knik River

Bold Peak ▲

Bashful Peak ▲

Pioneer Peak ▲

Benign Peak ▲

Eklutna Gl

Goat Creek

Eklutna Lake

Rock Gl

Mt. Rumble ▲

Icicle Gl

Mount Yukla ▲

Twin Peaks ▲▲

Eklutna Lake Rd.

Eklutna River

Thunderbird Creek

Peters Creek

Hurdygurdy Peak ▲

Trailhead

Thunderbird Falls Trail

Black Tail Rocks ▲

Eagle River Rd.

Eagle River

S. Fork of Eagle River

Eagle Lake

Symphony Lake

Ship Creek

Knik Arm

Mt. Baldy ▲

Meadow Creek

Old Glenn Hwy.

Glenn Hwy.

Hiland Dr.

Rendezvous Peak ▲

Ski Bowl Rd.

N

0   5

Scale in miles

Walking Makes up in Width What it Lacks in Height... and Length...and Distance... and Speed...and...

Sitting to the left beside me, an elderly woman pushed and pulled a bodkin gently through her needlepoint. The metal glistened in the small island of light that enveloped her like a small tent from the outlet above her head. Meanwhile, down the aisle, a movie— some nonsensical film about fishing starring Joe Pesci and Danny Glover—flickered on monotonously. But it was, for the most part, ignored by an audience that was largely asleep in what were now the small hours of the night.

Off to my right across the aisle and through the narrow window on the other side of two sleeping bodies, I could also just make out the full moon hovering in a small frame of planets and stars. I don't think the woman noticed it, though. Nor do I think too many other people, whether awake or asleep, noticed it either. Even for me it was hard to believe it was there.

"Is that really the same moon I saw rising only a few hours ago?" I wondered drowsily as I thought back to the last miles of the long day's hike.

"What a change," I murmured to myself as I closed my eyes.

"Amazing," was the last thing I think I said before drifting off.

Yet it was amazing. For throughout the whole time the woman worked at her needlepoint beside me and the silly movie wound on before us and the moon shone in the window beside us, the 727 we were on continued to roar relentlessly onward. Steadily holding its southwesterly course at an elevation of 30,000 feet and a speed of close to 700 mph, it pressed on through the night.

What a change: during the day, I'd never traveled two, three, and, at the fastest, five miles an hour, but now here I was, without any effort at all, traveling at speeds far greater exponentially than those earlier snail-like paces. Yet despite traveling so high and so fast, I was nowhere near seeing all that I'd seen on that hike I'd finished only a few hours before. In a mere twenty-five miles of hiking I saw—and smelled, and tasted, and felt, and even heard more (at a much lesser volume than the constant roar of a jet's engine) than I would not only on that 1:45 a.m. "red-eye" flight from Anchorage to Seattle, but on the other two legs of my journey to Boston as well.

Though far more efficient, flying is not nearly as effectual as walking.

> *I have met with but one or two persons in the course of my life who understood the art of Walking, that is, of taking walks, —who had a genius, so to speak, for sauntering: which word is beautifully derived "from idle people who roved about the country, in the Middle Ages, and asked charity, under pretense of going "a la Sainte Terre," to the Holy Land, till the children exclaimed, "there goes a Sainte-Terrer,"*
> *a Saunterer, —a Holy Lander.*
> (from <u>Walking</u> by H.D. Thoreau)

Hermetically sealed inside that metal tube, the passenger on a commercial airliner largely misses the simple process of movement in time and space unfolding in unison as the hike progresses. Yes, the passage of time can be felt in a plane as light of day and the dark of night alternate in the small windows, but the passage of time is all that a person on a plane at 30,000 feet feels. There is no sense of space or distance in that passage of time. One is simply too high up and too closed in to feel any dimension but time—and its often painfully slow passage.

The hiker, on the other hand, feels not only the passage of time, but also the unfolding of space. For the passage of time is felt through all the senses—not just that of sight:

> *In my walk I would fain return to my senses.*
> (H.D. Thoreau)

In addition to seeing the passage of time with each turn of the trail and each rise in the ridge, the hiker also hears, smells, feels, and even tastes it. He hears it in the rustle of leaves underfoot and the sigh of the wind overhead. He smells it in the blossoming flowers and the decaying dead wood. He feels it in the cold morning frost on the nose and the warm afternoon sun on the back. And he tastes it in the blueberry patches he wanders through, the springs he drinks from and even the very air he passes through. Thus, as the earth and sky unfold with the miles, the conversion of time into space and distance is far more acutely sensed by the hiker than by any other means of transportation—especially that of the jetliner. Yes, hiking is far less expeditious than flying, but it is also far more satisfying:

> *For I believe that climate does thus react on man, —as there is something in the mountain-air that feeds the spirit and inspires. Will not man grow to greater perfection intellectually as well as physically under these influences? Or is it unimportant how many foggy days there are in his life?*
> (H.D. Thoreau)

In the same amount of time, two and a half hours, it took the plane to reach Seattle, my five companions and I had already seen more while hiking than I'd see in the entire thirteen hours I'd spend flying—and maybe even far more than I'd see if I spent the next thirteen months flying.

"Sheep at 11 o'clock!" Steve called out as, soon after stepping off the end of Twin Peaks Trail and crossing one narrow rill, we were only seconds into plodding uphill across the browning tundra toward the 4,500 saddle above us. Everyone's eyes turned upward. Roughly a thousand feet above us, up on the slopes just below the base of the massive turret of East Twin Peak, little puff balls of white wool moved slowly across the broad, steep tundra. They appeared to be grazing.

We all stood momentarily mesmerized, though this was not by any means the first wildlife we'd seen. In the less than two hours of climbing up from Eklutna Lake we'd already—unintentionally—sent a half dozen angry red squirrels scurrying for cover, flushed three ptarmigan from cover, and stopped to watch from afar as a solitary eagle floated high over the lake's calm waters. Even before we left the parking lot, one lone raven had croaked at us from the nearby trees. Then, only a few steps up the trail, some of us had nearly stepped on some berry-filled bear scat—which was about as close as any of us wanted to come to the originator.

In our climb over the open tundra, we'd also been afforded views of Cook Inlet, shimmering at the far end of the valley opening to our north. To the south, we'd also been able to look well beyond the end of the lake, in itself more than eight miles away, to where, thirteen miles away, the gray snout of Eklutna Glacier pushed its way out of the high mountains. Lifting our eyes even farther, we could, in addition, look into the very heart of those mist-darkened mountains to where the extensive snowfields—the birthplace of many glaciers and the last bastion of long-past ice ages—stretched into the cloud-dappled distance.

> *Two or three hours' walking will carry me to as strange a country as I expect ever to see.*
> (H.D. Thoreau)

Once on the ridge itself, the views became even more extensive.

"Is that Palmer down there?" Georgia Gustafson asked, pointing down past the far shore of the braided Knik River toward the grid of thread-thin roads and dots of houses that spread northward across sunlit flood plains to the base of the Talkeetna Mountains.

Donna Schwirtz nodded.

"I didn't think it would be that close," Georgia said shaking her head. It wasn't that close, though, being ten air miles—and a good three- to four-hour hike—away.

What was close was the deep trough of the Goat Creek drainage dropping away at our feet and the dark mass of Pioneer Peak towering above its opposite side. Rising dominantly into the shadow of a small, solitary black cloud, the twin peaks of that one summit dominated the entire eastern sky. Only if we craned our necks to look around the silhouette of its steep southern slope, could we see where the long, snake-like length of Knik Glacier, like the Eklutna Glacier, wound down out of the innermost reaches of the highest and most remote of the ice-bound Chugach Mountains. Some of us even thought we could see Mount Marcus Baker, the highest and remotest of the Chugach, hovering just above the hazy horizon.

"It's always winter back there," I heard someone say.

Closer yet—literally on the earth we walked on and in the air we breathed—were evident details of the moist, ripe—and much milder— season we were moving through. It permeated the russet tundra and bulging black berries at our feet. It also, though not visible—and therefore not so obvious—filled the air with its contrary mix of sweet-smelling fruition and rancid-tasting decay.

> *When we walk, we naturally go to the fields and woods: what would become of us, if we walked only in a garden or a mall?*
> (H.D. Thoreau)

Then a slight breeze began to blow. The air suddenly took on a definite chill. The milder season of moments before had suddenly turned sharp. It was even enough for some of us to begin pulling gloves and wind-breakers from our packs.

Turning right (southeast) along the crest of the ridge, we began climbing again, only this time toward the high spur of an unnamed 5,450-foot summit that blocked our route along the ridge. Twenty minutes later when we crested that high ridge we could actually see almost our entire route, including all seven summits—all but the first being more than 5,000 feet in height—that our hike would carry us over.

It was certainly not an efficient route in regard to saving time and covering distance, but it was the one we had chosen.

> *Dulness is but another name for tameness.*
> (H.D. Thoreau)

First, in a big, elongated S-turn, the ridge we were on swung southwest for only a quarter mile or so to the closest and lowest summit, before continuing for another mile to where it reached the first and lowest of the 5,000-foot summits, a nondescript 5,080 lump on the ridge's crest. From there, the ridge turned northeast for another mile before cresting a

5,455-foot peak. Then it turned southeast again and soon climbed over a 5,285-foot summit. Turning once more northeast for another mile and a half, the ridge reached the fourth of six 5,000-foot summits, this one being a classically impressive 5,385-foot cone-shaped peak. From that high point, the ridge swung over the top of a much shallower hump. It continued, rising and falling over a number of shorter, gentler summits for the next two miles before finally climbing in one long, steady sweep to the highest summit along the whole ridge—a wide and long, hump-backed summit which at its farther end reached a height of 5,732 feet above sea level.

Even from this distance—more than five air miles away—that last and highest peak was an impressive sight. No other nearby peak of the many that fanned out around it even came close to challenging its preeminence. Silhouetted against the far horizon of the more distant snow-covered summits of the inner Chugach, its dark mass appeared like some great, beached behemoth.

That eye-stopping high point didn't mark the end of our hike, though. From the back of that highest summit, the ridge dropped once more down across a low saddle from where it climbed—once more—up and over one last 5,000-plus-foot peak at the northernmost corner of the Bold Peak valley. Once over that summit, we would then bushwhack down across the two or three miles of brush and brambles that still separated us from the Bold Overlook Trail, which we would follow the long way down to the Eklutna Lake Trail which we would, in turn, follow out to our cars now parked in the campground at the end of the lake.

It was a long, circuitous route, but such are the ways of the mountains: never level and never straight. Seemingly every route is like a sidewinding snake slithering across the grids of various maps as well as like a multi-humped camel stumping up and down against the contour lines. Our route was, of course, no different. First we hiked north, then we hiked south, then it was north again and then south again, and so on and so on, back and forth. And all the while we hiked, we also climbed. First we climbed up, then we climbed down, then it was up again and then down again, etcetera, etcetera.

But it was allright if the ridge we hiked along went back and forth and up and down. It would have surprised us if it hadn't. Expecting as much, we followed the route not because it was an inconvenience; but because it was an enhancement. It allowed us to see more, to touch more, and to hear more, and—despite being so high—even smell more than any of us would've ever experienced on even the longest airline flight.

> *Some, however, would derive the word [saunterer] from "sans terre," without land or a home, which, therefore, in the good sense, will mean, having no particular home, but equally at home everywhere. For this is the secret of successful sauntering. He who sits in a house all the time may be the greatest vagrant of all; but the saunterer, in the good sense is no more vagrant than the meandering river, which is all the while seduously seeking the shortest course to the sea.*
> (H.D. Thoreau)

By the time we were sitting over lunch at the beginning of the long section of the ridge leading up to the highest summit, we had hiked through a full day of experiences. We'd climbed up and over five 5000-plus-foot plus tundra-draped and rock-ribbed summits, and hiked seven miles along the cloudy and sunlight-dappled ridgetop. During that time we'd seen sheep grazing on nearby slopes and heard marmots whistling from nearby stones, stared at glaciers pouring out of gorges in distant mountains. We'd also smelt the decay of late summer in the forests below and tasted the crisp sharpness of the early autumn in the wind on the open alpine slopes above.

"Ahhh," Donna groaned with content as she laid her head back on her pack. Niles Wood, sitting a few feet away, was more content to stare at the broad north face of Bold Peak looking disdainfully down over the nearer, lower ridges from almost seven miles away. Streaked with dirty swaths of old snow and cloaked in swirling streamers of gray clouds, it looked every bit as formidable as it is.

Off to the east, Mount Marcus Baker was still just visible over the low saddle in the ridge that dropped at a right angle from the next high summit on the ridge before us. Though more than forty-five miles away and therefore not nearly as commanding a presence as the much nearer Bold Peak, it still held the eyes in awe. Towering above the white wilds of the perpetually snow-laden and glacier-girded inner Chugach, it dwarfed every other mountain that surrounded it.

Much nearer, the bronze light of the mid-August day glistened on the dry tundra by our reclining heads and on the lichen-stained stones at our stretched-out feet. A few ptarmigan darted overhead. A marmot whistled a warning from the stones just below us. We were in no hurry, though, to leave him in peace. The sun was too warm to get up and go just yet:

> *No wealth can buy the requisite leisure, freedom, and*
> *independence, which are the capital in this profession. It comes*
> *only by the grace of God.*
> (H.D. Thoreau)

An hour later, however, by the time we crested the highest peak on our hike, the clouds had shifted over our heads, cooling the landscape and dimming the views. Soon we were again pulling windbreakers and gloves from our packs. We didn't even think about taking them off for at least another hour. By then, after crossing the low saddle of the mountain's southern ridge, climbing over the next 5,430-foot summit and descending to the next saddle, we were finally turning off the crest of the ridge and just beginning the long bushwhack down to the Bold Overlook Trail. Not until then did we finally get out of the wind. Not until then did the sun come out again.

Like the ridge we just dropped off, the route down was far from direct. It's true that we could see the Bold Overlook Trail from the top of the ridge. Seeing the trail and getting to the trail, however, were two entirely different matters. For what the eyes could see, the body still had to reach. It was the body, after all, that had to connect the eyes (the seeing subject) with the trail (the object seen). To put a new twist in the old saw, "it was easier *seen* than done."

To make that connection, the body had to traverse down along the gravelly slope of the ridge, cross two deep, steep gullies, and stumble down through the first high bracken and brambles to the ridge's base. Then, from there, it still had to traipse down through the slightly lower willow and alders at tree line, wade across the stream flowing down the nadir of the valley, and then cross a mile-wide meadow of waist-high grass and brush, before crossing another stream and finally climbing one last steep embankment to the trail which lay just beyond:

> *Life consists with wildness. The most alive is the wildest. Not yet subdued to man, its presence refreshes him.*
> (H.D. Thoreau)

It was not an easy connection for any of us to make. For as it turned out, what our eyes could see in an instant, took anywhere from a hour to an hour and a half for our bodies to reach.

"Are we having fun yet?" Steve asked with a smirk as he, Donna and I finally sat in the long light of the evening by the trail's edge waiting for the others to catch up.

Neither Donna nor I answered. But, then, of course, we already knew the answer.

> *From the forest and wilderness come the tonics and bark which brace mankind.*
> (H.D. Thoreau)

Around us, the entire world was plated with hammered gold. Far above, the ridges were armored in gold. The grasses at our feet were sheathed in gold. Even the waters tumbling below were ribboned with gold. The whole world was ablaze with the sun's golden light. Even the soft underbellies of the clouds scattered in the blue heavens above were awash with gold.

None of this gold would make us any richer materially. It wouldn't fatten our bank accounts, or thicken our stock portfolios. We couldn't even put any in our pockets to jingle with our fingers on the long hike out. That was allright, though. Often one is richer just for the doing of something, and we had done enough to be far richer now than when we started. And our riches were far more fun to gather by walking than any fortune amassed by sitting in some office or working in some warehouse.

"Are we having fun yet?"

> *It requires direct dispensation from Heaven to become a walker. You must be born into the family of walkers.*
> (H.D. Thoreau)

372

No, there was no need to answer. As we made our way down the trail to the lake and then turned to follow the sinking sun back along the darkening shore of those flaming waters we all knew the answer.

In the same time it would soon take me to fly 5,000 miles at 30,000 feet, we had hiked only twenty-five miles without ever reaching more than 6,000 feet—and which eventually added up to a total elevation gain of still only 9,000 feet or so. Our hike wasn't easy or direct; nor was it always comfortable or enjoyable; but it was always changing, always interesting, and every moment a cornucopia for the senses and, in turn, a trouvaille for the mind.

> *So we saunter toward the Holy Land, till one day the sun shall shine more brightly than ever he has done, shall perchance shine into minds and hearts, and light up our whole lives with a great awakening light, as warm and serene and golden as on a bank-side in autumn.*
> (H.D. Thoreau)

This hike was also, in its own unique way, always fun. But we already knew that, though.

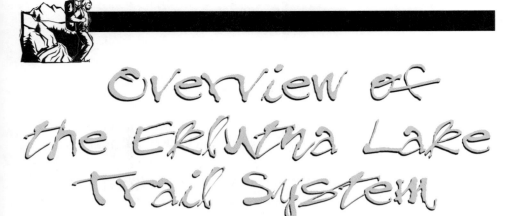

Overview of the Eklutna Lake Trail System

The Eklutna Lake area has more miles of trails per square mile than almost any other place in Alaska. Not only is there the Eklutna Lakeside Trail itself, but off this are other trails including Twin Peaks Trail, Bold Overlook Trail, East Fork Trail, a short spur trail leading to the base of Eklutna Glacier as well as other small trails leading to campsites and cabins just beyond the south end of the lake. These various trails are sufficient destinations in and of themselves for most people. But serious climbers will find that these trails provide superb access to some of the most magnificent—and difficult—peaks in the Chugach State Park, including Bashful Peak (8,005 feet), the highest mountain in the park. Some of these trails are predominantly flat and open, and therefore ideal for mountain biking while others are steep and/or rocky and therefore only accessible by foot. In between are a number of other trails with varying degrees of declivity and roughness. So no matter what level of ambition the hiker has when they get out of their car at the north end of Eklutna Lake, there is probably a trail to suit them somewhere in the valley.

Crossing a bridge on the Eklutna Lakeside Trail.

Eklutna Lakeside Trail

Trail Location: Drive north out of Anchorage to the Eklutna Exit at mile 26. At the end of the ramp, turn right. (Those coming from the north should turn left at the end of their ramp and cross back over the highway.) In less than a hundred yards turn right onto the frontage road and continue for less than half mile to a T intersection. Turn left here, following the directions of the signs for Eklutna Lake. This road, which begins as tar but soon turns to gravel, continues uphill for about ten miles to the shore of the lake where there is plenty of parking to be had for a small fee. Two of the trails in this picturesque valley begin in this parking area. Eklutna Lakeside Trail begins on the far left-handside of the parking area, continuing down the left shore of the lake. Twin Peaks Trail begins in the southeast corner of the second parking area which you will find by walking across a foot bridge to where a sign marks the beginning of the trail.

Trail Grade: Eklutna Lakeside Trail is a wide, rolling road that you should expect to share with horses, carriages, mountain bikers and—on given days of the week—ATV's and even automobiles. (To find out which days of the week motorized vehicles are allowed on the trail, call the Chugach State Park Headquarters. Their phone number can be found in Appendix 1 at the end of this book.) And if all these forms of transportation can be on this trail, it could be nothing more than a level 1. For those who want to avoid much of this traffic, there are sections of trail that drop periodically down to the lake shore. These side trails, upon which motorized vehicles are prohibited, will follow the edge of the lake for a half mile to a mile before again ascending to the main trail in the woods above. They are also level 1. Not only is the walking easy here, but there's also the added companionship of the lapping lake water and the views across the waters to the ridges far above—which, with no offense intended, is preferable to the traffic on the main trail above.

Trail Condition: As already stated, the trail is a dirt road so the walking conditions—though sometimes boring—are never less than excellent. The most difficult part of the trail is getting across the partially downed bridge over Eklutna River.

Trail Mileage: The one way hike to the base of Eklutna Glacier is 14 miles for a round trip total of 28 miles.

Total Elevation Gain: The climb from the parking area to the end of the trail entails a climb of only 200 feet, whereas to continue on to the base of the glacier entails an additional 200 foot climb, for a total climb of 400 feet.

High Point: It is 1,100 feet above sea level at the end of the trail and 1,300 feet above sea level at the base of the glacier.

Normal Hiking Time: Even the fastest hiker should expect to take 6 to 7 hours to make the 28 mile round trip to the glacier. Most other people should expect to take 2 days.

Campsites: There are cabins for rent and campsites available at the far end of the lake. Contact the Chugach State Park for details.

Best Time: Any time of year is a good time to either hike, ski or snowshoe this trail.

USGS Maps: Anchorage A-6.

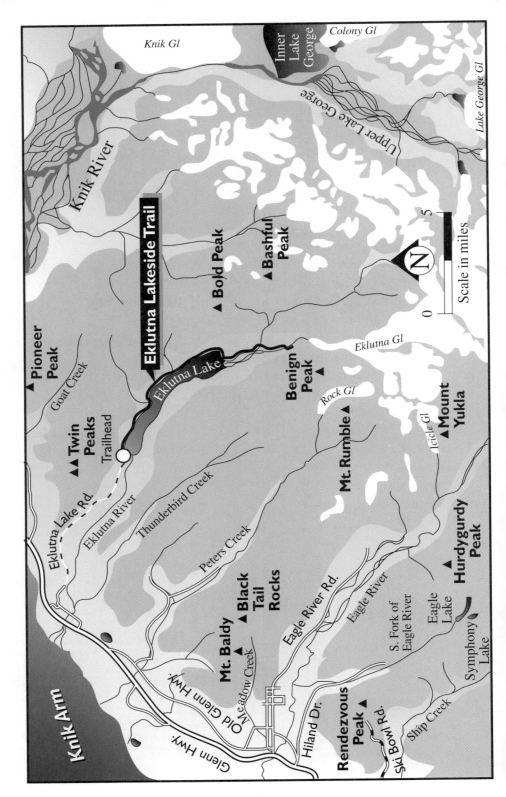

Knik Gl

Colony Gl

Inner Lake George

Lake George Gl

Upper Lake George

Knik River

Bold Peak ▲

Bashful Peak ▲

Eklutna Lakeside Trail

Eklutna Gl

N

Scale in miles

0   5

Pioneer Peak ▲

Goat Creek

Eklutna Lake

Benign Peak ▲

Rock Gl

Icicle Gl

Mount Yukla ▲

▲▲ Twin Peaks

Trailhead

Mt. Rumble ▲

Eklutna Lake Rd.

Eklutna River

Thunderbird Creek

Peters Creek

Hurdygurdy Peak ▲

Knik Arm

Black Tail Rocks ▲

Eagle River Rd.

Eagle River

S. Fork of Eagle River

Eagle Lake

Symphony Lake

Mt. Baldy ▲

Meadow Creek

Hiland Dr.

Old Glenn Hwy.

Glenn Hwy.

Rendezvous Peak ▲

Ski Bowl Rd.

Ship Creek

378

Lunch break on a ridge high above Eklutna Lake with Bold Peak in the background on the left and Eklutna Glacier visible in the distant right.

Trail Location: Although this may not be the official name of this trail because it is merely an extension of the Eklutna Lake Trail, it is different enough to warrant its own trail guide. Not only is it narrower, rockier and far rougher than the former, but it also has its own unique purpose—to get the hiker and biker as well as the ATV'er and moto-crosser who has already traveled the length of the Eklutna Lakeside Trail as close to the snout of Eklutna Glacier as possible. The problem is that the glacier has receded so much in the last few years that only a small corner of it can be seen from the end of this trail. However, this does not mean that this short trail is not worth hiking. The towering flanks of The Mitre (6,600-plus-feet) on the left and Benign Peak (7,200-plus-feet) on the left and the gray, foaming waters of Eklutna River rushing by below make this a raw and exciting trail to hike.

To get to this trailhead follow the Eklutna Lakeside Trail all the way to its very end (12.7 miles). (To get there, see WALK-ABOUT GUIDE TO EKLUTNA LAKESIDE TRAIL.) There, a sign indicating the dangers of the glacier and its environs is located. (The end of this trail is also obvious by the ATV turn-around that exists in front of the sign and the 12.7 mile marker just beyond it. This, where bike travel ends and foot travel begins, is where the Eklutna Glacier Overlook Trail begins.

Just beyond the 12.7 mile marker, a small footpath—which is the Eklutna Glacier Overlook Trail—leads along the right-handside of the river. Initially, this trail is very easy to walk. Before long, however, it is clambering over rocks and skirting along ledges. Though some care is definitely required in places, it is not extremely dangerous walking—except perhaps in wet weather when the rocks may be excessively slippery. Going up and down along the riverbank, it eventually climbs up over a small rise to where another sign is located. This is the end of the trail. A large, table, like rock just to the left of the sign offers a fine spot for a sit down picnic or just to stare at the overwhelming surroundings. Although some people may wish to explore further up the gorge, it is not recommended. The rocks and boulders are very unsteady and often move under foot and hand—which can make for very dangerous traveling. Not only that, but there is very little gorge left to explore: Within .25 miles, the bank comes up against an impassable sheer cliff. Dropping into the raging river on one side and towering into dangerous rock walls on the other, there is simply no place left to go—unless one is an experienced mountaineer. So for both safety reasons and the fact that the gorge up ahead makes it impossible to go very far, it is best not to venture any farther than the end of the trail.

Trail Grade: This trail, even though it is very rocky in places and full of short ups and downs—some of which are quite steep—still rates as a grade 2 hike. Don't let this low grade fool any one, though. It is a hard grade 2. For even though it is not long, it does gain quite a few feet in elevation. It is also very rough underfoot.

Trail Condition: The first section of this trail is flat and gentle. In a very short time, however, it becomes very rough as it winds up and down over the rocks and ledges above the river below and the cliffs above. Expect to use both hands in very many sections just to lift one's self up and down particularly sharp—but short—drops on and off the rocks.

Trail Mileage: The one way distance to the end of this trail from the end of the Eklutna Lakeside Trail is approximately .75 miles for a round trip total of 1.5 miles.

Total Elevation Gain: From the trailhead to the end of the trail, the total elevation gain is approximately 400 feet.

High Point: The highest point reached upon this trail is approximately 1,700 feet above sea level at the very end of the trail.

Normal Hiking Time: The round trip hike to and from the end of the Eklutna Lakeside Trail should take anywhere from 40 minutes to 2 hours, depending on the condition and ambition of the hiker(s) involved.

Campsites: There are no campsites anywhere along this trail. (Although some may find that the small turnaround at the very of the Eklutna Lakeside Trail may provide enough room for a tent, it is not recommended simply because of the traffic going back and forth along the trail. Instead, make reservations at one of the many campgrounds back along the Eklutna Lakeside Trail.)

Best Time: This trail is best hiked anywhere from mid-June to mid-September. However, if a particularly heavy snowfall may have occurred the winter before, it may be better not to begin hiking this trail until late June or even early August. This is because of the possible avalanches that may still be falling on the trail from the heights above.

USGS Maps: Anchorage B-6.

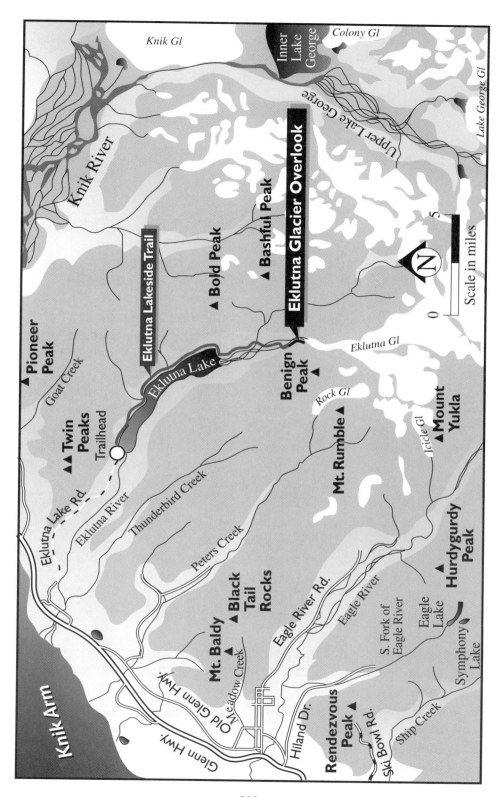

Twin Peaks Trail

Trail Location: Twin Peaks Trail begins at the edge of the second parking area at the north end of Eklutna Lake. (To get there, see WALK-ABOUT GUIDE TO EKLUTNA LAKESIDE TRAIL.) Walk across the foot bridge located at the southeast corner of the parking lot and look for the sign indicating the beginning of the trail. Turn left onto the trail, cross a road and begin climbing up through the woods. Occasional open areas provide views of the lakes below and the ridges and mountains above.

Many people end their hike at tree line, which is located at about 2,650 feet. Here just beyond the trail's end is a gentle meadow for a picnic down a steep embankment and across one stream through which runs a stream for soaking the feet. More ambitious hikers and climbers may prefer to continue up to the ridgeline far above (elevation 4,900 to 5,000 feet depending on the pass or summit reached). But be warned: the higher one gets, the rougher the footing and climbing gets. The view out over the Matanuska Valley from the saddle just south of the Twin Peaks, though, is worth the climb. Experienced mountaineers can also use this trail to reach East and West Twin Peaks (elevations 5,873 and 5,401 feet respectively).

Trail Grade: Though the footing is good on the trail, the elevation gain alone earns it a grade of 3.

Trail Condition: To tree line the trail is generally wide and dry. For those continuing above tree line, however, expect to encounter some rather irritating knee and waist high brush in the upper meadows and even some scree as the ridgeline is approached.

Trail Mileage: It is a 3 mile hike from the parking area to tree line, for a round trip total of 6 miles. To get to the ridgeline above entails a round trip hike of over 8 miles.

Total Elevation Gain: Hiking to tree line requires 1,800 feet of climbing, whereas the scramble to the ridgeline above requires 3,500 to 4,100 feet of climbing.

High Point: Depending on one's destination there are a variety of high points that can be reached: tree line is located at an elevation of 2,650 feet above sea level, the lowest pass in the ridge is 4,450 feet above sea level, the lowest summit on the ridge is 5,050 feet above sea level, West Twin Peak is 5,401 feet above sea level and East Twin Peak is 5,873 feet above sea level.

Normal Hiking Time: The round trip to tree line should take anywhere from 2 to 4 hours, whereas the hike up to the ridgeline and back should take 6 to 8 hours.

Campsites: None to speak of, but then because the hike is relatively short, none are really needed. However, those wishing to camp in a remote area may either find a level spot on the upper meadow which lies just down the steep embankment and across the stream at the upper trail's end, or even camp on one of the saddles far above.

Best Time: Because of the very real avalanche danger on the upper slopes of the valley, June to September are the best times to do this hike. And of these months, September is perhaps the best month to do it in because the leaves have been flying and the view is more expansive through the leafless trees.

USGS Maps: Anchorage B-6 NW.

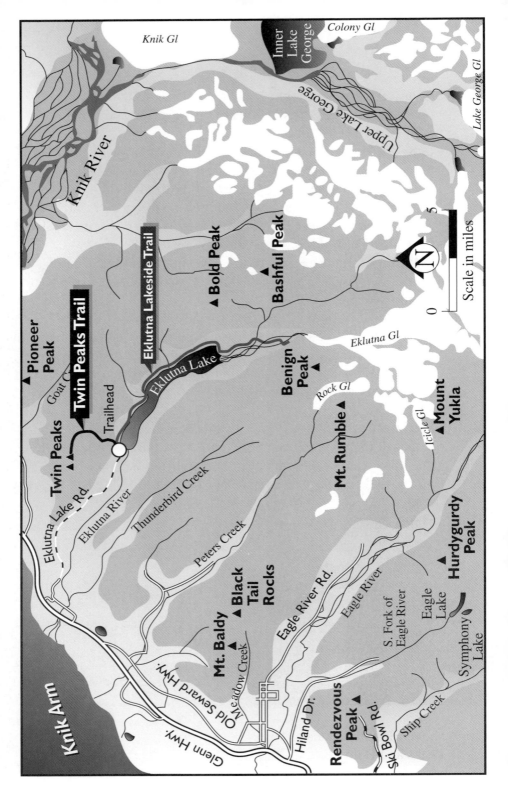

Knik Gl

Colony Gl

Inner Lake George

Lake George Gl

Upper Lake George

Knik River

Bold Peak ▲

Bashful Peak ▲

Eklutna Lakeside Trail

N

Scale in miles

0   5

Eklutna Gl

Pioneer Peak ▲

Twin Peaks Trail

Goat C

Eklutna Lake

Benign Peak ▲

Rock Gl

Icicle Gl

Twin Peaks ▲

Trailhead

▲Mount Yukla

Eklutna Lake Rd.

Eklutna River

Thunderbird Creek

Mt. Rumble ▲

Peters Creek

Hurdygurdy Peak ▲

Knik Arm

Black Tail Rocks ▲

Eagle River Rd.

Eagle River

Eagle Lake

Mt. Baldy ▲

Meadow Creek

S. Fork of Eagle River

Symphony Lake

Old Seward Hwy.

Hiland Dr.

Rendezvous Peak ▲

Ski Bowl Rd.

Ship Creek

Glenn Hwy.

High above Eklutna Lake's east shore on the ridge between East and West Twin Peaks and Bold Peak.

Bold Peak Overlook Trail

Trail Location: The Bold Peak Overlook Trail begins five miles in on the left, or east, side of the Eklutna Lakeside Trail. (To get there, see WALK-ABOUT GUIDE TO EKLUTNA LAKESIDE TRAIL.) There, 100 feet beyond where Bold Creek cascades beneath the road, a signpost stating "Bold Ridge Overlook 3.5 miles" marks the beginning of the trail. The trail leaves the road on the left-handside and climbs steadily for almost the entire 3.5 miles. For those ambitious and/ or strong enough to persevere to the end of the trail, they will be well-rewarded. The Bold Overlook Trail is one of the most breathtaking in the Eklutna Valley. For not only does it carry the hiker to well above tree line, but in doing so, it places them amid the broken moraine below the towering facade of Bold Peak. Here there is an entire glacier-carved valley to explore including ridges to scramble up, moraine to skip over and even a pass into the next valley to climb over. It's also an ideal place to just sit and gaze.

Trail Grade: Because it is a steady climb for almost its entire length, this trail is rated at level 3.

Trail Condition: The first mile or more of the trail, in which it parallels Bold Creek, is, though uphill, wide and easy to follow. This is very understandable considering that the trail utilizes an old roadbed. As it gets higher, however, the weeds begin to encroach more and more until they become so bad that in the last mile or so to tree line willow and alder have grown to so completely dominate the trail, they have forced hikers to climb out of the roadbed and create a new right-of-way up the embankments on either side. Once up on the moraine, however, the trail once again becomes easy to follow with few wet spots to jump and few weeds to avoid.

Once up on the moraine, the ambitious hiker(s) may wish to continue up valley and climb to the crest of Hunter Creek Pass. From this point one can see not only the pass's namesake, but also much of the Matanuska Valley, Knik River and Knik Glacier as well as some of the highest and most remote peaks in the Chugach Mountains including the highest—the 13,176-foot Mount Marcus Baker.

Trail Mileage: The one way hike from the beginning of the trail at mile 5 on the Lakeside Trail to the end of the trail in the Bold Peak valley is 3.5 miles for a round trip total of 7 miles, whereas the one way hike from the parking lot to the end of the Bold Overlook Trail is 8.5 miles for a round trip total of 17 miles. Hiking to the top of Hunter Creek Pass adds another 2 miles out and back to these totals.

Total Elevation Gain: Whether calculated from the parking lot or from the beginning of the trail itself, this hike entails a climb of 2,800 feet. The hike to the pass, however, entails an overall climb of 3,950 feet.

High Point: The highest point reached on the trail is 3,700 feet above sea level at the base of the moraine. The highest point reached if you also climb Hunter Pass is 4,850 feet.

Normal Hiking Time: From the parking lot, one should expect to spend anywhere from 7 to 10 hours to complete the round trip to the end of the trail and back. To climb to the top of Hunter Creek Pass will take an additional 2 to 4 hours.

Campsites: The upper valley below the massive shadow of Bold Peak is teeming with ideal campsites.

Best Time: Any time of the year is good time to hike this trail though most people prefer to do it in the warmer summer months from June to September. The additional climb to Hunter Creek Pass, on the other hand, should only be done from June to September due to the extreme avalanche danger.

USGS Maps: Anchorage B-6.

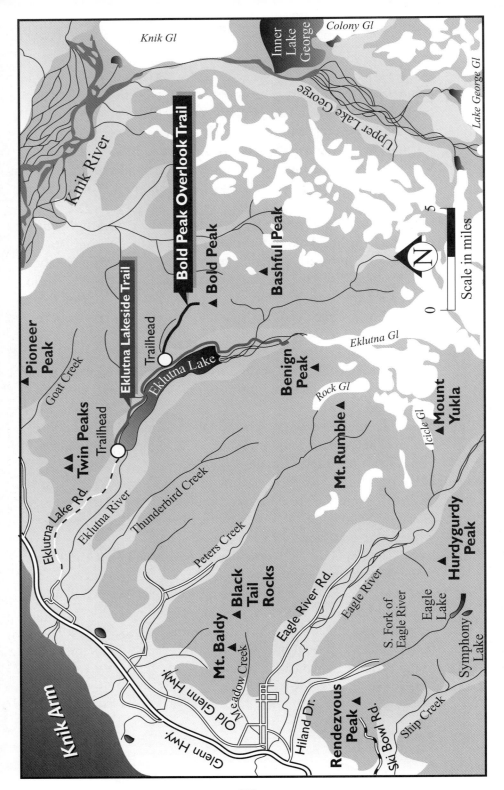

Knik Gl

Colony Gl

Inner Lake George

Lake George Gl

Upper Lake George

Lake George

Bold Peak Overlook Trail

▲ Bold Peak

Bashful Peak ▲

Eklutna Lakeside Trail

Trailhead

Eklutna Lake

Eklutna Gl

Knik River

Pioneer Peak ▲

Goat Creek

Twin Peaks ▲▲

Trailhead

Eklutna Lake Rd.

Eklutna River

Thunderbird Creek

Peters Creek

Benign Peak ▲

Rock Gl

Mt. Rumble ▲

Icicle Gl

▲ Mount Yukla

Hurdygurdy Peak ▲

N

Scale in miles

0   5

Mt. Baldy ▲

Black Tail Rocks ▲

Meadow Creek

Eagle River Rd.

Eagle River

S. Fork of Eagle River

Eagle Lake

Symphony Lake

Knik Arm

Glenn Hwy.

Old Glenn Hwy.

Hiland Dr.

Rendezvous Peak ▲

Ski Bowl Rd.

Ship Creek

390

On the Twin Peak Trail above Eklutna Lake.

Trail Location: The beginning of the East Fork Trail can be found on the left-handside of the Eklutna Lakeside Trail at mile 10.5. (To get there, see WALK-ABOUT GUIDE TO EKLUTNA LAKESIDE TRAIL.) A signpost marks the beginning of the trail, but if perchance you miss the turn-off, you'll know you've gone too far if you reach the bridge over the East Fork. Once on the trail, the hiker enters a different world. Not only is the road replaced by an actual trail, but the companionship of the calm lake is replaced by a frothing creek. Furthermore, instead of walking up a wide valley, the hiker is now climbing up a narrow vale over which loom some of the highest peaks in Chugach State Park, including the 8,005-foot Bashful Peak. It is not a trail suitable for bikes or ATVs, so the hiker is also, for the first time since leaving the parking lot, truly alone. From the trailhead, the trail winds along the creek's edge for 5.5 miles beneath the looming masses of Bold Peak, Baleful Peak, and Bashful Peak, the highest mountain in Chugach State Park. Some use this trail to approach the big climbs that these mountains offer, while others use it simply to explore to creek's end at the foot of a glacier-caped peak. No matter what the destination, however, the trail is worth seeking out.

Trail Grade: It is mostly a level trail, but because it is a rocky, rooted trail, it rates a grade 2.

Trail Condition: Rocks and roots underfoot and quick turns back and forth around trees and through rock falls, make the going relatively slow. There are also occasional muddy spots—as should be expected on any trail that borders a stream or creek— and brushy areas that will further hinder progress. So though it's level, it's difficult to do this trail fast.

Trail Mileage: The one way hike from where the East Fork Trail leaves the Eklutna Lakeside Trail to its end is 5.5 miles for a round-trip total of 11 miles. This makes the one way hike from the parking lot to the end of this trail 16 miles for a round trip total of 32 miles. (Bear in mind, though, that the first 10.5 of this hike is along the Lakeside Trail to the beginning of the East Fork Trail can be done on a bicycle.)

Total Elevation Gain: From the beginning of the trail to its end entails a total elevation gain of 1,100 feet. However, from the parking lot, where any outing on this trail must begin—whether its on bicycle or foot—the total elevation gain is 1,500 feet.

High Point: The highest point reached on the East Fork Trail is approximately 2,000 feet above sea level at the very at end of the trail at the base of an unnamed 6,810-foot glacier covered peak.

Normal Hiking Time: The round trip from the parking lot to the end of this trail can be done in one day, but most people should expect to take two or three—if for no other reason than to allow time to explore the East Fork valley. The 11 mile round-trip from where the trail leaves the Eklutna Lakeside Trail will take most people 4 to 7 hours.

Campsites: There are many places to pitch a tent along this trail, if you don't mind a few rocks and a few lumps beneath you. There is plenty of water to be had as well. Bear in mind, however, that any water taken out of the east Fork should be filtered before use because of its glacier origin.

Best Time: The best time to hike this trail is from mid-June to mid-September. It's not that it's too difficult or steep to ski or snowshoe in the winter, but simply because the avalanche danger from the steep, near slopes on either side of the trail make it extremely dangerous.

USGS Maps: Anchorage B-6, B-5 and A-6 and A-5.

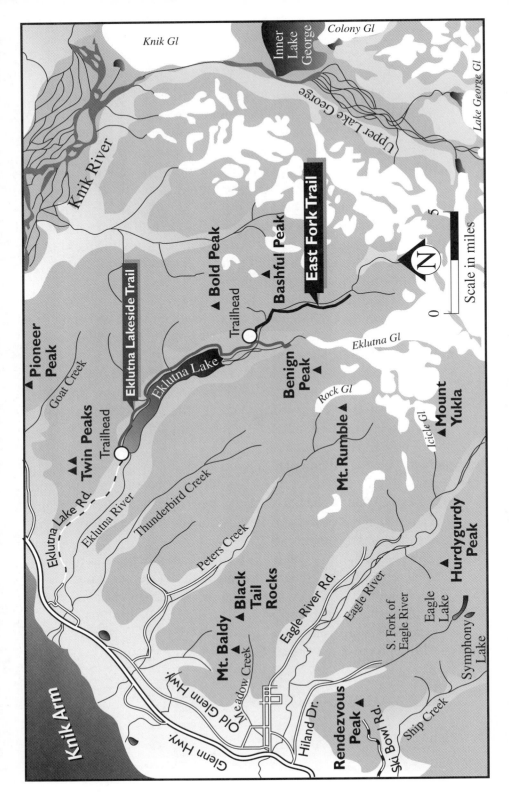

Knik Gl

Colony Gl

Inner Lake George

Lake George Gl

Upper Lake George

Lake George Gorge

Knik River

East Fork Trail

Bashful Peak

Bold Peak

Trailhead

Eklutna Lakeside Trail

Eklutna Lake

Eklutna Gl

Pioneer Peak

Goat Creek

Twin Peaks

Trailhead

Benign Peak

Rock Gl

Icicle Gl

Mount Yukla

Eklutna Lake Rd

Eklutna River

Thunderbird Creek

Mt. Rumble

Peters Creek

Hurdygurdy Peak

Knik Arm

Black Tail Rocks

Eagle River Rd.

Eagle River

Eagle Lake

Symphony Lake

S. Fork of Eagle River

Mt. Baldy

Meadow Creek

Old Glenn Hwy.

Glenn Hwy.

Hiland Dr.

Rendezvous Peak

Ski Bowl Rd.

Ship Creek

N

0   5

Scale in miles

394

Descending into the Bold Peak valley.

CHAPTER 18

New Year, Old Beliefs

No birds sang. No flowers bloomed. No shadows of sheep or fox crossed the snow-filled hollows below. No wings of birds crossed the sunlit slopes above. Nor was a single insect droning over the white winter wastes of the nearby tundra. We were alone. On the last day of autumn, the day before the first day of winter, the shortest day of the year, we were alone. Trudging up the high hump of a wide ridge, we were alone.

On one side of the ridge a hard, gray cornice of snow jutted out into space far above the cavernous Goat Creek valley. On the other side of the ridge the snow-dusted tundra and ice-sheathed rocks fell away into the wider, deeper Knik River valley. Behind us uncurled the long ridge we'd been climbing for the last four hours. Ahead of us towered the shattered twin summit of Pioneer Peak towards which we were still climbing. In the low, broken light of the late afternoon our own long, thin shadows, stretching for fifty feet at a diagonal behind us, followed us slowly upward as we made our way up the apex of that long ridge. Nothing else moved. We were alone. And being alone in one of the shortest days of the waning year can weigh upon the heart.

It wasn't that we couldn't see evidence of humankind. Far down to our right, down in the woods that bordered the wide, deep valley of the dark, braided flats of the Knik, we could at least see some scattered lights. We could even make out the headlights of a distant car spotlighting the woods as it wound down Knik River Road. Yet these few lights were insignificant compared to the blaze of electricity we could see farther down valley. There, partly blocked by the summit we were climbing toward, shone the far more numerous and much brighter clustered lights of Palmer. But even those lights were only an aberration, a momentary blink among the darker shapes of the nearby Chugach and the mist-blurred lines of the more distant Talkeetna Mountains that rose beyond.

Those lights, and the evidence they gave of other people, other lives, simply weren't enough to offset the atmosphere of magnificent loneliness that we felt as we continued to climb that high corniced ridge more than 5,300 feet above the land of the living below.

Usually not until spending a considerable amount of time out of doors does one begin to realize what power the sun has over the human mind and body. If enough time is spent under its direct influence, one may actually begin to recognize the sun in as wide a variety of manifestations as our not-too-distant Neolithic ancestors did. Perhaps the earliest as well as one of the most widespread of these seems to be the sun as the all-seeing eye. This representation of the sun can be found on dolmens and in cave paintings in Neolithic sights from all over Europe and the British isles. Later, the ancient Egyptians carved what seems to be the all-seeing eye on various solar discs that are believed to represent the head of a divinity. In even as late a play as <u>Oedipus at Colonus</u> by the fifth-century B.C. Greek playwright Sophocles, the tragic hero says just before going off to his own mysterious death, "may the all-seeing sun give thee and thine such a sad old age as mine." At other times the sun seems to be a divine ruler and preserver of justice. The famous Sphinx in Egypt is believed to represent King Cephron (a descendant of Cheops), the god-ruler of his people, in his role as the supreme sun. Even earlier, the Babylonians envisioned their sun-god Shamash as supreme judge and law-giver. This belief may have given rise to later religions' depiction of their supreme god as presiding over not only the individual judgment of newly deceased souls, but also the final judgment of all souls, which is God's role in Christianity. The later Greek god Apollo, who is often associated with the sun, was also the god of truth.

But the sun's most common and widespread role in Neolithic Europe was as guardian of both the living and the dead. In this last guise, the sun played a variety of seemingly dissimilar roles in a variety of early rites and rituals. But this dissimilarity was only superficial. In essence, all these ceremonies had only one underlying purpose: to call down the sun's life-giving light and warmth. Even by the later stages of the prehistory humankind was well aware of the fact that whether they lived or died depended almost solely upon the sun. Perhaps a wall carving of the Pharaoh Akhenaten and his wife and daughters dating from 1345 B.C. epitomizes this role of the sun best of all. Currently on display in the

Egyptian Museum in Berlin the carving depicts the Pharaoh and his wife, each holding one of their daughters, facing each other from either side while above them both in the center of the plaque shines the sun. From this sun extends a semi-circular group of spear-like rays that fill most of the space between the married couple with their representational light. One of these rays even connects with the Pharoah's head. These rays, called *ankhs*, were the symbol of life itself. Thus is the royal family bathed in divine light. Similar rays of light would later be used by Christian artists to represent the divine grace of the Holy Ghost, the last but certainly not least of the entities in the Holy Trinity, shining down on apostles and saints. But this is not due merely to imaginative conjurings of artists and sculptors.

From the very first doctrinal articulations of Christianity, the blessing of the Holy Ghost has been considered the supreme proof of God's grace and favor. For this reason alone the Holy Spirit is held sacred above all else.

> *All manner of sin and blasphemy shall be forgiven unto men:*
> *but the blasphemy against the Holy Ghost shall not be forgiven*
> *unto men.*
> (Matthew 12:31)

Bestowing direct and obvious evidence of God's favor, the Holy Ghost is the newest—and perhaps most potent—representation of the sun as guardian of life and death.

In light of the Holy Ghost (pun intended), it should not be surprising that the most important of Neolithic man's ceremonies revolved around the winter solstice. For it is at the winter solstice that the sun embodies both life and death—in fact, has control over life and death, not unlike later Christianity's Holy Ghost. In the moment between reaching its lowest point in the sky and beginning its six-month journey back to its highest point it contains all humankind's greatest fears and greatest hopes. Without the sun's warmth and heat, the earth would lie under perpetual snow. Crops wouldn't grow, livestock wouldn't increase and humankind would both starve and freeze. In the cold years of the last Ice Age, Neolithic man must've feared these possibilities if, for some reason, one year the sun might indeed fail to turn around. By the same token, if the sun didn't turn around at the height of the summer solstice, there would have been an endless harvest of crops in the fields and an always increasing number of livestock in the meadows. Humankind would've returned to Eden.

We had no delusions about returning to Eden when we started our hike down in that land of the living at the trailhead for Pioneer Ridge Trail. At about 10 a.m., when we were taking our first steps out of the parking lot, it was anything but warm and spring-like. A thick gray frost lay on the still night-shadowed woods and ice-misted meadows. Our own breaths rose in heavy clouds of crystal condensation. We had to almost jog up the trail just to generate some warmth in our still sleepy bodies. We knew, however, it would only get warmer as the day progressed— relatively speaking, of course. Already the first light rays of this all-too-short day in the year's last month were starting to thread their way through the mountains and ridges, the valleys and ravines that separated the low, distant sun from us. Soon after that, only a mile or so into the climb, the first rays of the distant sun were glazing the high summits to the south and east with warm, orange light. Across the Knik River valley that opened up behind and below us, the walls of the deeper, higher Chugach were awash with hazy diamond light. It would still, however, be a long time before any of that sunlight—if any at all—touched us.

We didn't mind having to wait, though. After all, we had a virtually snow-less trail before us on what was for all intents and purposes a balmy mid-December day in South-Central Alaska—relatively speaking again, of course. It was just over thirty degrees! Not only that, but the higher we climbed, the warmer it was getting—and not just from the exertion of the climb. There was not a breath of wind in the air, either. It was not Eden, but it was highly unnatural. And we were loving it!

But then there had been nothing natural about this winter so far. Only a few inches of snow had fallen since summer, and despite the one cold snap that bottomed out the thermometer regularly at fifteen and twenty-five degrees during much of mid- and late November, temperatures had been mild—mostly twenty to thirty degrees above, with some days even reaching into the high thirties and forties. Very unnatural.

Nor had it snowed much. Only a few inches had fallen since mid-October, and what had fallen hadn't stayed. Evaporation and convection had taken it all away by early December. Even in the high mountains there was very little snow to be seen, but mostly just gray rock and brown earth through which only an occasional swath of white powder could be discerned. Extremely unnatural.

Skiers and snowmachiners were moaning over the lack of snow; sports store managers were saddened over undiminished inventory of winter gear; and resort owners were shaking their heads in bewilderment over their idle lifts and near-deserted slopes. It had not been a winter for any paramour or protégé of snow. The lack of snow had even affected everyday life. Home owners were worried about frozen pipes. Snow plow operators and anyone else who made a living removing snow—including children going door to door with snow shovels in hand—were virtually out of work. Not only that, but the lack of bright snow had turned Anchorage into a dark, dreary, and dirty outpost on the fringes of the black sea. It was a cheerless place to be.

For hikers, though, it had been a great winter so far. No bears, no rain, no bugs and no mud. Conditions were nearly ideal. Places where one usually could not go were now accessible. I'd been told of people hiking and skating through muskeg and across bogs, up rivers and over lakes. The snow-less frozen conditions had opened up a whole new world of possibilities. It was unnatural—but that was all the more reason to take advantage of the unique opportunities the unnatural conditions offered. After all, such conditions did not come often and did not last long.

For prehistoric man, however, the world was always an unnatural place. It was, indeed, a wondrous place filled with mysterious and magical and unexplainable phenomena. Earthquakes that shook the earth, supernovas and comets that lit up the sky, as well as the rain and the lightning, and, in colder climates, the snow, sleet and hail that fell from that sky above to this earth below were all sources of amazement. Even the regular cycles of tides rising and falling, days and nights coming and going, and seasons following one after another in the turning of the year were a constant source of wonder. It all seemed so magical. And, for prehistoric and ancient man, the only means of appeasing or controlling such magic was to employ magic.

In his work <u>The Golden Bough</u>, Sir George Frazer classifies two major types of "sympathetic magic" used by man throughout history. The first type is called Homoeopathic or Imitative Magic. It is based on the Law of Similarity which believes "that like produces like, or that an effect resembles its cause" (11). The second type is what Frazer refers to as Contagion Magic. In contrast to the first, it is rooted in the belief "that things which have once been in contact with each other continue to act on each other at a distance after the physical contact has been severed" (11). Used in a large variety of rites and rituals throughout the world, both types of magic were practiced for almost exclusively one purpose: to compel the seemingly unnatural natural world to act beneficially on behalf of humankind. And what has always been most beneficial to humankind has been a good harvest. So it should not be surprising that most of the examples of these types of magic that Frazer includes in his book revolve around the fertilization and propagation of the earth.

Perhaps the most familiar examples of Homoeopathic or Imitative Magic are the hunting dances of many North American Indian tribes. In the Buffalo dance of prairie tribes such as the Sioux and Blackfoot, selected braves would don buffalo skins. During the course of the dance, these "buffalo" would be symbolically slain in the belief that their ritualized death would result in the real death of many buffalo when the hunt finally did take place. The same type of ritual was used by many northwest Indian tribes, such as the Haida, before they took their boats out to fish. Only instead of "slaying" human buffalo in their dance, they would "net" human fish. In ancient Europe as well as parts of the Far East, pregnant women of certain tribes or clans would spend the night in newly sown fields. Depending on local belief, this magic could work two ways: either the sown field would make the childbirth easy and the baby healthy or the pregnant women would insure a good harvest.

More often than not, however, Homoeopathic or Imitative Magic was used directly on the single power that had supreme control over the harvest: the sun itself. An example of one such ritual is described by Miranda Green in her work The Sun-Gods of Ancient Europe:

> *The ritual at Basse Kontz on the Moselle exemplifies the tradition; here, a wheel was set on fire and rolled down the Stromberg Mountain to the river, in magical imitation of the sun's descent from its highest point in midsummer. The idea was that if the wheel rolled unimpeded to the water, the local people would enjoy*

a lucky year and a good winter harvest. (19)

Perhaps the best example of Contagion Magic, on the other hand, can be found in the use of Voodoo dolls in the Caribbean—a practice still in use today. In Ireland, the Blarney Stone, whose properties are distilled with a kiss, is a major tourist attraction. But Contagion magic also plays a key role in many major religions. Sometimes that role is highly dubious, as in the buying and selling of relics in the Middle Ages. It is Contagion Magic that also compels Chaucer and his mix of holy and not-so-holy companions to make their famous pilgrimage to Canterbury. More often than not, however, Contagion Magic has been the root of honorable and truly devotional behavior. After all, it is why so many of King Arthur's knights took up the futile search for the Holy Grail. It is also the reason why so many Catholics have bathed in the waters of Lourdes where Bernadette received her vision of the Virgin Mary; and it why so many Christians have prayed at the base of Calvary or slept outside Christ's tomb in the Holy Land. For thirteen centuries now, Moslems the world over have sought at least once in their life to make the long trek to the holy city of Mecca and circumambulate the Kaaba where the Black Stone which the angel Gabriel gave to Abraham is kept. Mecca is such a holy city that no infidel, nonbeliever, is allowed inside its gates. Mount Sinai, on the other hand, has always been open to Moslem, Christian and Jewish pilgrims. Hindu's make the journey to Benares where beside the steps of the Bisheshwar Temple they bathe in the holy waters of the mighty Ganges River. And for over two and half millennia, Buddhists have journeyed for weeks, months, even years to sit beneath the Bo Tree where Gautama finally achieved enlightenment. These, and so many other places of pilgrimage not mentioned, all have their connection to Contagion Magic. Simply by touching or being near a thing or place associated with a saint, prophet or even god of their creed, the faithful hope to be healed physically or blessed spiritually.

There are, however, some rituals that contain elements of both Homoeopathic and Contagion Magic. Perhaps the best known of these is the ritual surrounding the Yule Log. Burning the Yule Log on midwinter's eve is a ritual whose roots are deep in European pre-history. By burning a conifer log on the shortest day of the year, practitioners, through Homoeopathic Magic, hoped to sympathetically coax the sun to return north after its six-month journey south. The practice was imitative in two ways: First, the conifer, because it was always green, was believed to somehow hold inside itself the warm, sun-filled days of summer. Second, the fire itself was believed to come directly from the sun. On the longest night of the shortest day the family would gather around the hearth. Then the log would be lit and perhaps some prayers or incantations said or sung. After the hearth cooled, the ashes of the Yule Log were carefully swept up and saved for numerous later rituals—rituals that had their basis in Contagion Magic. For these ashes, so closely associated with the sun and its power, were believed to aid in fertility and protect against lightning and thunder (though the connection between these two properties are somewhat obscure to most scholars). Depending on the tribe, these ashes were taken out on the equinox and mixed with the soon to be planted seeds. This mixture was then sprinkled over already planted seed, or even fed to livestock and young women to help bring about pregnancy. This was done simply because the mysterious sun, being the source of all life, was believed to make *all* things grow— regardless of whether those things are the seeds in the earth or the seeds in the womb.

With such beliefs did Neolithic man transform the natural world into a magical world. And the only way to contend with and try to control or appease a magical world was with magic—no matter what the time of year. Contrasting the domestic Yule fire of midwinter's day were the public bonfires of midsummer's day with their own distinct group of rites and rituals as well as the two equinoxes and numerous other prehistoric and ancient "holidays". Indeed, magic was a part of every hour of every day. In such a way did the ordinary become the extraordinary.

Tucker and I were, of course, not exploring anywhere out of the ordinary, though it was a bit extraordinary to be climbing where we were the day before the first day of winter. Snow and ice and the threat of avalanches usually make the Pioneer Ridge Trail very difficult and often dangerous in winter. That was not true this winter. Nor was it due to any magic. It simply hadn't snowed.

The only difficulties we encountered were the glaciated streams that blocked the trail like blue-green flows of solidified—and very slippery—lava. To cross these treacherous, frozen flows, we often had to pull ourselves across the ice by grabbing the branches of nearby trees, or, worse, if the ice was too steep and smooth, we had to trip and claw our way through the willows on either side of the trail to bypass the flow entirely. More than once we also got down on hands and knees, grabbing at ice-lodged sticks and weeds to pull ourselves over particularly wide and dirty sheets of frozen overflow.

As we climbed higher, the sunlit dome of Mt. McKinley appeared like a lopsided orange balloon hovering over the darker, nearer ridge line of the Talkeetnas. It was the only bright spot as far as the eye could see in that direction. All the rest of the world to the north was still wrapped in the shadowy mists of the gray winter morning—as were we.

"I wouldn't mind having a little bit of that sunlight down here," Tucker said turning to me. His red face framed by frost-whitened hair made me cold just looking at him.

I nodded in agreement.

Considering just the warming power of the sun alone, it is not surprising that early people venerated the sun as a deity. Certainly the sun became important with the dawning of the Neolithic Revolution. It was at that time, about 8,000 B.C., that the first agricultural discoveries were made and the practice of husbandry became more widespread, both of which soon led to the first establishments of towns and cities. Two of the oldest are believed to be Jericho in the Jordan Valley and Ali Kosh in western Iran, both of which were first settled some 13,000 years ago. Without a regular, cyclical sun, the crops would not grow and animals could not feed. Inevitably, famine would result—and did result. During the Bronze Age, dust and ash from volcanic eruptions in Iceland blocked out the sun over much of Europe for an extended period of time. Winters were suddenly colder and darker and summers were cooler and wetter; farmlands were ruined and people starved. These harsher conditions may have given rise to greater wanderings as people searched and fought for more hospitable climates and lands. Perhaps the thirteenth century B.C. Mycenaean sack of Troy which comes down to us in the romanticized settings of The Iliad and The Odyssey of Homer as well as in numerous other tales—including that of the famous Trojan Horse—was the result of such landgrabbing and piracy. Whether or not all the stories that evolved out of that historical event are entirely true, does not affect their merit as literature. Read in conjunction with all the archaeological evidence, they

404

do, however, point to the indisputable fact that all of Europe was in a state of semi-chaos. And all this social upheaval was almost entirely due to the partial blocking of the sun's life-giving rays. Little wonder, then, that the sun was an important—if not the all-important—deity to not only the first city dwellers, but to all people. By extension, this is probably why the Babylonians and Egyptians made the god associated with the sun their supreme deity.

Is it any wonder that ancient man thought highest of the sun when it was lowest in the sky? No doubt the winter solstice was a dreaded day for prehistoric man. After all, what would happen if the sun simply decided one year not to turn around?

But the sun represented more than light and heat to ancient man. It was also, by extension, the giver of life itself. Anybody who lives in the far north can easily understand this. Even with the modern conveniences of central heating and electric lights, the power of the sun to illumine and warm is evident. And that power must have been all the more evident ten, fifteen and even twenty millennia ago when heat and light both originated in the hearth of the rude hut, lodge or from a small fire in a cave that people called home. We often forget how necessary the sun is to our survival. Ancient man never forgot. That was why so many of his rites and rituals were associated with it—and why so many of those rites and rituals took place in the last days of the year when the sun was so low in the sky.

Evidence of these old rites and rituals can be found all across Europe—as well as in most of the rest of the world. In Neolithic Ireland, tombs such as that found at Newgate were often built so the sun would shine into the deepest recesses of the cave vault on the winter solstice. A Celtic altar from Nimes on the Lower Rhine has the solar wheel flanked by two thunderbolts carved into its base, and Stonehenge, built over a series centuries by numerous generations, was conceived as a calendar in which the winter and summer solstice play the most significant role. In the pre-Incan city of Tiwanaku in Peru, the Gateway of the Sun is the largest of several megalithic gateways that open on to sacred plazas. In the massive lintel of this simple, but impressive structure is carved, wearing an elaborate headdress, the sun god himself flanked by two attendants. In the pre-Aztec ruins of Teotihuacan in Mexico, the Pyramid of the Sun is the most dominant feature of the ruins. The inhabitants

believed that a natural cave over which the pyramid was built led down to
the underworld, which, according to their mythology, was the birthplace
of the human race—which is rather appropriate considering that the
entrance out of this womb-like birthplace lies under the life-giving sun.
The top of the pyramid, reaching a height of roughly 210 feet, making it
easily the highest point in the ruins, was also the first spot touched by the
sun's rays of the morning—which must've always been a heartening sight
to the local inhabitants.

Fifteen hundred years later, watching the first rays of the sun hit
the distant snowy summit of Mount McKinley was just as heartening—
and warming—a sight to us. McKinley was, for intents and purposes, our
Pyramid of the Sun. But then all people everywhere both before and after
Teotihuacan's centuries of glory have probably rejoiced in the daily—and
yearly—return of the sun. For many of these people—especially those of
prehistoric times—the rejoicing may have been all the more called for
simply because they were never sure if the sun would come back once it
set in the west or started its yearly journey south. But unlike many of
these early people, Tucker and I, having the benefit of countless
generations of observations and calculations behind us, never doubted the
sun would come back. It was only a matter of time. (Knowing this did
not necessarily make us any wiser than our ancient ancestors, only
smarter.) The problem was that it would take a considerable amount of
time on this particular day before that sun's light finally shone directly on
us.

Then there was actually a short period in which it seemed that the
shining summit of McKinley would be the only bright spot in the whole
day. For the cold, sunless morning was not the only problem we
encountered on the climb. In addition to the chilling cold we had to climb
through, there were the glaciated streams that we had to continually cross.
Admittedly, most of these were more of a minor inconvenience than a big
problem. There was one particularly wide and steep ice slope, however,
that did come close to being a big problem. Where it fell steeply across
the trail at a right angle, there were no branches, rocks or even roots
either imbedded in it or on hanging over either side of it with which we
could step or pull ourselves across it. Nor could we see any other way
around or across it after looking up or down from where we stood. To
step anywhere on its glassy, precipitous surface looked like it would've

quickly resulted in a slide of a hundred feet or more straight down. So we didn't even try.

Instead, seeing no way to cross it, we finally started climbing straight up through the willow that paralleled the ice fall. By doing so, we hoped—with a little bit of luck—to rejoin the switchbacking trail back on this side of the ice fall somewhere above. It wasn't easy pushing up against the down-slanting branches—it was like being a flea crawling against the hair's grain on a dog's broad, steep rump. Still, it was at least easier than it would've been in summer. Not only was the visibility better up through the leafless, brittle branches, but the devil's club, being leafless as well, had also lost much of their sting. The withered stalks of the stuff were still barbed, but without their spiked leaves, they were almost harmless, like defanged rattlesnakes.

Up through the trees we pulled ourselves until the last of the alder gave way to meadows of sporadic spruce. Soon after, with one more grunting pull up a steep, frozen slope of dirt and snow, we stumbled onto the trail again. Following the trail up two more narrow switchbacks, we soon passed above tree line and emerged onto the barren, sloped tundra above. Moments later—after one more steep scramble around a precipitous bend—we came level with the first of three picnic benches that were strategically located along the upper third of the trail. This one, for instance, was appropriately placed just above tree line, making a good benchmark of progress.

Now all we had to do was trudge up over a series of humps on the long, narrow spur we had just crested till we reached the intersection with the south ridge of Pioneer Peak proper. But this trudging only led us higher into more problems. First, the snow lay heavier underfoot the higher we climbed. It wasn't deep—maybe three or four inches at most—but it was crusty and uneven. Sometimes this crust would support us; sometimes it wouldn't. It was like walking on eggs—very cold eggs. Even more difficult was contending with the wind which had suddenly made its presence known the instant we popped our heads above tree line. Blowing off the cold, hard ice of Knik Glacier emerging out of the high mountains to the southeast behind us, it schussed up the barren tundra around us and, after blowing by us, slammed into the higher ridges overhead. And it seemed to only blow harder the higher we climbed. We both pulled up our collars and pulled down our hats as we continued upwards in silence.

Despite not stopping once—and actually trying to go faster to generate more warmth—we only got colder and colder. I got so cold that I finally had to stop to change socks. Over them, I even pulled some waterproof socks for additional warmth. Less than a hundred feet later, I stopped to change from gloves to mittens. Tucker put on a face mask. And still the south wind kept battering us broadside as we continued our slow, methodical march up the ridge over what seemed like a never-ending upward arching row of small humps.

A false summit just beyond the second picnic table didn't improve our moods much either. At first, thinking we were near the top of the ridge, we actually increased our pace. Tucker even managed to crack a joke. But I think it only pushed our moods lower than they originally were, however, when we topped it. For instead of being on top, we found ourselves only looking higher to another ridge line still a half mile away where the slate silhouette of the third and last picnic table stood out against the gray sky.

"I'm sorry, I should've remembered the picnic table," I said.

We stood there for a moment to let the disappointment register.

At least the wind's not as constant up here as it was below," I added without looking at Tucker.

"Yeah," was all he answered.

Then we commenced our march upward once again. Sometime together, sometime apart, we trudged wordlessly—almost mindlessly—up the snow-blasted trail. We were like two turtles who had suddenly retreated into the silence and solitude of their shells.

Finally, after one last grunt up one last, steep incline, we stood, at long last, where the long spur we had spent so long toiling up really did intersect with the south ridge of Pioneer Peak. The elevation here was 5,330 feet. We had made it. Beside us was the third and last picnic table. Below us was the T where our trail connected with another (unofficial) trail that continued in either direction up and down the crest of that high ridge. Behind was the Knik River valley which we'd been turning to look down upon all day. What was now before us, however, was entirely new to our sight. Instead of looking up only to see hump after hump of that long, cold, dark spur rising directly in front of us, there was now ridge after ridge and summit after summit of the Chugach Mountains extending away from us. They filled the whole southern and western skylines with their silent, serrated heights. Off to our left, we could pick out all the "B" peaks—Bold Peak and Bellicose Peak, Benign Peak and, the highest mountain in the state park, Bashful Peak—that rose above the far end of Eklutna Lake, as well as The Mitre. More directly in front of us, and slightly farther afield, we could easily make out Thunder Bird Peak and Mount Rumble, beyond the north ridge of which we could see the summits of Peeking, Corahusk and Yukla, the highest points on the ridge that separated Peters Creek from Eagle River. Beyond the gaps in those peaks, we thought we could see Polar Bear Peak and Eagle Peak. Tucker even thought he could make out Bird Peak way to the south toward Turnagain Arm, while I could have sworn I could see Temptation Peak in the Front Range above Anchorage. Among the closer mountains off to our left, we could also see the gray snows of Eklutna Glacier and a corner of Whiteout Glacier which wound back into the ever-frozen interior of the Chugach where seemingly countless other gray and misted spires could be seen rising against the great bank of dirty white clouds that welled up over the southeastern horizon like gray breakers on a stormy day on the North Sea.

"It's snowing some place," I said, thinking of Girdwood, Whittier and Portage that lay in the hollows of those great peaks in that direction, ". . .or raining," I added, thinking of the weird winter we'd had so far.

"Yeah," Tucker answered. "I'll bet some of those people wish they were here with us."

"Maybe," I answered dubiously. After all, we still had three miles and 1,100 feet to climb before we reached the South Summit of Pioneer.

Even if they didn't want to be with us, though, maybe they should have been with us. It would have been only appropriate if everyone were out moving on the day before the solstice. Whether it was walking, biking, running, climbing or—if enough snow could be found—even skiing, a collective effort to move could be used as a modern form of Imitative Magic to compel the sun to return to these northern climes all the sooner. After all, the sun itself has always been a wanderer. Whether from east to west on its daily cycles or north to south on its yearly cycles, the sun is a wandering pilgrim moving with a willful—and, according to many doctrines and myths, sacred—purpose. Nor is this a new concept of the sun. From the earliest depictions, it has been realized as a traveler, a wayfarer, a divine voyager moving across the sky. The Indo-Europeans were even using a spoked wheel to represent the sun two millennia before the wheel was introduced into central Europe. Later, after the introduction of the wheel into Europe, this spoked wheel became the wheel of a chariot or cart that supposedly carried the sun on its journeys back and forth across the sky.

One of the most impressive of these early sun vehicles is the Trundholm Chariot found in Denmark. Dating from the later Bronze Age and measuring twenty-four inches in length and twelve inches in height, this artifact is believed to have been used in a variety of homoeopathic and/or imitative rites associated with the sun. It's also important for being the earliest known representative of certain solar themes. For one, instead of a human rider, the chariot carries a large, gold-plated disc representing the sun. Gold-plated discs have been found at places of sun worship throughout Europe, Stonehenge being perhaps the most familiar. Second, the chariot is pulled by bronze horses which, along with the stag, are the animals most associated with the sun. This connection is further reinforced by the sun disc upon which the horse stands. Third, it's a chariot, a vehicle that throughout the Mediterranean basin was used almost exclusively by royalty—which makes this artifact one of the earliest depictions of the sun as a supreme ruler.

Both of these themes are evident in the later horse-drawn chariot of the Greek sun-god Helios. Centuries later, the Greek Xenophon noted that Persian royalty were the only people allowed to ride chariots. In a famous mosaic of Alexander the Great in battle, the Emperor Darius III is the only Persian in a chariot. In India, on the other hand, the sun rides a cart, while in Egypt, the sun god Ra rides in a boat, which is also what the Scandinavian sun god rides in. Usually the wandering sun also has a companion, which—not surprisingly—is usually a bird. But it's not just any bird. Royalty must have a royal bird, such as the swan or eagle. In this light, perhaps it's significant that Zeus took advantage of Leda in the form of a swan. Does this then make Helen, who along with the twins Castor and Pollux, was the offspring of that union and the cause of the Trojan War, a child of the sun? Was she just a symbol of what the Trojans and Greeks were really fighting for, the benefits of the sun, in other words, fertile land and a temperate climate?

Tucker and I didn't travel as far as we had for fertile land and a temperate climate—though they would've been nice. The only benefit of the sun we wanted was the light it could give us—light that there just wasn't enough of so late in the year. We had originally intended to climb over the South Summit of Pioneer Peak to the slightly higher North Summit. We even had carried up the rope and climbing hardware to do it. But now we wouldn't have time. There just wasn't enough light left in the day. It was already almost 1:00 p.m. which meant that this second shortest day in the last month of the passing year was almost over.

So thinking we wouldn't need it, we stowed the hardware under the picnic table. Then, after a short snack, we turned north to begin our march up the broad corniced back of the south ridge of the mountain. On our left, the narrow trough of the Goat Creek valley fell steeply away at our feet. On our right extended the wider, broader and deeper basin of the Knik River valley. Meanwhile, behind us rose the continuously darkening mass of rain clouds over the inner ranges of the Chugach. But though inspiring, none of the sights in any of these directions obsessed us as much as the bulk of Pioneer Peak which lay before us—and not just because we were facing it. Framed by the distant lights of Palmer, our goal also dominated our thoughts.

"Is the ridge really passable? Will we run into more ice falls? Maybe we should've brought the rope?" we asked ourselves along with a dozen other questions about time, light, rocks, and avalanches.

For the first mile after leaving the picnic table, we followed the inner edge of a dust-blasted cornice along the wide snow-free summit of the ridge. It was easy walking. Soon, however, the nearly level ridge narrowed to a spiny, rocky ridge. Now skirting above cavernous, declivitous ravines, we were finally beginning our last, long, laborious climb upward. But though the terrain was changing dramatically, we didn't seem to be getting any closer to the summit. It still looked as far away as it had back at the picnic table.

At least we were climbing, though. Any doubts we had on approaching the final summit cone were quickly forgotten in the simple effort of the climb itself. Scrambling over frozen mud and snow-hidden stones, we passed over one spire, then another and another. The world below dropped farther and farther away. Yet the summit above still didn't seem to be getting any closer.

411

We climbed on.

One particularly steep spire forced us out on the east face of the ridge in a long traverse. Pulling ourselves over a half dozen ice-sheathed rock ledges, and kicking steps up and across two wide, wind-drifted snow fields, we precariously made our way down and around that and the next spire. Then, after crossing one last snow ravine and scurrying nervously up one last chute, we were once again on the ridge crest. It was only then, when we stood to look up the rib of the final pyramid, that the summit now seemed suddenly, inexplicably—and almost menacingly— very close.

It was less than a hundred yards away. But between us and it was a dangerous maze of house-size boulders, cliffs and ravines. It actually looked much more difficult a climb up close than it had from a distance. But we had come this far. . .

"Let's go for it," Tucker said without a hint of doubt in his voice.

I nodded in agreement.

"I only wish we had a little more light," I answered.

"Yeah," Tucker said looking up at the dimming day around us.

Relaxing at home in our well-lighted and centrally heated houses it's easy to believe we've come a long way. It's easy to convince ourselves that our increase in scientific, astronomical, geographic and even psychological knowledge has given us a greater understanding of our place in the world as well as in the universe. It's easy to think such thoughts when we're warm and well fed. At such times, it's easy to believe that those ancient people who wandered through the cold and dark winters in northern Europe ten, twenty or even thirty centuries ago have little or no similarity to us. But to believe that is to believe wrongly. Those people are us.

Their similarity to us is very evident. If you take away our homes, lights and cars, and supermarkets, cinemas and schools, and all the other conveniences of modern life, that similarity would soon become very obvious. To stand naked on a high ridge before the cold and coming night is to realize that regardless of how much we know and have, how little we've actually changed. We still get cold, we still fear dark, and we still want rest.

We also still need gods and deities to guide and nurture our lives. And though their names and faces change from year to year and place to place, most of these gods and deities remain, essentially, the same. This is because the physical and, by extension, spiritual needs of humankind don't change. After all, the primary role we seek in our gods and deities is that of guide and nurturer. The ancient Mexicans even went so far as to call their sun-god Ipalnemohuani, "He by whom men live." That is why the sun has long been worshipped as an important—if not the all-important—deity in almost every society. (In this "light", I think it is no coincidence that so many monarchs throughout history have associated themselves with the sun—the pharaohs of Egypt and Louis XIV, "The Sun King", being the two examples that come to mind.) The sun, after all, is largely responsible for the creation of the food, shelter and water that sustain us. Nor did this remain unnoticed by early man.

Ever since man first started looking skyward, the importance of the sun has been recognized and, therefore, paid reverence. Nor has the importance of the sun as a life-giving deity diminished. Even surrounded by all our modern conveniences, we still feel the power of the sun today. This is true not only in regards to our physical well-being, as when harvests are ruined by too much and too little sun, but also our psychological well-being. Anyone living in Alaska knows how debilitating, even destructive, the lack of sunlight in the winter can be. There's even a disease associated with it, Seasonal Affective Disorder (S.A.D.).

I led the way up the first snowy boulders, picking a route as near to the ridge's crest as possible. Occasionally I'd come over one outcrop, or glance around another short cliff and come face to face with a near-vertical drop off the western side of the ridge. Then I'd back up a few steps and start up again, warning Tucker a few feet below not to follow my footsteps off to the left.

After climbing up through a cleft in one last rock face, we were on a short, wide plateau of pleasantly easy tundra. Then it was up into the rocks again. We topped one false summit. Then we crossed another. Finally after climbing up over one more wall of icy boulders and pulling ourselves up one last gully, we were standing in the snow-heavy summit. It was 3:30 p.m.

Directly before us was a deep, steep drop of more than 400 feet into a high pass that rose even steeper and rockier to the North Summit. We had neither the time or energy to even think about climbing that impressive heap. Instead we took a quick picture, stuffed some hard candies in our mouths and started our long descent into the waning day.

Behind us now, the lights of Palmer were blinking brighter in the rising twilight. Just below us to the left, the street lights along the wooded ribbon of Knik River Road had also clicked on.

Tucker pointed out a car's high beams flashing in the darkness between the isolated pools of light.

"He's probably going home," was all I could say.

Sometimes the way home seems so much longer than the way out. And this day was one of those "sometimes"—especially after a few breathless, but luckily short, falls down a couple of hard-packed gullies as we came down off the summit pyramid. These were followed by a few more slips on the ice-covered rocks along the narrow, spiny ridge that led back to the smoother corniced ridge beyond where the trail from below intersected with the ridge top. That was when time started to slow, even though we were moving as fast as we could in the fast-fading light. It was only 5 p.m. and already the long night on this next to shortest day of the year was closing in around us.

The power of the sun—even though we don't always realize it—still affects us profoundly. When did the people of this earth first realize how important the sun was to their lives? When did humankind first associate the bright ball in the sky with heat and light? Some archaeologists believe that worship of the sun extends far back into the Paleolithic and Mesolithic Periods. But no direct evidence of such early worship has been uncovered as yet. There is, however, much evidence of sun worship from the Neolithic Period—and it wasn't, as I've touched on before, sporadic or localized. Instead, it seemed that sun worship was almost universal.

But despite the artifacts that have been unearthed from this period, perhaps the strongest evidence of the power the sun played in the Neolithic period is the carry over of midwinter rituals and beliefs into written history—as well as into contemporary holidays. In the hieroglyphs of ancient Egypt, the Sanskrit of Vedic literature, and the runes of Scandinavia there are numerous allusions to the sun either as a deity—often the supreme deity—or at least an object of praise. In literature, Aeschylus makes reference to the sun in regards to the healing power of Apollo, a god often associated with the sun (<u>The Suppliants</u>

212-14 and <u>Eumenides</u> Prologue) and the Irish-Celtic god Lugh, whose name means "luminous one," appears at least once in all the major cycles of Irish stories—especially the Ulster Cycle and the King Cycle, the latter of which is supposedly about actual historical personages.

It took us a few minutes to find the picnic table in the rising darkness. When we did find it, though, we didn't stay long. Instead we stayed only long enough to pick up our stashed gear and prepare ourselves for the long hike down in the dark. In a matter of moments, Tucker, with the beam of his headlight bobbing on the crusty snow before him, turned down the trail. But though prepared, I still wasn't quite ready to go.

First, I took one last long look west down into the misty valley of Goat Creek. Then I lifted my eyes to the still silhouettes of the ridges and summits that disappeared over the southwest where the last thin ribbon of daylight hovered over the horizon. I watched until even that last light rolled away into darkness. To the north, the murky night was already deep and thick. Off to the west, however, far beyond the dark spires of East and West Twin peaks, and seemingly in defiance of the dying day and coming darkness, I could see the glow of Anchorage's lights. Like a huge, glassed dome, that light seemed the only haven of life.

"It won't be too long before we're back there," I muttered to myself.

Silence.

"That will be nice," I finally concluded.

What I didn't realize at the time was that though the sun was absent, its presence could be felt. No matter what the time of day or season in the year, the sun is always present. And it's always present for one purpose. From its first conception to its final resting place, the sun is the guardian of every living thing. Regardless of all disparaging depictions of the sun and rites associated with it, the sun is being sought out for one reason: to nurture all life. In ancient Greece, the sun was the preserver of seeds lying hidden under the earth during the winter. Perhaps this is also the reason why in ancient and medieval Sweden a sprig of mistletoe (an evergreen plant which, like many others, was believed to retain and contain the sun's power) was picked on the winter solstice because it was believed powerful enough to point to hidden treasure beneath the earth. Thus what was long buried—or dead—is brought to light—or life—again. It may at first seem contradictory that it is a spear of mistletoe that Loki gives to the blind god Hrothgar to throw at—and kill—the seemingly invincible god Balder. But mistletoe was the only plant that Balders' mother, the goddess Frigg, didn't ask to take a pledge not to kill her son. But out of this death comes life. For ever since, mistletoe has been venerated in Europe as a universal healer. The Druids in particular believed that a potion made of mistletoe would make barren animals bring forth young as well as serve as remedy against all poisons.

The living and the dead thus become united in the sun's power. The Celtic tomb at Maes Howe, along with previously mentioned one at Newgate, was oriented to the sunset of midwinter day, making them both not only tombs for the dead, but calendars for the living. But for ancient man perhaps there was little difference between living and dead. After all, in ancient Egypt, pharaohs were buried with all the amenities of this life because they may be wanted by the soul of the deceased in what was assumed to be a very similar afterlife.

Perhaps the sun as nurturer and guardian is best exemplified in the Greek myth of Prometheus. In his attempt to help primitive humankind, he defied the Titans and stole sparks from the fireball of the sun itself and brought them to earth where they were used for everything from ritualistic purification to the simple cooking of food. As such, that spark not only fed the soul, but also fed the body. Without that spark, humankind would've been destined to live in darkness and ignorance.

But the struggle between the powers of light and dark does not end with Prometheus's efforts. It has continued throughout history. It runs throughout the Old Testament, as well as in various myths, legends, and creeds, and some of the classic and most often studied works of literature. Though the sun is not mentioned explicitly, it is an implicit protagonist in the Norse epic <u>Beowulf</u>. On one level, the whole struggle between Grendel and humankind revolves around the struggle of light against darkness. On one side is Hrothgar, the ideal king who among his people and followers will

> . . . *give freely what God has provided*
> *share his wealth there shape borderlands,*
> *love and lead them in light against darkness.*
> (trans. by Frederick Rebsamen 71-3)

In Hrothgar's great mead hall Heorat,

> *They lived brightly . . .*
> *caught up in laughter till a creature brought them*
> *fear in the night an infernal hall-guest.*
>   (99-101)

This "infernal hall-guest" who is associated with Cain and all the powers of evil, is the monster Grendel, the epitome of evil and darkness, who, forever "palled in darkness" (115), visits the mead hall on his grisly visits not only just at night, but also just during the darkest and longest days of winter when the powers of evil were at their zenith.

    The association of darkness with the underworld and evil goes back long before the emissaries of Christianity first began to teach the tenets of their creed in the northern woods. This struggle is, in fact, the basic premise upon which the ancient religion Zoroastrianism was founded in Persia in the sixth century B.C. The struggle or opposition between light and darkness is also a major themes in the earliest writings and beliefs of Judaism, Mohammedanism and Hinduism—as well as in many much more ancient mythologies and religions.

    The sun, being the source of light is, of course, always symbolizes what is good and right in the world. For contemporary Christians, the epitome of the sun as the source of good is found in the association of Jesus of Christ as the "Son of Man." And in conjunction with this title is the time of year in his birth. Christ's day birth, however, wasn't always December 25. Biblical evidence actually points to the fact that he was born sometime in the spring. But early Church fathers moved it to December 25 which, significantly enough, was the winter solstice in the old Julian Calendar. It was also the Church's way of overshadowing an older sun deity, Mithra, an extremely popular Persian deity, whose festival was held on that same day.

    This festival was called Nativity of the Sun. According to Frazer, on the midnight of the solstice, followers of Mithra would emerge from hidden sanctuaries crying, "The virgin has brought forth! The sun is waxing!" "The Egyptians," Frazer goes on to say, "even represented the newborn sun by the image of an infant which on his birthday, the winter solstice, they brought forth and exhibited to his worshippers." Retaining many trappings of this older ritual, the Church made it easier for many people to accept and convert to their new doctrine. Thus Nativity of the Sun became Nativity of the Son.

But even after Christmas caught on, aspects of the older Mithraic holiday still lingered. Early in the 4th century, Emperor Constantine was still worshipping the "the unconquerable sun." In 312 A.D. on his way to Milvin Bridge to fight Maxentius for control of the empire he had his famous vision of a cross superimposed on the sun—the "son and sun combined.

"Conquer in this," he heard a voice say.

And he did.

But though memories of all the early sun rites and rituals still linger in thought—and even some practice—it is the holiday of Christmas that has come to dominate the last days of the year. It has even come to overshadow its origin, the solstice itself. But the connection between the two is still there: both are times of birth, of the end of death and the beginning of life. No doubt, Christmas is the best known and most widely practiced holiday of the western world. But the beliefs it rests upon extend far back through centuries and millennia, through countless generations of people who wanted to do more than just live. They also sought to understand. Christmas grew out of this desire and need to understand.

Yes, the world did appear lifeless to me. But only when seen through weak human eyes. For though I couldn't see them, there were, no doubt, moles burrowing under the turf, rabbits and ptarmigan huddling in the brush below and probably even a hawk cruising out of sight just over the next ridge. We even surprised a lone ptarmigan in the darkness just below tree line on our long descent. It flitted away in the small field of light spread by Tucker's head lamp.

Yes, even in the long night before the darkest day of winter there is life. It is not spectacular. It is not always even obvious. More often than not, it may not even be awake—or even seem alive. It is there, though, and it is very much alive. Just knowing that was almost enough to make me actually believe in magic. It was certainly enough to dispel the long, lonely hours at the exhausted end of that long, dark hike.

On the ridge just south of Pioneer Peak looking out over Knik Glacier.

Pioneer Ridge Trail

Trail Location: The Pioneer Ridge Trail begins at the edge of a small parking lot located at mile 3.9 on the Knik River Road. To get there from Anchorage drive north on the Glenn Highway to the Old Glenn Highway Exit just beyond mile 25, and just shy of the Knik River Bridge. (For those traveling from the north, take the Old Glenn Highway—just south of the Knik River bridge, and cross back over the highway onto the Old Glenn Highway.) From here, follow the Old Glenn High for almost 9 miles to its intersection with Knik River Road. Turn right onto Knik River Road and follow it for 3.9 miles to the small parking lot on the right-hand side of the road. The trail begins at the back, right-handcorner of the parking lot. Simply go under the wood framed door and you're on the trail.

The Pioneer Ridge Trail, which begins only a few hundred feet above sea level and ends at the highest point reached by any trail in the Chugach State Park has, consequently, the highest elevation gain of any trail in the park. But though long and time consuming, it is not a boring climb. For as it steadily winds upward—sometimes switchbacking and sometimes going straight up the ridgeline—this trail passes through the flora and fauna of various climate zones. From the temperate hardwood forests at the trail's beginning to the arctic tundra at its end, it is a botanist's and biologist's delight. But if the specimens of botany and biology in their natural state aren't stimulating enough, there are also the wide and deep views to the east and north on the climb up. (Even down low, the woods are sparse enough to be able to look out at the scenic world beyond.) Once the top of the ridge is reached, the view not only becomes omni-directional—with new vistas opening up to the west and south—but also far more expansive.

The trail ends at the picnic table located on the crest of the ridge—the last of three such tables that are passed on the way up.

Trail Grade: Because of the continuous climbing virtually from beginning to end, this trail is rated a grade 3.

Trail Condition: This trail is well-cut and nicely switchbacked but no matter how well maintained a trail is in Alaska, one should expect to encounter mud and rocks, and the Pioneer Ridge Trail is no exception. Above tree line, though, the trail dries out considerably, making for very enjoyable walking-even though one is still climbing.

Trail Mileage: The one way climb to the third picnic table located at the end of the trail at the top of the ridge is 6 miles for a round trip total of 12 miles.

Total Elevation Gain: The climb from the parking lot to the top of the ridge is 5,100 feet—making it a daunting almost 900 feet per mile climb.

High Point: It is 5,330 feet above sea level at the third and final picnic table.

Normal Hiking Time: it should take 5 to 10 hours to do this round trip depending on the ambition and condition of the hiking party.

Campsites: Though there are no official campsites on this trail, the top of the ridge and some spots above tree line are certainly scenic enough and just level enough to pitch a tent—though water at those heights is very scarce.

Best Time: June to September are the best times to do this hike. It can, however, also be done in winter if some care is exercised to avoid potential avalanche areas—very few of which are on the trail itself—and enough extra clothes are carried to combat the cold.

USGS Maps: Anchorage B-6, C-6 SE.

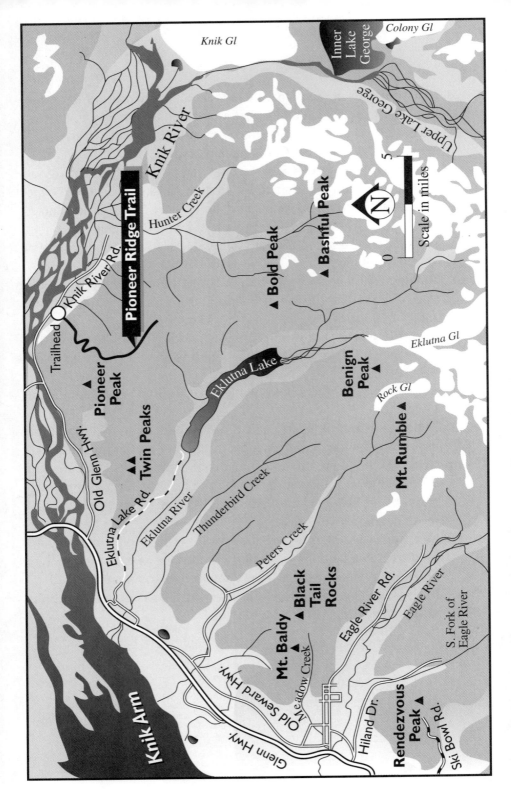

Knik Gl

Colony Gl

Inner Lake George

Upper Lake George

Knik River

Pioneer Ridge Trail

Hunter Creek

▲ Bold Peak

▲ Bashful Peak

N

0   5

Scale in miles

Eklutna Gl

Knik River Rd.

○ Trailhead

Pioneer Peak ▲

Eklutna Lake

Benign Peak ▲

Rock Gl

Old Glenn Hwy.

Eklutna Lake Rd.

▲▲ **Twin Peaks**

Eklutna River

Thunderbird Creek

Peters Creek

Mt. Rumble ▲

Knik Arm

Mt. Baldy ▲

Black Tail Rocks ▲

Meadow Creek

Old Seward Hwy.

Eagle River Rd.

Eagle River

S. Fork of Eagle River

Glenn Hwy.

Hiland Dr.

Rendezvous Peak ▲

Ski Bowl Rd.

On the ridge south of Pioneer Peak.

SOUTH SUMMIT OF PIONEER PEAK

Trail Location: From the end of the Pioneer Ridge Trail, a decent trail
follows the crest of the ridge north toward the twin summits of
North and South Pioneer Peak. (To get to Pioneer Ridge Trail, see
WALK-ABOUT GUIDE TO PIONEER RIDGE TRAIL.) The
South Summit is the nearer— and easier of the two to climb. To
continue from the South Summit to the North Summit entails not
only descending into and climbing out of a 400-foot col, but also
requires technical equipment and expertise.

Trail Grade: Beginning at grade 2, this climb, as it gets closer to the
summit, also ascends through all the grades up to level 6.

Trail Condition: Beginning on gentle tundra, this climb becomes more
difficult as more rocks and more scree and more gendarmes and
rock ribs are encountered as the summit gets closer.

Trail Mileage: The one way climb from the parking area to the South
Summit of Pioneer Peak is 9 miles—3 more miles than the hike to
the last picnic table at the crest of the ridge—for a round trip total
of 18 miles.

Total Elevation Gain: The total elevation gain from the parking lot is
6,190 feet. The total elevation gain from the last picnic table is
1,060 feet.

High Point: The South Summit of Pioneer Peak is approximately 6,350
feet above sea level. The elevation of the North Summit is 6,398
feet above sea level.

Normal Hiking Time: From the parking lot to the South Summit should
take one long day or two days. From the last picnic table to the
South Summit should take anywhere from 3 to 6 hours.

Campsites: Despite the lack of water, there are many level and scenic

424

spots along the ridge crest to pitch a tent.

Best Time: The best time to do this climb is anywhere from mid-June to mid-September. Experienced snow and ice climbers, however, may find this climb a spectacular challenge during any one of the long, cold months of winter.

USGS Maps: Anchorage B-6, C-6 SE.

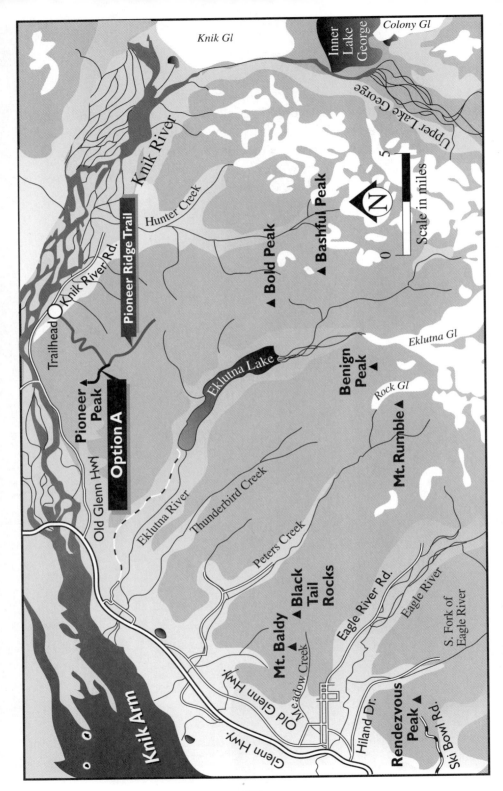

Knik Gl

Colony Gl

Inner Lake George

Upper Lake George

Knik River

Hunter Creek

Pioneer Ridge Trail

Knik River Rd.

Trailhead

Bold Peak

Bashful Peak

Eklutna Gl

5

N

Scale in miles

0

Eklutna Lake

Benign Peak

Rock Gl

Pioneer Peak

Option A

Old Glenn Hwy

Mt. Rumble

Eklutna River

Thunderbird Creek

Peters Creek

Black Tail Rocks

Mt. Baldy

Meadow Creek

Eagle River Rd.

Eagle River

S. Fork of Eagle River

Knik Arm

Old Glenn Hwy

Glenn Hwy

Hiland Dr.

Rendezvous Peak

Ski Bowl Rd.

Looking down Bold Creek alongside the Bold Overlook Trail to Eklutna Lake.

PIONEER RIDGE TO EKLUTNA LAKE TRAVERSE

Note: This trip requires the spotting of a car at the trailhead of the Eklutna Lakeside Trail on the north end of Eklutna Lake. The hike itself hugs the crest of the ridge far above some of the most scenic and wild country in the Chugach Mountains. Expect to see Dall Sheep, possibly a bear or two and maybe even a wolf. Also expect to do a lot of up and down climbing along the long ridge that leads from Pioneer over to Hunter Creek Pass.

Trail Location: From the last picnic table at the upper end of the Pioneer Ridge Trail, a marked trail leads left and south down the ridge. (To get to Pioneer Ridge Trail, see WALK-ABOUT GUIDE TO PIONEER RIDGE TRAIL.) The first few miles are flagged by orange markers, but even after they peter out, there is a fine sheep trail still remaining which can be followed all the way to Hunter Creek Pass. From the pass, one can then descend into the Bold Overlook valley, down the lower end of which you can pick up the Bold Overlook Trail which leads in 3.5 miles down to the Eklutna Lakeside Trail which, in turn, leads in 5 miles out to the parking lot.

    If one doesn't have the time or energy to go all the way to Hunter Creek Pass, the experienced hiker—and none but experienced hikers should attempt this traverse—can cut a corner by descending directly to the Bold Overlook Trail from the first peak reached upon entering the Bold Peak valley.

Trail Grade: The marked trail and goat trail walking are grades 2 and 3. Other trail-less sections rise no higher than grades 4 and 5. Once on the Bold Overlook Trail, the level once again reverts to grade 2, and then even lower to grade 1 on the Eklutna Lakeside Trail.

Trail Condition: This traverse is mostly on tundra with sporadic sections of rock scrambling and even some bush whacking in the Bold Peak valley.

Trail Mileage: The traverse from the parking lot of the Pioneer Ridge Trail to the parking lot at Eklutna Lake is 20 to 23 long miles one way.

Total Elevation Gain: The total elevation gain from the beginning of the Pioneer Ridge Trail to the parking lot at Eklutna Lake is only 700 feet, but in between lies not only the 5,100 foot climb to Pioneer Ridge, but also climbs over a variety of other 5,000 foot summits which entail ascents of anywhere from 200 to 1,000 feet with numerous other climbs of varying heights in between which go up and over ledges and in and out of gullies. So the estimated overall elevation gain is anywhere between 9,000 and 10,000 going in either direction.

High Point: There are eight peaks along the ridge listed at more than 5,000 feet above sea level in elevation with the highest being 5,745 feet.

Normal Hiking Time: Though this hike can be done in one long ,hard day, many might prefer to take two or even three easy days to enjoy it.

Campsites: The ridge is—except for one or two sometimes dry tarns—waterless so fill all available water bottles if the intent is to camp high up on any portion of the ridge. There is, however, plenty of water to be had in the Bold Peak valley and even all the way down to the parking lot.

Best Time: June to September are the best months in which to do this traverse. It might, however, be a good idea to wear bright clothes during hunting season from late August into September.

USGS Maps: Anchorage B-6.

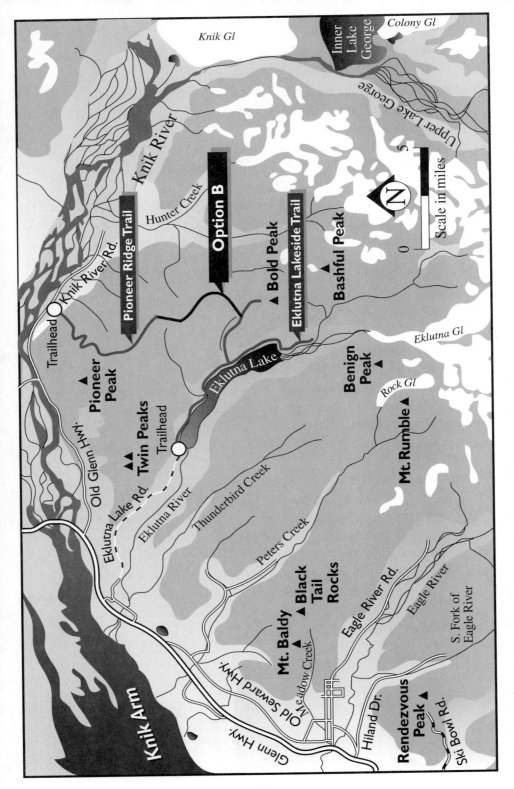

Descending off a ridge into the Bold Peak valley with Eklutna Lake just
visible in the deeper valley beyond.

APPENDIX 1:

INFORMATION SOURCES

ALASKA PUBLIC LANDS INFORMATION CENTER
605 West Fourth Avenue Anchorage, AK 99501
(907) 271-2738

LAND MANAGERS

ALASKA DEPARTMENT OF FISH AND GAME
Anchorage Area Office
333 Rasberry Road • Anchorage, AK 99518
(907) 267-2100

ALASKA DIVISION OF LAND
South-central Region
3601 C Street P.O. Box 10-7005 • Anchorage, AK 99510-7005
(907) 762-2253

BUREAU OF LAND MANAGEMENT
Anchorage District Office
6881 Abbott Loop Road • Anchorage, AK 99507
(907) 267-1246

ALASKA DIVISIONS OF PARKS
AND OUTDOOR RECREATION

CHUGACH STATE PARK

Potter Section House: Park Headquarters
Mile 115 Seward Highway HC 52, Box 8999 • Indian, AK 99540
(907) 345-5014

CHUGACH NATIONAL FOREST

3301 C Street, Suite 300 • Anchorage, AK 99503
(907) 271-2500   TDD (907) 271-2504

Cabin Reservations: Alaska Public Lands Information Center,
(907) 271-2599 or through any U.S. Forest Service district office
in the state.

Girdwood District Office: P.O. Box 129 • Girdwood, AK 99587
(907) 783-3242

ADDITIONAL SOURCES OF INFORMATION

ALASKA DEPARTMENT OF NATURAL RESOURCES
Public Information Center
Frontier Building
3601 C Street, Suite 200 • Anchorage, AK 99503
(907) 269-8400

ALASKA PUBLIC LANDS INFORMATION CENTER
605 West 4th Avenue • Anchorage, AK 99501
(907) 228-6214   TDD (907) 271-2738

EAGLE RIVER NATURE CENTER
(managed by the non-profit Friends of Eagle River Nature Center, Inc.)
32750 Eagle River Road
Eagle River, AK 99577
(907) 694-9255

ALASKA DEPARTMENT OF TRANSPORTATION AND PUBLIC
FACILITIES
P.O. Box 196900 • Anchorage, AK 99519-6900
Numbers to call for highway and road conditions:
Anchorage: (907) 243-7675
Main Number (Maintenance Division): (907) 266-1735
Matanuska-Susitna District: (907) 745-2159

ALASKA DIVISION OF TOURISM
P.O. Box 110801-0801 • Juneau, AK 99811
Juneau: (907) 465-2010   Anchorage: (907) 563-2167
Ask for the "Vacation Planner," an annually revised publication that lists names, addresses, and phone numbers of businesses and services that cater to any and all who visit Alaska, whether they want to just rent a car or take a ten day rafting trip.

U.S. GEOLOGICAL SURVEY
Earth Science Information Center
4230 University Drive • Anchorage, AK 99508-4664
(907) 786-7011
Alaska topographical maps are available to the public through this office.

FORT RICHARDSON MILITARY RESERVATION
Military Police
(907) 384-0823
This is the number to call for permission to hike and camp on military lands.

ALASKA MOUNTAINEERING CLUB
P.O. Box 102937 • Anchorage, AK 99510

ALASKA AVALANCHE SCHOOL
Alaska Mountain Safety Center
9140 Brewster Drive • Anchorage, AK 99516
(907) 345-3566

APPENDIX 2:

CABIN RENTALS
The cabins in Chugach State Park and State Forest are maintained by three separate groups. For the most part, the location of the cabin—whether it's on State Park land or State Forest Land—determines what office to contact. The exception to this rule is the Public Use Cabin and Yurt located 1.5 miles from the Eagle River Nature Center along Eagle River Trail and Albert Loop Trail, respectively. Though located on State Park land, they are maintained by the 'Friends' through whom reservations can be made. Because all the cabins in the Chugach Mountains are popular, it is best to make reservations early. Rental fees may vary from organization to organization.

ALASKA DEPARTMENT OF NATURAL RESOURCES
PUBLIC INFORMATION CENTER
Frontier Building 3601 C Street, Suite 200
Anchorage, AK 99503
(907) 269-8400
Reservations for cabins in Chugach State Park may be made through this office or at the nearest State Park office (see their park headquarters address and phone number listed in Appendix 1).

ALASKA PUBLIC LANDS INFORMATION CENTER
605 West 4th Avenue • Anchorage, AK 99501
(907) 228-6214
TDD (907) 271-2738
Reservations for cabins located on National Forest land may be made through this office.

EAGLE RIVER NATURE CENTER
(managed by the non-profit Friends of Eagle River Nature Center, Inc.)
32750 Eagle River Road • Eagle River, AK 99577
(907) 694-9255
Reservations for their new privately owned Public Use Cabin and Yurt located 1.5 miles from the Center along the Eagle River Trail, may be

made through this organization.

APPENDIX 3:

PARKING PERMITS

As of March, 1998, a parking fee is required at all but one Chugach State Park trailheads, campgrounds and picnic areas. (The one exception is the parking area outside the privately leased Eagle River Nature Center whose policy is described below.) This fee of $5.00 (which is subject to change) must be paid each time one parks. An alternative to this pay-when-you-park routine is to buy a season pass which is good for all but the one parking area at Eagle River Nature Center in Chugach State Park. This season pass may be purchased for $25.00 from Chugach State Park Headquarters (the address of which can be found in Appendix 1). If more than one permit is bought at one time, there is, upon request, a discount for the second permit.

Eagle River Nature Center, which is managed by a non-profit organization (Friends of Eagle River Nature Center, Inc.), also charges a fee for parking outside their facility (the address of which can be found in Appendix 1). This fee, which is $3.00 as of June 1998, is separate from the State Park fee. Unlike the State Park, one cannot buy a season parking ticket. However, for the $35.00 it costs to become a member of the Friends of Eagle River Nature Center, one not only gets free year-round parking, but a newsletter and regular updates on special affairs taking place at the center.

Anchorage Ski Club, which manages and maintains a section of Arctic Valley Road, has also initiated parking fees for Alpenglow parking area. Currently that fee is $3.00 per car. A seasonal permit can also be purchased through the ski club.

A hiker stays on the high ridge as friends fill water bottles in the lake below.

About the Author

    Shawn Lyons is, by vocation and avocation, a person of many parts. As a professional classical guitarist, he plays dinner music every Thursday through Saturday at Villa Nova Restaurant in Anchorage. When he is not playing guitar at Villa Nova, Shawn is a part-time instructor of guitar at the University of Alaska in Anchorage where he also teaches Music History, English Composition and Literature. Shawn is also an avid hiker and hill scrambler. So much that after many long hikes through many a valley and over many a summit, he has become the hiking guru of South-Central Alaska. Nor is this all he does in the outdoors. As an ultra-athlete, he is an eight-time winner of the Iditashoe wilderness show-shoe race, and three time winner of the 100 mile Coldfoot Classic held each year on Halloween above the Arctic Circle. Shawn's narratives about his hikes and races will often appear in a weekly hiking/climbing column he writes for the Anchorage Daily News.